D1221516

The Spirit of the Constitution

The Spirit of the Constitution

*John Marshall and the 200-Year Odyssey
of McCulloch v. Maryland*

DAVID S. SCHWARTZ

OXFORD
UNIVERSITY PRESS

OXFORD
UNIVERSITY PRESS

Oxford University Press is a department of the University of Oxford. It furthers
the University's objective of excellence in research, scholarship, and education
by publishing worldwide. Oxford is a registered trade mark of Oxford University
Press in the UK and certain other countries.

Published in the United States of America by Oxford University Press
198 Madison Avenue, New York, NY 10016, United States of America.

© David S. Schwartz 2019

All rights reserved. No part of this publication may be reproduced, stored in
a retrieval system, or transmitted, in any form or by any means, without the
prior permission in writing of Oxford University Press, or as expressly permitted
by law, by license, or under terms agreed with the appropriate reproduction
rights organization. Inquiries concerning reproduction outside the scope of the
above should be sent to the Rights Department, Oxford University Press, at the
address above.

You must not circulate this work in any other form
and you must impose this same condition on any acquirer.

Library of Congress Cataloging-in-Publication Data
Names: Schwartz, David S., author.
Title: The spirit of the Constitution : John Marshall and the 200-year
odyssey of McCulloch v. Maryland / David S. Schwartz.
Description: New York : Oxford University Press, NY 2019. |
Includes bibliographical references and index.
Identifiers: LCCN 2019004959 | ISBN 9780190699482 (hardcover : alk. paper)
Subjects: LCSH: Implied powers (Constitutional law)—United States. |
Legislative power—United States. |
Marshall, John, 1755–1835—Influence.
Classification: LCC KF4565 .S39 2019 | DDC 342.73/052—dc23
LC record available at https://lccn.loc.gov/2019004959

1 3 5 7 9 8 6 4 2

Printed by Sheridan Books, Inc., United States of America

For Beth,
Everything and always.

CONTENTS

PREFACE

This book is a work of revisionism, and by questioning certain cherished beliefs as revisionism inevitably does, it creates potential anxiety for both its author and its readers. My argument questions the belief that John Marshall, the Great Chief Justice, was a "nation builder," and that his great decision in *McCulloch v. Maryland* laid the constitutional foundations for the modern welfare state. I found that I had touched a nerve early on. When I was presenting an early version of Chapters 1 through 3 at a workshop, the first comment I received was, "We have to ask... whose side are you on, anyway?" The question was jocular, but my anxiety was increased some months later when I discovered that a radical states'-rights website applauded my paper, by then published as a law review article, for supposedly proving that the modern welfare state was unconstitutional because John Marshall would have thought so.

That, of course, was a blatant misreading of my paper, though perhaps a predictable one. I happen to believe that the post–New Deal welfare state *is* constitutional, but not because of what John Marshall did or did not think. In writing this book, I've adhered to the belief that historical inquiry should strive to translate and understand the past on its own terms before deploying it for present-day purposes. The reactions of my workshop interlocutors and the states'-rights website had less to do with my argument, or the *McCulloch* case, or Marshall's beliefs, than with the view that present-day constitutional arguments should depend on which side of the argument would be supported by Marshall. Canonizing Marshall and his opinions, casting fundamental constitutional questions in the form of WWJMD—"what would John Marshall do?"—begs important questions about judicial supremacy, constitutional history, and the right of later generations to adapt constitutional meaning to their own times. Marshall, a man of unusual personal humility relative to his station in life, is known for his statement in *McCulloch* that the Constitution is "intended to endure for ages to come." Ironically, he might well have agreed that hanging on his every word is not the best approach to constitutional interpretation.

Work on this project has been scattered across the past several years, giving me the opportunity to experience the way that scholarship is a community enterprise. The University of Wisconsin Law School has generously supported my research, both with direct research grants and through the Foley & Lardner-Bascom professorship. I am grateful to Dean Margaret Raymond and Associate Dean Susannah Tahk for their support. I benefited greatly from the assistance of several law librarians and student research assistants: Bonnie Shucha (now Law Library Director), Jay Tucker, Kris Turner, and Peter Wehrle of the University of Wisconsin Law Library; history graduate student Athan Biss; and law students Hayley Archer, Nancy Cruz, Austin Doan, AJ Fabianczyk, Kathryn Fifield, Cecilia Kress, James Meadows, Chelsey Metcalf, Olivia Radics, and Charis Zimmick. I received expert editorial advice from Pamela Haag. The Harvard Law School Library Historical and Special Collections Department provided access to the James Bradley Thayer Papers, and its staff, especially Lesley Schoenfeld, provided invaluable assistance. The staff of the Bentley Historical Library at the University of Michigan assisted by providing access to the Frank Murphy Papers.

I am grateful for feedback from numerous colleagues who have read various parts of the book in various stages: Rebecca Aviel, Steven Barkan, William Baude, Eric Berger, R.B. Bernstein, Mary Bilder, Tonya Brito, Peter Carstensen, Bernard Chao, Roberto Corrada, Anuj Desai, Sam Erman, Keith Findley, Mark Graber, Paul Halliday, Charles Hobson, Alexandra Huneeus, Nancy Isenberg, Sam Kamin, Neil Komesar, Heinz Klug, Sophia Lee, Nancy Leong, Eric Lomazoff, Gwendolyn Leachman, Gerard Magliocca, Justin Marceau, Megan McDermott, Richard Monette, Ion Meyn, Robert Mikos, Sheldon Nahmod, William Nelson, Yaron Nili, Richard Primus, Asifa Quraishi-Landes, David Marcus, Toni Massaro, Lori Ringhand, Cristina Rodriguez, Carol Rose, Victoria Saker-Woeste, Christopher Schmidt, Miriam Seifter, Mitra Sharafi, Matthew Steilen, Robert Yablon, and Jason Yackee. John Mikhail was especially helpful and encouraging with advice and comments. Alison LaCroix and Mark Killenbeck gave invaluable feedback and support to this project at both the book proposal and manuscript stages. Kent Newmyer's excellent scholarship on Marshall comes in for a fair amount of criticism in my book, but that is a testament to its great influence and iconic status; he was extremely gracious in our brief exchange of emails. Edward Purcell's excellent book *Brandeis and the Progressive Constitution* inspired me at the outset to understand that a single important case could be the vehicle for a book-length exploration of U.S. constitutional development. He read the whole manuscript and offered incisive comments. So did Sanford Levinson, with whom I conducted a sort of internal dialogue in my mind as I shaped the argument in the book. Brad Snyder, though several years my junior, has perfected the art of what I call "reverse-mentoring." In addition to offering insightful comments on the whole book, Brad provided advice and promotional activities on my behalf, without which this book might never have found a publisher. Andrew Coan read all of the underlying articles and the full book manuscript. He was meticulous in closely reading my arguments, always pushing me toward greater clarity and coherence, and also picking up my spirits during the inevitable low points of a lengthy writing project. Most of all, my wife, BethAnne Yeager, contributed superlative research assistance and read the manuscript cover to cover multiple times. She provided superlative editorial guidance, in addition to her patience, support, and encouragement. I could not have completed this book without her.

Certain portions of the book have appeared in earlier and different forms, in the following publications:

David S. Schwartz, *An Error and an Evil: The Strange History of Implied Commerce Powers*, 68 American University Law Review 927 (2019).

David S. Schwartz, *A Question Perpetually Arising: Implied Powers, Capable Federalism and the Limits of Enumerationism*, 59 Arizona Law Review 573 (2017).

David S. Schwartz, *Misreading* McCulloch v. Maryland, 18 University of Pennsylvania Journal of Constitutional Law 1 (2015).

Introduction

"The Letter and Spirit of the Constitution"

In June 2012, the United States Supreme Court came within one vote of striking down the Affordable Care and Patient Protection Act of 2009. Known as "the ACA" for short, and "Obamacare" in public discourse, the law was the signature legislative achievement of the eight-year Obama Administration. Even after running a legislative gauntlet, which reached back across more than fifty years of debate over national health care, the ACA had one more obstacle to overcome. Soon after the ACA's enactment, opponents brought a court challenge, arguing that the law exceeded the Constitution's limits on the powers of the national government. In *National Federation of Independent Business ("NFIB") v. Sebelius*, the Court issued a sharply divided five-to-four decision, barely upholding the law as constitutional under the federal taxing power, while deciding that the law would have been unconstitutional under the federal commerce power. Curiously, the parties' briefs and oral arguments in the 2012 case debated the meaning of *McCulloch v. Maryland*, a constitutional law decision written by Chief Justice John Marshall in 1819 that upheld the constitutionality of the Second Bank of the United States. The *NFIB* justices, too, discussed *McCulloch* at some length and were closely divided about whether Marshall's decision meant the law was constitutional or not. Why did the parties and Justices on both sides of this issue base arguments on *McCulloch*? Why did both sides of the argument each believe *McCulloch* supported their view? Why did an 1819 case about a bygone institution, the Second Bank of United States, have any bearing on healthcare legislation in 2012?

The answer to these questions reveals a basic feature of our constitutional system, but also a mystery. Constitutional lawyers debating whether Congress has the power to enact a particular law, like the ACA, are trained to believe that *McCulloch* provides the authoritative answer. They typically begin their inquiry by looking to this language from Marshall's opinion:

Let the end be legitimate, let it be within the scope of the constitution, and all means which are appropriate, which are plainly adapted to that end, which are not prohibited, but consist with the letter and spirit of the constitution, are constitutional.[1]

The basic feature of our constitutional system is that debates over the distribution of powers between the national and state governments—federalism—are, as Marshall said in *McCulloch*, "perpetually arising, and will probably continue to arise, as long as our system shall exist."[2] These debates have done more to shape American constitutional law than any other issue, and have surfaced in hundreds of Supreme Court cases. The arguments made by the challengers to the ACA were the same, in their essence if not their details, as those made in earlier years to try to strike down the monumental Civil Rights Act of 1964, the New Deal–era Social Security Act, National Labor Relations Act, and Fair Labor Standards Act, and many other laws since the Constitution was ratified in 1789. The mystery is why the ongoing debates over federalism are thought to be authoritatively answered by the 200-year-old case of *McCulloch v. Maryland*.

John Marshall is widely regarded as the greatest jurist in American history. If George Washington is "father of his country," and James Madison the "father of the Constitution," then John Marshall is the "father of American constitutional law." Marshall was not the first chief justice of the United States, but comparing his long and illustrious judicial career with the obscure, short, and uneventful tenures of his three predecessors, he might as well have been. It was Marshall who established the Court's prestige and made the Court an institutional player in the nation's constitutional politics. Marshall's constitutional rulings tended to be cases of first impression—literally, without judicial precedent—giving Marshall the historical reputation of the original and authoritative "Expounder of the Constitution."

McCulloch v. Maryland is generally regarded by constitutional scholars as not only Marshall's "greatest decision,"[3] but also as "the richest and most important single opinion of the United States Supreme Court in our entire history."[4] Decided on March 6, 1819—thirty years almost to the day after the United States Constitution went into effect on March 4, 1789, and celebrating its 200th anniversary at the time of this writing—*McCulloch* ruled that Congress had the power to create a national bank even though the power to do so was not expressly granted in the Constitution. According to Marshall's opinion, the Constitution granted implied powers, not specified in the Constitution, that were "appropriate" and "plainly adapted" to implementing the Constitution's purposes. Today, *McCulloch* is taught to every law student as *the* foundational case, introducing the fundamental topic of the constitutional powers of Congress. Indeed, *McCulloch* has effectively "displaced the views of the Framers as the authoritative source on the scope of Congress's power."[5]

Yet the story of *McCulloch v. Maryland*'s rise to glory in constitutional law is puzzling. *McCulloch* upheld the constitutionality of the Second Bank of the United

States, successor to the original national bank created by Alexander Hamilton in 1791. But the case decided just two important but unglamorous technical issues: the power of Congress to charter corporations, and the immunity of federal instrumentalities from state taxation. These hardly account for the case's fame.

In its first seventy years, *McCulloch* did not appear destined to become a canonical case. The scope and extent of the powers of Congress were debated frequently in these tumultuous decades, as were questions about the nature of the Constitution's union of states and the supremacy of federal law. Yet from 1819 to 1892, *McCulloch* was rarely invoked as a foundational statement of these principles in the Supreme Court. *McCulloch* was frequently cited (thirty-six times) in Supreme Court cases involving the powers of the federal and state governments to tax each other. But subsequent Supreme Court majority opinions presented *McCulloch* as a significant national powers precedent only in a few cases, mostly involving the federal government's power to issue paper money. The case now regarded as the greatest constitutional law decision was for many decades viewed primarily as a decision about "intergovernmental tax immunity" and currency regulation.

Even after *McCulloch*'s perceived importance emerged toward the end of the nineteenth century, its meaning was subject to dispute. What did it mean to say that a law was "appropriate" and "plainly adapted"? And what was the "spirit" of the Constitution that might be relied upon to say that a law was unconstitutional? Present-day constitutional lawyers and scholars believe that *McCulloch* "provides an enduring nationalist interpretation" of the Constitution "which has laid the foundation for the living Constitution, . . . and an almost infinite increase in the powers of the federal government."[6] But *McCulloch* has not always been interpreted this way, and its role in laying the constitutional foundations for present-day national power is far from clear.

What was so great about *McCulloch*, anyway? The dominant understanding of constitutional lawyers and scholars is that *McCulloch* is the most important case in constitutional law because it has been a creative force, shaping constitutional debates and guiding constitutional development. But it neither produced nor even encouraged expansive national policies for decades; it failed to convince subsequent Supreme Court justices to interpret national legislative power broadly; and it did not even save the Second Bank from later constitutional attack and dissolution. The opinion is praised for its brilliance, but it did not develop a single new idea. Marshall rehashed the arguments of great statesmen, like Alexander Hamilton and Daniel Webster, as well as members of Congress and constitutional litigators of less enduring fame. The opinion is praised for its boldness, but in fact it was hedged about with caution. Marshall's writing has been praised for its logic, stylistic virtue, and crystal clarity. Sanford Levinson, one of the most insightful constitutional law thinkers in the present day, calls *McCulloch* a "prose poem."[7] Yet wholly aside from the highly elliptical style of early-nineteenth-century legal writing, Marshall's opinion is conceptually clouded and ambiguous. For example, Marshall used more

than twenty different words and phrases to define the key concept in the case, "necessary and proper," and he subsequently felt the need to clarify his *McCulloch* analysis in a newspaper editorial. Marshall was a great judge, and a nationalist, but he
was not a visionary who foresaw the modern American nation.

McCulloch is a great case because many years after the decision was largely dead
and buried, lawyers and judges said it was a great case. They found material in it
that was useful to their constitutional arguments, and they had come to believe that
John Marshall was an iconic figure whose words carried great weight. *McCulloch*
has thus been given a central role in a modern-day foundation myth for constitutional law. The United States Constitution, the charter of American government
and the fundamental law of our democratic republic, is also the basis for an ideology
of American constitutionalism—some have called it our "civic religion." This myth
holds that the Constitution sets forth two fundamental principles that define our
system: a strong central government recognized by all to be the supreme, unifying
authority and wielding the power to address all national problems; and a Supreme
Court with the authoritative and final say over what the Constitution means, to
safeguard our individual liberties by keeping our democratically elected representatives within constitutional limits. American constitutional history is viewed as a
march toward our present-day understandings of broad national powers and judicial supremacy. While acknowledging occasions of "one step backward," the myth
finds that these have always been followed by two steps forward. The deference to
states' rights and the slave power in the antebellum period was "swept aside by the
great impulse of national feeling born of the Civil War," in the words of renowned
twentieth-century liberal Justice William J. Brennan.[8] The re-emergence of stringent limits on national power during the late-nineteenth-century era of laissez-faire
(deregulatory) jurisprudence was swept aside by the New Deal jurisprudence of
1937–42, which constitutionalized the modern welfare state. And the re-emergence
of states'-rights theory in support of Jim Crow was eradicated by mid-twentieth-
century Civil Rights Era jurisprudence. Calling Marshall "the expounder of the
Constitution," the standard story of U.S. constitutional history credits Marshall's
"great" decisions, such as *Marbury v. Madison*, but above all *McCulloch v. Maryland*,
as embodying, consolidating, and settling the role of the Supreme Court as the supreme interpreter of the Constitution, and establishing the supremacy and breadth
of national power in the Constitution's structure of federalism.[9] This standard story,
taught to law students and relied upon by judges and professors as a background assumption for much constitutional argument, has some truth to it, but oversimplifies
matters to an extent that obscures much of the truth of our constitutional history.

* * *

This book proceeds in thirteen chapters, divided into three parts. Part I offers a revisionist interpretation of Marshall Court jurisprudence, focusing on *McCulloch* and

its subsequent treatment by Marshall and his Court. I argue that, despite its expansive potential for national powers, *McCulloch* was deeply ambiguous. Marshall left *McCulloch*'s most nationalistic features vague and underdeveloped, resulting in an opinion that in its day functioned in a far more cautious and "defensively" nationalistic manner than we read it today. Chapter 1 lays out terms of the argument, in particular distinguishing between "defensive nationalism" aimed at resisting radical states'-rights interpretations of the Constitution, and "affirmative nationalism," authorizing expansive exercises of national legislative power. Chapters 2 and 3 examine the *McCulloch* decision closely, in its historical context, to show that Marshall stopped short of clearly embracing the more nationalistic arguments and positions available to him. Chapter 4 explains the curious disappearance of *McCulloch* from later Marshall Court decisions and reinterprets *Gibbons v. Ogden*, Marshall's other famous decision on national legislative powers. *Gibbons* is conventionally understood as an expansive "affirmative nationalism" decision, but I show that in *Gibbons* the Marshall Court retreated from the more expansive ideas of implied powers expressed in *McCulloch*.

Part II traces the disappearance of *McCulloch* from Supreme Court jurisprudence and constitutional politics during the Jacksonian era—the presidency of Andrew Jackson and his antebellum successors—and its gradual re-emergence later in the nineteenth century. The spirit of the Constitution in the post–Marshall Court nineteenth century was dominated by a consistent adherence to a conception of reserved state powers that tended to thwart the development of *McCulloch*'s expansive potential for legislative powers, even after the Civil War generated new and stronger sentiments of constitutional nationalism. Chapter 5 shows how the Court under Marshall's successor Roger Taney essentially overruled *McCulloch* in fact, albeit not in name. Chapters 6 and 7 trace the glimmerings of *McCulloch*'s reemergence in the halls of Congress during the Civil War and Reconstruction while the Supreme Court largely continued to ignore the case. Chapter 8 shows how the Court endorsed post–Civil War nationalism without embracing *McCulloch* or a broad conception of implied legislative powers. Chapter 9 explains that the Supreme Court's recognition of *McCulloch* as a canonical case arose as part of a John Marshall revival movement designed to protect the Court's assertion of judicial supremacy in anticipation of Populist political attack.

In Part III, we see that while the twentieth- and twenty-first-century legal establishment has uniformly viewed *McCulloch* as a canonical case, debates over the spirit of the Constitution have often been framed as disagreements over the proper interpretation of *McCulloch*. For progressives (Chapter 10) and New Dealers (Chapter 11), the spirit of the Constitution was its adaptive capacity to empower Congress to address newly emerging national problems, and they interpreted *McCulloch* accordingly. But the Supreme Court tended to read *McCulloch* as support for a conservative judicial activism that construed national legislative powers narrowly. Strangely, neither the Court nor progressive lawyers or legislators consistently applied *McCulloch* to the Commerce Clause to develop a theory of implied commerce powers. Such a theory was not recognized until the late New Deal jurisprudence of the 1940s, as we will see in Chapter 12. That chapter also examines the emergence of a *McCulloch*/implied-powers approach to the Reconstruction Amendments, which had been rejected by the post-Reconstruction Supreme Court. In Chapter 13, I show that the apparent triumph of *McCulloch*'s doctrine of implied powers in the mid-twentieth century represented a high-water mark for *McCulloch*'s influence on the development of constitutional law, as the "long conservative" Court from 1969 to the present has tended to treat the case more as a symbol than a binding precedent. Most recently, the Court has shown signs of bending *McCulloch*'s nationalism back, at least slightly, toward a renewed emphasis on limited national powers.

My use of the term "nationalism" throughout the book requires explanation. In present-day common parlance, nationalism is an imprecise term meaning that the nation-state is the optimal unit of autonomous governance, or that nations do or should pursue self-interest in world affairs. Some use "nationalism" to cover such beliefs as patriotism, jingoism, or nativism. In this book, I use the term "nationalism" as it is used in American constitutional law discourse, particularly federalism discourse, to refer to the belief that the national government created by the Constitution is the supreme sovereign authority in the United States, while the states are subordinate entities with limited sovereignty rather than fully sovereign, independent governments. These two nationalisms—popular and constitutional nationalisms, perhaps—are at times related, but significantly different.

* * *

Knowing the story of *McCulloch*'s 200-year odyssey, from 1819 to the 2012 decision in the Affordable Care Act case, and beyond to the present day, helps us understand how our constitutional order has answered the basic questions of judicial supremacy and federalism. If the "spirit" of the Constitution is an expression of an unwritten interpretive ethos, then that spirit is something that has been transfigured repeatedly throughout the eras of U.S. constitutional history. *McCulloch* has been interpreted, or ignored, to fit the varying spirits of the Constitution.

PART I

DEFENSIVE NATIONALISM

"The Case Now to Be Determined"

John Marshall and *McCulloch v. Maryland* in Constitutional History

On March 6, 1819, an expectant audience packed into a cramped courtroom in the basement of the national Capitol building directly below the Senate Chamber. They were there to hear Chief Justice John Marshall deliver the Court's opinion in *McCulloch v. Maryland*, the first major case to reach the Supreme Court in which advocates of states' rights challenged the scope of Congress' legislative power. *McCulloch* came before the Marshall Court in early 1819 as a test case to decide the fate of the Second Bank of the United States. Created in 1816 by an act of Congress and signed into law by President James Madison, the Second Bank was a private corporation chartered by the U.S. government to act as a nationwide central bank and administer the government's finances. It was called the Second Bank because it was successor to the original Bank of the United States, the brainchild of Treasury Secretary Alexander Hamilton that had been created by act of Congress in 1791. The Second Bank had quickly become unpopular, and in 1819 the Maryland legislature tried to drive the Bank's Baltimore branch out of business by imposing prohibitive taxes on it. The precise legal question before the Court was whether a state could tax an entity acting on behalf of the federal government. But to establish that the Bank was a bona fide agent of the federal government, the Court had to consider whether Congress had the power to create the Bank in the first place.

Marshall had written this opinion himself, as he had done for nearly all the Court's decisions since he had been appointed in 1801 to become the nation's fourth chief justice. "In the case now to be determined," he read aloud, "[t]he constitution of our country, in its most interesting and vital parts, is to be considered; the conflicting powers of the government of the Union and of its members, as marked in that constitution, are to be discussed; and an opinion given, which may essentially influence the great operations of the government." One can imagine him pausing for dramatic effect before continuing, "No tribunal can approach such a question without a deep sense of its importance, and of the awful responsibility involved in its decision." Noting that the case involved a conflict between the respective powers of the federal and state governments—"a sovereign State, denies the obligation of a law enacted by the legislature of the Union"—Marshall asserted that the Court was to play a pivotal role in quieting the sentiments of disunion that cropped up episodically in the early Republic. The federal-state power conflict "must be decided peacefully, or remain a source of hostile legislation, perhaps of hostility of a still more serious nature; and if it is to be so decided, by this tribunal alone can the decision be made. On the Supreme Court of the United States has the constitution of our country devolved this important duty."[1]

The 10,000-word *McCulloch* opinion has two main parts. Marshall stated the first question simply: "has Congress power to incorporate a bank?" Because the federal government "is acknowledged by all to be one of enumerated powers," Marshall acknowledged, "the principle, that it can exercise only the powers granted to it, would seem too apparent" to be disputed. Nevertheless, the express powers granted to the federal government were written in broad, general language, and they also carried with them *implied* powers. The Bank's validity depended on the implied powers of Congress, because the power to incorporate a bank is not expressly granted. Implied powers are the means by which Congress executes the great powers granted in the Constitution. They are necessarily left to implication, because a constitution is necessarily written in broad outlines. Maryland's counsel argued that implied powers must be limited to those without which an express power would be nullified—"nugatory" in the words of strict constructionists of the period. Marshall rejected that contention. Congress, he said, must have discretion to choose among any means convenient or well adapted to implementing the granted power. Reading the Constitution in the narrower sense would undermine its adaptability to unforeseen crises and its ability to endure over time. Implied powers, Marshall observed, would thus exist under any sensible interpretation of the Constitution, but their existence was confirmed by the Necessary and Proper Clause. That clause, coming at the end of the enumeration of the powers of Congress in Article I, section 8, explicitly authorizes Congress "[t]o make all laws which shall be necessary and proper for carrying into execution the foregoing powers, and all other powers vested by this Constitution in the government of the United States, or in any department or officer thereof." The Bank was constitutional, Marshall concluded, because "it is a convenient, a useful, and essential instrument" in conducting the national government's "fiscal operations."[2]

Having determined that the Bank was constitutional, Marshall then considered whether Maryland could tax it. The question had to be analyzed against the backdrop of federal supremacy, whose essence is to remove all obstacles to federal government action within its sphere of authority. State taxation was a potential obstacle: taxation is essentially a power to regulate and even destroy what is taxed, limited only by the political wishes of the state's constituents. But the states' sovereign power of taxation extends only to powers that can be conferred by the state's constituents, which did not include a power over the national government. Therefore, states could not tax operations of the general government, just as a part cannot control the whole.

Marshall knew this ruling was an important one, but it seems doubtful that he saw *McCulloch* as a timeless "landmark case." The First and Second Banks of the United States had been the subjects of recurring political controversy, and *McCulloch* set out important principles regarding implied powers. But *McCulloch* was not the first case in which the Marshall Court recognized implied powers—his now-obscure 1805 decision in *United States v. Fisher*[3] had that distinction—and Marshall probably assumed *McCulloch* would not be the last. Ongoing arguments from strict constructionists over the scope of implied powers, Marshall acknowledged, meant that "the question respecting the extent of the powers actually granted, is perpetually arising, and will probably continue to arise, as long as our system shall exist."[4] Indeed, several more federalism cases arose during Marshall's tenure, yet Marshall would virtually ignore *McCulloch* for the last sixteen years of his judicial career, never referring back to its discussion of implied powers. He probably would have been surprised to learn that posterity would come to regard *McCulloch* as "the richest and most important single opinion of the United States Supreme Court in our entire history."[5]

* * *

In a Boston courtroom eight decades later, Marshall was once again the center of attention. On February 1, 1901, in the Supreme Judicial Court of Massachusetts, Chief Justice Oliver Wendell Holmes Jr., presiding, hundreds of would-be spectators had braved a severe snowstorm to attend the proceedings for "John Marshall Day," a nationwide observance of the centennial of Marshall's appointment as chief justice. Leading the ceremony in the Massachusetts locale, Holmes gave a fifteen-minute address, one of the dozens of speeches made around the country to honor Marshall. While the other speeches celebrated Marshall's greatness, Holmes adopted a slightly skeptical tone, reflecting on the accidents of history that contribute to one man's greatness. Marshall had been in the right place at the right time to become the "expounder of the constitution," and Holmes felt "doubt whether, after Hamilton and the Constitution itself, Marshall's work proved more than a strong intellect, a good style, personal ascendancy in his court, courage, justice and the convictions of his party." Holmes's summation struck a note of irony: "I do fully believe that if American law were to be represented by a single figure, sceptic and worshipper alike would agree without dispute that the figure could be one alone, and that one, John Marshall."[6]

Marshall's biography is far and away the most impressive of the 115 men and women who have served as Supreme Court justices, particularly his life before his appointment as chief justice at the age of forty-five.[7] Marshall participated in numerous key events of the Founding era. The only justice with a significant record as a combat veteran (other than Holmes himself), Marshall fought in several of Washington's major battles in 1777–78 and spent the harsh winter of that year with the Continental Army at Valley Forge. Marshall went on to develop a successful law practice, arguing several cases of national importance. He served in prominent legislative and executive posts in the Virginia government, and played a key role in favor of the Constitution at the all-important Virginia ratifying convention. Marshall was the friend or acquaintance of many of the Founding Fathers and the close confidant of Presidents Washington and Adams. Later, while chief justice, Marshall wrote and published a multivolume biography of Washington that for many years was viewed as definitive. He was the hero of the "XYZ Affair," one of the most famous and controversial diplomatic missions in U.S. history, in which Marshall bested the legendary French foreign minister Talleyrand in a battle of wills, facing down Talleyrand's efforts to extort bribes and loans from the U.S. envoys. Fame from this episode propelled Marshall into election to the House of Representatives, where in a brief career of a few months, Marshall made a significant mark and emerged as the leader of the moderate Adams wing of the Federalist Party. He performed superlative service in his brief tenure as Secretary of State at the end of the Adams administration. Only then did he begin his thirty-four-year tenure as chief justice, one of the longest Supreme Court careers in U.S. history, and far longer than that of most of his contemporaries.

Marshall's humble origins—he was born in a log cabin in a frontier village—add to the mythic quality of his life. Marshall's personal charm and affability, down-to-earth demeanor, and personal humility were legendary. These qualities are captured in William Wetmore Story's bronze sculpture of Marshall, which now adorns the lobby of the Supreme Court building. Though he is wearing his judicial robe, Marshall's hand is extended in a friendly invitation, as he slouches cross-legged in his chair.[8] Jefferson, revealing his own aristocratic side, tried to turn these qualities into a vice, referring contemptuously to Marshall's "lax, lounging manners." But Marshall's combination of greatness and humility are superbly suited to the lore of a democratic republic. So Holmes was quite right: if it were necessary to put a human face on the institutions of the Supreme Court and judicial review, John Marshall would be the only conceivable choice. *If* it were necessary.

* * *

In yet another Marshall celebration, this one in 1955, the 200th anniversary of Marshall's birth, Felix Frankfurter asserted that "the conception of the nation which Marshall derived from the Constitution and set forth in *M'Culloch v. Maryland* is his greatest single judicial performance."[9] Frankfurter was describing a consensus among constitutional lawyers that dated back to the turn of the century, and that continues to the present day.* To constitutional scholars, *McCulloch* is "possibly the most far-reaching decision ever handed down by the Supreme Court," and the "most canonical of cases" in American constitutional law—that is, the case most essential and most important for members of the legal profession to read and to know.[10] Indeed, *McCulloch* is presented as the leading case in every current constitutional law casebook, usually introducing the central topic of congressional power under Article I.[11]

Two versions of John Marshall have come down to us from history. To constitutional lawyers, Marshall "was not just creating doctrine but building a nation."[12] Constitutional law literature is filled with such references.[13] The implication is that Marshall was a Washington or Hamilton of the judicial branch, creating or shaping the nation's institutions beyond the Court itself, including even its territories or infrastructure. In this view of things, *McCulloch* was Marshall's "greatest single judicial performance" because it was his signature "nation-building" achievement. *McCulloch* expressed a "sweeping nationalist vision" that established the constitutional foundation for "the extraordinary expansion of federal authority" in the aftermath of the New Deal.[14]

A handful of historians of the Marshall Court have offered a more complex and ultimately more accurate picture of Marshall's jurisprudence in general and the *McCulloch* decision in particular. To these historians, Marshall tried to avoid political controversy in his judicial opinions by expressing his nationalistic views only when they commanded broad political support, while taking pains where possible to make concessions to opposing forces. Marshall's nationalism was "a critique of reserved state sovereignty" rather than an endorsement of modern "plenary federal regulatory power." In *McCulloch*, Marshall did not "so much affirm a 'broad' (a term he did not use) construction of Congress's powers as reject the restrictive construction adopted by Maryland's counsel." Thus, "[a]s an expression of nationalism, *McCulloch* is not to be understood as a prescient anticipation of the modern liberal state."[15]

Despite the caveats of these historians, it is the lawyers' version of John Marshall that predominates in American constitutional ideology. No doubt Marshall is of greater interest to lawyers, who have a stronger claim to "ownership" of his legacy and to the training deemed necessary to read and understand the texts that make

---

* Frankfurter's spelling of the case name with an apostrophe, "M'Culloch," requires comment. The official reports spelled the name "M'Culloch," using an upside-down and backward apostrophe, because that was how nineteenth-century printers rendered a lowercase superscript "c," which was itself part of an abbreviation, with the uppercase "M," for "Mc" or "Mac." Eventually that turned-around apostrophe was turned right-side up and retained in many modern references to the case despite the general abandonment by printers of the superscript "c" practice. Michael G. Collins, *"M'Culloch* and the Turned Comma," 266. I prefer to spell out the name rather than adhering to a bygone typographical convention, but I retain the apostrophe in direct quotations.

up that legacy. Historians are better equipped to understand Marshall in the context of his own time, and they have provided us a far more detailed and nuanced view than the lawyers' broad-brush hero. But the historians are deferential—if not diffident—in their conclusions. Rather than explaining how and why the lawyers' view of Marshall has strayed from historical fact, many historians seem unable in the end to resist getting swept up in the lawyers' hyperbole of the aggressively nationalistic, nation-building John Marshall. After describing Marshall's political centrism and caution, the historians nevertheless conclude that Marshall "made great law," "defined [the] nation," and led the Supreme Court's "heroic age."[16] Some otherwise careful historians have exaggerated *McCulloch*'s nationalistic impact on the crucial issue of Congress's power over economic development projects, claiming that *McCulloch* "gave impetus, not mere approval" to a legislative program of national economic development: protective tariffs, a national bank, and infrastructure projects (known as "internal improvements").[17] Not even revisionist legal historians who question the scope of Marshall's legacy are immune from the aggressive nationalist reading of *McCulloch*, seeing in the case "a commitment to Hamiltonian political economy."[18] For example, Michael Klarman writes that *McCulloch* "vindicated an almost limitless conception of national government authority," making it "difficult to imagine a politically plausible congressional exercise of power that would exceed constitutional limitations." Klarman insightfully demonstrates that *McCulloch* did not have a great influence on subsequent antebellum constitutional questions, but he then argues that that was only because Congress was far more cautious than the nationalistic Marshall.[19]

These broad interpretations see John Marshall and his *McCulloch* decision as charting a path through history that leads inexorably to where we are now. They make an implicit, unexamined claim about courts' ability to contribute directly to the creation of national culture, wealth, and power. The claims about Marshall and the meaning and influence of *McCulloch* need a much closer examination.

* * *

The nature and extent of Supreme Court citations to *McCulloch* can provide important information about *McCulloch*'s influence on constitutional law. Supreme Court decisions become binding law—"case law"—through the system of precedent, according to which later decisions should conform to rules set down by earlier ones. Lower courts are obligated to follow Supreme Court precedents in good faith. The Supreme Court can overrule or disregard its own precedents, but it rarely does so, generally adhering to the principle of *stare decisis*—literally "to stand by what has been decided." Under the common-law method of judicial opinion-writing that flows from this doctrine, court opinions cite precedents, sometimes to state the controlling case law, and sometimes to bolster their arguments by claiming the authority of respected precedents. Judicial opinions and legal briefs bristle with citations to "authority"—the names and page numbers of prior cases and other legal materials.

If numbers of citations alone tell us anything, they seem to support the broad claims about *McCulloch*'s influence—at least at first glance. *McCulloch* has been cited in 387 Supreme Court opinions, far more than any other Marshall Court case, including *Gibbons v. Ogden* (291) and *Marbury v. Madison* (269). Only *Brown v. Board of Education* has been cited with greater annual frequency than *McCulloch*, and that not by much.[20] But we need to look behind the numbers to ask what constitutional lawyers and historians are talking about when they talk about *McCulloch*.

There are several legal conclusions for which *McCulloch* can be, and has been, cited, but not all of them explain *McCulloch*'s place in constitutional history. The result of *McCulloch* was to hold that Maryland could not tax the Bank, and about one-third of the Supreme Court's citations to *McCulloch* are to make a point about this issue, which has been categorized as "intergovernmental tax immunity"—the limitations on the power of the federal and state governments to tax one another. This is an important subject, to be sure, but it is hard to imagine constitutional scholars waxing lyrical about the Supreme Court case that tells us whether, for example, a state can tax federal bonds held in a state bank.[21]

Nor is *McCulloch* especially famous for deciding that the federal government has the power to charter a corporation to assist in particular government functions. Again, this is an important point, but not the basis for *McCulloch*'s fame. The First and Second Banks of the United States were highly important and controversial institutions, and their opponents vigorously argued that the federal government lacked the power to charter a corporation. *McCulloch* settled this question so successfully that it did not remain a viable source of constitutional argument. Yet constitutional scholars don't celebrate *McCulloch* today because it empowers Congress to create entities like the Federal Deposit Insurance Corporation.

A third issue in *McCulloch*, one of continued concern to present-day readers, is federal supremacy. Why is it that Maryland could not tax the Bank? The Supremacy Clause of the Constitution states, "This Constitution, and the laws of the United States ... shall be the supreme law of the land."[22] This clause has been understood in part to mean that state laws are "preempted" (essentially, nullified) when they conflict with federal laws. *McCulloch* was an early instance of the Court applying this concept, and Marshall explained it thoroughly. The essence of federal supremacy is to remove all obstacles to federal government action within its sphere. Taxation is a potential obstacle: it amounts to a power to regulate and even destroy what is taxed, and it is limited only by the political wishes of its constituents. States' sovereign power of taxation extends only to powers that can be conferred by the state's constituents and does not include a power over the national government. The United States government "is the government of all; its powers are delegated by all; it represents all, and acts for all," Marshall declared. "Though any one State may be willing to control its operations, no State is willing to allow others to control them.

The nation, on those subjects on which it can act, must necessarily bind its component parts."[23] Because the Bank was created by the whole people of the United States, Maryland could not tax it. Otherwise, the people of Maryland would be exerting authority over the people of the rest of the states, who were not represented by Maryland's government.[24]

Excellent as it is, Marshall's succinct structural analysis of the principles underlying the Supremacy Clause only begins to suggest why McCulloch is the canonical case. Marshall's statement of the supremacy principle—"that the government of the Union, though limited in its powers, is supreme within its sphere of action"[25]—already commanded a broad antebellum consensus. Even critics of the Bank and the McCulloch decision agreed with it. A leading contemporary critic who attacked McCulloch's interpretation of implied powers nevertheless agreed that the Bank, if constitutional, could not be taxed by Maryland.[26] The Second Bank's foremost enemy, Andrew Jackson, sustained the principle of federal supremacy during the 1832–33 Nullification Crisis (Chapter 5). Likewise, the Taney Court treated McCulloch as authoritative on the taxation point, even as it ignored McCulloch's implied powers holding.[27]

In sum, McCulloch's discussions of taxation, federal corporate charters, and federal supremacy are not what inspired later generations to canonize the case as having "set forth" a "conception of the nation," in Felix Frankfurter's words.[28] We don't celebrate McCulloch as "the Great Intergovernmental Tax Immunity Case," "the Great Federal Incorporation Case," or "the Great Federal Preemption Case." These are important points of law, and account for approximately half of the Supreme Court's citations to McCulloch. But these issues fail to capture any long-running and fundamental constitutional conflicts, and tell us little about McCulloch's enduring influence.

* * *

The prevailing present-day understanding of McCulloch can be called the "aggressive-nationalism thesis" after legal historian Richard Ellis's book about the case, Aggressive Nationalism. Ellis encapsulated a consensus view, arguing that McCulloch "provides an enduring nationalist interpretation of the origins and nature of the Constitution and the union and a broad definition of the necessary and proper clause . . . , which has laid the foundation for the living Constitution, and with it the means for an almost infinite increase in the powers of the federal government."[29] The aggressive-nationalism thesis thus has two elements: McCulloch (1) embodies broad nationalist principles, and (2) established those principles in our constitutional doctrine once and for all. To test the truth of this claim, we need to unpack the two elements to identify their premises.

What does it mean to say that McCulloch embodies nationalist principles? McCulloch has been celebrated for three nationalist elements of the opinion. First, the opinion famously asserts a *nationalist theory* of the United States Constitution, rejecting the so-called compact theory. Second, *McCulloch* embraces a permissive view of *implied powers*, and suggests that the Court will generally defer to Congress's interpretation of the scope of its own implied powers. Third, *McCulloch* endorses what can usefully be called a *capable Constitution* theory, by which the Constitution should be interpreted flexibly to empower the national government to address unforeseen national problems through changing times and circumstances.

To understand these nationalist elements in *McCulloch*, we first have to distinguish between "negative" or "defensive" nationalism, and "affirmative" or "aggressive" nationalism. Marshall's "defensive nationalism," as Marshall scholar Charles Hobson calls it, meant preserving the Union against extreme states'-rights theories that would pull it apart. In the circumscribed role of a judge who could issue rulings only on legal disputes brought into his court, Marshall's tools were limited. His primary contribution was in developing doctrines to justify the Supreme Court's power to review state laws and actions that conflicted with the Constitution.[30]

But the predominant claims about Marshall by constitutional scholars—the lawyer's John Marshall—are that Marshall Court decisions were affirmatively, aggressively nationalistic. This stance requires something more than fending off attacks from radical states'-righters. "Aggressive nationalism" implies a willingness to push the boundaries of constitutional politics in a pro-nationalist direction, expanding the constitutional limits of federal government authority beyond what would have been acceptable to the political mainstream. It suggests a Court relying on its institutional protections, such as judicial life tenure, to take bold positions and perhaps even withstand attacks from the political center.

Interpreters of Marshall's jurisprudence, and of *McCulloch* in particular, have not always been careful to distinguish between these two types of nationalism. Of course, judicial review is inherently negative insofar as its direct impact stems from striking down laws, and rarely if ever affirmatively mandates legislative action. But while the Marshall Court could not have *required* the chartering of a national bank, or the building of a national road, it permitted the former and could have permitted the latter. With this in mind, we can consider the three nationalist elements of the opinion.

The Nationalist Constitution. Marshall began his argument in *McCulloch* by asserting that the government of the United States "proceeds directly from the people" rather than from a compact of sovereign States. He indicated that the need to address this point was forced on the Court by counsel for Maryland, who asserted instead that the Constitution was a compact with the states. The compact theory, which formed the core of states'-rights constitutionalism throughout the antebellum period, argued that states retained their sovereignty under the Constitution as they had under the Articles of Confederation. While the arguments spun out of this theory—strict construction, nullification, and secession—do not follow as logical corollaries, compact theory was nevertheless a dominant mode of argument against the assertion of national powers over the states. Here, Maryland's counsel used compact theory to argue that implied powers should be restricted to those "absolutely necessary" to the enumerated power, without which the enumerated power would be "nugatory."[31]

Marshall rejected compact theory in *McCulloch*. The people met in state conventions as a convenience, Marshall admitted, but that did not make the state conventions into the equivalent of sovereign state legislatures. On the contrary, the state legislatures assented to yielding the state's sovereignty to the constitutional scheme by "impli[cation] in calling a Convention and thus submitting that instrument to the people." Rather than reconstituting a league in which sovereign states yielded bits of their sovereignty, Marshall said, echoing *The Federalist* No. 37, the Constitution emanated directly from the people. This emanation created a government whose "powers are granted by them, and are to be exercised directly on them, and for their benefit." [32]

The Capable Constitution. Some of the most celebrated quotations from *McCulloch* express broad and abstract ideas that might usefully be called "the capable Constitution." More of an interpretive approach to constitutional problems than a specific doctrine, the capable Constitution is one that should be amenable to adaptation, and interpreted flexibly to allow the national government to address the nation's problems.[33] This idea overlaps with, but differs from, "the living Constitution," a term generally used by legal scholars to suggest that open-textured constitutional provisions, often emphasizing those involving rights, should embody evolving societal values.[34]

McCulloch expressed the capable Constitution idea in various ways, but most famously in this passage:

> A constitution, to contain an accurate detail of all the subdivisions of which its great powers will admit, and of all the means by which they may be carried into execution, would partake of the prolixity of a legal code, and could scarcely be embraced by the human mind. It would probably never be understood by the public. Its nature, therefore, requires, that only its great outlines should be marked, its important objects designated, and the minor ingredients which compose those objects be deduced from the nature of the objects themselves. That this idea was entertained by the framers of the American constitution, is not only to be inferred from the nature of the instrument, but from the language. . . . It is also, in some degree, warranted by their having omitted to use any restrictive term which might prevent its receiving a fair and just interpretation. In considering this question, then, *we must never forget, that it is a constitution we are expounding*.[35]

Justice Felix Frankfurter called this last sentence "the single most important utterance in the literature of constitutional law—most important because most comprehensive and comprehending."[36] Marshall's arresting sentence is amenable to different interpretations. In context, it seems to reaffirm that a Constitution must be deemed to have implied powers, since specific legislative means can't be specified in advance. But it can be given a loftier meaning, that a written Constitution must be interpreted expansively and adaptably.

The latter meaning draws support from a different passage, making essentially the same point about implied powers. The Necessary and Proper Clause, which affirms the existence of implied powers, should not be strictly construed "in a constitution intended to endure for ages to come, and, consequently, to be adapted to the various crises of human affairs."[37] Finally, Marshall suggests in several places that Congress should be accorded the discretion to interpret its legislative powers "in the manner most beneficial to the people." Marshall refers to the "beneficial exercise" of legislative power several times in the opinion, and elsewhere observes that "a government, entrusted with such ample powers, on the due execution of which the happiness and prosperity of the nation so vitally depends, must also be entrusted with ample means for their execution."[38]

Implied Powers. In contrast to the abstract and somewhat amorphous nationalist Constitution and capable Constitution elements, *McCulloch's* principles regarding implied powers offer a doctrinal rule with great potential to expand national legislative powers. A federal law challenged as exceeding Congress's enumerated powers can be upheld as an implied power under the Necessary and Proper Clause if it is "appropriate" or "plainly adapted" to implementing a power vested in the national government. Whether a particular law is a well-adapted means to execute a given power—the "degree of its necessity"—is a matter for the discretion of Congress. The Court cannot strike down a law because it deems the law ineffectual or otherwise bad policy. The Hamiltonian theory of implied powers affirmed in *McCulloch* held great potential for expanding the scope of federal legislative power, particularly if applied to "vast" powers such as the Commerce Clause.

The implied powers and capable Constitution elements offer the clearest support for the aggressive-nationalism interpretation that has made *McCulloch* a canonical case. *McCulloch's* nationalist constitutional theory, in contrast, hovers ambiguously between aggressive and defensive nationalism. The latter argument complements Marshall's ultimate conclusion that the states cannot tax the Bank, because they do not represent the whole people—a fundamentally defensive nationalism point. One could imagine using the theory as a basis to argue that national powers, intended to be exercised for the people's benefit, should be liberally construed. Marshall didn't go quite that far, deploying the theory to rebut strict construction and to argue for "fair" construction of the Constitution's grants of powers.[39] Still, Marshall's nationalist theory at least atmospherically supports an aggressive nationalist interpretation of the case.

* * *

The second part of the aggressive-nationalism thesis contends that *McCulloch* established its nationalist principles once and for all. What might this mean? The conventional story of *McCulloch* is that it built the constitutional foundations of the nation. That story implies claims about influence and historical causation. Constitutional scholars who praise *McCulloch* have used a cavalcade of verbs implying that *McCulloch* played an important causal role in building the constitutional foundations of the modern American nation. *McCulloch* "*buil[t]* a nation," "*implemented* a nation-building agenda," "*laid* a foundation," "*established* an expansive view of national power," "*gave* impetus," and so on.[40] Even more judicious claims—*McCulloch* "*creat[ed]* doctrine," "*resolves* a number of important questions"[41]—imply that *McCulloch* shaped constitutional law directly.

But these accounts are typically vague about the details of historical causation, blurring or confusing at least three ways in which that influence may have come about. The most ambitious claim is that *McCulloch* shaped the course of politics by defining the constitutional law in which that politics took place. An example of this characterization is the suggestion that by establishing the constitutionality of broad congressional powers, *McCulloch* was a causal agent in congressional policy decisions to build U.S. infrastructure and develop the domestic economy. Second, and less ambitious is a claim that *McCulloch* was a source of ideas that, adopted or internalized, shaped the thinking of important political actors or guided their debates. Third, *McCulloch* may have "made *law*," by establishing constitutional doctrines that bound and directed later Supreme Courts through the mechanism of judicial precedent.[42] The chapters that follow will show that all three of these causal arguments for *McCulloch*'s historical influence are greatly exaggerated, if not false. For the moment, I will suggest criteria for assessing these claims.

The first claim, that *McCulloch* shaped the course of politics, is the most ambitious. It adopts an exceedingly jurocentric world view in which judicial decisions shape events. Yet it is readily apparent that judicial review acts primarily to block government actions rather than to affirmatively require them, and the Supreme Court has never *required* Congress to exercise its powers more nationalistically. The Court could have tried to block Congress from building a road; it could not have ordered Congress to build a road.

A more plausible version of this claim about *McCulloch*'s impact is that the Court encouraged or "invited" Congress to exercise its powers to an aggressively nationalistic degree. The antebellum Congress frequently debated proposals that formed a legislative program of national economic development that was eventually dubbed "the American System" by its leading proponent, congressman and later senator Henry Clay. Only one case directly involving an element of the American System ever came before the Court—the national Bank, in *McCulloch*—and only a handful of cases raised such issues peripherally.[43] Nevertheless, several constitutional law scholars read *McCulloch* as a kind of constitutional pre-approval letter for the nation-building legislation of the American System.[44] Our assessment of this claim will have to examine whether the Marshall Court made the most of its limited opportunities to promote nationalist principles and the American System, in *obiter dicta* (statements reaching beyond the precise issues of the case), or to build *McCulloch* into a nationalist doctrinal edifice for posterity.

The claim that *McCulloch* contributed significantly to constitutional debates suggests that ideas expressed in the decision were influential, irrespective of the extent to which courts or elected officials felt obligated to follow *McCulloch*. This claim further suggests that we should find direct references to *McCulloch* in political speeches or state papers, language that echoes Marshall's opinion, or other traces of its influence. Although Marshall's ideas in *McCulloch* were wholly derivative, the opinion may still have been a conduit by which the ideas were delivered to others.

The claim that *McCulloch* "made law" seems the most natural effect we would expect from a judicial decision, and should be the easiest to prove. To assess the claim that *McCulloch* made law in an "aggressive nationalism" sense, we would need to examine whether the more nationalistic elements of the decision were viewed as binding on subsequent constitutional interpreters. Did political actors or Supreme Court justices believe themselves to be constrained by Marshall's ruling? This constraint can occur at more specific and more general levels. Every judicial decision at a minimum resolves the immediate controversy between the litigating parties; what elevates the judicial function beyond mere arbitration to lawmaking is the effect beyond the individual case. We could ask whether the dispute between Maryland and the Bank was authoritatively resolved; whether parties similarly situated to Maryland (other states) felt themselves bound by the ruling to refrain from imposing unconstitutional taxes on the Bank; and whether political actors felt themselves bound to apply the underlying principles of *McCulloch* to comparable situations, such as by acknowledging other implied powers of Congress. To be sure, some of the Court's most influential decisions have met with resistance by government officials or the public. But we can ask whether that resistance eventually gave way to consensus and stability, or even grudging compliance, and whether one can draw a direct line between the case and the eventual consensus. *Brown v. Board of Education* may be an example of the consensus phenomenon, and *Roe v. Wade* of grudging compliance.

McCulloch is more difficult to judge along these lines, because its nationalistic elements did not involve judicial orders to refrain from conduct. *Brown* ultimately led to judicial directives to cease segregation practices, and *Roe* required states to desist from enforcement of blanket prohibitions of abortion. *McCulloch* implied a judicial directive to cease efforts by states to impose taxes on Bank operations, but this is not the case's most celebrated element. Again, the doctrinal claim for aggressive nationalism is that the Court established permission for broad federal legislative powers whose exercise it could not compel.

We can also ask to what extent *McCulloch* bound subsequent decisions of the Supreme Court. A Supreme Court decision can be said to make law in a doctrinal sense if it becomes a binding judicial precedent. Exactly what "binding judicial precedent" means is a point frequently taken for granted, and rarely analyzed, by legal scholars. The mechanism of judicial precedent and stare decisis is a species of historical claim. It presumes continuity. Consider the *Civil Rights Cases* (1883),[45] which established the state action doctrine under the Fourteenth Amendment. I consider it one of the more discreditable rulings ever rendered by the Supreme Court (see Chapter 7), but it is an excellent example of a strong precedent. It has been continuously adhered to for over a hundred years, the Court declined to overrule it when requested, and its doctrine was relied on as recently as 2000 to strike down a key provision of the Violence Against Women Act.[46]

The following three qualities seem like sensible criteria for a Supreme Court decision to "make law" in the technical sense of a binding precedent:

1. stability: the decision becomes a stable precedent within a few years;
2. adherence: the decision's force as precedent constrains later constitutional actors (including the Court itself) largely because of the court's own institutional power or prestige;
3. non-malleability: the decision articulates a rule that constrains behavior and cannot be made to "mean all things to all people."

As *an argument about historical causation* of present-day constitutional nationalism, the aggressive-nationalism account of *McCulloch* is almost entirely wrong. *McCulloch* had little impact on constitutional debates prior to the New Deal, though it received some noteworthy if not pervasive attention during the Civil War and the Progressive era. As a judicial precedent, *McCulloch* failed all three of the lawmaking criteria just noted. Its nationalist holdings were ignored by the Supreme Court for the next fifty years after its issuance. The Marshall Court never cited *McCulloch*'s nationalism principles, and the Taney Court effectively overruled *McCulloch*, albeit not formally by name. Where *McCulloch*'s theory of implied powers had the most to contribute to constitutional development—in expanding Congress's powers to legislate under the Commerce Clause and the Reconstruction Amendments—the Supreme Court either ignored *McCulloch* or construed it narrowly, citing *McCulloch* as frequently to strike down as to uphold an exercise of federal legislative power. Arguments suggesting that *McCulloch* has been interpreted and followed consistently over time should be viewed with caution, because they probably result from ideologically motivated historical accounts.

As *a textual interpretation* of *McCulloch*, the aggressive-nationalism thesis is not entirely wrong. *McCulloch* contains several important passages that can validly be read as supporting a broad nationalist vision. Marshall's apparent concession to the Jeffersonian-Madisonian concept of limited enumerated powers can be read as grudging and ambiguous. Moreover, *McCulloch*'s theory of implied powers could, if pushed to its logical conclusion, be read to legitimate most exercises of legislative power by Congress to address national problems. Even under a theory of limited enumerated powers, the logic of implied powers spelled out in *McCulloch* could, when applied to the Commerce Clause, justify all present-day federal regulation of the economy.

Yet the nationalist implications of *McCulloch* are themselves ambiguous. Marshall did not clearly commit himself to the most nationalist positions that the opinion touched on. Significantly, Marshall himself shrank from applying his own doctrine of implied powers to the Commerce Clause, even in *McCulloch* itself. And the *McCulloch* opinion is filled with phrases that lend themselves to restrictions on the exercise of national legislative power. Time and again, in the two centuries following *McCulloch*, the Supreme Court has seized on those limiting phrases and concepts to strike down contested exercises of congressional authority.

In the end, what can be said about the aggressive-nationalism thesis as a reading of *McCulloch* is that it is a valid and perhaps even the best reading, but it isn't the only valid reading. Frankfurter's choice of words, placing *McCulloch* in "the literature of constitutional law," is revealing. *McCulloch* is like a great but forgotten piece of literature that was rediscovered, dusted off, and newly appreciated. But like great works of literature, *McCulloch* has been subject to varied and even contradictory interpretations. Indeed, it may be that this ambiguity—the ability of both sides of the constitutional argument to claim *McCulloch*'s "true" interpretation—has contributed as much as anything to its canonical status.[47] Each generation of constitutional interpreters since 1819 has interpreted *McCulloch* differently, and in ways that reveal the generation's own interpretive "spirit" of the Constitution.

In the chapters that follow, we will see that *McCulloch*'s journey since 1819 to become the Great Case is a tortuous, fascinating odyssey that has much to tell us about the nature of American constitutional law and how that law is made.

2

"The Question Perpetually Arising"

Constitutional Law and Politics, 1819

The United States government, Marshall explained early in the *McCulloch* opinion, is "one of enumerated powers," and therefore "can exercise only the powers granted to it." Although this axiom was "too apparent" to require extended argument, he added, "the question respecting the extent of the powers actually granted, is perpetually arising, and will probably continue to arise, as long as our system shall exist."[1] This evocative phrase was at once a history and a prophesy.

In the antebellum United States, the dispute over the respective powers of the national and state governments over questions of domestic policy—what we now call "federalism" questions—defined the major political line of division. Public debates over policy questions were frequently cast as questions of constitutional interpretation.[2] The federalism divide emerged as a recurring theme during Washington's presidency, and remained the dominant theme of constitutional politics during Marshall's tenure on the Court. Marshall himself traced this division to the debate over the first Bank of the United States in 1791. In the fourth and final volume of his *Life of Washington*, published in 1807, Marshall wrote that two parties had emerged, one that "retained the opinion that liberty could be endangered only by encroachments upon the states," and the other that "sincerely believed that the real danger which threatened the republic was to be looked for in the undue ascendency of the states." The debate over the national bank, Marshall concluded, "made a deep impression on many members of the legislature; and contributed, not inconsiderably, to the complete organization of those distinct and visible parties, which, in their long and dubious conflict for power, have since shaken the United States to their centre."[3] But by 1819, the national bank wasn't the only highly contested question dividing advocates of national power and states' rights. Equally important were debates over "internal improvements" (federally subsidized infrastructure projects) and slavery.

It is naive to think of the Supreme Court and constitutional law as insulated from politics. Marshall's observation about the Bank controversy reflects a wider phenomenon usefully understood as *constitutional politics*. Public policy controversies that reflect fundamental differences over the nature of government are typically framed as arguments over constitutional principles. These debates make up constitutional politics. As Marshall suggested, they often settle into political party differences. Constitutional *law* refers to the doctrines and arguments by which our institutions—often, but not exclusively courts—attempt to settle these debates.[4] This chapter describes the major questions of constitutional law and constitutional politics that in 1819 set the stage for the *McCulloch* decision.

* * *

An axiom of American constitutionalism holds that the government of the United States is one of limited powers. In the Founding era, the nature of these limitations was contested. A significant number of Framers and members of the first Congress believed that Congress's authority was limited only insofar as its legislation had to deal with matters of national rather than local concern. Under this view, the Constitution's enumeration of powers was a non-exhaustive list, and Congress had broad implied powers to legislate for "the general welfare."[5] An opposing view maintained that the Constitution limited the national government to its enumerated powers. This view, which I call "enumerationism," won out in the sweeping victory of the Jeffersonian Republicans in the 1800 elections, and has been the orthodox view ever since, in form if not in substance.[6]

Nevertheless, implied powers are all but unavoidable with a written Constitution, even one of limited enumerated powers. As Marshall would write in *McCulloch*, a constitution's "great outlines" and "important objects" will be stated expressly, but the means to implement them must be "deduced."[7] The first Congress, 1789–91, understood the practical necessity of implied powers: It enacted regulations of merchant ships and seamen, and maintained a nationwide system of navigational aids ("lighthouses, beacons, buoys, and public piers") deemed "incidental to commerce"—that is, necessary and proper to, or implied from, the power to regulate commerce.[8] When the first Congress debated the constitutionality of Alexander Hamilton's proposed Bank of the United States in early 1791, proponents argued that the power to create a bank was implied from several enumerated powers. Hamilton summarized the theory of implied powers in his famous 1791 memorandum to President Washington on the Bank's constitutionality, asserting that "every power vested in a Government is in its nature sovereign, and includes by force of the term, a right to employ all the means requisite, and fairly applicable to the attainment of the ends of such power."[9] In an 1812 judicial opinion, James Kent, the preeminent jurist and constitutional scholar who was then a judge on New York's highest court, "willingly accede[d]" to the idea that the national government's powers "whether express *or implied*, may be plenary and sovereign" and "may even be liberally construed in furtherance of the great and essential ends of the government."[10] The existence of implied powers was thus well established by the time *McCulloch* reached the Court in 1819.

Without implied powers, it would be difficult if not impossible to implement the enumerated powers. The power to collect taxes, for example, implies the power to hire tax collectors, which in turn implies the power to make it a crime to assault a tax collector in the line of duty, and so on. Thus, even hard-line Jeffersonians, who believed in construing the Constitution strictly to limit federal powers, had to acknowledge the existence of implied powers. But they tried to limit the scope of implied powers by arguing that the Constitution permitted only those implied powers "strictly" or "absolutely" necessary to implementing an enumerated power. "Strictly necessary" implied powers were those, the Jeffersonians argued, without which the enumerated power would be useless—"nugatory" in the language of the day.[11] This approach would not only hamstring Congress by denying it the ability to make reasonable legislative choices; it was also paradoxical. Opponents of Hamilton's whiskey tax, for example, might have argued that the implied power to tax whiskey is not *strictly* necessary, because the taxing power could be exercised, and revenue raised, by an excise tax on carriages instead. But the carriage tax would likewise be unnecessary because of the availability of the whiskey tax. Marshall made this point in *United States v. Fisher* (1805),[12] the Court's first effort to construe the Necessary and Proper Clause. Strict necessity could not be the test, Marshall argued, because "[w]here various systems might be adopted for [a legislative] purpose, it might be said with respect to each, that it was not necessary because the end might be obtained by other means."[13] Strict constructionists never came up with a workable definition of "strict" or "absolute" necessity, but merely employed the idea when it suited them to oppose some proposed legislation.

The conflicting constitutional views about implied powers play out in the text of the Tenth Amendment, which states, "The powers not delegated to the United States by the Constitution, nor prohibited by it to the states, are reserved to the states respectively, or to the people." When the Tenth Amendment was debated in the first Congress in 1789, the House rejected an effort to add the modifier "expressly" before "delegated," a move that might have stripped Congress of implied powers and gone a long way toward reverting the Constitution to the terms of the Articles of Confederation, which had limited the powers of Congress to those "expressly granted."[14] Congress thus recognized the need for implied powers, and made clear that they are "delegated" to the United States by the Constitution. This delegation made manifest the tension between implied powers and "states' rights." By negative implication, powers delegated to the United States are not "reserved to the states." Conversely, if some specific set of powers was deemed "reserved to the states," it could not be impliedly delegated to the United States. This tension would be played out again and again in constitutional disputes until 1941.

* * *

Even taking as axiomatic that the Constitution is "the supreme law of the land," the idea of federal supremacy, and the competing concept of states' rights, raised several vexatious questions about the respective roles of Congress, the Supreme Court, and state governments in the interpretation and application of the Constitution. For example, are states bound by unconstitutional federal laws? And who decides whether those laws are unconstitutional?

The Alien and Sedition Acts of 1798 provoked these questions. The Acts were pushed through Congress by the anti-French Federalist majority, which was riding a wave of public outrage against France in the wake of the XYZ Affair. The Alien Act authorized the president to deport foreigners deemed dangerous to the United States. Though a standardless and ill-advised attack on the rights of noncitizens, it was at least arguably constitutional under the standards of the time. The Sedition Act, which made it a crime to publish "seditious libel" critical of the national government, was an indefensible infringement of free speech at any time since the Founding. The Federalists overreached in passing these laws, and the reaction against them reverberated in American politics throughout the nineteenth century as a rallying cry for states' rights.[15] The episode fed the dubious idea that authorizing states to decide the constitutionality of federal laws for themselves was essential to preserving individual liberty.

The rallying cry was expressed in the Virginia and Kentucky Resolutions of 1798, ghostwritten for the state legislatures by Madison and Jefferson, respectively. Both resolutions identified the United States Constitution as a "compact," with the states as parties. Madison's Virginia Resolution, asserted that states had the right and duty "to interpose for arresting the progress of" federal laws that were a "deliberate, palpable, and dangerous exercise" of powers "not granted" by the Constitution. In the Kentucky Resolution, Jefferson asserted that it was "despotism" for "the general government" to act as "the exclusive judge" of its delegated powers. The states "who formed" the compact "being sovereign and independent, have the unquestionable right to judge of its infraction." Madison did not explain how a state would "arrest" an unconstitutional law, while Jefferson hinted darkly at the possibility of seeking, albeit as a last resort, the "dissolution" of the Union. Despite the subtle distinctions between the two resolutions, succeeding generations read them as a single document, and they became the ideological forbears for radical states'-rights theories of "interposition," "nullification," and ultimately secession. Both before the Civil War and for several decades after, states'-rights advocates in the Democratic party continued to celebrate the Virginia and Kentucky Resolutions, often referred to as "the principles of '98."[16]

The Resolutions' suggestion that states had the power—whether through their legislatures or their courts—to issue binding interpretations of the U.S. Constitution within their own borders challenged both the operations of federal statutes and instrumentalities, and the authority of federal courts. The Marshall

Court twice found it necessary to reaffirm its own basic authority to review state court interpretations of federal law, even though that power was plainly granted by section 25 of the 1789 Judiciary Act. The cases, *Martin v. Hunter's Lessee* (1816) and *Cohens v. Virginia* (1821), are two of the Marshall Court's most renowned nationalism cases, and exemplify defensive nationalism. But *Martin* and *Cohens* did not manage to settle the issues raised by the Virginia and Kentucky Resolutions to Marshall's satisfaction: the Resolutions' anti-unionist sentiment preoccupied Marshall throughout his chief justiceship.[17]

* * *

In discussing the supremacy principle in *McCulloch*, Marshall stated "that the government of the Union, though limited in its powers, is supreme within its sphere of action." The idea of separate "spheres" of state and federal regulatory power "command[ed] the universal assent of mankind."[18] Antebellum states' righters worried continuously that an expansive federal sphere would lead inexorably to a "consolidated government"—a national government that exercised all legislative power. But their resistance to federal regulation was not motivated by laissez faire, the preference for minimizing all government regulation. As legal historian William Novak has shown, antebellum constitutionalists believed in a "well-ordered society," characterized by dense networks of laws, known as state "police power" or "municipal legislation," that promoted the general welfare and regulated property to prevent one owner impinging on the rights of others.[19] Instead, the states'-rights anxiety about federal power reflected a concern that an enlarged federal sphere would nullify these state and local laws, leaving nothing in their place.

Antebellum constitutionalists created a conceptual problem for themselves by assuming that most grants of power to the national government were *exclusive*. That is, a grant of power to the federal government—in nineteenth-century parlance, the "general" or "national" government—meant a denial of that power to the states. The exclusivity problem was not particularly a matter of federal *laws* preempting state laws—Congress enacted relatively few regulatory laws in the antebellum era. Rather, the problem was the belief that the Constitution's mere grant of a federal power could be deemed exclusive in its "negative" or "dormant" state—that is, by virtue of the grant per se, even in the absence of federal legislation.

Today, these fears might seem odd, since modern federalism so easily accepts the idea that the federal and state governments exercise concurrent powers—they can regulate the same subject matter simultaneously. Coordination of overlapping federal and state jurisdiction is handled through preemption doctrine, which for the most part tolerates the simultaneous pursuit of non-conflicting policies by the two levels of government. Some antebellum constitutionalists realized this, though they were in the minority.[20]

To most antebellum constitutional thinkers, concurrent powers presented an insoluble puzzle. Justice Bushrod Washington, a member of the Marshall Court and George Washington's nephew, captured the common understanding in an 1820 opinion for the Court: "I am altogether incapable of comprehending how two distinct wills can, at the same time, be exercised in relation to the same subject, to be effectual, and at the same time compatible with each other."[21] The Constitution's Tenth Amendment seems to corroborate the view of separate and non-overlapping spheres of federal and state power in providing that "The powers . . . reserved to the states" are those "not delegated to the United States by the Constitution."[22] Similarly, the Articles of Confederation declared that "Each state retains . . . every power, jurisdiction, and right, which is not by this Confederation expressly delegated to the United States, in Congress assembled."[23] Constitutional lawyers and judges believed that states "surrendered" those powers that *were* delegated (or expressly delegated) to the national government.[24] The Constitution's grant of a power to the federal government created a strong presumption that states were precluded from exercising that same power concurrently, and the Marshall Court struggled inconclusively with this issue.[25] In a world of mutual exclusivity, keeping federal powers "few and defined," as Madison put it in *The Federalist*,[26] could be essential to preserving state authority to regulate.

* * *

Article I, section 8, clause 3 of the Constitution empowers Congress "To regulate commerce with foreign nations, and among the several states, and with the Indian tribes." These thirty-three words, known as "the Commerce Clause," form what has become the Constitution's broadest grant of regulatory power to the federal government. With few exceptions, a general antebellum consensus acknowledged that Congress should have plenary power to regulate relations with foreign governments, commercial and otherwise. But Americans disagreed about the breadth of Congress's power to regulate *interstate* commerce.

In contrast to today, when established Supreme Court doctrine authorizes Congress to regulate most economic activity under its commerce power, many constitutional interpreters in 1819 understood interstate commerce primarily to mean sales or shipments of trade goods across state lines. Liberal construction of the Commerce Clause might broaden this understanding to include passenger traffic or even immigration, and recognition of implied commerce powers might make the reach of Congress broader still. Nevertheless, commerce was defined sufficiently narrowly to exclude productive activities such as labor, manufacturing, and agriculture. These activities were viewed as distinct from buying-and-selling transactions, and therefore not in themselves commerce, even though they produced goods for interstate markets or required the interstate purchase of tools and supplies.

Strict constructionists sought to rein in Congress's power over interstate commerce by arguing that it was intended to be significantly narrower than the power over foreign commerce. While *foreign* commerce might be subjected to protective tariffs to promote the position of domestic industries in foreign trade, strict constructionists maintained that Congress lacked affirmative power to promote the domestic economy by regulating *interstate* commerce. They further argued that while Congress could prohibit foreign commerce through an embargo—like Jefferson's embargo of trade with Britain in 1807–8—the power "to regulate" *interstate* commerce did not permit its prohibition. These latter arguments were convenient for Republicans wanting to reconcile support for Jefferson's foreign policy with states'-rights arguments that would protect against regulation of slavery under the Commerce Clause.[27]

Nationalists disputed these interpretations, arguing that there was no difference between the scope of the powers to regulate foreign and interstate commerce, and that the interstate commerce power extended to domestic economic development policies.[28] Even under a narrow definition in which "commerce" meant "trade," the commerce power held potential for wide-ranging affirmative regulation by Congress. As we will see, advocates of a national bank argued that a federal power to charter such a bank could be implied from the Commerce Clause. More generally, almost all business could be tied to commerce, which could in theory give extensive implied powers to Congress.[29]

Nationalist interpretations of the Commerce Clause did not necessarily contemplate a lot of affirmative federal regulation. Many antebellum constitutionalists recognized that interstate commerce under the Confederation had been hampered by discriminatory regulations and taxes imposed by states trying to favor their own merchants. State import duties at coastal ports handling foreign trade were a particular irritant.[30] To address these problems, the new Constitution prohibited states from laying tonnage duties and from using import and export taxes as a source of revenue, in addition to authorizing Congress to regulate foreign and interstate commerce.[31] Daniel Webster and some other constitutional interpreters saw the Commerce Clause as intended to create a domestic free-trade zone, unencumbered by state protectionism, to be achieved by striking down state laws under the *dormant* Commerce Clause.[32]

Because the Commerce Clause had the greatest potential of any enumerated power to preempt state laws, the debate over its scope was especially contentious. In 1812, the New York Court for the Correction of Errors decided *Livingston v. Van Ingen*,[33] a federal dormant commerce challenge to the Livingston-Fulton steamboat monopoly on the Hudson River. A decade later, this monopoly would be struck down by the U.S. Supreme Court in *Gibbons v. Ogden*. In the 1812 case, however, the New York court upheld the monopoly, and the lead opinion by James Kent rejected the idea of dormant Commerce Clause exclusivity. Kent pointed to the array of state laws that would be nullified by such exclusivity, including control of turnpike roads, regulations of peddlers and paupers, liquor licensing, inspection and export laws, health and quarantine laws, and laws "prohibiting the importation of slaves." Nothing would be more "preposterous and extravagant" than to see these regulations as void because they might *possibly* "interfere with the power granted to Congress to regulate commerce."[34]

* * *

Debates over the scope of commerce and other constitutional doctrines were not esoteric, abstract questions. They had profound, tangible implications for important national policies—including internal improvements and slavery, both of which could theoretically be regulated under the federal commerce power.

At least as dominant as the slavery question in antebellum constitutional politics was a debate over "internal improvements." This term covered what we now call infrastructure, and referred specifically to means of transportation and communication. Internal improvements formed a key element of a broad program for national economic development, also including a national bank and protective tariffs, that eventually became known as the "American System." Nineteenth-century internal improvements projects included the building or maintenance of roads, canals, bridges, navigable waterways, navigation facilities, and later, in the century, railroads and telegraphs. The improvements were "internal," because in contrast to earlier infrastructure projects to improve coastal navigation, these were aimed at improving transportation, communication, and commerce between the American seaboard and its expanding interior. The Cumberland Road (also known as the National Road), America's first national highway, was authorized in 1806 with the intention of linking the newly admitted state of Ohio with the east. New impetus for nationwide internal improvements projects materialized in 1815. The end of the War of 1812 early that year generated a wave of national feeling, while the war had painfully illustrated how a lack of good roads could hamper national defense. And, of course, continued westward expansion increased the demand for communications with the east. Internal improvements were contested on policy grounds, of course, based on questions of feasibility and expense, or objections by state or regional representatives to spending the nation's treasure for the benefit of other states or regions. States dominated by elite plantation owners did not necessarily feel a strong interest in paying taxes to improve the commercial opportunities for smallholding farmers or local merchants. As was typical in the antebellum era, these policy objections were turned into constitutional ones.[35]

The constitutional challenge to the Second Bank of the United States in *McCulloch* was interwoven with the debates over internal improvements between 1815 and 1819. In successive December annual messages to Congress in 1815 and 1816, President Madison called on Congress for legislation to undertake "a comprehensive system" of road and canal building. In doing so, Madison was continuing

a policy of mixed messages about internal improvements established by his prede-
cessor. President Jefferson had called for federal internal improvements legislation
while also expressing doubts about the constitutionality of such programs, sometimes asking for constitutional amendments to permit them, other times simply
overcoming his scruples. Perhaps Jefferson and Madison's presidential perspective
created a tension with their states'-rights views, or perhaps they were just trying to
please a diverse national constituency. In any event, Jefferson signed two bills for
the Cumberland Road project and allowed his treasury secretary to recommend
an ambitious road- and canal-building program to Congress. Madison, for his part,
expressed constitutional qualms even as he suggested vaguely that Congress might
nevertheless have power to pursue such projects.[36]

Congress promptly responded to Madison's December 1816 message by
passing the "Bonus Bill" at the end of its lame-duck session in March 1817. The
law chartering the Second Bank in March 1816 had required the Bank to pay the
Treasury a $1.5 million "bonus" as consideration for its monopoly privileges. The
Bonus Bill proposed to use this as seed money for a long-term federal internal
improvements fund. But Madison vetoed the Bonus Bill on his last day in office,
flatly asserting that the bill was unconstitutional. The next day, Madison's newly
elected successor James Monroe gave his inaugural address, announcing his view
that internal improvements were unconstitutional, but advocating a constitutional
amendment to permit them. The conflict-averse Monroe, hoping to usher in an era
of nonpartisan politics, was trying to head off contentious debate by preemptively
implying that he would veto a new bonus bill. He was only partially successful. When
the new Congress convened in December 1817, Monroe's suggestion about a constitutional amendment went nowhere, as nationalists recognized it as a poison pill
that would imply acceptance of strict construction of the existing Constitution.[37]
But a new bonus bill in the House was quickly tabled and substituted with a set of
abstract resolutions on the constitutionality of internal improvements. In a series of
close votes in March 1818, the House approved a resolution stating that Congress
had the power to *appropriate money* to construct roads and improve waterways
under its spending power, but voted down resolutions stating that Congress had the
power to *construct* roads and canals under the war, postal, or commerce powers.[38]

The debates over these resolutions canvassed the constitutional arguments at
length. Since they occurred just one year before *McCulloch*, Marshall was undoubtedly aware of them. Virginia Republicans led the congressional opposition to internal improvements, and Marshall, whose permanent home was in Richmond,
remained highly sensitive to the anti-federalist or states'-rights sentiments and
maneuvers emanating from his home state. Many of the key speeches were reprinted
in the *National Intelligencer*, a leading Washington newspaper that Marshall read.[39]

What were the constitutional objections to internal improvements? Opponents
made strict constructionist arguments against implied powers or in favor of narrow
constructions of granted powers. The power to establish post roads was not to build

them, they argued, but merely a power to designate existing state roads as postal routes. The power "to regulate" commerce meant only a power to "prescribe the manner, terms, and conditions, on which that commerce should be carried on"— not a power to promote commerce. Under such restrictive views, Congress had no peacetime power to build roads, and the war powers could not justify building roads when there was no war on.

Strict constructionists believed that the building of a federal road could quite literally make an inroad into state jurisdiction.[40] Supporters of internal improvements repeatedly found themselves trying to reassure opponents that federal jurisdiction over such roads would extend only to maintaining them, while states would retain jurisdiction "[i]n regard to all other matters occurring on the road, whether of crime, or contract, etc."[41]

The political and intellectual leader for internal improvements in Congress was Henry Clay of Kentucky. Born in 1777, Clay was a statesman of the first rank and leader in Congress for four decades, from 1811 until 1850, where he led the nationalist wing of the Republican party—the "National Republicans"—that eventually coalesced into the Whig party. Clay's career included negotiating the peace treaty with Britain after the War of 1812, engineering the Missouri Compromise of 1820, and running as a major-party candidate for president four times (unsuccessfully).

As Speaker of the House from 1815 through 1820 and again from 1823 through 1825, Clay took a leading role in some of the most important internal improvements debates in Congress. In several speeches, he laid out an economic development theory asserting that the end of the Napoleonic wars in 1815 shrank the war-dependent trade opportunities with Europe; accordingly, the United States had to develop a thriving internal market with a national bank, protective tariffs, and an ambitious program of internal improvements. He eventually called this program "the American System." Clay believed that state-managed internal improvements were insufficient. A state's constitutional power to improve its internal infrastructure was undoubted, and states undertook many such projects—the Erie Canal being the most famous example. But states often lacked the money or self-interest to pursue ambitious projects. A road through a state, or a canal connecting navigable waterways, might disproportionately benefit the terminal points of the route without significantly benefiting the states in between.[42] Therefore, it was essential for the national government to oversee internal improvements.

Clay's 1818 speeches on internal improvements placed great emphasis on constitutional arguments. Described by Marshall in 1823 as "an enlightened statesman," Clay was also an accomplished lawyer and sophisticated constitutional thinker who argued several major cases before the U.S. Supreme Court.[43] Clay's constitutional theory was shaped by his experience as a commercial lawyer and entrepreneur in Kentucky, which at that time was the heart of the American west. The overriding purpose of the Constitution, Clay argued, was to strengthen the bonds of Union, which were continually stretched by westward expansion. Congress had a constitutional duty to ensure that "the population of the east and of the west" remained a united "community in interest and in feeling." Only a well-developed network of roads and canals could accomplish this goal. Clay paid lip service to the doctrine of limited enumerated powers: he had "imbibed" the constitutional principles of Madison and the Virginia Resolution of 1798, he said. But the powers of Congress included those "fairly incident to the express grant," which had to be given "a liberal construction" to promote the overriding constitutional end of uniting a geographically diverse people. The Constitution was less threatened by excesses of national powers than it was by "the water gruel regimen" of strict construction that would render the Constitution "a dead letter." "We . . . are not legislating for this moment only, or for the present generation, or for the present populated limits of these states," Clay declared, "but our acts must embrace a wider scope; reaching northwestwardly to the Pacific, and more southwardly to the river Del Norte. . . . [S]ee how essential is the power, how important its exercise, of connecting" these reaches "by means of roads and canals."[44]

Pursuant to his liberal construction of the Constitution, Clay argued that roads and canals were authorized by the postal, war, and commerce powers. The power to "establish post roads" was not a mere power to deliver the mails along designated state roads. Rather, it was a power to *build* federal roads "to diffuse information, to circulate intelligence, for commercial, military and social purposes, that all parts of the country might derive the benefits intended from the constitution." Clay argued at length that "establish" as used in the Constitution was "a creative power," and therefore the power to build roads was directly granted by the postal power. Further, the war power implied a power to build roads and canals to facilitate the movement of armed forces for national defense. Finally, Clay argued that an internal improvements power could be implied from the Commerce Clause. There was no basis in the Constitution to conclude that the power to regulate interstate commerce was less than the power to regulate foreign commerce, he contended. The two commerce powers were "conferred on Congress in precisely the same terms," and "therefore must have an equal latitude of construction." The power "to regulate" interstate commerce necessarily included a power to facilitate and promote it, because that construction promoted the Constitution's purpose of strengthening the Union. Just as the power to build maritime improvements such as lighthouses, buoys, piers, and custom houses "had been incidentally derived" from the power to promote, and therefore regulate, foreign commerce, so Congress could build roads and canals to facilitate interstate commerce.[45]

Clay took up the question of implied powers under the Necessary and Proper Clause, which would be the one of the central issues decided in *McCulloch*. He denied the position of the Virginia Republicans that only those implied powers "strictly" or "absolutely" necessary were allowable. But, he continued, "whatever language you may choose to express it, there must be a certain degree of discretion left to the agent who is to apply it." There was no security from an excessive exercise of implied powers in verbal formulas, because that discretion lay entirely with Congress. The security against abuse lay within Congress itself, "in the fact of our being members of the same society, equally affected ourselves by the laws we promulgate," by "the oath which is taken to support the constitution," and finally "that, at the end of every two years, the members must be amenable to the people." Finally, there was "the last resort" for "extreme cases"—the right of revolution. Clay did not include the Supreme Court as a check on Congress's abuse of its discretion over implied powers.[46]

* * *

Slavery loomed over the constitutional politics of the antebellum era, shaping, distorting, and constraining virtually all discussions of the Constitution's distribution of powers between the national and state governments—even when slavery was not explicitly mentioned. In theory, slavery could have been the subject of four constitutionally distinct levels of regulation: the international slave trade, the interstate slave trade, the states' internal policies governing slavery and race, and the extension of slavery to new territories and states.

A broad consensus held that Congress could prohibit Americans' participation in the international slave trade. At the Constitutional Convention in 1787, South Carolina and Georgia bargained for a twenty-year moratorium on a congressional prohibition of the international slave trade. The moratorium was set forth in the Constitution's "Migration and Importation Clause."[47] But the foreign slave trade was unpopular even with many slave owners, who believed their slaves would have higher value in an interstate slave market free from foreign competition. Without even waiting for the twenty-year moratorium to expire, Congress in 1794 made it illegal to fit out any ship for the importation of slaves, banned ships sailing from U.S. ports to engage in slave trafficking abroad, and strictly regulated the size of ships transporting slaves in "the coasting trade"—commercial transport within U.S. territorial waters.[48] Later, acting on a reminder in President Jefferson's December 1806 annual message, Congress made it a crime to import slaves from abroad, effective January 1, 1808, the first day the prohibition would be permitted under the Migration and Importation Clause.[49] Yet there was no expressly granted power to do this; it was simply assumed on all hands that importing slaves was a form of foreign commerce subject to regulation, including prohibition, under the Commerce Clause.

If Congress could regulate or prohibit foreign commerce in slaves, why could it not do the same for interstate commerce in slaves? The text of the Commerce Clause makes no distinction between the kinds of things that can be regulated under the foreign and interstate commerce powers. Under straightforward logic, Congress would have the power to regulate or prohibit the interstate slave market. Even under a narrow definition of commerce limited to the buying and selling of goods, the relationship between slavery and commerce regulation should not have been far-fetched. The consensus opinion in the early nineteenth century recognized that the Commerce Clause was designed to empower Congress to maintain a level playing field for interstate trade, something even the pro-slavery Taney Court believed.[50] A perception that plantation-based slave labor offered competitive advantages over freehold agriculture fueled anti-slavery politics in the antebellum era.[51] In theory, that belief might have led to regulation or prohibition of interstate buying and selling of slave-made goods. It could even have been argued that state slave codes obstructed free labor and therefore violated the dormant Commerce Clause.

Yet antebellum legal thinkers did not develop such constitutional arguments for regulating or abolishing slavery under the Commerce Clause. As early as 1794, when it rebuffed an anti-slavery petition by a Benjamin Franklin–led group of Pennsylvania abolitionists, the House of Representatives resolved that "Congress have no authority to interfere in the emancipation of slaves or in the treatment of them within any of the states, it remaining with the several states alone, to provide any regulation therein, which humanity and true policy may require."[52] Starting from this bedrock assumption, the commerce power was interpreted accordingly. While some abolitionists eventually argued for a commerce power to regulate the interstate slave trade in the 1830s and 1840s, this was a minority view even within abolitionism, which itself was a fringe movement with little political clout.[53] Most northerners accepted southern slavery as a reasonable price to pay for the Union. Southern states enacted slave codes, which stripped slaves of the most basic human protections and imposed draconian behavioral restrictions on them. Northern states enacted laws to keep slaves out and to resist cooperation with slave catchers pursuing alleged runaways, but some northern states also enacted laws restricting the rights of free black people. The antebellum constitutional order assumed that free black people had no rights by default, as white people did, but rather only those rights enacted by law.[54] The "purely internal" buying and selling of slaves within a state was understood to fall entirely outside the enumerated commerce power. The same could be said for slave labor. The doctrine that slavery was a "municipal" matter within the reserved powers of the states was accepted and acted upon in both the North and the South. It was not dictated or even suggested by the language of the Constitution; it was rather a mindset of constitutional politics.

Despite this entrenched constitutional consensus protecting slavery from federal regulation, southern constitutionalists perceived nationalist constitutional doctrines as threats to slavery. Many legal thinkers viewed a power over internal improvements as a threat to the state's internal regulatory system of police powers in general, and its regulation of slavery in particular.[55] In 1825, the eighty-two-year-old Jefferson complained that "the three ruling branches" of the national government" were conspiring to strip their colleagues, the State authorities, of the powers reserved by them, and to exercise themselves all functions foreign and domestic. Under the power to regulate commerce, they assume indefinitely that also over agriculture and manufactures, and call it regulation to take the earnings of one of these branches of industry—and that, too, the most depressed—and put them into the pockets of the other—the most flourishing of all. Under the authority to establish postroads, they claim that of cutting down mountains for the construction of roads, of digging canals, and, aided by a little sophistry . . . a right to do . . . whatsoever they shall think or pretend will be for the general welfare.[56]

Jefferson's reference to agriculture may have been an oblique allusion to plantation agriculture and slavery. Other Virginians expressed concern about the adverse effect on "agriculture" if a congressional internal improvements power were recognized.[57] John Randolph, a congressman from Virginia and scion of the illustrious Virginia Randolph family, was more direct. Speaking in opposition to a major internal improvements bill, Randolph connected the themes of implied powers, the Commerce Clause, and internal improvements to the slavery question. If the power "to regulate commerce" were given "a *liberal* construction" to include a power to build roads and canals, then it would also include a congressional power to "*prohibit* altogether the commerce between the States, or any portion of the States" or to "declare that it shall be carried on only in a particular way." If Congress possessed such implied powers, Randolph warned, it "may emancipate every slave in the United States."[58]

Although Congress never attempted to assert a commerce power to regulate slavery, its power to prohibit slavery in the territories was expressly asserted and sharply contested, and would ultimately become the prime mover toward southern secession and the Civil War. [59] Opposition to the expansion of slavery into the territories was far broader in northern states than abolitionism. Many northerners willing to tolerate slavery within the states where it existed were strongly opposed to its territorial expansion. The idea that new territories and states should be reserved for free white labor, free from the burden of economic competition with slave agriculture and of status competition with the social pretensions of slave owners, was compatible with the most virulent white racism.[60]

The territorial question had not generated extensive controversy prior to 1819. But when Missouri applied to Congress for statehood in December 1818 with a pro-slavery constitution, its admission threatened to upset the existing balance of eleven slave and eleven free states, thereby creating a majority of slave states for the first time since New Jersey abolished slavery in 1804. This would worsen the existing disproportion of slave-state power in national politics. Not only was a new state entitled to two Senators despite its relatively small population, but slaveholding representation was enhanced in the House and the electoral college by the "three-fifths clause," the Constitution's formula counting slaves as three-fifths of a person for purposes of determining population-based electoral representation.[61] To prevent a slave-state majority, representative Tallmadge of New York introduced an amendment to the Missouri admission bill in February 1819 to condition Missouri's entry into the Union on its abolishing slavery in its state constitution. This proposal touched off an intense national debate that was not resolved until the Missouri Compromise of 1820. The compromise ultimately provided that Missouri would be admitted as a slave state, but that slavery would be prohibited in the remainder of the Louisiana territory north of the 36° 30' latitude line that demarcated Missouri's southern boundary. In addition, the district of Maine, ceded by Massachusetts, would be admitted as a free state, preserving the balance in the Senate between slave and free states.[62]

The Missouri debate opened just a few days before oral argument in *McCulloch*. The floor debate in the Senate was going on literally right above the justices' heads in late February and early March 1819, since the Supreme Court chamber was located in the Capitol basement directly below the Senate chamber.[63] Plainly, the justices knew of this debate when they decided *McCulloch*. Did it influence the decision? The most immediately relevant constitutional provisions to the Missouri debate, the Territories and New States clauses, were only tangentially relevant to *McCulloch*.[64] But the justices may have believed that the question of implied commerce powers could have implications for a congressional power to regulate slavery.

* * *

The *McCulloch* decision was one episode in a long-running constitutional struggle over the question of federal control over national currency and monetary policy, a question that was not fully settled for 150 years after the founding of the republic.[65] The Constitution's provisions on this are suggestive, but incomplete. Congress is authorized to coin money and regulate its value; to punish counterfeiting; and to borrow money on the credit of the government. States are forbidden to "coin money; emit Bills of Credit; [or] make any Thing but gold and silver Coin a Tender in Payment of Debts."[66] The grant of congressional power to determine the value of coin, which implicitly denied that power to the states, continued a policy established under the Articles of Confederation. But the other prohibitions on state issues of money, either as coin, paper, or negotiable debt instruments, were new. Taking these clauses together, the Constitution strongly suggests that the nation's money supply should be regulated by the national government, not the states.[67]

Alexander Hamilton, as the nation's first Secretary of the Treasury, addressed aspects of this issue in a comprehensive set of proposals to rationalize the nation's finances and promote domestic industry. The First Congress passed a bill adopting the recommendations in Hamilton's *First Report on the Public Credit* to assume and refinance state revolutionary war debts, on December 14, 1790. Shortly thereafter it received Hamilton's *Second Report on the Further Provision Necessary for Establishing Public Credit*, also known as the *Report on a National Bank*.[68] Hamilton argued that a national bank would be an integral part of "the general system of the political economy." Administratively, a national bank would provide a reliable source of loans to the government, and facilitate revenue collection. Taxes could be paid at local branches in each state, using deposit credits or paper banknotes rather than "specie"—gold and silver coin. Taxpayers would not have to cart gold and silver around the country, a doubly disadvantageous practice, since it exposed the precious metals to robbery and took them out of circulation during transit. Hamilton also understood that an inadequate money supply slowed the pace of commercial transactions and therefore hindered the economy. The Bank would manage the nation's money supply through prudent lending and the circulation of reliable banknotes. The resulting "increase [in] the active capital of [the] country" would make the Bank a "nurser[y] of national wealth." At the same time, Hamilton proposed that the Bank would be primarily a private corporation (the federal government would own 20% of the Bank's stock). As such, it would not be subject to "the temptations of momentary exigencies" that tend to push governments to overdraw their treasuries.[69]

A Senate committee adopted Hamilton's recommendations and reported out a bill to incorporate a Bank of the United States. Senate debates at this time were secret, but the legislative record shows that the proposal was vigorously debated in the House of Representatives, where Virginia congressman James Madison led the nascent Jeffersonian faction in opposition. Madison and his followers focused primarily on policy arguments. A national bank would favor mercantile over agrarian interests, and its state branches would compete with state banks and interfere with states' banking regulation. More worrisome, a national bank would induce corruption, as had happened in the reviled British system: legislators and officials would be irresistibly tempted to speculate in bank stock, thereby becoming beholden to moneyed interests at the heart of the central government. This concern was prescient: thirty members of Congress would eventually invest.[70]

Late in the debate, Madison offered constitutional objections. First, he argued against a liberal construction of implied powers. A bank was "convenient," but not necessary to conduct the government's financial functions, because state banks could fulfill the national government's banking needs. Second, and more importantly, chartering a bank was "a distinct, an independent and substantive prerogative, which not being enumerated in the constitution could never have been meant to be included in it." Without explaining why a corporate charter was such a power, Madison argued that recognizing such "important" powers by implication would cause "[t]he essential characteristic of the government, as composed of limited and enumerated powers, . . . [to] be destroyed." Further, no powers could be inferred from the nature or needs of a sovereign national government. The failure of the Constitution to specify any needed national power must either be "lamented, or supplied by an amendment of the constitution."[71] Significantly, Madison ignored the Commerce Clause as an applicable enumerated power. In his first speech, on February 2, he simply omitted mention of it. In his second speech, on February 9, after the Commerce Clause was raised by the bank bill's supporters, he replied summarily and lamely, "but what has this bill to do with trade? Would any plain man argue that this bill has anything to do with trade?"[72] According to the startling recent discovery by constitutional scholar Richard Primus, Madison concocted all these constitutional arguments at the eleventh hour to block passage of the bank bill. Constitutional objections had not guided the opposition at the outset, and Madison's suggestion that the enumerated powers limited what Congress could do was not in fact the consensus view. With the Pandora's box of constitutional objections having been opened, other Jeffersonians joined in to argue against the bank proposal's constitutionality.[73]

Supporters of the bank bill responded by arguing for implied legislative powers. "[T]he constitution had expressly declared the ends of legislation; but in almost every instance had left the means to the sober and honest discretion of the legislature," said Massachusetts Federalist Theodore Sedgwick. The power to charter a bank was implicit in the commerce, war and borrowing powers, as well as the power to pay the debts of the United States.[74]

The Senate passed the bank bill on January 20, 1791 and on February 8, the House passed the bill by a wide margin, thirty-nine to twenty. The vote roundly rejected Madison's novel critique of implied powers. Madison would later be enshrined as the "father of the Constitution," but his contemporaries apparently did not take his views as authoritative original intent. The bill was submitted to President Washington, who took his full allotment of ten days, as provided by the Constitution's Veto Clause, to consider it.[75] He asked his Secretary of State Thomas Jefferson and his Attorney General Edmund Randolph to write opinions on its constitutionality.[76] Both argued that the bank bill was unconstitutional and urged Washington to veto it. Randolph argued that, although the powers of Congress should not be strictly construed, incorporating the Bank pushed them too far. According to Jefferson, unless implied powers were limited "to those means without which the grant of power would be nugatory," Congress would be permitted "to take possession of a boundless field of power, no longer susceptible of any definition."[77]

Washington then asked Hamilton for a written response.[78] With only a few days before Washington's constitutional deadline to veto or sign the bill, Hamilton provided a point-by-point response to the arguments of Randolph, Jefferson, and the bank's congressional opponents. Hamilton began by arguing that the opponents' narrow interpretation of the federal government's powers "would be fatal to the just & indispensible authority of the United States." The Constitution's grant of powers, "especially those which concern the general administration of the affairs of a country, its finances, trade, defence, etc. ought to be construed *liberally*, in advancement of the public good." This interpretation included recognition that the

Constitution conferred implied as well as enumerated powers. As a "decisive example" of implied powers, Hamilton referred to the first Congress's recent act "concerning light houses, beacons, buoys & public piers." A power to build and deploy them was implied, even though they were not strictly necessary to regulating interstate and foreign commerce. By this logic, the power to create a national bank could be derived from the powers to collect taxes and borrow money, to raise and support armies and navies, and to make "all needful rules and regulations concerning the property of the United States."[79] Should an economic crisis produce a drain of gold reserves from the nation, or a potential war suddenly require "large sums . . . to make the requisite preparations," loans from individuals or small banks would be inadequate, making a national bank necessary. The government must have the power to provide against such foreseeable crises before they arise.[80]

Significantly, Hamilton argued that the power to incorporate the bank was also implied from the Commerce Clause. "Money is the very hinge on which commerce turns," he asserted, restating in detail the mercantile advantages outlined in his Bank Report. Congress could regulate commerce by chartering a corporation, whether a bank or a trading company like the East India Company. Both the bank's charter and its banking activities were "to be regarded as a regulation of trade. . . ." Finally, Hamilton advanced a synergistic interpretation of congressional powers. Taking "an aggregate view of the constitution," Hamilton argued "that it is the manifest design and scope of the constitution to vest in congress all the powers requisite to the effectual administration of the finances of the United States." Furthermore, banks and corporations are a means implicitly residing within the sovereignty of all governments. Therefore, "little less than a prohibitory clause can destroy the strong presumptions" supporting the power to create a bank.[81] Washington was convinced, and signed the bank bill into law on February 25, 1791.

By most accounts the First Bank fulfilled its intended functions effectively over the next twenty years. Branches were opened in several cities beginning in spring of 1792. The Bank acted as fiscal agent of the Treasury, making payments of interest on public debt and salaries of government officials (including Jefferson), brokering sales of new issues of government securities, collecting taxes and customs duties, supplying gold bullion and foreign coins to the U.S. mint, brokering foreign exchange, and serving as the principal depository of government funds. The Bank also served a central banking function, moderating the outflow of specie to foreign countries and providing a widespread and uniform circulating medium, since its notes were legal tender for debts due the government. The initial opposition faded as Jeffersonians became reconciled to the Bank or saw its advantages. Even Jefferson himself gave in: as President, he signed a bill authorizing the Bank to establish a New Orleans branch office, and another to punish the counterfeiting of the First Bank's notes. And of course, the Bank assisted in financing Jefferson's Louisiana Purchase.[82]

But by early 1811, with the First Bank's charter set to expire, the politics of the Bank had turned again. Madison—now President—had come around to see the advantages of the Bank and supported the charter renewal. But new opposition to the First Bank arose within Republican ranks. A growing demand for easy credit and prolific banknote issues by emerging businesses led to an increase in state-chartered banks from four in 1791 to over 100 by 1811. In its central banking role, the First Bank restrained profligate lending practices, generating resentment among the more speculative or reckless banks and their customers. These voted Republican.[83] Fueled by this new source of opposition, bills to renew the First Bank's charter for another twenty years were defeated by a single vote in both the House and the Senate, in January and February 1811.[84]

With the First Bank dissolved, the number of state banks exploded from 100 to nearly 260, and their banknote circulation more than doubled. The War of 1812 greatly worsened the inflationary impact of this profusion of new paper money, as the export and domestic coasting trade fell off sharply, reducing both the volume of economic transactions and the federal government's main revenue source. To finance the war, the government now depended on depreciating state banknotes, and loans negotiated piecemeal with numerous state banks on various terms. Funds were not necessarily available where the government needed them, if the loans could be obtained at all. In August 1814, the British raids on Washington and Baltimore touched off a run on the banks around the country, and a corresponding suspension of payments in specie. Soldiers were paid in depreciated paper currency (sometimes in notes that the government would not itself accept in payment of taxes) and the Treasury found itself "obliged to borrow pitiful sums" simply to keep basic government operations going—to pay its stationery bill, for example. The disuniformity in value of these depreciated state banknotes—by now, the dominant form of circulating money—had become a currency crisis.[85]

This experience converted President Madison, the First Bank's erstwhile opponent, into an ardent supporter of a new national bank. In his December 1815 annual message, Madison asked Congress to charter a Second Bank and authorize it to issue paper money to address the problem of currency disuniformity. But what gave the federal government the power to issue a uniform paper currency, either through a private bank or the Treasury? Madison, whose constitutional principles were heavily mixed with pragmatism, cagily declined to specify the constitutional grounds, leaving the arguments to his treasury secretary and congressional supporters of a Second Bank.[86] These Bank supporters came up with two arguments. To appeal to hard-line Jeffersonians, Madison's treasury secretary argued that chartering a new national bank was authorized under the Coinage Clause of the Constitution for the limited purpose of restoring the value of specie as the national circulating medium. It was hoped that this argument would be consistent with otherwise strict construction of federal powers, since it purported not to rely on the Necessary and Proper Clause, even though it seems difficult to connect a Bank to the value of coin without an implied-powers argument. Ironically, strict constructionists and hard-money advocates would argue in later decades that the Coinage Clause implied a prohibition against the national government's issuance of paper money.[87]

An argument aimed at centrists more open to nationalistic views was supplied by South Carolina Representative John C. Calhoun, who introduced the bill desired by Madison on January 8, 1816. Calhoun had begun his political career as a "national Republican" and staunch advocate of the American System. A decade or so later he would change his political stripe and become the apostle of states' rights, but in his February 26, 1816 floor speech supporting the bank bill, Calhoun was positively Hamiltonian in outlook. Calhoun explained the national currency crisis in detail. State banks were circulating banknotes with such "prodigality" that "this paper was emphatically called trash or rags." The resulting disuniform currency "was a stain on public and private credit," causing payment of government debts in depreciated currency, and creating inequalities in taxation since the Treasury would accept depreciated banknotes at face value. A vicious circle was created as depreciated paper money caused a flow of gold and silver out of the country, leading banks to suspend specie payments, leading to further depreciation of their notes. The numerous state banks lacked the ability or incentive to act in concert to address the problem. But a new *national* bank *could* address the problem by conscientiously redeeming its own notes for specie, and imposing discipline on state banks by refusing to accept their non-redeemable notes.[88]

Calhoun argued that the national government's power to charter a national bank was beyond question. The power "to give a steadiness and fixed value to the currency of the United States" was properly implied, not only from the delegated power "to coin money," but also "as an attribute of sovereign power, a sacred and important right." It had to exist somewhere, and at the moment, the monetary power was being "exercised by two hundred and sixty banks, scattered over every part of the United States, not responsible to any power whatever for their issues of paper." The Constitution had to be interpreted to adapt to unforeseen circumstances. The Framers could not have predicted the "extraordinary revolution in the currency of the country," in which state banks "would have multiplied from one to two hundred and sixty; from a capital of four hundred thousand dollars to one of eighty millions." The undisciplined circulation of paper money from private state-chartered banks was no different, in spirit, from state treasury notes expressly prohibited by the Constitution. The inability of the states to produce a uniform national currency, due to a state race-to-the-bottom in banking regulation, created "a strong presumption [that] this power was intended to be exclusively given to Congress."[89] In sum, a national power to impose a uniform currency was not simply a power to issue national treasury notes or banknotes, but also necessarily entailed a power to regulate the money supply by exerting control over the nation's banking system. Because a chaotic state banking system had emerged since Hamilton's time, Calhoun could see more clearly than Hamilton that a national bank had a central banking function to exercise: disciplining state banks' creation of money.[90]

* * *

The bill to charter the Second Bank passed both houses in March and April 1816, after a few weeks of limited debate in which the Republicans overcame the internal divisions that had scuttled the First Bank in 1811. The bill was signed by Madison on April 10, 1816. The Second Bank, like the First, was fundamentally a private corporation, with some government participation. Of its twenty-five directors (all of whom were required to be U.S. citizens), five were to be appointed by the president, and 20% of the Bank's stock would be owned by the federal government.[91]

The Second Bank promptly established branch offices in sixteen states, which enabled it to fulfill one of its functions of moving federal funds around the country. Otherwise, the Second Bank did not get off to a good start. At times ineptly managed financially, the Bank also made political enemies by aggressively competing with state-chartered private banks for commercial lending business. Several state legislatures, whose members very likely had political or even financial stakes in their state-chartered banks, sought to retaliate or improve their state banks' competitive position by imposing taxes on the Bank's operations. The Second Bank also found itself overextended by its aggressive lending, and in late 1818 it abruptly began calling in many of its loans as the economy entered a downturn. The rapid contraction of credit exacerbated (if it did not cause) the nation's first major depression, which became known as the Panic of 1819. The public perception of the Bank turned increasingly negative. The *McCulloch* case arose in this setting.[92]

* * *

The constitutional politics of 1819 established a set of arguments that would bear directly on the *McCulloch* case. Nationalists like Hamilton, Clay, and Calhoun had developed arguments recognizing implied commerce powers broad enough to encompass federal control over the money supply and internal improvements. While paying lip service to the idea of limited enumerated powers, they argued for "liberal" construction of the Constitution's grants of powers, and suggested the existence of implied powers from sources other than those expressly granted. Powers could be implied from the nature of sovereignty, from reading several constitutional provisions synergistically, or from recognizing national needs that could not be met by the states. Jeffersonian Republicans, led by presidents and congressmen from Marshall's home state of Virginia, met these arguments by advocating strict construction and states' rights. Doctrinally, they opposed implied powers, particularly implied commerce powers, and hoped to confine them within a narrow test of strict necessity. Their pragmatic motivation was opposition to internal improvements, particularly road building. Looming in the background of these constitutional and policy arguments was the fear that increased federal power would threaten state control of slavery. Marshall was undoubtedly aware of all of these issues as he pondered his decision in *McCulloch*.

"Has Congress Power to Incorporate a Bank?"

The *McCulloch* Litigation and Opinion

At the beginning of Marshall's tenure in 1801, the U.S. Supreme Court was not a prestigious institution. John Jay, who resigned as first chief justice in favor of other public pursuits in 1795, declined Adams's attempt to nominate him to a second tenure as chief justice in 1801, citing the institution's lack of prestige and authority.[1] The appointment then went to Marshall, who reshaped the Court into a respected and vital branch of government through a combination of artful political navigation, skilled administrative oversight, and his own lengthy tenure and personal leadership. Most importantly, Marshall curtailed the former practice of seriatim opinions, in which each justice wrote his own legal analysis in support of the judgment. The new practice of issuing a single "opinion of the Court" gave the rulings more authority. The opinion would represent the majority of the justices (who then numbered six),[2] but Marshall always strove for unanimity. Marshall could not prohibit separate concurrences or dissents, but he worked hard to gain his colleagues' agreement. He wrote most of the Court's opinions himself, thus taking on the lion's share of the workload. Another factor was convincing his judicial colleagues to live in the same Washington, D.C. boardinghouse during the short, six-week Supreme Court sessions. There, he could bring his conviviality and his excellent store of Madeira to bear on his brethren as they held case conferences over communal meals. After 1811, all of Marshall's fellow justices were appointees of Marshall's ideological opponents. It is a testament to Marshall's personal charm and talent for compromise that he was able to win unanimity on so many cases until the late 1820s, when that unanimity finally began to fray.[3]

While it is not true that Marshall personally dominated his colleagues, his influence on the Court's substantive output was far greater than that of any other justice before or since. This influence is particularly true of constitutional cases. Not only did he write most of the important constitutional opinions, but there was also not a lot of opportunity to receive substantive input from judicial colleagues. The Marshall Court issued its opinions quickly, typically within a few days following the oral argument, and draft opinions were thus usually not circulated among the justices beforehand. In this sense, opinions written by Marshall were Marshall opinions to a greater degree than is true of majority opinions today.[4]

McCulloch was one of these opinions, written toward the end of the Marshall Court's so-called golden age, from approximately 1810 to 1825. By the time the case was heard, nearly thirty years of debates over a national bank had created a rich record of factual, policy, and constitutional arguments that supported not only the Bank's constitutionality, but also potentially broad interpretations of several congressional powers. Marshall knew this record well. In researching his *Life of George Washington*, published in installments between 1804 and 1807, Marshall closely studied the documentary history of the 1791 debates over the first Bank, including the House debates and the internal cabinet memoranda. He described them in detail in the finished work. Hamilton's memorandum to Washington, Marshall wrote, contained "a copious and perspicuous argument on the policy of the measure."[5]

* * *

McCulloch v. Maryland was argued before the U.S. Supreme Court, beginning on February 22, 1819. James McCulloh (McCulloch was a misspelling by the Court clerk) was the "cashier" (the manager) of the Baltimore branch of the Second Bank.[6] Under his management, the Baltimore branch sought to evade control of the central Bank office, and was particularly aggressive in extending easy credit to outcompete state banks for commercial lending business. McCulloh and his cronies also used the branch to engage in widespread financial manipulation and outright fraud. In February 1818, Maryland enacted a law "to impose a Tax on all Banks or Branches thereof in the State of Maryland not chartered by the [Maryland] Legislature." The tax was imposed on notes issued by the bank, ranging from 10 cents to $20, depending on the amount of the note. Failure to pay the tax was punishable by fines of $100 for each offense. The Bank could obtain a waiver of the tax by paying a $15,000 annual fee. These costs may or may not have been prohibitive by themselves, but there is little doubt that they would have undermined the Bank's competitive position vis-à-vis state-chartered banks for lending business within Maryland.[7] When the law went into effect in May 1818, McCulloh issued notes without paying the tax, and a Maryland treasury official brought an action for debt against McCulloh, as Bank cashier, to collect $2,500 in penalties on five notes. Both Maryland and the Bank wanted the case resolved by the Supreme Court, and apparently cooperated in litigating the case on agreed facts in the Maryland courts, which upheld the tax, to fast-track the case to the U.S. Supreme Court.[8]

The contemporary importance of the case was emphasized by the makeup of the legal teams for the two sides. For Maryland, Luther Martin, at seventy-one, was one of the few surviving members of the Constitutional Convention, where he had been a leading advocate for limited national power. He was attorney general for Maryland over many years, had defended Aaron Burr at the latter's 1807 treason trial, and had argued twenty-five cases before the Supreme Court prior to *McCulloch*, his last Supreme Court argument. Joseph Hopkinson had defended Justice Samuel Chase in the latter's impeachment trial in 1804, co-counseled the *Dartmouth College v. Woodward* case with Daniel Webster, and had served as a congressman from Pennsylvania, where he would later be appointed to a federal judgeship. Walter Jones, who was serving as United States Attorney for the District of Columbia, was a Supreme Court regular, arguing 169 Supreme Court cases between 1815 and 1835. Representing the Bank was Daniel Webster, who was beginning to establish his reputation as "Godlike Daniel," the nation's foremost orator, and a preeminent advocate before the Supreme Court. He would argue 168 cases between 1814 and 1852. William Wirt, a successful Virginia attorney and man of letters, had been handpicked by Jefferson to prosecute Aaron Burr for treason in 1807, and later became the longest-tenured U.S. Attorney General in history, serving the full terms of presidents Monroe and Adams, from 1817 through 1829. All these luminaries were outshone by the third and final member of the Bank's team. Before arguing the *McCulloch* case, William Pinkney had served as U.S. Attorney General for three years under Madison, as U.S. envoy to Britain and Russia, and as a member of the House from Maryland from 1815 to 1816, during which he voted for the charter of the Second Bank. The recognized leader of the Supreme Court bar until his premature death in 1822, Pinkney had been described by Marshall as "the greatest man he had ever seen in a Court of justice."[9]

The lawyers followed what were by 1819 fairly predictable lines of argument. Maryland's attorneys argued that the Constitution was a compact whose spirit was to protect state sovereignty. Accordingly, enumerated powers had to be narrowly construed, and implied powers limited to those absolutely or indispensably necessary to executing enumerated powers. Chartering a bank was a sovereign power that could not be implied. None of Maryland's counsel explicitly advanced Madison's 1791 House argument, perhaps to avoid embarrassing the elder statesman Madison, who as president had eventually come around to supporting the Bank. Instead, Jones offered a simpler and less coherent version, arguing that an implied power cannot be "greater than those which are expressly granted." Martin advanced a more aggressive and far-fetched claim that the enumeration of certain powers that were means to executing other enumerated powers demonstrated that the "framers of the constitution intended to leave *nothing* to implication."[10]

Webster, Wirt, and Pinkney, representing the Bank, each argued that the Congress had an implied power to charter a bank to assist the government's fiscal operations, but they went on to offer more far-reaching arguments previously made by Hamilton, Calhoun, and others. Pinkney argued that the Bank had "a close connection with the power of regulating foreign commerce, and that between the different States" by "provid[ing] a circulating medium, by which that commerce can be more conveniently carried on. . . ." Webster and Wirt agreed.[11]

Maryland's counsel tried to turn the Bank's commerce-promoting virtue into a vice, describing a parade of horribles that would follow any interpretation of the Commerce Clause broad enough to sustain the Bank. Jones argued that upholding the Bank charter as commerce regulation would authorize the establishment of "an East or a West India company, with the exclusive privilege of trading with those parts of the world." Even worse, in Jones's view, if Congress could incorporate a bank to regulate commerce, it could "create corporations for the purpose of constructing roads and canals; a power to construct which has been also lately discovered among other secrets of the constitution, developed by this dangerous doctrine of implied powers."[12] Here, Jones threw down a gauntlet on the commerce clause issue. By explicitly linking the Bank's fate to internal improvements, he essentially dared the Marshall Court to issue a decision that would sustain both.

The Bank's legal team took up Jones's challenge on the internal improvements issue by echoing the argument by Hamilton and various congressmen in support of implied powers. "[L]ight houses, beacons, buoys, and public piers have all been established under the general power to regulate commerce," Pinkney reminded the Court. These improvements were "not indispensably necessary to commerce," thereby demonstrating a congressional understanding that implied powers extended beyond the narrow confines of strictly necessary measures.

The *McCulloch* argument lasted an unprecedented nine days, until March 3. Three days later, the Court issued its decision, unanimously upholding the implied power of Congress to incorporate the bank, and ruling that Maryland's attempt to tax the bank was unconstitutional. Both the length of the oral arguments, and quickness of the Court's decision are instructive. Lawyers did not submit written briefs in the Marshall Court era, but instead delivered their arguments as lengthy speeches. Marshall would take copious notes of these oral arguments, and rely on them heavily in drafting his opinions. Marshall's opinions were sprinkled with phrases like "it has been said," or "truly said" or "argued at the bar," which contemporary readers understood to signal that Marshall was paraphrasing part of an oral argument. Even when these signals were absent, Marshall paraphrased a great deal. To Marshall, speed and substance were more important than originality.[13]

* * *

A revealing moment in the history of *McCulloch* occurred during the 2012 oral argument in the Affordable Care Act case, in an exchange between the lawyer for the Act's challengers, Paul Clement, and Justice Stephen Breyer.

JUSTICE BREYER: So I'm focusing just on the Commerce Clause . . . And I look
back into history, and I think if we look back into history we see sometimes
Congress can create commerce out of nothing. That's the national bank,
which was created out of nothing to create other commerce out of nothing.
I look back into history, and I see it seems pretty clear that if there are
substantial effects on interstate commerce, Congress can act . . .

MR. CLEMENT: Well, Justice Breyer, let me start at the beginning of your
question with *McCulloch*. *McCulloch* was not a commerce power case.[14]

Clement was correct: *McCulloch* was "not a commerce power case," in the sense
that it did not base the constitutionality of the Bank on the Commerce Clause. But
Breyer's confusion on this point—if it was confusion—is understandable, because
Marshall was so elusive on the question. *McCulloch* is conventionally read to mean
that an implied power must be derived from specified enumerated powers, but
Marshall never clearly identified the enumerated powers from which he derived the
implied power to incorporate a bank. At the critical juncture in the opinion, Marshall
referred vaguely to the Bank as "a means to effect the legitimate objects of the government," and asserted further that it is not "necessary to enter into any discussion
in order to prove the importance of" the Bank to those "legitimate objects."[15] This
omission has frustrated generations of law students, as well as the few present-day
legal scholars who have bothered to notice it.[16] The omission did not pass unnoticed
by Marshall's contemporary critics, who charged that "[the Bank's] friends have not
yet agreed upon the particular power to which it is to be attached!"[17]

The closest Marshall came to identifying a particular enumerated power was to
say that the Bank is "a convenient, a useful, and essential instrument in the prose-
cution of [the national government's] fiscal operations." But "fiscal operations" as
such are not an enumerated power, and the phrase does not seem to refer to high
financial policy or regulation of interstate trade or the money supply. "Fiscal operations" probably refer to the treasury functions of collecting taxes, borrowing, and
disbursing funds appropriated by Congress.[18]

When Marshall did refer to specific enumerated powers, he used vague general
terms not directly addressing the constitutionality of the Bank. Marshall mentioned
the Commerce Clause (indeed, the word "commerce") only twice in the entire opinion, both times to make a general point about implied powers. First, he
rebutted Madison's 1791 House argument, even though that had not been advanced
by Maryland's lawyers: a power to charter corporations "is not, like the power of
making war, . . . or of regulating commerce, a great substantive and independent
power, which cannot be implied as incidental to other powers."[19] Second, the great
enumerated powers require implied powers for their execution.

Although, among the enumerated powers of government, we do not find
the word "bank" or "incorporation," we find the great powers to lay and

collect taxes; to borrow money; to regulate commerce; to declare and conduct a war; and to raise and support armies and navies. The sword and
the purse, all the external relations, and no inconsiderable portion of the
industry of the nation, are entrusted to its government. It can never be
pretended that these vast powers draw after them others of inferior importance, merely because they are inferior. . . . [A] government, entrusted
with such ample powers, on the due execution of which the happiness and
prosperity of the nation so vitally depends, must also be entrusted with
ample means for their execution. The power being given, it is the interest
of the nation to facilitate its execution. It can never be their interest, and
cannot be presumed to have been their intention, to clog and embarrass its
execution by withholding the most appropriate means.[20]

This passage contains suggestive nationalist atmospherics, and the reference to
the "industry of the nation" seems to give tacit approval to protective tariffs. But
the quoted passage doesn't actually say that the Bank is justifiable under all—or
any—of these powers. Rather, Marshall's point was that the express grant of great
powers in general does not imply general permission to assume all inferior powers
willy-nilly, but does imply a broad range of means to carry out the great powers.
Elsewhere, Marshall referred to other enumerated powers—such as the postal
power—but only as illustrations, not directly as sources.[21] The Bank could easily
have been shown to meet *McCulloch*'s necessary and proper test in connection with
the taxing, borrowing, war, or commerce powers, or even the territories clause. But
to Marshall's way of thinking, any of these options might have embroiled the Court
in needless controversy.

Marshall's slipperiness about naming a specific enumerated power to sustain
the Bank can be read, and is perhaps best read, to have aggressive nationalism
implications. Marshall defined implied powers as means that must be conducive
or adapted to legitimate ends. But he never stated that those ends must all be
enumerated powers. Despite his polite bow to the idea that "[t]his government is
acknowledged by all to be one of enumerated powers," Marshall did not say that
the government is "limited" to its enumerated powers; rather, the government is
"limited" to its "granted" powers, which include implied—that is, un-enumerated,
powers.[22] Nor did he ever clearly say that implied powers must be attached to
enumerated powers. Instead, he spoke more amorphously of "legitimate ends,"
"objects" and "great powers" of which the enumerated powers are *illustrations*—
"such ample powers." This leaves open the possibility that one implied power
could be derived from another unenumerated power. The Necessary and Proper
Clause itself is not clearly limited to the enumerated powers. It grants Congress the
power "[t]o make all laws which shall be necessary and proper for carrying into
execution the foregoing powers, *and all other powers* vested by this Constitution
in the government of the United States, or in any department or officer thereof."[23]

"Vested" powers may refer to "granted" powers, which are not necessarily limited to "enumerated" powers. And some undisputed governmental powers are not clearly means to exercising enumerated ends: for example, a broad, general power to conduct foreign affairs, which has never been doubted, is not a means to the end of making treaties, but rather the reverse.[24] Was Marshall offering a subtle gift to nationalists, who would interpret the Constitution to permit Congress to legislate broadly for the general welfare? Perhaps Marshall meant to subtly undermine the doctrine of limited enumerated powers.[25]

But if Marshall meant to resist enumerationism, his point was undermined by excessive subtlety. Because Marshall was writing in a political environment in which Jeffersonian-Madisonian enumerationism was ascendant, his readers would expect to see the Bank attached to one or more enumerated powers. In this context, Marshall further offset the nationalist implications of *McCulloch* by his evident unwillingness to attach the concept of implied powers to the broadest of all enumerated powers, the Commerce Clause. *McCulloch* presented a clear opportunity for Marshall to recognize implied commerce powers, which would have placed the Court squarely behind a doctrine that could greatly enlarge the constitutional space for federal legislation. The arguments for doing so were clearly mapped—even invited and provoked—for Marshall. The Bank's advocates had all asserted that the Bank was justified as an exercise of implied commerce powers. Marshall himself had written in his *Life of Washington* that "the utility of banking institutions" was demonstrated by the fact that "In all commercial countries they had been resorted to as an instrument of great efficacy *in mercantile transactions*."[26] Through its central banking functions, the Bank could regulate the loan practices of the nationwide network of state banks, thus affecting all corners of the economy. Indeed, the controversy swirling around the Bank in early 1819 stemmed precisely from its precipitate calling in of loans to the state banks—an action that contributed to the Panic of 1819.[27] Marshall could also have addressed the related issue of the national government's power to impose a uniform national currency. As we have seen, both Hamilton in 1791 and Calhoun in 1816 had argued that such a power was an inherent attribute of sovereignty, that could also be implied by interpreting the Constitution's money provisions synergistically—reading multiple constitutional provisions together to infer a power greater than the sum of its parts.

Marshall avoided all of this. By focusing on the Bank's usefulness to the "fiscal operations" of *the government*, Marshall declined to recognize—or to give the Court's blessing to—the Bank's role as a regulator and facilitator of interstate private enterprise. *McCulloch* said nothing about the Bank's usefulness to regulating currency, imposing discipline on state banks, or even issuing banknotes to serve as a uniform national currency. This latter omission is particularly strange, since the *McCulloch* litigation arose over a state tax on the issuance of national banknotes. And despite his suggestion that implied powers questions should "depend on a fair construction of the whole" Constitution,[28] Marshall did not actually employ a synergistic interpretation. The "fiscal operations" on which Marshall grounded the Bank are logistical elements attaching independently to each of several powers (taxing, borrowing, spending, war, etc.), but do not constitute a more general power implied by combining those several. Nor did Marshall embrace the idea that the United States government possesses a general sovereign power to create and regulate a uniform national currency. The connection between a national bank, the regulation of interstate commerce, and the national government's money powers was so obvious to all involved, Marshall included, that Marshall's avoidance of these issues is striking.

An implied power to charter a national bank to facilitate commerce could easily be extended to a power to charter corporations to build roads and canals to facilitate commerce. If Marshall were a nation-builder, then surely we could expect him to suggest that Congress can build a road. But again, Marshall was evasive. Some scholars have interpreted the following passage from *McCulloch* as an endorsement of internal improvements:

> Throughout this vast republic, from the St. Croix to the Gulph [sic] of Mexico, from the Atlantic to the Pacific, revenue is to be collected and expended, armies are to be marched and supported. The exigencies of the nation may require that the treasure raised in the north should be transported to the south, that raised in the east conveyed to the west, or that this order should be reversed.[29]

Here, Marshall echoed Henry Clay's 1818 speeches on internal improvements, and we could put on nationalist glasses to read this as an approval of Clay's argument that the war power implies a power to build roads for defense. While Marshall's geographical description is perhaps more poetic than Clay's, it lacks Clay's bold assertiveness about a federal power to build roads. Many who conceded the implied powers to carry treasure or march armies did not concede that this implied a power to build a road, and Marshall made no effort to contradict this view. Here, Marshall avoided even saying the word "roads." Later in the opinion, in his only reference to "roads," Marshall addressed the enumerated power "to establish post offices and post roads." This power, he said, was limited to "the single act of making the establishment," which implied the powers to "carry[] the mail along the post road" and "punish those who steal letters . . . or rob the mail."[30] As we have seen, Clay and his opponents placed great emphasis on whether "establish" in the Postal Clause authorized building post roads or merely designating postal routes on existing state roads. Marshall flagged this controversy without taking a position. It is hard to read *McCulloch* as a "roads and canals" case when Marshall would not even suggest a federal power to *build* a post road.[31]

The most revealing indication of Marshall's failure to endorse internal improvements is found in the two-page passage in which he offers strikingly modest examples of implied powers. In addition to the just-mentioned postal powers,

Marshall referred to a federal criminal code as a set of implied powers—though he mentioned no specific crimes except perjury and falsifying court records. Finally, Marshall mentioned the power to require that officeholders take an oath.[32] Missing from this list is the legislative precedent for a congressional power to *build* "lighthouses, beacons, buoys and public piers." Hamilton and Clay had identified these as definitive legislative implied-powers precedents for internal improvements and the Bank itself, and Pinkney raised the example at oral argument. Had Marshall deployed this example, he might have cemented the connection between *McCulloch* and internal improvements. Pinkney encouraged Marshall to do it. Jones dared Marshall to do it. But Marshall shrank from the challenge.

Marshall's avoidance of implied commerce powers and internal improvements may have been politically savvy, and was certainly consistent with his legendary penchant for keeping the Court out of unprofitable political controversies. Avoiding those issues may also have helped him tread carefully around the slavery question. And it might have seemed politically tone deaf to expressly recognize a federal power to control the nation's currency and commercial credit through a national bank that had so recently contributed to the nation's economic depression by precipitously calling in debts. Finally, given the antebellum conception of exclusivity of federal powers, a recognition of implied commerce powers could have raised questions about the constitutionality of numerous state laws regulating economic activity then viewed as intrastate: agriculture, manufacturing, labor relations, or slavery. In short, Marshall may have had very good reasons to avoid adopting the most nationalistic arguments available to him. But prudently safeguarding the political position of the Supreme Court, whatever its long-term benefits to the strength of national institutions, resulted in an opinion whose nationalism was more defensive than aggressive.

* * *

As a matter of constitutional doctrine, *McCulloch* discusses the test for implied powers—how to tell whether a law is "necessary and proper"—and who is to judge. These elements are more ambiguous than the conventional reading of *McCulloch* suggests. No one seriously argued for a complete denial of implied powers, but Marshall nevertheless took pains to demonstrate their existence, producing one of *McCulloch*'s most celebrated passages. Quoted in Chapter 1, the passage began by asserting that the Constitution could not specify how Congress might implement its enumerated powers without becoming mired in "the prolixity of a legal code," and therefore the Constitution's Framers necessarily left those details to implication. It was, after all, "a constitution we are expounding," a broad framework document rather than a statute book.[33]

The controversy surrounded, not the existence of implied powers—admitted by all sides—but how to limit them in the manner consistent with the idea of limited enumerated powers. Maryland's argument, as summarized by Marshall, held that the Necessary and Proper clause "limit[ed] the right to pass laws for the execution of the granted powers, to such as are indispensable, and without which the power would be nugatory"; and that "it excludes the choice of means, and leaves to Congress, in each case, that only which is most direct and simple." Marshall rejected this argument in a lengthy explanation. "Necessary" in ordinary speech can mean "convenient, or useful, or essential" and the Constitution elsewhere uses the modifier "absolutely" when intending to use the word "necessary" in a more restrictive sense.[34] Further, the clause's inclusion among the Article I, section 8 powers, rather than the Article I, section 9 limitations of Congress refuted the idea that the clause is a limitation.[35] After this, Marshall circled back to his broader argument from constitutional interpretation:

> The subject is the execution of those great powers on which the welfare of a nation essentially depends. It must have been the intention of those who gave these powers, to insure, as far as human prudence could insure, their beneficial execution. This could not be done by confiding the choice of means to such narrow limits as not to leave it in the power of Congress to adopt any which might be appropriate, and which were conducive to the end. This provision is made in a constitution intended to endure for ages to come, and, consequently, to be adapted to the various crises of human affairs. To have prescribed the means by which government should, in all future time, execute its powers, would have been to change, entirely, the character of the instrument, and give it the properties of a legal code. It would have been an unwise attempt to provide, by immutable rules, for exigencies which, if foreseen at all, must have been seen dimly, and which can be best provided for as they occur. To have declared that the best means shall not be used, but those alone without which the power given would be nugatory, would have been to deprive the legislature of the capacity to avail itself of experience, to exercise its reason, and to accommodate its legislation to circumstances.[36]

In short, Marshall argued, a good-faith grant of power necessarily implies a grant of sufficient freedom of action to implement the power effectively. Maryland's strict limitation on the scope of implied powers would thus undermine the Constitution's express grants of powers. As *McCulloch* makes plain, the "strictly necessary" argument was really not made in good faith. Rather, it was one of the several efforts, repulsed by Marshall throughout his tenure as chief justice, to undermine the efficacy of the national government and reduce the Constitution to the functional equivalent of the Articles of Confederation.

The breadth of *McCulloch*'s endorsement of implied powers depends on how one reads numerous ambiguous passages. On the one hand, Marshall supplied soaring rhetoric about the "great," "ample" and "vast" powers of the national government, often phrasing these in terms that sound broader than the powers enumerated in Article I, section 8: the "great" enumerated powers "to lay and collect taxes; to borrow money; to regulate commerce; to declare *and conduct* a war; and to raise and support armies and navies" give rise to even broader-sounding national authority over "[t]he sword and the purse, all the external relations, and no inconsiderable portion of the industry of the nation."[37] On the other hand, Marshall refrained from adopting the most nationalistic descriptions of how to interpret the Constitution. Hamilton and Clay had both argued that the Constitution must be liberally construed to serve its purposes and benefit the people.[38] Pinkney, in the *McCulloch* hearing, likewise argued that "It is the duty of the Court to construe the constitutional powers of the national government liberally. . . ."[39] Marshall agreed, less emphatically, that the "beneficial execution" "of those great powers on which the welfare of the nation essentially depends" could be insured by a "fair" or "just"— not a "liberal"—construction.[40] Pinkney had proposed that the enumerated powers were themselves merely means to accomplish the "national objects" stated in the Constitution's preamble. Indeed, "all laws are but means to promote the legitimate end of all government—the felicity of the people."[41] In Pinkney's account, implied powers need not be subordinate to enumerated powers, making it unnecessary to pin down elusive distinctions between laws that resemble "substantive" or "independent" powers and those that don't. But as noted previously, Marshall embraced this suggestion ambiguously at best, while reaffirming the Republican orthodoxy that "[t]his government is acknowledged by all to be one of enumerated powers."[42]

The breadth of implied powers in *McCulloch* also depends on how "necessary and proper" is interpreted, and by whom. A doctrine interpreting these words very broadly, or giving great deference to Congress's own claims about the scope of its constitutional powers, would tend to be expansive. Notwithstanding the wide acclaim for Marshall's clarity in legal exposition, his effort to formulate the "necessary and proper" test for implied powers was not entirely clear. Marshall used over twenty different expressions to interpret "necessary and proper," creating ambiguities about the scope of the implied powers.[43] Words and phrases like "convenient," "useful," "conducive," "adapted," and "free use of means" suggest more latitude for Congress.[44] Those such as "direct," "needful," "requisite," "required" and "essential" seem more restrictive.[45] Other terms fall somewhere in the middle, but suggest some room for judicial second-guessing of Congress. His occasional use of superlatives seemingly suggests that Congress's discretion should aim at choosing "the best," "most convenient," "most appropriate" or "most advantageous[]" means,[46] while other terms suggest some sort of scrutiny of the congressional decision-making or an objective test of necessity: "*really* calculated," "*plainly* adapted," "ordinary," "usual," or "appropriate."[47]

The Bank's lawyers argued that the Court should adopt a deferential posture toward congressional power. Deferring to legislative precedent acknowledges the authority of the elected branches to create precedential interpretations of the Constitution, and the Bank's lawyers argued that the Bank's constitutionality was settled by long-standing legislative acceptance. Further, Webster argued the Court should set a very high bar for striking down an act of Congress, doing so only when the challenger shows that the law "has no fair connection with the execution of any power or duty of the national government, and that its creation is consequently a manifest usurpation." Pinkney argued even more assertively, "The vast variety of possible means excludes the practicability of judicial determination as to the fitness of a particular means." A Court can hold a law unconstitutional on this basis only if it appears to be "violently and unnaturally forced into the service, or fraudulently assumed, in order to usurp a new substantive power of sovereignty." Therefore, "Congress is, *prima facie*, a competent judge of its own constitutional powers."[48] Strikingly, Pinkney said "powers," not "implied powers," which presumably included enumerated powers as well.

McCulloch settled on a less deferential formula, albeit equivocally. After asserting that it was the Supreme Court's role to "decide[] peacefully" questions of "the conflicting powers of the government of the Union and of its members," Marshall promptly backtracked. Because four presidents and numerous Congresses had affirmed the Bank's constitutionality, "[i]t would require no ordinary share of intrepidity to assert" that the Bank "was a bold and plain usurpation, to which the constitution gave no countenance."[49] This language suggested a high bar for striking down an act of Congress, at least an act of long standing, and reflected ambiguity—or perhaps ambivalence—about the roles of the Court and Congress. The ambiguity persisted throughout *McCulloch*. Congress has "that discretion" over legislative means "which will enable that body to perform the high duties assigned to it, in the manner most beneficial to the people." But in the next sentence, Marshall wrote, "*Let the end be legitimate, let it be within the scope of the constitution, and all means which are appropriate, which are plainly adapted to that end, which are not prohibited, but consist with the letter and spirit of the constitution, are constitutional.*"[50] This statement seems to leave room for a significant judicial role in limiting legislative discretion. Whether "the end [is] legitimate" is nearly always the contested question when a law is challenged as exceeding the powers of Congress. If commerce does not include domestic manufactures, then promoting domestic manufactures is not a legitimate end that can justify the means of building a road or bridge. Marshall did not actually say it is for the Court to determine whether the end is legitimate—his style was to hedge—but subsequent interpreters have assumed it is for the Court.

Even if the end is legitimate, the means might run afoul of a constitutional prohibition. Here, Marshall indicated, express prohibitions may be supplemented by prohibitions *implied* from the "spirit" of the constitution. What were these implied, "spirit"-based limitations—did they flow from the reserved powers of the states? Whatever they were meant to be, Marshall's phrase would later be quoted time and again in support of judicially created limitations on congressional powers, as we will see in the ensuing chapters.

In the other famous passage on this theme, Marshall perpetuated these ambiguities by reformulating the statement about congressional discretion and judicial review:

> But, were [the Bank's] necessity less apparent, none can deny its being an appropriate measure; and if it is, the degree of its necessity, as has been very justly observed, is to be discussed in another place. Should Congress, in the execution of its powers, adopt measures which are prohibited by the constitution; or should Congress, under the pretext of executing its powers, pass laws for the accomplishment of objects not entrusted to the government; it would become the painful duty of this tribunal, should a case requiring such a decision come before it, to say that such an act was not the law of the land. But where the law is not prohibited, and is really calculated to effect any of the objects entrusted to the government, to undertake here to inquire into the degree of its necessity, would be to pass the line which circumscribes the judicial department, and to tread on legislative ground. This court disclaims all pretensions to such a power.[51]

The passage suggests Congress has unreviewable discretion to determine whether a particular law is a necessary and proper means. Or does it? The Court will undertake the "painful duty" to invalidate a law that is not "really calculated" to an end within the enumerated powers. Is "really calculated" the same as or different than "plainly adapted," "convenient," or "essential"? Marshall seems to have said that the degree of necessity is not to be judged by the Court at all—twice in fact in the paragraph just quoted. And in the same paragraph, he says that it is.

A second layer of ambiguity surrounds the idea of legislative ends. Marshall implied that the Court reserves this question for itself ("let the end be legitimate"), and then said so more directly (the "painful duty"). But the word "pretext" in this passage muddies the waters. How would the Court decide that Congress has passed a law under a "pretext" of acting within its enumerated powers? Suppose Congress were to enact a law for the building of an intrastate road whose terminus was an interstate or international port. Congress could argue that the road was "convenient" or "plainly adapted" to promote interstate navigation—something Marshall deemed indisputably a matter of commerce. But it might have been argued in the 1820s that road travel, in contrast to navigation, is not commerce; and that the navigation hook was a mere pretext for internal improvements, which in turn could be labeled an illegitimate end that violated the "spirit" of the Constitution. In order to reach such a conclusion, a court would have to reason that the road was not sufficiently "necessary" ("convenient," "conducive," etc.) to navigation—thereby, judging the "degree of its necessity" non-deferentially. The word "pretext" implies a lack of deference, a second-guessing of a claimed legislative justification; and such an analysis spills over into a judgment of the relation of means to that end.

The *McCulloch* opinion thus gives plenty of ammunition to both sides of a debate over the role of the Court and the standard which it will apply. Each time Marshall claimed that the Court must defer to Congress's legislative choices, he tempered that claim by asserting the Court's power to scrutinize the choice. Unsurprisingly, *McCulloch* has frequently been cited by later Courts in non-deferential decisions, in just this manner, to justify striking down acts of Congress on matters that arguably fell well within its discretion about means.[52] Legal scholars have likewise disagreed about how rigorous the test is, thereby underscoring the ambiguous nature of Marshall's purported deference to Congress.[53]

* * *

In the end, Marshall wrote an opinion whose ambiguous language offered something to both nationalists and moderate Jeffersonian Republicans. The only losers were the hard-line Jeffersonians, who hoped to reduce the Constitution to the weakness of the Articles of Confederation with an unworkably strict construction of implied powers. The *McCulloch* opinion had language that could be interpreted in support of a very broad conception of national powers. Even under an enumerationist interpretation of the Constitution, *McCulloch*'s logic of implied powers held hugely expansive potential for national legislative authority, if only the Court would apply that logic to broad enumerated powers such as the Commerce Clause. It is thus significant that Marshall did not follow that logic to its conclusion in *McCulloch*.

Marshall stopped short of aggressively nationalistic grounds for upholding the Bank. The lawyers for the Bank laid out unmistakable invitations to place the constitutionality of the Bank on the broadest terms, which would endorse a theory of implied powers untethered from the enumerated powers. They also offered a less aggressive but still highly nationalistic theory of implied commerce powers that would support internal improvements. Lawyers for Maryland dared Marshall to adopt that view. While Marshall at times used soaring language that suggested a conception of "the capable Constitution" in the abstract, he stopped short of putting those ideas into practice. Marshall's studied avoidance of the Commerce Clause was almost certainly intended to avoid committing the Court to a concept of implied commerce powers, with all that might entail: the validation of a federal internal improvements power, the displacement of state police powers, and perhaps even the recognition of a federal power to regulate slavery. This is not to say that Marshall would have used judicial review to strike down congressional assertions of such powers. Marshall did not close any doors to more expansive assertions of congressional power. But neither did he invite Congress to step through.

4

"As Far as Human Prudence Could Insure"

Marshall's Retreat from Implied Commerce Powers

If Chief Justice Marshall had been engaged in an ambitious nation-building project through his constitutional decisions, then we would expect him to build on his greatest nation-building case: *McCulloch*. That didn't happen. In *Gibbons v. Ogden* (1824),[1] Marshall famously construed the term "commerce" in the Commerce Clause to include navigation, and struck down a state monopoly over steamboat travel. *Gibbons* is widely understood as setting forth an expansive interpretation of the Commerce Clause. It and *McCulloch* are said to be "the twin pillars of constitutional nationalism," in which Marshall laid the constitutional foundations for a powerful national government with broad legislative powers.[2] Yet *Gibbons* makes no mention of *McCulloch* and, as we will see, marks a significant *retreat* from *McCulloch*'s conception of implied powers. Indeed, from the issuance of *McCulloch* in 1819 to the end of Marshall's chief justiceship on his death in 1835, the Marshall Court rendered several decisions to resolve power disputes between the federal government and the states—issues that went to the core of the *McCulloch* decision. Marshall thus had ample opportunity to reaffirm and extend *McCulloch* as a constitutional precedent. Yet *McCulloch* was rarely cited by the Marshall Court after 1819, and no Marshall Court case ever cited *McCulloch*'s discussions of constitutional interpretation, nationalist constitutional theory, or implied powers.

What accounts for Marshall ignoring his own "greatest case"? In *McCulloch*, Marshall had written that the Framers of the Constitution had intended "to insure, as far as human prudence could insure, the[] beneficial execution" of the Constitution's granted powers.[3] But for Marshall after 1819, "human prudence" required stepping back from the potentially broad implications of implied powers. In particular, Marshall's studied refusal to endorse implied commerce powers are best explained as resulting from his desire to keep the Court out of two incendiary issues of constitutional politics—internal improvements and slavery.

* * *

The Marshall Court discussed *McCulloch* at length in only one subsequent case, *Osborn v. Bank of the United States* (1824),[4] and there only because the case relitigated a constitutional challenge to the Bank. Aside from *Osborn*, the Marshall Court cited *McCulloch* substantively in just three other cases.[5] Each dealt with constitutional challenges to state and local taxes. Two additional cases cited *McCulloch* completely insubstantially, bringing the total to six citations in sixteen years.[6] The Marshall Court never cited *McCulloch*'s discussions of implied powers or constitutional nationalism, even though it decided several cases that involved those issues.

True, the modern practice of generous citations to prior precedents was not well established in this era. Readers of Marshall's constitutional opinions in particular have frequently noticed and commented on the paucity of citations.[7] In *McCulloch* and *Gibbons*, Marshall cited no authorities whatsoever. In a late-career opinion in *Willson v. Blackbird Creek* (1829), Marshall seemed to discount the value of precedents, citing three cases "expressly in point" but noting that they established the point of law only "as far as precedents can establish any thing."[8] An anecdote reported in an early Marshall biography, and often repeated, has it that Marshall followed his public reading of one of his opinions with this quip: "These seem to me to be the conclusions to which we are conducted by the reason and spirit of the law. Brother Story will furnish the authorities."[9]

Marshall's admirers have tended to turn this apparent vice—a lack of scholarly discipline—into a virtue. Praising Marshall's vigorous intellect, stylistic clarity, and analytical brilliance, modern legal scholars have explained the absence of citation as characteristic of a "grand style" of judicial writing. As applied to Marshall's constitutional decisions, the Grand Style is taken to mean direct logical exposition of the Constitution itself, rather than interpretation of previous judicial interpretations of the Constitution.[10] As crystalized by an early admirer, Chancellor Kent, the Constitution "furnishes essentially the means of its own interpretation; and to resort to it was the practice of the late Chief Justice Marshall, in [his] clear and admirable judicial views. . . ."[11] Heavy reliance on citations gives an impression of a reluctance to expound the Constitution boldly and forthrightly, connoting a cautious, even mincing, incrementalism.

There are more prosaic explanations for the relative absence of citations. The relative newness of the Constitution meant that there were often few applicable precedents. The nineteenth-century judicial mind may have tended to confine what precedents there were to their specific facts and to regard the discussion of constitutional principles as *obiter dicta*—non-precedential verbiage. Even more mundanely, the lack of citation might simply have reflected the unavailability of a good law library. In 1824, Marshall wrote to President Monroe to seek a $3,000 appropriation for a law library for the Court, but Congress didn't provide that money for another eight years.[12]

Even taken together, however, these observations do not satisfactorily explain *McCulloch's* virtual disappearance from Marshall Court jurisprudence. Although the Marshall Court infrequently cited any of its constitutional opinions in subsequent cases, it did cite them sometimes. A partial survey of citations shows: *Fletcher v. Peck* (1810) (thirteen subsequent citations); *Martin v. Hunter's Lessee* (1816) (ten); *Marbury v. Madison* (1803) (nine); *Sturges v. Crowninshield* (1819) (six); *McCulloch v. Maryland* (1819) (six); *Dartmouth College v. Woodward* (1819) (four); *Cohens v. Virginia* (1821) (three); *Gibbons v. Ogden* (1824) (one). *McCulloch's* six subsequent citations place it in the middle of the pack, and five of these were in cases authored by Marshall himself. In *Brown v. Maryland* (1827), Marshall relied on *McCulloch* as authority to hold that a federal commerce statute preempted a state tax. Marshall "deem[ed] it unnecessary" to re-argue federal immunity from state taxation "because the subject was taken up, and considered with great attention, in *McCulloch v. The State of Maryland*, the decision in which case is, we think entirely applicable to this."[13] Significantly, this application of *McCulloch* required a stretch to analogize the Bank to a private merchant operating under a federal trade license but not conducting federal business. In *Weston v. Charleston* (1829),[14] Marshall extended *McCulloch* to strike down a state tax on federal treasury bonds. In *Providence Bank v. Billings* (1832),[15] Marshall upheld a state tax on a state bank against a Contracts Clause challenge, citing *McCulloch* for the proposition that the democratic process provided the best safeguard against excessive taxation where no federal constitutional provision restrained the tax. These cases tell us that Marshall knew where to find the *McCulloch* opinion and how to rely or build on it as precedent, when he felt the need.

Marshall made no reference to *McCulloch* in *Cohens v. Virginia* (1821),[16] one of his most celebrated defensive-nationalism decisions. The Cohen brothers were federal contractors licensed by Congress to sell lottery tickets to raise revenue for the municipal government of Washington, D.C. On trial in the Virginia courts for illegally selling their lottery tickets in Virginia, the Cohens argued unsuccessfully that the federal license superseded the state law. The Virginia high court upheld their convictions, adding defiantly that the U.S. Supreme Court had no appellate jurisdiction over the state tribunal. The Virginia prosecutors pressed this argument before Marshall's Court, where they were roundly rebuffed. Marshall's opinion famously reaffirmed that the Supreme Court had authority, under section 25 of the 1789 Judiciary Act, to review any state court decision on a question of federal law, whether statute, treaty, or the Constitution itself. Story's opinion in *Martin v. Hunter's Lessee* (1816)[17] had established this principle in cases between private parties, and *Cohens* extended it to cases where the state is a party. Because the validity of the Cohens' criminal convictions depended on interpreting the federal license, the case raised a federal question and was reviewable on its merits in the Supreme Court. Here, the good news for the Cohens ended. Reaching the merits, Marshall construed the federal license to permit their lottery ticket sales only inside the District of Columbia.

Therefore, the state law, and the criminal conviction, stood. This was an example of what modern commentators see as Marshallean tactics, mollifying potential critics by sacrificing the narrow case result in order to win the larger jurisprudential point.

Marshall's omission of *McCulloch* is not plausibly explained by general citation practice, given that his *Cohens* opinion cited both *Marbury v. Madison* and *Martin v. Hunter's Lessee*.[18] Yet the *Cohens* decision revisited every major nationalist theme in *McCulloch*. Supreme Court control over potentially disuniform state court interpretations of federal law was essential to maintaining the Union, Marshall argued. To drive this point home, Marshall took the opportunity to reprise his nationalist constitution theory, reassert the supremacy of federal over conflicting state laws, and reaffirm that "a constitution is framed for ages to come. . . ."[19] Most of all, *Cohens* raised an issue of implied powers. Virginia's lawyers argued that Congress had no power to give extraterritorial effect to municipal ordinances for Washington, D.C. But Marshall, rejecting this claim, held that the power to legislate for the national capital "carries with it all those incidental powers which are necessary to its complete and effectual execution"—including the power to give the lottery law extraterritorial effect.[20] Marshall's failure to cite *McCulloch* is truly striking, and indeed revealing, when we consider that the defiant Virginia court opinion had been written by Judge Spencer Roane, whose editorial attack on *McCulloch* two years before had inspired Marshall's only published effort to defend *McCulloch's* celebrated nationalism elements—as we will now see.

* * *

Marshall held a deep and ongoing anxiety about the future of the Union, throughout his post-*McCulloch* years. He believed that the anti-federalist forces that had opposed ratification of the Constitution had now coalesced into a major element of Jeffersonian republicanism. "[C]ertain restless politicians of Virginia," Marshall wrote, viewed the Constitution with a "zealous and persevering hostility" and "vindictive hate" that "seems never to have been appeased." They "desire to strip the government of those effective powers, which enable it to accomplish the objects for which it was created; and, by construction, essentially to reinstate that miserable confederation. . . ."[21]

The hard-core states'-rights ideologues who most concerned Marshall were predominantly Virginians. Known to modern-day historians as "Old Republicans" or "Virginia Republicans," these men were former opponents of ratification of the Constitution, or their ideological heirs. As previously noted, it was a group of Virginia congressmen who dominated the opposition to internal improvements in the 1818 House debates. The epicenter of this movement was Richmond, and its leadership was a small but influential group of Virginia politicians known as the Richmond Junto. Spencer Roane, a Junto leader, was a judge of the Virginia Supreme Court of Appeals, and in that role had issued opinions rejecting the U.S.

Supreme Court's appellate authority over state courts on federal questions, both in the *Martin v. Hunter's Lessee* litigation prior to *McCulloch*, and in *Cohens v. Virginia* after. The Junto was encouraged by Jefferson, who by then had retired from public office to his role as "sage of Monticello"—or, in Marshall's words, "the Great Lama of the Mountain."[22] Given a platform by Thomas Ritchie's Richmond *Enquirer*, the Junto members denounced all and sundry expressions of nationalism as "consolidation." This was a term of opprobrium in antebellum political discourse, and meant the destruction of sovereign states and the absorption of the entire American people into a single consolidated government.[23]

The Richmond connection should not be underemphasized. Marshall had deep roots there, having settled in Richmond after the Revolutionary War and built one of the most successful law practices in the state. Richmond was still his permanent year-round home, and Junto members were Marshall's neighbors and social peers in a community of fewer than 12,000.[24] Marshall had held public office in Virginia for many years prior to his chief justiceship, and continued to be highly attentive to Virginia politics, either as an observer or, as in Virginia's 1829 constitutional convention, a participant. Perhaps these connections may have exaggerated Marshall's sense of the national importance of the Junto's activities, but Virginia was the third most populous state in the Union, and still arguably the most politically powerful.

From late March to late June 1819, the Richmond *Enquirer* ran two series of pseudonymous essays by Richmond Junto members that assailed the *McCulloch* decision. The first salvo consisted of two editorials by state lower-court judge William Brockenbrough under the name "Amphictyon." In May and June, Roane published four essays under the name "Hampden." Whereas Amphictyon's essays were comparatively mild in tone and substance, Hampden's were much more extreme, and Marshall knew they were written by Roane.[25] Marshall believed that *McCulloch* had "brought into operation the whole antifederal spirit of Virginia," and that "if the principles which have been advanced" in the attacks "were to prevail, the constitution would be converted into the old confederation." [26] Marshall replied to "Amphictyon" in April 1819 with two essays under the name "A Friend to the Union," and to "Hampden" in a nine-essay series in late June and July as "A Friend of the Constitution." Both essay series were published in the Alexandria [Virginia] *Gazette*, where Marshall hoped they would help forestall a Virginia legislative resolution condemning *McCulloch*. [27]

Marshall's essays, though remarkable as an unusual public relations campaign by a sitting Supreme Court justice, are less remarkable for their ideas: Marshall's editorial style was more pedestrian than in *McCulloch* itself, and he let his critics draw him into disputing arcane points. Still, they contain a few revealing passages. While they reflect Marshall's continuing commitment to constitutional nationalism, the essays hint at some creeping doubts about *McCulloch*'s theory of implied powers.

In *McCulloch*, Marshall had described all legislation as "means," which were implied powers that would be constitutional if plainly adapted to a legitimate end.

But in a curious passage in the third "Friend of the Constitution" essay, Marshall explained that legislative "means" referred to "the *direct execution* of the principle [enumerated] power," but not to implied powers. For example, he observed, regulating a post office or designating a post road were means to implement the enumerated power to establish post offices and post roads. "With these means the doctrine of incidents has nothing to do." Moreover, "[n]o court has a right to enquire whether" such means "are necessary or unnecessary. The means are appropriate, and congress may, constitutionally, select and vary them at will." These, Marshall now said, were different from "incidental or implied powers," which are "additional" or "appertaining" to an enumerated power. Thus, in contrast to postal regulations, "the right to punish those who rob the mail is an incidental power, and the question whether it is fairly deducible from the grant is open for argument."[28]

Perhaps this distinction makes some sense, but it is a curious way to explain *McCulloch*, which did not draw it, and for a very good reason. The difference between direct and indirect means of executing an implied power will more often than not be blurry, and shouldn't matter in a regime where, as *McCulloch* said, Congress has an "ample" "choice of means." The distinction, moreover, tends to backtrack from the idea of broad congressional choice, producing more room for disputing the appropriateness of a claim of implied powers. Consider that, in *McCulloch*, Marshall had cited Congress's power to punish mail robbers as so plain that it demonstrated unassailably the existence of implied powers. Here, Marshall conceded that an implied power to punish mail robbers was "open for argument." More generally, he continued,

> [i]n the exercise of an incidental power, we are always to enquire whether "it appertains to or follows the principal"; for the power itself may be questioned; but in exercising one that is granted there is no question about the power, and the very business of a legislature is to select the means.

But who is to inquire? If the courts, then Marshall would be walking back from *McCulloch*'s conclusion that Congress had broad discretion to determine the appropriateness of implied powers. Marshall concluded the essay by further muddying the waters:

> It is not pretended that [Congress's] right of selection may be fraudulently used to the destruction of the fair land marks of the constitution. Congress certainly may not, under the pretext of collecting taxes ... alter the law of descents; but if the means have a plain relation to the end—if they be direct, natural and appropriate, who, but the people at the elections, shall, under the pretext of their being unnecessary, control the legislative will, and direct its understanding? [29]

Was Marshall here discussing "means" in his new sense of directly executing an enumerated power, or was he speaking of implied powers?

This confusion aside, the essays contained numerous subtle assurances that *McCulloch's* doctrines would not be pushed too far. Marshall expressly disavowed any effort in *McCulloch* to endorse "liberal" construction of the Constitution—"a palpable misrepresentation of the opinion of the court"—again emphasizing that the Court sought only a "fair" construction. His brief reference to the postal power to "designat[e] post offices and post roads," said nothing about building them, and conceded that any implied postal powers would be "open for argument." (In the courts?) And the previously quoted suggestion that Congress could not, as an implied power, "alter the law of descents" would have been pregnant with meaning to Marshall's Virginia audience. Inheritance laws were a major vehicle by which slaves were conveyed from one generation to the next, and Marshall seemed to want to signal that these—and perhaps other state laws regarding slavery—were safe from federal interference.

Despite such reassurances, Virginia Republicans continued to view *McCulloch* and its doctrine of implied powers as a threat to slavery, either as a direct source of regulation under the commerce power, or indirectly through recognition of an internal improvement power. The Virginia Republicans seemed to view Supreme Court decisions as broad statements of doctrinal principle, much as we do today. In this, they were either ahead of their time as legal theorists, or else their states'-rights, pro-slavery antennae were so sensitively attuned that they would see threats from further off than other constitutional interpreters of their day. Spencer Roane, in the June 1819 Hampden essays, warned that *McCulloch's* expansive conception of implied powers would in effect authorize "the representatives of Connecticut in congress . . . to make laws, on the subject of our negro population."[30] Although Marshall, in his nine "Friend of the Constitution" essays, responded point by point to most of Hampden's arguments, he did not directly address that one. In an 1820 book published by Thomas Ritchie with Jefferson's encouragement, Virginia Republican essayist-politician John Taylor of Caroline made an emphatic (albeit turgid and incoherent) argument connecting *McCulloch*, the Bank, and implied powers with the emerging movement to prohibit slavery in new states.[31] And as we saw in Chapter 2, in the 1824 House debate on internal improvements, Virginia representative John Randolph—another distant cousin of Marshall, and a friend—had warned that an implied commerce or war power over internal improvements would lead inexorably to recognition of a congressional power to emancipate slaves.[32]

The slavery issue was percolating in the lower federal courts around this time, to Marshall's concern. In early August 1823, Francis Deliesseline, the sheriff of Charleston South Carolina, boarded the British merchant vessel *Homer*, forcibly removed one of its crew, Henry Elkison, and threw him in the city jail. Elkison, born in the British colony of Jamaica, was black, and his presence on board ship came within South Carolina's Negro Seamen Act. The law, enacted in December

1822 in the wake of the abortive Denmark Vesey slave rebellion earlier that year in South Carolina, stated that any "free negroes or persons of color" serving as crew members on a ship coming into South Carolina must be taken off and held in jail, at the captain's expense, for as long as the ship remained in harbor. Elkison eventually obtained the help of an attorney, who filed various writs for his release. The case came before U.S. Supreme Court Justice William Johnson sitting as circuit judge. Johnson, though a Jefferson appointee from South Carolina, was something of a maverick nationalist.[33] In *Elkison v. Deliessline*,[34] Johnson held the South Carolina law unconstitutional as a clear violation of the exclusive federal power over foreign and interstate commerce.

The case pointedly demonstrated how the federal commerce power could be perceived as a threat to state regulation of slavery. Despite conceding that the state could pass laws restricting black sailors' freedom to move about on shore, Johnson's ruling outraged the press and politicians. In a September 1823 letter to Justice Joseph Story, Marshall commiserated over the harsh political backlash against their colleague. Marshall wrote that he had decided a similar circuit case in 1820 under a Virginia statute that was the "twin brother" of the South Carolina law. Marshall "escaped" the explosive constitutional question "on the construction of the act," because "I am not fond of butting against a wall in sport."[35] He was referring to *The Wilson v. United States* (1820),[36] where he indeed had faced a similar issue with a Virginia statute that prohibited "import[ing] or bring[ing]" black sailors ashore in Virginia ports. Marshall construed "import or bring" to be inapplicable to crew members temporarily going ashore, and thus avoided having to rule on the constitutional issue. In the letter to Story, Marshall expressed specific concern that such a case might reach the Supreme Court, and that pro-slavery critics were "continually adding [fuel] to the fire . . . to roast the judicial department." [37]

There is little doubt that Marshall had the courage of his convictions and the fortitude to stand up to his Virginia critics. But even Marshall's admirers recognize that he picked his battles and seemed inclined throughout his judicial career to avoid unnecessary fights. Marshall's motivations may be due for a reassessment by historians and biographers for the light they may shed on his jurisprudence. *McCulloch's* critics and political opponents among Virginia Republicans were Marshall's peers, neighbors, and relatives. His willingness to provoke them, and his stomach for fighting with them, may well have had their limits. Moreover, he may have had more in common with them socially and politically than his admirers have credited. Historian Paul Finkelman's 2018 study demonstrates that, contrary to the prevailing myth, Marshall was a major slave owner, who took a dim view of free black people, bought and sold slaves throughout his life, bequeathed them on his heirs, and probably owned more than two hundred slaves at one time or another, never freeing a single one. Marshall was heavily invested in land and slaves in northern Virginia and Kentucky, and his less famous decisions reveal pro-slavery leanings.[38] These revelations put various statements by Marshall—such as his insistence that implied powers could not alter the law of inheritance—in a new light. We have to consider the possibility that when the Virginia Republicans warned that *McCulloch's* theory of implied powers threatened slavery, Marshall took the warning to heart.

Whether his motivation was self-interested or merely conflict-avoidant, Marshall was well aware that a nationalist interpretation of the Commerce Clause had the potential to impinge on slavery and create a political backlash. He had reason to know that *McCulloch* was provocative to his pro-slavery Virginia Republican neighbors, who had a penchant for interpreting the decision in an alarmist fashion, as a broad statement of principles about implied powers. This recognition may account for his failure to reaffirm *McCulloch* in response to Spencer Roane's challenge in *Cohens*. And *Gibbons* would be decided less than six months after Marshall's expression of concern about pro-slavery forces roasting the judiciary.

* * *

As for internal improvements, no case directly ruling on their constitutionality ever came before the Marshall Court. But events beyond the Court suggest that Marshall and his colleagues were ambivalent on this question and did not believe that Congress had the power to build roads and canals as part of an implied power to regulate or promote commerce, *McCulloch* notwithstanding. In early 1822, the Cumberland Road was back on the congressional agenda. With the road still incomplete but nevertheless in serious need of repair, Congress sent a bill to President Monroe in May to erect tollgates and use the tolls to pay for road repairs. The use of tollgates for road revenues was long established on public and private roads within the states, but an additional provision making it a federal crime to evade the tolls touched a nerve. This was the sort of assertion of land-based jurisdiction that made strict constructionists view federal road building as an unconstitutional threat to state sovereignty.

Monroe vetoed the bill, supplementing his short veto message with a 29,000-word pamphlet.[39] Monroe's main objection was that a power to build and regulate a federal road, by cutting across dry land, implied a "system of internal improvement" requiring the unconstitutional assertion of powers to condemn the underlying land; to build tollgates or tollhouses, and collect tolls; and to assert federal criminal jurisdiction over the road. Without naming the case, Monroe disregarded *McCulloch's* formulation of implied powers and the Necessary and Proper Clause: "Whatever is absolutely necessary to the accomplishment of the object of the grant [of power to Congress], though not specified, may fairly be considered as included in it. Beyond this the doctrine of incidental power cannot be carried." Monroe stingily interpreted enumerated powers, rejecting the war, postal, territories, and commerce powers as grounds from which a road-building or internal-improvements power could be implied. He asserted an extreme states'-rights interpretation of the Commerce Clause,

arguing that it authorized Congress to regulate interstate commerce only incidentally to regulation of foreign commerce.[40]

Nevertheless, Monroe was attentive to the aspirations of the nationalist wing of
his party and wanted federal participation in some sort of road-building program.
As a compromise solution, he proposed that the federal government could pay for
roads and other internal improvements. The basis for this was Article I, section 8,
clause 1—the power "to provide for the general welfare," which (perhaps partly because of this episode) has become known as "the spending power." So long as those
projects served "great national" rather than "strictly local" purposes, Congress could
underwrite them. The federal government simply could not thereafter regulate the
roads thus built. This position eventually became Jacksonian orthodoxy, embraced
by President Jackson and the Taney Court.[41]

Monroe sent copies of his pamphlet to members of Congress and to the justices
of the Supreme Court. Three of the justices, including Marshall, sent letters to
Monroe in reply. Story did not "feel at liberty to express any opinion as it may here-
after perhaps come for discussion before the Supreme Court."[42] Justice Johnson
responded far less circumspectly:

> Judge Johnson has had the Honour to submit the President's argument on
> the subject of internal improvement to his Brother Judges and is instructed
> to make the following Report. The Judges. . . . are all of opinion that the de-
> cision on the Bank question completely commits them on the subject of
> internal improvement, as applied to Postroads and Military Roads. On the
> other points, it is impossible to resist the lucid and conclusive reasoning
> in the argument. The principle assumed in the case of the Bank is that the
> granting of the principal power carries with it the grant of all adequate and
> appropriate means of executing it. That the selection of these means must
> rest with the General Government, and as to that power and those means
> the Constitution makes the Government of the U.S. supreme. Judge Johnson
> would take the liberty of suggesting to the President that it would not be
> unproductive of good, if the Secretary of State were to have the opinion of
> this Court on the Bank question, printed and dispersed through the Union.[43]

Johnson's letter may or may not have accurately represented the views of "his brother
judges," but it is remarkable as a sort of unprecedented advisory opinion. [44]

Also remarkable is that while Johnson extolled *McCulloch* as committing the
Court on the question of implied powers, Marshall's own letter to the President
did not:

> I have received the copy of your message to Congress on the subject of
> internal improvements which you did me the honor to transmit me, and
> thank you for it. I have read it with great attention and interest.

This is a question which very much divides the opinions of intelligent men; and it is not to be expected that there will be an entire concurrence in that you have expressed.[45] All however will I think admit that your views are profound, and that you have thought deeply on the subject. *To me they appear to be most generally just.*

The general power over internal improvement, if to be exercised by the Union, *would certainly be cumbersome to the government, & of no utility to the people.* But, to the extent you recommend, it would be productive of no mischief, and of great good. I despair however of the adoption of such a measure.[46]

Could Marshall's denial of a "general" internal improvement power have simply referred to the absence of an enumerated power? That is possible, but unlikely. Not only was the absence of such an enumerated power too obvious to bear mention, but "cumbersome" and "of no utility" are not words Marshall would have used to describe the absence of an enumerated power. They are opposites of the sorts of adjectives—like "conducive," "convenient," "plainly adapted"—that he used in *McCulloch* to describe implied powers. "Cumbersome" and "of no utility" would for Marshall be characteristics of laws that failed his test for "necessary and proper" legislative means. In other words, Marshall's denial of a "general power over internal improvement" probably meant to negate an implied internal-improvements power under the Commerce Clause, which was far more "general" a regulatory power than the more specialized war or postal powers.

While it is possible that he was trying to be agreeable rather than candid in writing to his old friend Monroe, Marshall's denial of "a general" commerce-based "power over internal improvement" was probably his actual view.[47] This becomes clearer in a March 1828 exchange of letters between Marshall and Timothy Pickering, the eighty-three-year-old elder statesman of the defunct Federalist party.[48] Pickering wrote to Marshall to share a few "suggestions on the construction of the Constitution," arguing that legislative precedents supported an implied internal improvements power under the Commerce Clause. Marshall replied that

> there is a great difference between a general power and a power to make them for military purposes or for the transportation of the mail. For these objects the power may be exercised to great advantage and, there is much reason for thinking, consistently with the constitution; farther than this, I know not why the government of The United States should wish it, nor do I believe it is desired.[49]

In other words, Marshall equated an internal improvements power under the Commerce Clause with a "general" internal-improvements power, as distinct from one implied from the postal and war powers. As a private citizen, Marshall invested

in roads and canals, and lobbied for internal improvements to the Virginia legislature.[50] It seems that Marshall agreed after all with Johnson that Congress could
build military and post roads. But a "general" (i.e., Commerce Clause-based) power
of internal improvement would be "cumbersome" and "of no utility to the people,"
as Marshall wrote to Monroe—and thus fail *McCulloch*'s test of necessary and
proper laws.

The constitutional controversy over internal improvements persisted right up
until the *Gibbons* decision. *Gibbons* was argued from February 4 to 9, 1824, and
Marshall issued the Court's decision on March 2.[51] During this time, Congress was
debating a bill to undertake nationwide surveys for roads and canals that would be
signed into law in April 1824 as the General Survey Act.[52] In the House debates in
January and February, several members discussed implied powers at some length in
debating whether an internal improvement power could be implied from the postal,
war, or commerce powers. *McCulloch* appeared to have a modest impact on the debate. No one referred to Marshall's decision explicitly, and opponents—most of
them again from the Virginia delegation—simply ignored *McCulloch*, offering their
own interpretations of the Necessary and Proper Clause in its place.[53] In January,
John Randolph made his speech connecting internal improvements to slave emancipation in opposing this bill, and other Virginia delegates attacked the idea of implied commerce powers.[54] A few speeches in support of internal improvements
showed at least traces of influence from *McCulloch*.[55]

Henry Clay once again led the supporters of the bill. In his remarkable January
14, 1824 speech, Clay repeated his theme that internal improvements promoted
"intercourse" connecting the people of the west "with our friends and brethren" in
the east. And he articulated a theory of the capable Constitution. The states were
incapable of national internal improvements projects, because they lacked the resources and the ability to subordinate their local interests to those of the nation. Yet
such internal improvements were highly beneficial to the people. If Congress arguably had such a power by reasonable construction of the Constitution, but failed
to exercise it, given its benefit to the people and the incapacity of the states, then it
was a breach of public trust—indeed, "treachery"—not to exercise it.[56] *McCulloch*
might have been in Clay's mind—he was preparing to argue in the Supreme Court
on behalf of the Second Bank in the upcoming case of *Osborn v. Bank of the United
States*—but one can find no more than a faint echo or two of *McCulloch* in Clay's
speeches.[57] Clay saw no need to adopt Marshall's formulation for "necessary and
proper" laws: as in 1818, Clay again argued that the definition was academic, because Congress had exclusive discretion to judge the question.

What is most striking in comparing Clay's speech to *McCulloch* is how much
bolder and more specific Clay was on the subject of internal improvements and
implied commerce powers. In contrast to Marshall's vague references to the postal
power, Clay asserted, "Mails certainly imply roads, roads imply their own preservation, their preservation implies the power to preserve them, and the Constitution

tells us, in express terms, that we shall establish the one and the other."[58] Clay laid out a clear theory of implied commerce powers, arguing that "[t]he power to regulate commerce among the several States, if it has any meaning, implies authority to foster it, to promote it, to bestow on it facilities similar to those which have been conceded to our foreign trade." The powers of the national government, Clay argued, "should be interpreted in reference to its first, its best, its greatest object, the Union of these states." The Union, he continued, was "best invigorated by an intimate, social, and commercial connexion between all the parts of the confederacy," which was best attained "by the application of federative resources."[59] Clay's speeches and others from the 1824 General Survey Act debates were once again reprinted in the National Intelligencer, and thus probably available to Marshall. These debates provide another useful frame of reference for understanding Marshall's opinion in *Gibbons* written just a few weeks later.

* * *

The litigation in *Gibbons v. Ogden* arose out of more than a decade of legal wrangling over the rights to operate steam-powered vessels on the Hudson River. Steamboats enabled travel against the current of navigable rivers, the main interstate highways in the early nineteenth century, and could revolutionize interstate commerce. They offered potentially enormous profits to holders of state-issued monopolies. A partnership of Robert Livingston, a statesman with great political influence in New York, and Robert Fulton, an engineer who had advanced steamboat technology, had won such a monopoly from the New York legislature. After losing a legal battle challenging the monopoly, Aaron Ogden purchased a license from the Livingston-Fulton partnership to operate a lucrative steamboat passenger service between New York City and Elizabethtown, New Jersey. Thomas Gibbons, a former partner of Ogden's who was now locked in a personal feud with him, began running his own steamboats on that route. Ogden sued to block Gibbons from continuing to do so, winning an injunction in the state chancery court. The decision was upheld in the chancery appellate court by the renowned Chancellor James Kent, and from there went to the U.S. Supreme Court.[60]

Daniel Webster and William Wirt, two of the three lawyers for the Bank in *McCulloch*, teamed up once again to represent the nationalist interest as lawyers for Gibbons. They argued primarily that the power to regulate navigation fell within an exclusive federal commerce power—the dormant Commerce Clause. For a fallback argument, Webster and Wirt pointed to Gibbons's possession of a federal license to engage in the coasting trade. They argued that this license gave its holder a federal right to engage freely in coastal navigation, which included the cities at the mouth of the Hudson. So interpreted, the federal license would void the state monopoly under the Supremacy Clause. Webster and Wirt placed little faith in this argument, because it had a glaring weakness: the apparent purpose of the federal licensing law

was merely to identify American-owned vessels, in order to give them lower tonnage and import duties than foreign-owned ones. Ogden's lawyers pointed out that
problem. So had Kent in his lower-court opinion.[61]

The Supreme Court held the New York steamboat monopoly unconstitutional.
While that result was not wholly unexpected, Marshall's opinion surprised the
litigants by deciding that Gibbons's coasting license was indeed a free-navigation
permit. Marshall might have reached this result by the simple assertion that a power
to regulate navigation was necessary and proper to the regulation of trade, that is,
an implied commerce power. Instead, Marshall went to some lengths to hold that
navigation was *not* an *implied* commerce power, but rather was entailed by the *definition* of commerce:

> [C]ounsel for the appellee would limit [the meaning of "commerce"] to
> traffic, to buying and selling, or the interchange of commodities, and do
> not admit that it comprehends navigation. This would restrict a general
> term, applicable to many objects, to one of its significations. Commerce,
> undoubtedly, is traffic, but it is something more: it is intercourse. It
> describes the commercial intercourse between nations, and parts of na-
> tions, in all its branches, and is regulated by prescribing rules for carrying
> on that intercourse. The mind can scarcely conceive a system for regulating
> commerce between nations, which shall exclude all laws concerning navi-
> gation, which shall be silent on the admission of the vessels of the one na-
> tion into the ports of the other, and be confined to prescribing rules for the
> conduct of individuals, in the actual employment of buying and selling, or
> of barter. [62]

This is the core of *Gibbons's* famous holding. Post–New Deal courts and
commentators have interpreted this passage as committing American constitutional
law to a broad construction of the Commerce Clause. In *Wickard v. Filburn* (1942),
the crucial post–New Deal decision that established the broad, modern "substantial
effects" test for interpreting the Commerce Clause, the Court said that, in *Gibbons*,
"Chief Justice Marshall described the federal commerce power with a breadth never
yet exceeded."[63]

The outcome of the decision, viewed in its most nationalistic light, was to broadly
affirm the federal government's sovereignty over the nation's navigable waterways.
Moreover, Marshall pointed out, "Commerce among the States, cannot stop at the
external boundary line of each State, but may be introduced into the interior," and
thus "The power of Congress . . . must be exercised within the territorial jurisdiction of the several States." The commerce power covered not only the New York–
New Jersey terminus of the steamboat route, but also its intrastate New York
segments: "if a foreign voyage *may* commence or terminate at a port within a State,
then the power of Congress may be exercised within a State."[64]

Why did Marshall treat the federal power over navigation as part of the *defini-tion* of commerce, rather than as a power *implied* from the Commerce Clause? In short, why did Marshall ignore *McCulloch*—he did not even cite it—when writing *Gibbons*? There is no conventional answer, because the question has never been asked. Only the lawyers for Ogden cited *McCulloch*, in their case *against* federal power.[65] Although Marshall did not speak of implied commerce powers, he did mention the Necessary and Proper Clause, which he curiously referred to as a *"lim-itation* on the means which may be used" by Congress to implement its enumerated powers.[66] This statement seems at odds with *McCulloch*, in which Marshall had emphatically asserted that the Necessary and Proper Clause "is placed among the powers of Congress, not among the limitations on those powers," and is "an addi-tional power, not a restriction on those already granted."[67]

A superficial "aggressive nationalism" reading of *Gibbons* would presume that Marshall believed he was simply expanding the commerce power by adding nav-igation to the definition of commerce. But there is an alternative explanation. By making navigation part of the definition of commerce, rather than an implied power under the Commerce Clause, Marshall was better able to *confine* the expansion of the commerce power in a way that would be palatable to states'-rights advocates.

Marshall introduced the famous, previously quoted "commerce is . . . inter-course" passage with this language: "The subject to be regulated is commerce; and our constitution being, as was aptly said at the bar, one of enumeration, and not of definition, to ascertain the extent of the power, it becomes necessary to settle the meaning of the word."[68] Subsequent commentators have overlooked the self-contradiction in this passage: Commerce can't be defined, Marshall says, so let's de-fine it. What "was aptly said at the bar" was Daniel Webster's argument that "[i]t was in vain to look for a precise and exact definition of the powers of Congress," because they were granted in broad terms, "in few words" rather than "exact definitions." A "general, or complex" power like commerce "must necessarily be judged of, and limited, by its object, and by the nature of the power." The purpose of the Commerce Clause was to get rid of the "divers restrictions" such as "monopolies of trade and navigation" by which states sought commercial advantage over one another, and institute "an uniform and general system." In sum, Webster argued, because com-merce regulation potentially "cover[ed] a vast field of legislation," it was better not to define commerce but rather to apply exclusivity to any commerce-related matter where federal control could operate "with more advantage" to "the public good."[69] Clearly, Webster believed that leaving "commerce" undefined created a broader space for federal power. What is more, Webster was making a disguised implied-powers argument, echoing *McCulloch's* argument that the broad and vast sweep of potential legislative means could not be provided for in express grants of powers.

In defining commerce to include navigation, Marshall not only ignored Webster's plea. He also pushed against the prevailing understanding that navigation was inci-dental to commerce, rather than included within its definition. Founding-era writers

commonly referred to "commerce" and "navigation" as distinct things.[70] They typically viewed the regulation of navigation as *incidental to* the regulation of commerce,
and repeatedly cited navigation regulation as a leading and uncontroversial illustration of the constitutional existence of implied powers. Recall that Hamilton and
members of Congress arguing for the constitutionality of the First Bank had cited
federal laws erecting "lighthouses, beacons, buoys" and other navigation aids as legislative precedent for implied commerce powers. Members of Congress repeatedly
referred to navigational aids as authorized by implied commerce powers, right up to
the 1824 General Survey Act debates.[71]

Likewise, courts had viewed navigation as an implied commerce power. In
United States v. The William (1808), an important district-court decision upholding
Jefferson's Embargo Acts, the court reasoned that the term "commerce" in the
Constitution "does not necessarily include shipping or navigation; much less does it
include the fisheries." Yet such navigation and maritime laws were within the powers
Congress because they were "incidents to commerce, and intimately connected with
it," and thus "necessary and proper, for carrying into execution" the enumerated
commerce power.[72] In his 1823 *Elkison* circuit decision, Justice Johnson stated that
"the navigation of ships has always been held, by all nations, *to appertain* to commercial regulations."[73] The word "appertain" refers to implied powers.[74] Marshall
himself leaned toward analyzing navigation as an implied commerce power in the
"twin brother" of Johnson's case, *The Brig Wilson v. United States* (1820). "From the
adoption of the constitution, till this time," Marshall wrote, "the universal sense of
America has been, that the word 'commerce,' as used in that instrument, is to be
considered a generic term, comprehending navigation, *or,* that a control over navigation is necessarily incidental to the power to regulate commerce."[75] But viewing navigation as incidental to commerce seemed to strike him as more plausible. "There
is not, in the constitution, one syllable on the subject of navigation," he wrote,
echoing his assertion in *McCulloch* that "[a]mong the enumerated powers, we do
not find that of establishing a bank or creating a corporation."[76] Instead, the power
to regulate navigation was implicit. First, the power had to exist somewhere and
couldn't reside in the states. Second, Congress's "unlimited power over the cargoes"
meant that it could also "control the vehicle in which they are imported."[77] These are
implied-powers arguments.

The view that a federal power to regulate navigation could be *implied* under the
commerce power was so well established by 1824 that counsel for Ogden had to
concede in the *Gibbons* oral argument that navigation laws "are all exercises of the
implied powers derived from that of regulating commerce."[78] Marshall would have
to go out of his way to avoid this conclusion.

It might be argued that an implied-powers approach would have been narrower
and therefore less aggressively nationalistic than the definitional approach adopted
by Marshall. Before *Gibbons*, this argument would go, implied powers would be
constrained by the narrow "trade-only" understanding of commerce; whereas after

Gibbons, implied commerce powers could be attached to a broader base. But this is unpersuasive. Given the broad consensus that Congress could regulate navigation as an implied commerce power, it is hard to see how moving "navigation" into the definition of commerce expands congressional power over things it could not have regulated before.

It might also be argued that the breadth of *Gibbons* is to be found in Marshall's claim that "Commerce, undoubtedly, is traffic, but it is something more: it is intercourse." Some modern commentators have argued that Marshall meant "intercourse" to refer to all human interactions bearing on the national wealth or economy.[79] Henry Clay certainly used "intercourse" that way in his internal improvements speeches, and Marshall may well have intended to invoke Clay's words. Yet no sooner did Marshall use the word "intercourse" than he narrowed it down to "commercial intercourse . . . regulated by prescribing rules for . . . navigation."[80] And the only concrete example of intercourse provided in *Gibbons* was commercial passenger navigation. The most one can say about the extremely broad understanding of "intercourse" is that the word is ambiguous, and even the modern Court has only partially embraced the broader view. The understanding that "intercourse" meant passenger transportation prevailed in the Supreme Court for the next hundred years and more, and the dominant reading of *Gibbons* until the mid-twentieth century was that the word "commerce" in the Commerce Clause meant "trade-plus-navigation."[81]

Consider in contrast how *Gibbons* might have been written if Marshall *had* built on *McCulloch* rather than treating the issue as "one of definition" of the term "commerce." The following hypothetical revision of *Gibbons*'s key language (indicated in bold and strikeouts) illustrates my point:

> The subject to be regulated is commerce; and our constitution being, as was aptly said at the bar, one of enumeration, and not of definition, to ascertain the extent of the power, it ~~becomes necessary~~ **is vain** to settle the meaning of the word. The counsel for the appellee would limit it to traffic, to buying and selling, or the interchange of commodities, and do not admit that it comprehends navigation. This would **unduly** restrict a general ~~term~~ **delegation of power**, applicable to many objects, to one of its ~~significations~~ **applications**. Commerce, undoubtedly, is traffic, but ~~it~~ **the power of Congress to regulate commerce** is something **much** more. ~~it is intercourse.~~ **As this Court said in *McCulloch v. Maryland*, the legislative powers of the government extend to all legislative means, "which are appropriate, which are plainly adapted" to executing the enumerated powers; in this case, the power to regulate trade among the states or with foreign nations or Indian tribes.** ~~It describes the commercial intercourse between nations, and parts of nations, in all its branches, and is regulated by prescribing rules for carrying on that intercourse.~~ **As was**

> aptly said at the bar [by Webster], almost all the business and inter-
> course of life may be connected, incidentally, more or less, with com-
> mercial regulations. Whatever else may be comprehended by "that
> vast mass of incidental powers which must be involved in" the regula-
> tion of commerce, *see McCulloch*, those incidental powers over com-
> merce undoubtedly include the power to regulate navigation. The
> mind can scarcely conceive a system for regulating commerce between na-
> tions, which shall exclude all laws concerning navigation. . . .

Gibbons presented Marshall with a clear opportunity to reaffirm and build on *McCulloch* by endorsing the idea of implied commerce powers, with its hugely expansive potential for federal legislative power. But Marshall not only declined to cite *McCulloch* in his *Gibbons* opinion. At times he wrote as if *McCulloch's* implied powers holding did not even exist. If the definition of "commerce" did not include navigation, Marshall argued, then "the government of the Union has no direct power over that subject, *and can make no law prescribing what shall constitute American vessels, or requiring that they shall be navigated by American seamen.*"[82] This assertion makes no sense—indeed, is plainly wrong—according to *McCulloch's* understanding of implied powers. Under *McCulloch*, the absence of a "direct" (read, "enumerated") power does not negate an implied power over navigation. Had he applied *McCulloch's* analysis of implied powers to the Commerce Clause in *Gibbons*, Marshall could have thrown the door open to a wide array of legislative means deemed by Congress to be "appropriate" and "plainly adapted" to the regulation of interstate trade. This application could extend to internal improvements, and the regulation of agriculture, manufactures—and slavery.

And that was undoubtedly the problem. Applying *McCulloch* to the Commerce Clause was too expansive for Marshall. By instead making the question turn on the definition of commerce, *Gibbons* in effect suggested that each assertion of regulatory power onto a new object other than navigation, whether internal improvements, agriculture, or slavery, would require a new definitional battle over the meaning of commerce. It would be far more difficult to say that road-building *was in itself* commerce than to show that building roads was an implied power "plainly adapted" to regulating commerce.[83] *McCulloch's* implied-powers analysis is based on a much looser concept of relatedness than the addition of dictionary meanings to a word or phrase. In effect Marshall shifted the commerce-power inquiry from a deferentially reviewed congressional determination of "appropriate" or "plainly adapted" means to a rigorous judicial determination of the definition of a word in the Constitution.

* * *

The aggressive nationalism reading of *Gibbons* derives much of its force from Marshall's statements that the commerce power can reach "into the interior" of the states. There is little doubt that this concept could expand federal regulation. It was emphasized in post–New Deal jurisprudence creating the modern "substantial effects" test under which Congress can now regulate many subjects that were formerly deemed within the reserved powers of the states. But *Gibbons* was ambiguous about what internal state matters could be reached under the commerce power.

The scope of the Commerce Clause, Marshall began, implicitly excludes (by not enumerating) a power to regulate "the exclusively internal commerce of a State."[84] This interpretation raised a factual problem regarding the steamboat monopoly: New York claimed that the Hudson River was an entirely New York waterway, so that most of the route controlled by the monopoly was intrastate. Its interstate element occurred only at the New Jersey ferry terminal.[85] Looked at one way, the monopoly regulated intrastate commerce and only incidentally touched on interstate commerce, and one possible resolution would have been to let the monopoly stand as far as it concerned service entirely within New York. But the Court wanted to embrace Webster's argument that intrastate sections of navigable waterways could not be separated from the system of free interstate navigation, which therefore had to be kept free even from intrastate obstructions. "Every district has a right to participate" in interstate commerce, Marshall wrote. "The deep streams which penetrate our country in every direction, pass through the interior of almost every State in the Union, and furnish the means of exercising this right."[86] Thus, Marshall had to say that federal commerce power could reach at least some intrastate commerce.

In making this point, Marshall wrote two key passages whose ambiguity charted the divergent course of Commerce Clause jurisprudence for the next two centuries. In the first passage, Marshall crucially asserted, "Commerce among the States, cannot stop at the external boundary line of each State, but may be introduced into the interior." But he immediately qualified this by reaffirming that "[t]he completely internal commerce of a State, then, may be considered as reserved for the State itself," and that congressional power over such matters "would be inconvenient, and is certainly unnecessary."[87] The rhetorical emphasis is on *restriction* of the federal power, and the backhanded allusion to *McCulloch*, in the negative form of the words "convenient" and "necessary," suggests that "reserved" state powers could negate claims of implied federal power. This subtle, almost between-the-lines suggestion would be turned into one of the dominant ideas of the Court's states'-rights jurisprudence under the Chief Justiceship of Marshall's successor, Roger Taney.

The second key passage is designed to reassure states that their police powers will be safe from Commerce Clause exclusivity. Marshall cited state inspection laws as a leading example of "that immense mass of legislation, which embraces every thing within the territory of a State, not surrendered to the general government: all which can be most advantageously exercised by the States themselves." This "mass" also included "quarantine laws, health laws of every description, as well as laws for regulating the internal commerce of a State, and those which respect turnpike roads, ferries, &c . . ." Congress lacked a "direct general power over these objects," which thus "remain subject to State legislation" and can only be reached by Congress under a law that is "*clearly* incidental to some power which is expressly given."[88] Why "clearly" incidental? That suggests that implied powers would be viewed more restrictively when they reached into reserved state powers. As an example of a "clearly incidental" implied commerce power, Marshall suggested that a federal navigation license for voyages "from one port to another, in the same State" would be constitutional as incidental to the commerce power, but "implies no claim of a direct power to regulate the purely internal commerce of a State, or to act directly on its system of police."[89] In this example, an implied commerce power merely reaches more commerce—intrastate commerce, yes, but still only trade or navigation. Nothing in Marshall's discussion here indicated that implied powers could reach further into reserved state powers to regulate intrastate matters that are not themselves commerce—the states' "system of police." Nothing in *Gibbons* contradicts the idea that internal improvements ("turnpike roads, ferries, &c.") are part of a "mass" of state reserved powers outside the reach of implied commerce powers.

Finally, Marshall affirmed the concept of separate regulatory spheres in a manner not wholly unsatisfactory to advocates of states' rights. The fact that the federal and state governments might use legislative means resembling one another's powers, Marshall reasoned, did not prove that they possessed one another's powers concurrently.[90] A significant implication of this passage was the notion that states have incidental powers to engage in what looks like commerce (or other federal) regulation when exercising their police power. The Taney Court would make much of this, as we will see.

Marshall's suggestion that federal commerce regulations may follow trade goods or navigation across state lines into the interior of a state does not necessarily suggest that Congress may, under its commerce power, build roads or regulate slavery. One could exploit *Gibbons*'s suggestion that commercial intercourse is commerce, and argue that such intercourse includes commercial traffic on roads. But objections to such an analogy would be easy to make: exercises of power on dry land and on water were viewed as different in antebellum constitutional thought, as we have seen. Daniel Webster knew his judicial audience, and he carefully distinguished between navigation, an acceptable commercial power, and internal improvements, a controversial one. "It is a common principle, that arms of the sea, including navigable rivers, belong to the sovereign," Webster argued, but he then conceded that the commerce power did not authorize Congress to establish "turnpikes, bridges, &c. and provide for all this detail of interior legislation."[91]

Marshall embraced this distinction between navigation and overland transportation, revealing a conservative edge to the definitional approach. Marshall asserted, quite accurately, that "[a]ll America understands, and has uniformly understood, the word 'commerce,' to comprehend navigation."[92] Rivers and coastal waters were the nation's highways in 1824—the Cumberland Road notwithstanding—and navigation seems thus to have been unique in its national character. And the distinction would encourage future Supreme Courts to reject novel or contested definitions of commerce; it certainly cuts against readings of *Gibbons* suggesting that the case offered leading rather than lagging interpretations of congressional power.[93] However much *Gibbons* may have encouraged later Congresses to push the boundaries of its powers, it invited later Courts even more to refuse to extend the definition of commerce beyond trade-plus-navigation. In fact, the latter is exactly what happened over the next fifty years.

* * *

Marshall's opinion in *Gibbons* did not resolve the question of whether the commerce power was exclusive. Famously, Marshall recited Webster's exclusivity argument at great length only to stop short of implementing it. He concluded, "There is great force in this argument, and the Court is not satisfied that it has been refuted." There, the exclusivity discussion ended, and Marshall pivoted to a lengthy inquiry whether the steamboat monopoly grant "come[s] into collision with an act of Congress, and deprived a citizen of a right to which that act entitles him."[94]

Why would Marshall flirt so extensively with a broad negative commerce argument only to veer away sharply and rely on a statutory preemption argument? Scholars have debated this question for decades.[95] One answer is that Marshall was understandably reluctant to endorse a doctrine that all state police-power laws affecting interstate commerce were excluded by the dormant commerce power. The problem was that many, if not most, exercises of state police powers did have such an effect. A general theory of commerce power exclusivity would therefore raise vexed questions about invalidating the reserved powers of the states to regulate health, safety, morals—and race. Marshall had not worked out a general exclusivity theory that could invalidate selected state police powers, while preserving others so as to avoid explosive controversies.

These difficulties bring us back to Marshall's choice not to treat navigation as an implied power. Marshall was uncertain about the exclusive effect of federal statutes. It was contentious enough to hold that an express constitutional grant of federal power could make such an inroad. But to hold that *implied* powers could make this inroad would have raised a yet more difficult question. Could an *unexercised* implied power be field-preemptive in the same way that at least some enumerated powers were? In the *Gibbons* hearing, Ogden's lawyer Thomas Oakley did not challenge Congress's power to enact the coasting license law, but argued instead that the power to regulate navigation was an implied commerce power. "All implied powers are, of course, concurrent," Oakley contended, because to hold otherwise "would deprive the States almost entirely of sovereignty, as these implied powers must inevitably be very numerous, and must embrace a wide field of legislation."[96] In other words, clever lawyers might challenge state laws by arguing that as-yet unexercised implied powers were exclusive of state laws. As Chancellor Kent had warned in *Livingston v. Van Ingen*, this threat of exclusivity might leave state legislatures guessing about what laws might be preempted: "Such a doctrine would be constantly taxing our sagacity, to see whether the law might not contravene some future [congressional] regulation of commerce."[97]

Oakley's co-counsel, Thomas Emmett, pushed the argument even further. If the commerce power were exclusive and, as *McCulloch* held, extended to "all the means which are appropriate and plainly adapted to the execution of that power," then "what becomes of the State control over our canals, the craft on them, or the tolls from them?"[98] Implied powers could make Commerce Clause exclusivity unmanageable. Recognizing this, Wirt and Webster did not refer to *McCulloch*, their great Supreme Court victory of just five years earlier. Neither did Marshall. By making navigation an element of a definition of the word commerce in the Constitution, Marshall made the potential scope of the Commerce Clause more concrete and *smaller* in order to reduce the potential displacement of state laws were the Court ever to adopt an exclusive commerce theory. By 1824, *McCulloch* had become more of a conceptual albatross than a source of pride.

* * *

Marshall continued to ignore *McCulloch*'s discussion of implied powers in Commerce Clause cases following *Gibbons*. Two weeks after deciding *Gibbons*, the Court decided *Osborn v. Bank of the United States* (1824).[99] This case was in essence *McCulloch II*, arising out of an aggressive effort by the state of Ohio to drive its Second Bank branch out of the state. Ohio had levied a $50,000 tax on the Bank's Ohio branch, seized the money from the branch's vault, and ignored lower-federal-court injunctions attempting to enforce *McCulloch*'s tax-immunity principle.[100] But by the time the case reached the Supreme Court, Ohio's lawyers had softened the state's position. They conceded that the Bank was constitutional, and that it was immune from state taxes when conducting the federal government's business; they merely argued that the state could tax the Bank's in-state for-profit operations, such as commercial lending, that were not federal government business. Significantly, the public/private character of the Bank had been questioned in the *McCulloch* oral argument by Maryland's lawyers, who argued that the Bank's private aspect made it unnecessary and taxable. Pinkney replied at length, channeling arguments that had been made by Hamilton and Calhoun, that the Bank "could not be rendered effectual" without its private aspect because an "altogether a government bank" would not be creditworthy.[101] Marshall had neglected to address this question in *McCulloch*, leaving a loose end that he now had to tidy up in *Osborn*.

Marshall rejected Ohio's argument, but again declined to adopt the most aggressively nationalistic position. Although the Bank was created by the federal government for the primary purpose of conducting the government's fiscal operations,

Marshall reasoned, its private activities supported that purpose. If the Bank did not engage in the "trade" of banking, it would not have the capital and the machinery to serve the government's fiscal needs. Therefore, the Bank's engagement in nongovernmental transactions did not affect its immunity from state taxation. Referring vaguely to the Second Bank as serving "the purposes" or "the fiscal operations of the government," Marshall once again failed to connect the Second Bank to potentially broad federal powers over commerce and the money supply.[102]

Marshall's avoidance of recognizing a broad federal power over the money supply stands in sharp contrast to Justice Johnson's concurring opinion. Johnson recognized the opportunity and seized it. "A specie-paying Bank, with an overwhelming capital, and the whole aid of the government deposits," Johnson proclaimed, "presented the only resource to which the government could resort, to restore that power over the currency of the country, which the framers of the constitution evidently intended to give to Congress alone."[103] The "power over the currency" does not stem from a single enumerated power, but is most plausibly derived from a synergistic reading of the various finance clauses, and perhaps the Commerce Clause. Marshall did not make such readings; Johnson clearly did. So too, shortly after Marshall's death, did Justice Story, who asserted in his 1837 dissent in *Briscoe v. Bank of Kentucky* that state banknotes were "subject always to the control of Congress, whose powers extend to the entire regulation of the currency of the country."[104] Marshall's majority opinion in *Osborn* thus took a less nationalistic view of Congress's powers relating to currency and the money supply than did at least two of his colleagues.

The Marshall Court decided only two important Commerce Clause cases after 1824. In *Brown v. Maryland* (1827),[105] discussed briefly at the start of this chapter, a Baltimore importer challenged the constitutionality of a state duty on his imports. Marshall's opinion for the unanimous Court held the tax unconstitutional both as a violation of the Constitution's express ban on state-imposed import taxes, and because the tax "would obviously derange the measures of Congress to regulate commerce." Federal law granted a license to importers who paid the federal tariff. Once again, as in *Gibbons*, Marshall flirted with Commerce Clause exclusivity, only to rely on a federal licensing statute, this time interpreting the federal importing license as a free-trade right that conferred immunity from state taxes. Marshall reasoned that the goods retained their character as foreign commerce so long as they remained inside their "original package," and became subject to state regulations and taxes only when removed from their original package. Maryland's tax was therefore void as a conflict with federal law. Marshall cited *McCulloch* only for its discussion of tax immunity.[106] *Brown* became famous for its creation of the "original package doctrine," and before 1900 this now largely forgotten case was cited by the Supreme Court almost as frequently as *McCulloch*.[107]

Marshall's last commerce decision, *Willson v. Blackbird Creek Marsh Co.* (1829),[108] upheld a state's power to obstruct commerce by damming a small but navigable tidal stream. Dams and other improvements were "undoubtedly within" the reserved powers of the states, wrote Marshall, since they could increase property values and protect health. In the absence of a federal statute seeking to control such waterways, the state had concurrent authority to authorize the dam. Modern commentators have tended to read *Willson* as evidence that the Marshall Court "reined in its earlier nationalism" to adapt itself to the "age of Jackson."[109] Marshall's very short, unanimous opinion omitted *Gibbons*, but the two cases are entirely consistent. *Willson* concluded that commerce exclusivity did not apply in "the circumstances of the case," where one could readily distinguish swampy tidal creeks from rivers like the Hudson. But *Gibbons* had not established commerce exclusivity either, and both cases acknowledged state police powers. *Willson* is better understood as an illustration of the limits of *Gibbons*.

* * *

The Marshall Court never ruled on the constitutionality of internal improvements. Had a case come before the Court challenging a federal internal improvements law as unconstitutional—if Monroe had signed the Cumberland Road bill, rather than vetoing it, for example—it seems likely that the Marshall Court would have upheld it: not because Marshall and his colleagues were active promoters of the American System, but rather because it was not Marshall's jurisprudential approach to impose limits on the powers of Congress. The Court would not take the lead, but neither would it obstruct any nationalist impulses forthcoming from Congress. *McCulloch* could be read to support internal improvements, as an implied power under the postal, war, or even commerce powers, but the justices did not lay out a map.

Their equivocation was captured by Joseph Story in his famous treatise, *Commentaries on the Constitution*, first published in 1833. Story devoted a chapter to Internal Improvements, in which he laid out the arguments. On one side, under the reasoning of *McCulloch*, "Congress may . . . authorize the making of a canal, as incident to the power to regulate commerce," to "facilitate the intercourse between state and state." But under "a strict construction of the constitution. . . . The power to regulate commerce cannot include a power to construct roads and canals, and improve the navigation of water-courses in order to facilitate, promote, and secure such commerce[.]" Story claimed that "the liberal interpretation has been very uniformly asserted by congress," whereas "the strict interpretation has not uniformly, but has upon several important occasions been insisted upon by the executive." Where was the Court in all this? "In the present state of the controversy, the duty of forbearance seems inculcated upon the commentator; and the reader must decide for himself upon his own views of the subject."[110] Story wrote a lengthy and touching dedication of his *Commentaries* to Marshall, whom he loved and admired, and took pains to finish the work during Marshall's lifetime. Marshall told Story that the *Commentaries* were "a comprehensive and accurate commentary on our constitution" that should be "read by every statesman, and every would-be statesman in the United States."[111] Story's commentary is a fitting epitaph for the Marshall Court's elusiveness on internal improvements.

* * *

It would be silly to argue that Marshall shrank the reach of the Commerce Clause in *Gibbons*. But it is misleading to argue that *Gibbons* expanded commerce *power*—the Commerce Clause plus any powers implied from it—in the open-ended fashion retrospectively credited to Marshall's opinion. While seeming to expand the enumerated power over interstate commerce, Marshall effectively shrank the power that might be *implied* from the Commerce Clause.

Marshall offered hints and phrases that readers could, and eventually did, turn into the modern substantial effects test, authorizing Congress to enact broad regulation of the economy. At the same time, *Gibbons* is chock full of language suggesting more limited interpretations. The opinion can be read to place boundaries on the Commerce Clause and to suggest that implied powers could not reach things that were not deemed "commerce." This is how *Gibbons* would be understood at the turn of the century. And the opinion can even be understood to mean that state laws can be immunized from preemptive federal commerce regulation if they are properly characterized as police power laws. This is how *Gibbons* would be understood by the Taney Court. Indeed, a sign of the limits of *Gibbons's* nationalism, or at least its profound ambiguity, is its favorable reception in the Jacksonian-dominated Taney Court. While ignoring or even flouting *McCulloch*, Taney Court justices celebrated *Gibbons* as the leading case and authoritative interpretation of the Commerce Clause.[112] The Taney Court's comfort with *Gibbons* supports the notion that the case easily fit into a Jacksonian jurisprudence that believed in preserving the Union while tilting heavily toward state sovereignty.

PART II

DISAPPEARANCE AND REVIVAL

"The Baneful Influence of this Narrow Construction"

McCulloch in the Age of Jackson, 1829–1860

In *McCulloch*, Chief Justice Marshall warned that the "baneful influence" of unduly narrow constructions of the Constitution's enumerated powers would "render[] the government incompetent to its great objects."[1] In this, he repeated Hamilton's warning to Washington that the strict construction—the indispensable necessity test for implied powers—urged by Jefferson and later by Maryland in the *McCulloch* argument "would be fatal to the just & indispensable authority of the United States."[2] After the 1828 election of Andrew Jackson, *McCulloch* and its principles came under attack, but Marshall's decision itself was rarely defended—even by the Marshall Court.

Following Marshall's death in 1835 until the eve of the Civil War, the Court under Marshall's successor, Roger B. Taney, pursued an agenda of rolling back Marshall Court nationalism by embracing strict construction and a strong theory of reserved state powers. To the Taney Court, the fundamental jurisprudential problem was to identify and expand the scope of reserved state powers. These are mentioned but left unspecified by the Tenth Amendment: "The powers not delegated to the United States by the Constitution, nor prohibited by it to the states, are reserved to the states respectively, or to the people." As Marshall made clear in *McCulloch*, the absence of the word "expressly" to modify "delegated" in this amendment is consistent with the idea that the powers delegated to the United States include implied powers. At the same time, powers reserved to the states, being unspecified in the Constitution, are all in a sense implied powers. The result, as Marshall implicitly recognized in *Gibbons*, is a gray area in which federal implied powers and reserved state powers compete. The Taney Court sought to ensure that reserved state powers would prevail in this competition. This would require, in essence, not overruling but actually reversing the direction of *McCulloch*—confining implied federal powers while expanding the scope of implied state powers. The prime mover of this new "spirit of the Constitution" was the perceived need to protect the constitutional position of slavery.

The Taney Court's pro–states'-rights agenda was made easier by the ambiguous qualities of Marshall's decisions in *McCulloch* and *Gibbons*. Those opinions had refrained from committing the Court on any significant question of congressional powers other than the Bank and a regulatory power over navigation. *Gibbons* in particular refrained from setting a precedent for implied commerce powers, or from authoritatively resolving the concurrent powers problem in a way that would make implied commerce powers workable. Marshall's opinion left doors ajar in both directions—for more national legislative power, and for more aggressive statements about reserved powers of the states. The Taney Court could treat *Gibbons* as the authoritative interpretation of the Commerce Clause while moving toward states' rights. *Gibbons* also invited the Taney Court to ignore *McCulloch* and implied powers when interpreting the Commerce Clause. And this is precisely what the Taney Court did.

* * *

A crucial political test of *McCulloch*'s principles came in 1832, at the end of Andrew Jackson's first term as president. The events of 1832 created a perfect storm of federalism issues. First, "Indian removal," the signature policy of Jackson's first term, defined his states' rights agenda as he supported Georgia's right to expel the Cherokee nation from the western part of the state in spite of federal treaties and Supreme Court decisions. Second, Jackson's hostility to the Second Bank of the United States—the "Monster Bank" as Jackson called it—came to a head in June 1832 as Congress passed, and Jackson vetoed, a bill to recharter the Bank for a new twenty-year term. Finally, the Nullification Crisis, South Carolina's resistance to enforcement of federal law that had been brewing since 1828, came to a climax in December 1832.

Consequently, when Marshall issued the Court's opinion in *Worcester v. Georgia*[3] in March 1832, the moment seemed opportune for a vigorous reaffirmation of *McCulloch*. As part of its assault on the Cherokee, the Georgia legislature had passed a law prohibiting whites from trading or living with the Cherokee without the state's permission. Two missionaries living in Cherokee lands under federal license had been arrested, tried, and convicted by Georgia authorities and were serving lengthy prison terms at hard labor. The structure of the case paralleled *McCulloch*: the federal trading license was appropriate legislation pursuant to Congress's power to make treaties with the Indian nation, and to regulate commerce "with the Indian tribes" under the Commerce Clause. The state obstructed these federal powers by direct legislative attack. At a minimum, Marshall could have cited *McCulloch* for the more general proposition—asserted in both *McCulloch* and *Worcester*—that a state law "repugnant to the constitution, laws and treaties of the United States" is void.[4] The Court did indeed hold that the convictions of the missionaries were unconstitutional (though Georgia infamously ignored the judgment, and Jackson did nothing to enforce it). But Marshall did not cite *McCulloch* for any substantive point.[5] He did not even try to defend *McCulloch* against the swipe taken at it by his recently appointed colleague, Justice John McLean. "The constitution of the United States," McLean wrote in a concurring opinion, "was formed, not... as some have contended,"—namely, the Court in *McCulloch*—"by the people of the United States, nor, as others, by the states; but by a combined power, exercised by the people, through their delegates, limited in their sanctions, to the respective states."[6] Perhaps Marshall no longer disagreed with McLean's position: in *Gibbons*, he had written that the Constitution was formed when the sovereign states "converted their league into a government."[7] The explanation for Marshall's omitting *McCulloch* cannot simply be his conflict avoidance: historians agree that Marshall wanted to make *Worcester* into an "election manifesto," hoping to give the Whig presidential candidate running against Jackson another election issue by branding Jackson's highly divisive Indian removal policy unconstitutional.[8]

Four months later, the Whig party created what it hoped would be the next major election issue by passing a bill to recharter the Second Bank. The Bank's supporters calculated that the Bank had sufficient political support that Jackson would either sign the charter renewal reluctantly or veto it and give his presidential opponent Henry Clay a winning campaign issue. The bill to recharter the Bank was introduced in Congress in January, and for the first and only time before the Civil War, *McCulloch* was receiving considerable attention in Congress. The Bank's supporters extolled Marshall's decision, while the Bank's opponents either attacked it or attempted to reinterpret it against the recharter bill.[9] The occurrence of this debate while *Worcester* was being argued and decided adds to the strangeness of Marshall's failure to reaffirm *McCulloch's* substance.

The recharter bill was eventually passed in July 1832, at which point it was subjected to the most famous presidential veto in U.S. history.[10] Jackson's veto message asserted that it is the President's right to interpret the Constitution independently, without being bound by a decision of the Supreme Court: "The authority of the Supreme Court must not ... be permitted to control the Congress or the Executive when acting in their legislative capacities. . . ." But the veto message followed this seemingly bold assertion of departmentalism with a surprisingly fair and even respectful reading of *McCulloch*, one that simply fails to live up to the universal perception that the bank veto defied the Supreme Court. In fact, Jackson discussed objections to the bank bill "[w]ithout commenting on the general principle affirmed by the Supreme Court." According to Jackson, *McCulloch* had recognized that it was "the exclusive province of Congress and the President" to decide whether any particular legislation was necessary and proper.[11] Jackson then laid out a litany of objections to the bill. Jackson did not say that *McCulloch* was wrong to decide that the federal government had an implied power to charter a national bank. He did not even challenge Marshall's definition of "necessary and proper." Instead, Jackson said that a national bank with the *particular features* in the 1832 bank bill was not "necessary and proper."[12] While he contended that some features violated specific provisions of the Constitution that had not been considered by *McCulloch*, he couched most of his objections as legislative policy judgments that specific provisions of the bank bill failed *McCulloch*'s test for necessity. This was a lawyerly reading of *McCulloch*, if perhaps a narrow one. *McCulloch* did not set out to compel congressional judgments about a national bank's necessity, but to give Congress room to make such judgments and perhaps constrain judicial second-guessing them. The twist Jackson put on *McCulloch*, if there was one, was to assert that as president, he was entitled to participate in that legislative judgment—a claim that certainly finds support in the grant of presidential veto power.

Historians uniformly emphasize Jackson's assertion of the president's independent power to interpret the Constitution, reading it as the leading statement of "departmentalism," the theory that each "department" of the federal government—legislative, executive, and judicial—has equal authority to interpret the Constitution.[13] But taken in its entirety, the bank veto message is less a bold statement of departmentalism than a cagey example of Jackson's transformation of the veto power. Washington and his presidential successors had held to a tradition of reserving use of the veto power for constitutional objections. Jackson is known for being the first president to veto bills on policy grounds.[14] Jackson's bank veto was a hybrid of constitutional and policy reasons rather than an all-out attack on *McCulloch*. But whatever Jackson may have been trying to signal by the careful and lawyerly effort to harmonize his veto with *McCulloch*, he failed: the bank veto was uniformly interpreted from the moment of its issuance to the present day as a flat-out rejection of *McCulloch*.[15]

The ambiguous undercurrent of the bank veto message yields an important insight into the legal thought of Jackson's Attorney General, Roger B. Taney, who four years later would succeed Marshall as chief justice. Significant portions of the veto message were ghostwritten by Taney, who had argued in the Cabinet that *McCulloch* had decided only that Congress had the power to charter a national bank while leaving the particulars to legislative discretion.[16] Taney's reluctance to attack *McCulloch* head on in the bank veto message was consistent with his later practice as chief justice. His judicial opinions rarely if ever criticized Marshall Court precedents and never argued to overrule them. His practice, instead, was to reinterpret them to support his positions, or simply ignore them.[17] The bank veto laid out a road map by which a future Jacksonian Supreme Court could strike down a future bank bill by distinguishing *McCulloch*. All this should give pause to legal historians who have asserted that Taney was eager to overrule *McCulloch*, and would have done so had a suitable case arisen.[18] As we will see, suitable cases did arise, and Taney didn't.

* * *

McCulloch played surprisingly little role in constitutional debates other than the Bank debate. This was evident during the Nullification Crisis of 1832–33. The Nullification controversy had been brewing since the enactment of an 1828 tariff— the so-called Tariff of Abominations—whose maldistributed burdens fell heavily on cotton and rice producers, particularly in South Carolina. In November 1832, South Carolina convened a Nullification Convention that passed an ordinance declaring that the federal tariffs of 1828 and 1832 were unconstitutional, void, and uncollectible within South Carolina. President Jackson, whose support for states' rights was counterbalanced by his support for the Union, reacted strongly and swiftly. He immediately proclaimed nullification to be unconstitutional and unlawful, declared his intention to continue collecting customs duties in South Carolina ports, and asked Congress for authorization to use force to suppress state resistance to federal authority.[19]

The doctrine of nullification, which came to be called "the South Carolina Doctrine" by its opponents, had been articulated in its most developed form by John C. Calhoun. In 1828, Calhoun was still a nationalist clinging to presidential aspirations and was elected Andrew Jackson's vice president. Yet he was beginning his conversion into the apostle of states' rights. That year, to avoid becoming politically isolated in his home state, Calhoun ghostwrote a treatise for the South Carolina legislature, laying out a theory of nullification entitled "The South Carolina Exposition." Then in 1831, spurned by Jackson and with his presidential aspirations evaporating, Calhoun used his own name in publishing his "Fort Hill Address,"[20] the leading theoretical statement of nullification.

Calhoun and other South Carolina nullifiers refused to acknowledge the idea, espoused in *McCulloch*, that the people directly delegated power to the general government. The United States, Calhoun asserted, was not a unified government, properly understood, but rather a "joint commission or agency" created by the "compact between sovereigns" and "appointed to superintend and administer" the joint interests of the states. As such, the U.S. government had no rights in resolving a dispute over Constitution's distribution of powers. Like any agency agreement, the Constitution could not delegate to the agent—here, the national government—the power to decide the extent of its own powers. And like an agent, the national government was not a party to the agreement; the states were its only principals. "On no sound principle can the agents have a right to final cognizance, as against the principals, much less use force against them to maintain their construction of their powers,"[21] Calhoun argued. Purporting to expand on the idea of a state power to "arrest" unconstitutional laws, as stated in the Virginia and Kentucky resolutions of 1798, Calhoun maintained that a state could declare a national law void within its borders if the state determined the law to be a "palpable" violation of the Constitution. Such a determination by the state would trigger an "appeal" to Article V of the Constitution (the amendment process), in which the nullifying state's determination would stand unless overruled by a constitutional amendment. The practical effect of this doctrine would be to give each state a limited veto, in the form of final and binding authority to determine the applicability of federal laws to itself, subject only to the Constitution's cumbersome amendment process requiring a ratification by three-fourths of the states. Nullification was a constitutional review power on a par with the Supreme Court's, differing primarily to the extent that a state could nullify the federal law's applicability only to itself rather than nationwide.

Although *McCulloch* was written more than a decade before the Nullification Crisis, disunion was an ongoing anxiety for Marshall, who by 1819 had lived through at least three high-profile secession threats.[22] The *McCulloch* case raised a problem very much like nullification, insofar as Maryland sought to nullify the bank within its state boundaries through prohibitive taxation. Marshall's rejection of compact theory, his argument that the people met in their state conventions as an administrative convenience rather than as a demonstration of state sovereignty, and his assertions that the people delegated powers directly to a national government supreme within its sphere of action, all tended to refute nullification.

But the two leading anti-nullifiers, Daniel Webster and Andrew Jackson, omitted any mention of *McCulloch*, John Marshall, or Marshall Court decisions. In his December 1832 proclamation denouncing nullification, Jackson advanced a hybrid view of the Constitution's formation, similar to McLean's concurrence in *Worcester*. "The people of the United States formed the constitution acting through the state legislatures in making the compact, to meet and discuss its provisions, and acting in separate conventions when they ratified those provisions." But the result was a national government because the lower House and president are chosen by "the people of the states" and who therefore represent "the people ... and not the states." Jackson thus added a presidentialist twist, arguing that the system for electing a president for the whole people demonstrated that the Union is a government independent of the states, and not its "creature" or "agent," as Calhoun would have it.[23] Webster laid out his anti-nullification arguments in two famous speeches—"Second Reply to Hayne" (1830) and "The Constitution Is Not a Compact" (1833). Webster stressed that nullification would result in a minority ruling the majority, thereby subverting the cardinal republican principle of majority rule.

Although Webster rejected the "compact" characterization of the Constitution while Jackson embraced it, they agreed that nullification was unconstitutional. Both Webster and Jackson placed great reliance on the structural argument that one state's power to nullify a national law was incompatible with the existence of the Union and contrary to the letter, spirit, and purposes of the Constitution. Webster and Jackson also agreed that, contrary to Calhoun's assertion, the Constitution did indeed specify a procedure for settling disputes over constitutional interpretation, giving authority to the federal judiciary with final authority to the Supreme Court.[24] One can find Marshall's representation theory in their arguments, but neither simply rephrased Marshall's statements of nationalism. To give Marshall credit for these arguments requires some squinting.

Both Jackson and Webster also advanced an argument that was gaining currency at the time to the effect that the sovereignty of the states did not predate the existence of the Union. This argument was based on the theory that the states declared their sovereign independence collectively, through the Continental Congress. This argument did not come from Marshall, who was "particularly struck" by it when he first heard it from John Quincy Adams in 1831.[25]

Despite putting the Supreme Court in charge of resolving constitutional disputes, neither Webster nor Jackson referred to *McCulloch* or any Marshall Court judicial opinions making the same claim. In Jackson's case, perhaps this omission is unsurprising, given his recent bank veto. In Webster's case, it is more surprising, in light of his role as advocate of nationalism in cases before the Court, including *McCulloch*. Or maybe it isn't surprising: Webster may well have believed that Marshall was simply recapitulating Webster's own arguments.[26] Either way, neither Jackson nor Webster found it advantageous to invoke the authority of Marshall or *McCulloch* against nullification.

* * *

The process of burying *McCulloch*, arguably started by Marshall himself, was completed by the Court of his successor, Chief Justice Taney. Marshall died on July 6, 1835, at the age of seventy-nine, and the expressions of mourning around the nation seem to have greatly exceeded that accorded to modern-day justices. Even some of Marshall's fiercest opponents, such as Andrew Jackson or Richmond Junto editor Thomas Ritchie eulogized him. Jackson wrote that Marshall expressed his opinions "with the energy and clearness which were peculiar to his strong mind, and gave him a rank amongst the greatest men of his age." Perhaps such eulogists were being politic or personally magnanimous, but Ritchie's had a ring of sincerity: "There was about [Marshall] so little of 'the insolence of office,' and so much of the benignity of the man, that his presence always produced the most delightful impressions. There was something irresistibly winning about him."[27] Marshall's stature was such that a myth soon arose that the Liberty Bell in Philadelphia cracked when tolling for his death.

Eight months later, Roger B. Taney was sworn in as chief justice, on March 28, 1836. Born in 1777 to a Maryland tobacco plantation-owing family, Taney combined personal antislavery views—in contrast to Marshall, he actually freed his own slaves—with a strong identification with southern plantation culture and states' rights. After joining the Maryland bar in 1799, Taney entered Maryland politics as a Federalist, but switched to the Republican party after the War of 1812. He served one term in the Maryland state senate, was appointed Maryland attorney general in 1827, and joined Andrew Jackson's cabinet as U.S. Attorney General in 1831. A staunch opponent of the Second Bank, Taney served as acting Treasury Secretary and implemented Jackson's order to remove federal Treasury funds from the Second Bank in 1833–34, effectively killing the Bank before its charter expired in 1836.[28]

Taney's appointment as Chief Justice completed a transition from the Marshall Court to a Jacksonian Court. By the time the Court began hearing cases again in December 1836, Joseph Story was the only surviving member of the Marshall Court's golden age. Other than Story and Smith Thompson, a moderate states'-rights Republican appointed by Monroe, the 1837 Court consisted of five Jackson appointees. On the last full day of Andrew Jackson's presidency, March 3, 1837, Congress enacted the most aggressive "court-packing" law in U.S. history. The law reorganized existing federal circuits, and created two new ones, the Eighth and Ninth Circuits. Since each Supreme Court seat at that time was filled by a resident of each circuit, the system was designed to make the Court into a regionally representative body. The 1837 reorganization law gerrymandered the judicial circuits so that five of them—and therefore five seats on the Court—would comprise slave states.[29] This move gave Jackson's successor, Martin Van Buren, two immediate Court appointments from slave states.

The states'-rights orientation of the Court was further shaped by the dominance of the Jacksonian Democrats in presidential politics. After Taney, the next six members of the Court, through 1850, were appointed by staunch Jacksonian successors. Following Story's death in 1845, the Court consisted of nine Jacksonian appointees leaning more or less heavily toward states' rights. All except John McLean were Jacksonian Democrats; McLean, though a moderate opponent of slavery and not a Jackson supporter, was nevertheless a reliable believer in reserved state powers. Only one other Whig, a moderate nationalist, would be appointed to the Court before the Civil War, in 1851.[30] This was the Court that interpreted and applied Marshall-era precedents, and the fact that this Court embraced *Gibbons* is more a reflection of *Gibbons*'s consistency with Jacksonian ideas than it is to the power of Marshall to control constitutional law from the grave.

The Taney Court wasted little time in undermining *McCulloch*, finding its first opportunity in Taney's first term on the bench. *New York v. Miln* (1837)[31] involved a challenge to a New York law that required the master or owner of any ship landing in New York harbor to submit a written report providing the name, birthplace, residence, age, and occupation of all foreign or interstate passengers, and to post a bond for the costs of maintenance or removal of impoverished immigrants. The law plainly regulated navigation, which was commerce under *Gibbons*, and indeed Congress had already imposed similar regulations on arriving immigrants. But the Court, over the lone dissent of Justice Story, upheld the law by concluding that it was not a regulation of commerce, but a "police" regulation designed to aid the state's ability to "guard against" "the moral pestilence of paupers, vagabonds, and possibly convicts" by controlling immigration. This conclusion made it unnecessary to decide whether the federal commerce power was exclusive.[32] But the conclusion was unconvincing: regulating passengers at the point of debarkation plainly regulated the preceding journey.

Justice Philip Barbour, a states'-rights firebrand from Virginia, made his *Miln* opinion into a states'-rights manifesto. Barbour asserted that when a state acts within "the legitimate scope of its power as to the end to be attained, it may use whatsoever means, being appropriate to that end, it may think fit; although they may be the same, or so nearly the same, as scarcely to be distinguishable from those adopted by congress acting under a different power[.]" Absent a direct collision with federal law—and the Court found none in this case—the state had "not only the right, but the bounden and solemn duty ... to advance the safety, happiness and prosperity of its people, and to provide for its general welfare, by any and every act of legislation, *which it may deem to be conducive to these ends*[.]" When it came to "all those powers which relate to merely municipal legislation, or what may, perhaps, more properly be called internal police, ... the authority of a state is *complete, unqualified, and exclusive.*"[33]

This language in *Miln* represented a reversal of *McCulloch* in two respects. First, it suggested that the states' reserved powers could defeat at least some plausible claims of implied powers under *McCulloch*. Recall that an implied power is one that is not expressly granted to Congress, but can nevertheless cut into presumedly reserved state powers if it is conducive to executing a granted power. Yet Barbour said that state police powers are "exclusive," suggesting that reserved state powers might defeat a claim of federal implied powers. Even more moderate Taney Court justices agreed with this proposition.[34] Second, *Miln* argued that state police powers carry implied powers that may extend into the ambit of the federal commerce power. The New York passenger-report law was not in itself a regulation of foreign paupers entering the state, but a regulation of navigation used as means to that end. So long as the end was legitimate—within state police powers—states could use legislative means that were indistinguishable from commerce regulation.[35] This was truly *McCulloch* in reverse.

Miln's anti-*McCulloch* essence was to build up a robust concept of reserved state powers that neutralized implied federal powers. This conception would dominate constitutional jurisprudence for the next century. Under it, the Court would uphold state laws, irrespective of their effect on foreign or interstate commerce, if they could plausibly be characterized as police regulations. The Taney Court decided three major Commerce Clause cases in the 1840s that struggled with the tension between the Commerce Clause and reserved state powers. Following *Miln*, the Court upheld state laws barring slave importation, in *Groves v. Slaughter* (1841),[36] and regulating liquor sales, in the *License Cases* (1847).[37] In the *Passenger Cases* (1849),[38] the Court struck down a tax on interstate and foreign passenger arrivals. The issue in each case was whether the federal commerce power, either in its dormant state or in light of a federal statute or treaty, nullified a state law exercising the state's "police power." These cases showed the Taney Court at its most perplexed, producing nineteen separate opinions and thus effectively abandoning Marshall's practice of issuing a clear opinion of the Court. Despite the seeming cacophony, the three cases and nineteen opinions are unified by a single theme—the power of states to keep out undesirable persons or things—so it will be more useful to discuss the cases thematically rather than as a chronological progression. When it came to the primacy of the states' core reserved powers, particularly the power to control slavery and race matters, the Taney Court justices showed remarkable unanimity.

While *Miln* and later Taney Court commerce decisions treated *Gibbons* as the leading case for construing the Commerce Clause, they construed *Gibbons* with a significant twist. In *Gibbons*, Marshall had emphasized that state quarantine and inspection laws were police-power laws rather than commerce regulations. His point was that the incidental effect such laws might have on interstate commerce did not prove that states had power to regulate such commerce. In *Miln*, the Taney Court turned this notion inside out: because the laws came from the state's police powers, no resulting intrusion on interstate commerce would make the state laws unconstitutional. The Court would uphold the state law as noncommercial by emphasizing its purpose as regulating health, safety, or morals. In the *License Cases* (1847), for example, the Court upheld state laws regulating liquor sales despite their obviously commercial nature. As one of the justices put it, "the true question presented by these cases, and one which I am not disposed to evade, is, whether the States have a right to prohibit the sale and consumption of an article of commerce which they believe to be pernicious in its effects, and the cause of disease, pauperism, and crime."[39] Taney himself put the matter more bluntly in a later case: "disease, pestilence, and pauperism are not subjects of commerce."[40]

A broad Taney Court consensus held that the concept of reserved state powers "has its foundation in the sacred law of self-defence, which no power granted to Congress can restrain or annul."[41] Taney Court justices from both northern and southern states agreed that state health and safety laws "are not regulations of commerce, but acts of self-preservation. And although they affect commerce to some extent, yet such effect is the result of the exercise of an undoubted power in the State."[42] Thus, although, "[a] concurrent power in the States to regulate commerce is an anomaly," said one justice, "[i]t does not follow, as is often said, with little accuracy, that, when a State law shall conflict with an act of Congress, the former must yield. On the contrary, except in certain cases named in the federal Constitution, this is never correct when the act of the State is strictly within its powers."[43]

This notion that conflicts between federal and state law might be resolved in favor of the states—contrary to *McCulloch* and *Gibbons*—commanded a consensus on the Taney Court. How this idea would be harmonized with the Supremacy Clause, the Taney Court never worked out.[44] According to one justice in the *License*

Cases (1847), state police-power laws "are from their very nature of primary importance; they lie at the foundation of social existence; . . . and necessarily compel all laws on subjects of secondary importance, . . . to recede, when they come in conflict or collision. . . ."[45] This suggestion that courts weigh the relative importance of federal laws against state police-power laws seems at first blush to undermine the principle of federal supremacy. But it can be viewed as somewhat compatible with the Supremacy Clause, and mostly as subverting *McCulloch*, so long as the federal laws of "secondary importance" are viewed as implied powers. If federal commerce power and state police powers were viewed as "separate spheres," it is only implied federal powers that could be said to make inroads into state reserved powers. The principle overrules *McCulloch* without naming the case.

Taney Court justices were far more concerned with practical outcomes than with consistency in the doctrine of federal supremacy. The first practical concern was to preserve state police-power regulation in general. The practical policy standing behind the doctrine of commerce exclusivity was one of nationwide domestic free trade. Story's *Miln* dissent embraced the free trade theory of commerce power, in which "the regulation of a subject . . . produces a uniform whole, which is as much disturbed and deranged by changing what the regulating power designs to leave untouched, as that upon which it has operated."[46] But replacing the dense web of state and municipal health, safety, and morals laws with a federal regime of sparse regulation could disorder society. One justice expressed this anxiety plainly, arguing that Commerce Clause exclusivity "would overthrow and annul entire codes of State legislation" and "expunge more State laws and city corporate regulations than Congress is likely to make in a century on the same subject."[47]

The Taney Court maintained unwavering consistency on one point: the states' power to regulate slavery. This position became increasingly clear throughout the 1840s. *Groves v. Slaughter* (1841)[48] raised the connection between interstate commerce exclusivity and slavery in the starkest possible fashion. *Groves* involved a suit by a slave trader to collect on promissory notes he had received for slaves sold on credit to residents of Mississippi. The debtors claimed that the promissory notes were void because the sales violated a Mississippi constitutional amendment that prohibited the commercial importation of slaves. This ban on interstate slave sales was by no means an antislavery law, but rather a discriminatory commercial measure designed to bolster Mississippi's internal slave market. Daniel Webster and Henry Clay, representing the slave dealer, advanced the irrefutable argument that the Mississippi provision thus represented the very type of protectionism that the dormant Commerce Clause was designed to eliminate. But to nullify the Mississippi law by applying dormant commerce exclusivity, as Webster and Clay urged, would be to recognize that the interstate slave trade was within the regulatory power of Congress under the Commerce Clause. This acknowledgment would raise serious concerns, both for slave-exporting states like Virginia and for free states. The former would fear a congressional ban on the interstate slave trade, while the latter would worry that their laws against slave importation would be deemed unconstitutional.

The majority opinion decided that the Mississippi constitutional provision could not void the out-of-state slave sales in the absence of implementing legislation, of which there was none. This stratagem resolved the case without having to decide the federal constitutional issues. Nevertheless, the justices went on to issue four concurring opinions explaining additional grounds for reaching the result of upholding the slave sales. In in the end, six of the seven participating justices agreed that the power to regulate slave trading was reserved to the states, even if the trading crossed state lines.[49] The gist of this position was expressed by Taney, who asserted that "the power over this subject" of slavery rested "exclusively with the several states." Each state could "decide for itself" whether to permit slavery within its borders, "and the action of the several states upon this subject, cannot be controlled by Congress, either by virtue of its power to regulate commerce, or by virtue of any other power conferred by the Constitution of the United States."[50] While some of the justices seemed to view slavery as legally unique—as though there were a slavery exception to the Commerce Clause—others appeared to view slavery as a particularly strong form of reserved state power in a conception of reserved powers that could fend off other forms of federal regulation as well. The distinction made little practical difference.

Slavery loomed in the background whenever the Court reviewed a state law aimed at protecting the inhabitants of the state from a perceived external evil. In the License Cases, dealing with regulation of liquor sales, Justice Story's successor from Massachusetts, Levi Woodbury, expressly likened the temperance laws at issue to those regulating slaves and immigrants.[51] The connection between slavery and immigration was built into the Constitution by the Migration and Importation Clause, and reinforced by the fear that admitting free black people into southern states would stir up slave insurrections.[52] This was made clear in the Passenger Cases, where a five-to-four majority struck down municipal taxes on immigrants, on the grounds that federal policy favored open immigration, and therefore nullified restrictive state immigration laws that were not especially targeted toward "paupers, vagabonds, or fugitives from justice."[53] In dissent, Chief Justice Taney emphatically asserted the state's power to exclude "any person, or class of persons, whom it might deem dangerous to its peace, or likely to produce a physical or moral evil among its citizens," whatever such a state law's incidental effect on foreign commerce. Taney claimed to be concerned primarily with the "disease and pauperism . . . daily brought to our shores in emigrant ships." But he was more worried about maintaining state control over slavery. Striking down the state immigration controls, Taney argued, meant that "the emancipated slaves of the West Indies have at this hour the absolute right to reside, hire houses, and traffic and trade throughout the Southern States, in spite of any State law to the contrary; inevitably producing the most serious discontent, and ultimately leading to the most painful consequences."[54] To the dissenters, states required power to exclude immigrants both to prevent the migration or importation of slaves into free states, and to prohibit the migration of free black people into both slave and free states.[55]

Still, the *Passenger Cases* made clear that the Court's pro-slavery consensus was so strong that it transcended sharp disagreements on other jurisprudential issues. Justices voting in the majority took pains to reassure the dissenters that their holding would not undermine the protection of slavery. Justice Grier reaffirmed "the right of any State, whose domestic security might be endangered by the admission of free negroes, to exclude them from her borders."[56] To Justice Wayne, the fear that "the United States may introduce into the Southern States emancipated negroes from the West Indies and elsewhere" was groundless, because the Court would always interpret the Constitution so as not "to dissolve, or even disquiet, the fundamental organization of either of the States."[57] All nine justices were committed to preserving slavery.

More abstract doctrinal questions were left unresolved. The Taney Court finally reached a compromise on commerce exclusivity in *Cooley v. Board of Wardens* (1852),[58] where the Court upheld a municipal pilotage law requiring ships arriving at Philadelphia to hire local pilots to steer them into port. Municipal pilot laws were inescapably regulations of navigation and hence of commerce, but a seven-to-two majority rejected once and for all a rule of across-the-board Commerce Clause exclusivity. Instead, exclusivity would be determined on a case-by-case basis. The Court expressly declined to state opinions about "what other subjects, under the commercial power, are within the exclusive control of Congress, or may be regulated by the States in the absence of all congressional legislation[.]"[59] In the end, doctrinal consistency in abstract principles regarding commerce exclusivity was far less important to the justices than preserving reserved state powers in general and control over slavery in particular.

* * *

The Taney Court's compulsion to reject *McCulloch*'s permissive approach to implied powers also surfaced in cases involving internal improvements. In *Searight v. Stokes* (1845),[60] for example, the Court considered a constitutional challenge to tolls imposed by Pennsylvania on private contractors using the Cumberland Road to carry U.S. mail along with private goods and passengers. The contractors argued that the tolls were barred by *McCulloch*'s prohibition of state taxation of federal functions, even when intermingled with private business.[61] Taney's majority opinion invalidated the tolls, but he ignored *McCulloch*, relying instead on a "compact" between Pennsylvania and the federal government in which Pennsylvania had agreed to waive tolls on all carriages conducting federal business. Although Taney noted that the case did not require the Court to opine on the constitutional power to build the Cumberland Road, he did venture in dicta that "[i]f the state had made this road herself, and had not entered into any compact upon the subject with the United States," it would have been entirely free to charge tolls on vehicles conducting federal business.[62] This assertion implied that because roads are purely state instrumentalities, they are within the regulatory sphere of the state, and federal use of the road must be on whatever terms the state imposes, so long as the terms are nondiscriminatory (i.e., the same as those imposed on private parties).

The Taney Court worried that an implied commerce power over internal improvements would threaten states' domestic institutions, notably slavery, and made this fear quite plain in *Veazie v. Moor* (1853).[63] Little known to history, *Veazie* was the Taney Court's most aggressive and comprehensive states'-rights statement on internal improvements and the Commerce Clause. There, the Court unanimously upheld a monopoly for steamboat travel on the Penobscot River, issued by the state of Maine to the Moor brothers. Although navigable, the river was "situated entirely within" the state and "not subject to the tides ... near its mouth." Presumably, this purely intrastate character was sufficient to distinguish the case from *Gibbons*, which the Court did not bother to discuss or quote. If *Gibbons* had at least suggested that the commerce power could reach intrastate navigation, that suggestion was effectively overruled in *Veazie*, in which the Court flatly asserted that "the term commerce in its broadest acceptation. . . . can never be applied to transactions wholly internal, between citizens of the same community, or to a polity and laws whose ends and purposes and operations are restricted to the territory and soil and jurisdiction of such community."[64] Commerce regulation— whether by an expansive definition of commerce, or through the notion of implied powers—could never extend to the internal concerns of a state, because "[a] pretension as far reaching as this, would extend to contracts between citizen and citizen of the same State, would control the pursuits of the planter, the grazier, the manufacturer, the mechanic, the immense operations of the collieries and mines and furnaces of the country." Because the products of "these avocations" would inevitably "be borne either by turnpikes, canals, or railroads" to interstate or foreign destinations, the logic of implied powers would make their regulation incident to commerce. An implied commerce power to regulate land-based internal improvements could place the law on a slippery slope to federal regulation of "the planter"[65]—read, "slave owner." This doctrinal logic had to be shut down, and the Court determinedly stated that the Commerce Clause "excludes" federal "control over turnpikes, canals, or railroads, or the clearing and deepening of watercourses exclusively within the States, or the management of the transportation upon and by means of such improvements." Instead, the purpose of the commerce power was merely "to establish a perfect equality amongst the several States as to commercial rights," and to prevent interstate commercial discrimination.[66] Once again, the Taney Court was reasoning backward from its guiding interpretive ethos to protect slavery.

* * *

Despite assertions in various Taney Court opinions suggesting a neutral orientation to states' rights to permit or exclude slavery, the Taney Court found such neutrality unsustainable. When push came to shove, the Taney Court deemed protection of slavery to be a higher value than states' rights as such. Since the rights of slave and free states could collide over slavery—particularly over the issue of the return of fugitive slaves—states'-rights jurisprudence alone could not protect slavery. In *McCulloch*, Marshall's idea of a capable federal government with adequate implied powers and supremacy of federal over state law was intertwined with a foundational narrative of a government created by the people rather than by a compact of sovereign states. The Taney Court required an alternative foundation narrative of federal supremacy that did not rely on *McCulloch* or a Constitution formed by and for the people.

This set of issues emerged in *Prigg v. Pennsylvania* (1842), a case arising out of the tragic story of Margaret Morgan. In the 1810s, Morgan's enslaved parents were permitted by their Maryland owner, John Ashmore, to move to Pennsylvania with young Margaret to live as free people. Becoming Margaret Morgan after her marriage to a free black man, Morgan continued to live in Pennsylvania as a free person with her husband and two children. But Ashmore had never bothered to formally manumit Morgan or her parents. After Ashmore's death, his son-in-law Nathan Beemis traveled to Pennsylvania in 1837 with three slave catchers to re-enslave Morgan. Beemis went before a local magistrate to obtain a recapture certificate under the 1793 federal Fugitive Slave Act to carry the entire Morgan family into slavery. Morgan's husband and both children were free born, and Morgan herself, having lived with her former owners' permission as a free person for over two decades, had a strong claim to freedom under both Pennsylvania and Maryland law. The magistrate denied the recapture certificate. Beemis then kidnapped Margaret and her two children and forcibly brought them to Maryland, where they were sold to slave traders and probably spent the rest of their lives as slaves. The kidnapping violated an 1826 Pennsylvania law, a "personal liberty law" designed to prevent this very situation, the wrongful seizure of claimed fugitive slaves. A Pennsylvania grand jury indicted Beemis and his three accomplices, but Maryland refused to extradite them to stand trial. After extended negotiations between the governors of the two states, Maryland agreed to extradite one of the slave catchers, Edward Prigg, who was tried and convicted in the Pennsylvania courts.[67]

Cases like Morgan's raised large questions of human rights and federalism. The Constitution's Fugitive Slave Clause provided that "[n]o person held to service or labor in one state, under the laws thereof, escaping into another, shall, in consequence of any law or regulation therein, be discharged from such service or labor, but shall be delivered up on claim of the party to whom such service or labor may be due."[68] The Clause was incorporated into the Constitution with little debate other than an insistence that a circumlocution be used in place of the word "slave." The Clause was undoubtedly meant to negate the international law principle from *Somerset's Case* (1772),[69] a well-known British precedent that a slave became free by setting foot on free soil. This principle might have applied between sovereign states in the absence of a contrary constitutional provision.[70] It is far from clear that the Fugitive Slave Clause was intended to go beyond negating the *Somerset* principle by placing any further restrictions on states or obligations on the federal government. The second Congress enforced the Fugitive Slave Clause by passing the Fugitive Slave Act of 1793, which provided that slave owners could present an affidavit or other proof to a federal or state magistrate and obtain a certificate authorizing them to recapture their claimed runaway slaves. The Act also imposed fines on persons who hid escaped slaves or interfered with the recapture process. But the statute left unclear whether states could add additional procedural safeguards to prevent kidnapping of free black people. Many states did enact such laws, which came to be known as "personal liberty laws." Some personal liberty laws permitted alleged fugitive slaves to give testimony, to file writs of habeas corpus, or to have a jury trial, while others extended the crime of kidnapping to prevent slave catchers from bypassing proper procedures.[71] The constitutionality of these personal liberty laws presented a complex legal question.

While personal liberty laws may have made a tremendous difference in the lives of individuals, they did not pose a major threat to the institution of slavery. A few hundred slaves escaped to free states each year, while fifty times that many went missing and remained within slave states.[72] However, southerners deemed it a point of honor and principle that the Fugitive Slave Act be enforced—more than that, it was deemed to be symbolic of the North's commitment to keeping southern states in the constitutional compact.

Prigg's case reached the U.S. Supreme Court in *Prigg v. Pennsylvania* (1842),[73] raising three nettlesome federalism questions. First, did the Fugitive Slave *Clause*, whose terms created only a private recapture right, and not an express grant of legislative power, authorize Congress to enact the Fugitive Slave *Act*? Second, if so, did those laws override state personal liberty laws? And, finally, were state officials obligated to enforce either a federal fugitive slave statute or the Fugitive Slave Clause itself? Prigg argued that the state personal liberty law was unconstitutional, on the ground that it conflicted with both the Clause and the Act. All nine justices agreed that Prigg's conviction should be reversed. Justice Story's opinion for the Court held that the Fugitive Slave Clause provided that every slave owner was "clothed with entire authority, in every State in the Union, to seize and recapture his slave, whenever he can do it without any breach of the peace, or any illegal violence." Moreover, the Clause gave Congress exclusive power to legislate the procedure to enforce that right. State personal liberty laws, like Pennsylvania's, were therefore unconstitutional: "no state law or regulation can in any way qualify, regulate, control, or restrain" the constitutional right to recapture a fugitive slave. In a limited concession to free states, however, Story observed that this exclusive congressional power precluded states from passing fugitive slave laws to assist in *enforcement* of the recapture right, not just laws hindering that right. Moreover, state officials were not obligated to enforce the federal Fugitive Slave Act and could obey state directives to refrain from doing so.[74] Justices Taney and two others agreed with the pro-slavery aspects of the ruling, but disagreed with the limitations that Story said followed from federal exclusivity. States could certainly pass laws to protect slaveholders' recapture rights, they argued, and state officials were duty bound to cooperate in enforcing the constitutional right even in the absence of state legislation.[75]

Joseph Story in 1842 was a Whig with antislavery leanings, and he would have been at least personally answerable for this pro-slavery opinion to the antislavery sentiments of his social milieu back home in Boston. As later recounted by his son, Story apparently believed that he had significantly tempered the pro-slavery thrust of the decision with the exclusivity and state non-obligation aspects of his ruling. The compromise nature of the decision reflected an attitude typical of many northern Whigs, who saw this as the price of Union. A decade earlier, in his *Commentaries on the Constitution*, Story had observed that "many sacrifices of opinion and feeling are to be found made by the Eastern and Middle states to the peculiar interests of the south." As the price of Union, "[t]his forms no just subject of complaint; but it should for ever repress the delusive and mischievous notion, that the south has not at all times had its full share of benefits from the Union."[76]

One opinion that Story sacrificed in *Prigg* was his deep admiration for *McCulloch*. The power of Congress to enforce the Fugitive Slave Clause was plainly not enumerated and thus could only be an implied power. Answering Pennsylvania's argument that the 1793 Act exceeded the enumerated powers of Congress, Story pointedly responded that Congress "has, on various occasions, exercised powers which were necessary and proper as means to carry into effect rights expressly given, and duties expressly enjoined thereby. The end being required, it has been deemed a just and necessary implication, that the means to accomplish it are given also. . . ."[77] That Story did not discuss *McCulloch* here, and had to content himself with discussions of other Marshall Court decisions, shows how far *McCulloch* had fallen into disfavor among his colleagues.[78] Even the lawyers refrained from mentioning *McCulloch*, instead quoting the passage from Story's *Commentaries* that summarizes *McCulloch*.[79]

On a practical level, *Prigg* nationalized the southern-state legal presumption that black people were slaves: the right of northern state law to protect any black person from being kidnapped as a purported slave was cast in doubt.[80] On an abstract level, *Prigg* articulated a pro-slavery principle of constitutional interpretation. The conclusion that the Fugitive Slave Clause and the 1793 Fugitive Slave Act were incompatible with state personal liberty laws was plausible, but not inevitable. That interpretation assumed that both the Clause and the statute were intended to guarantee a fast and cheap recapture remedy for slaveholders. But nothing in either the Fugitive Slave Clause or Act gave slave owners a right to mistakenly "recapture," i.e., kidnap and enslave, free black people, and both the statute and the constitutional clause could easily have been interpreted to permit states to add procedural protections to prevent such tragic injustices. States could have been permitted to afford black people a presumption of freedom (analogous to the "presumption of innocence" in criminal law) coupled with significant procedural protections to prevent their erroneous enslavement. True, this protection would have made recapture more difficult and costly for slave owners, but it theoretically should have aligned well with a doctrine neutrally recognizing the states' sovereignty over their own race laws.

Prigg is often read out of context by constitutional scholars as an affirmance of federal over state power. But when contrasted with *McCulloch*, which placed federal supremacy on broad structural principles, *Prigg*'s nationalism can be seen as limited to the "peculiar institution" of slavery. For the Taney Court, "states' rights" were better understood as slave-states' rights. Neutral principles of state sovereignty were subordinated to the protection of slavery. The Court chose to justify the pro-slavery interpretation of the Fugitive Slave Clause by indulging in historical fiction. Story accepted the idea that a right to recapture fugitive slaves was deemed by the Framers to be "so vital to the preservation" of slavery "that it constituted a fundamental article, without the adoption of which the Union could not have been formed." The Fugitive Slave Clause was "adopted into the Constitution by the unanimous consent of the framers of it; a proof at once of its intrinsic and practical necessity."[81] Justice Wayne of Georgia, in his concurring opinion, claimed that "[w]hen the three points relating to slaves"—the Three-fifths, Migration and Importation, and Fugitive Slave clauses—"had been accomplished, every impediment in the way of forming a constitution was removed." Had these concessions not been made to the slave states, the constitutional convention "would have been dissolved, without a constitution being formed."[82] In other words, the proper interpretation of an ambiguous constitutional provision like the Fugitive Slave Clause was to be determined by the justices' surmise of how the slave states would have wanted it interpreted in framing and ratifying the Constitution.

This was made-up history. The historical record did not support the claim that southern states would have refused to ratify the Constitution in the absence of *Prigg*'s guarantee of a fast and cheap slave-recapture procedure, one that created a high risk of erroneously enslaving free black people.[83] There was every reason to believe that southern states would have been satisfied with the Clause's abrogation of the free-soil doctrine of *Somerset's Case* without further concessions. Whether or not the Taney Court justices actually believed their own historical gloss, their interpretation in fact had more to do with the views of slave states in 1842 than in 1789.

Pro-slavery jurisprudence in whatever national form tended to involve a negation of the principles of *McCulloch*. This can be seen in *Dred Scott v. Sandford* (1857),[84] the Taney Court's best-known case and perhaps the most reviled Supreme Court decision ever. The Missouri Compromise should have been a strong legislative precedent supporting the power of Congress to prohibit slavery in U.S. territories. But when the battle over slavery in the territories was reignited by the acquisition of territories from Mexico in 1848, the constitutional question was reopened. The package of legislative measures that made up the Compromise of 1850 included a provision to determine slavery in the new territories of Utah and New Mexico on the basis of the majority will of their inhabitants, under Senator Stephen A. Douglas's pet doctrine of "popular sovereignty." In 1854, the Kansas-Nebraska Act extended "popular sovereignty" to the remaining Louisiana Purchase territories, an act that required repeal of the Missouri Compromise and opened territories north of the compromise line to the possible admittance of slaves.

In *Dred Scott*, the Supreme Court presumed to settle the power of Congress to prohibit slavery in the territories once and for all. Dred Scott was a slave owned by a military surgeon named Emerson, who over several years brought Scott with him to postings in the free Wisconsin territory (now Minnesota) and Illinois before returning with him to Missouri. After Scott's offer to buy his freedom was rebuffed by Emerson's widow, Scott sued for his freedom. The resulting litigation became a decade-long test case, heard in both the state and federal courts. Scott's basic claim was that his long residence on free soil due to the voluntary actions of his owner made him free under the laws of both Illinois and the Wisconsin territory. Illinois was a free state and Wisconsin, as Louisiana Purchase land, was a free territory under the Missouri Compromise.

The Court rejected Scott's claim by a seven-to-two vote, in a complicated ruling. The Missouri state courts had rejected Scott's claim by deciding that the case was governed by Missouri law, which did not recognize the free-soil doctrine that Scott's argument depended on. Since most Taney Court justices agreed with this law, they could simply have affirmed on that basis. Instead, Taney and a majority of his colleagues decided to reach two other issues. The lead opinion, written by Taney, held that Scott had no basis to invoke the jurisdiction of a federal court. Black Americans, Taney ruled, could never be citizens of the United States, and indeed "had no rights which the white man was bound to respect."[85] Taney made clear that his motivation in making this ruling was to clear up a loose end in slavery jurisprudence. The Privileges and Immunities Clause provides that "[t]he citizens of each state shall be entitled to all privileges and immunities of citizens in the several states."[86] This clause was and is understood to include the right of citizens to travel freely and take up residence in states of their choosing. If free black people were citizens, they would have a right to travel in slave states, where their presence might stir up slave rebellion. Reprising the reasoning of *Prigg*, Taney reasoned that the southern states would never have agreed to the Constitution had it been intended to confer such a right. Therefore, Scott was not a citizen of the United States or of any state for U.S. constitutional purposes, and had no right to sue in federal court. That ruling, too, could have disposed of the entire case. But Taney and five of his colleagues went on to decide that Congress had no power to prohibit slavery in the territories.[87] This decision meant that the Missouri Compromise was unconstitutional, and thus that Wisconsin territory was not free soil after all. (Note that this ruling did not dispose of Scott's claim on the basis of residence in Illinois—meaning that it was even more gratuitous.)

The portion of the case striking down the Missouri Compromise demonstrates the status of *McCulloch* in the late Taney Court. Taney argued for the Court that the territories clause, under which the Missouri Compromise had been enacted, applied only to territories possessed by the United States at the time of ratification of the Constitution—the territories covered by the Northwest Ordinance and those ceded by North Carolina and Georgia. That argument eliminated both the textual basis for a congressional power to bar slavery from the territories and the argument based on the Northwest Ordinance as a precedent for prohibiting slavery in the territories. But Taney could hardly argue that Congress lacked all power to acquire and govern new territories; his agenda was to invalidate the Missouri Compromise, not the Louisiana Purchase. If the Territories Clause did not authorize federal regulation of territories, what did? Without the Territories Clause, Taney was forced to pursue an implied-powers theory, and he argued that the power to govern territories was implied from the New States Clause ("New States may be admitted by the Congress into this Union"). This theory allowed Taney to argue, further, that Congress did not govern territories as if it were a state government with general powers— including a power to bar slavery—as was commonly believed.[88] Rather, Congress acted as a sort of trustee for a state government-in-waiting. As such, Congress could not ban slavery and thereby prejudice that future state government's power to opt for slavery, "on equal terms with the other States as a member of the Union."[89]

Taney thus acknowledged an implied congressional power to govern territories, but of course without acknowledging *McCulloch*, and he imposed a sharply restricted view of the scope of that implied power. Perhaps banning slavery was not strictly necessary to governing a territory in preparation for statehood, but it certainly would meet *McCulloch*'s more expansive test for implied powers. According to *McCulloch*, "needful" was synonymous with "necessary and proper," and "[t]he power to 'make all needful rules and regulations respecting the territory or other property belonging to the United States'" was sufficient to empower Congress to exercise such sovereign powers as creating corporations and territorial governments.[90] But Taney implicitly rejected this interpretation,[91] and his negation of *McCulloch* did not go entirely unnoticed. Justice McLean, one of the two dissenters, argued, "If there be a right to acquire territory, there necessarily must be an implied power to govern it." Citing *McCulloch* for the proposition that Congress possessed discretion over legislative means, McLean argued, "If Congress should deem slaves or free colored persons injurious to the population of a free Territory, as conducing to lessen the value of the public lands, or on any other ground connected with the public interest, they have the power to prohibit them from becoming settlers in it."[92] In other words, the power to prohibit slavery was not only implied from the power to govern territories, but should be judged by *McCulloch's* broad and permissive test for "necessary and proper" laws.

* * *

In *McCulloch*, Marshall had said that the "important duty" of peacefully arbitrating power disputes between the national government and the states had been granted to the Supreme Court "alone." Both Marshall and Taney believed the Court had a role in keeping the Union together. The difference between them on this point was that Marshall believed in a wider range of federal interests that would take precedence over state sovereignty. For Taney and his court, the federal government was supreme in a far more limited sphere, primarily one that protected free interstate navigation and slavery. Moreover, Marshall perceived the strength of federal institutions as the lynchpin of preserving the Union. In the milieu of the Taney Court, where the threat to the Union was the sectional crisis over slavery, the key to preserving the Union was to ensure that the southern states continued to receive the benefit of their supposed bargain in joining the constitutional "compact."

Taney and his colleagues undoubtedly came to the Court with this belief, which was only reinforced by the 1837 court-packing law and political developments in the 1850s. The new Fugitive Slave Act, part of the Compromise of 1850, gave the southern states what they wanted in the form of a more favorable slave recapture procedure, with a new corps of federal commissioners to enforce it. President James Buchanan's March 1857 inaugural address urged adherence to the Supreme Court's pending decision in the *Dred Scott* case, promising that it would settle the sectional crisis over slavery once and for all. These developments must have fed the Supreme Court's exaggerated and misguided (megalomaniacal?) sense that it was the only institution with the authority and legitimacy to save the Union.

In this overheated context, the Court decided *Ableman v. Booth* (1859).[93] Sherman Booth, an abolitionist, was arrested for aiding a fugitive slave in violation of the 1850 Fugitive Slave Act, and held in custody by the United States Marshal for the federal district of Wisconsin. Booth petitioned the Supreme Court of Wisconsin for writs of habeas corpus, and the Wisconsin court issued two successive writs directing the U.S. Marshal to release him. The first writ ordered Booth's release from pretrial custody, and the second ordered his release after his conviction in a federal district court trial. According to the Wisconsin court, the Fugitive Slave Act was unconstitutional, and therefore the marshal's actions were illegal. The U.S. Supreme Court unanimously reversed those orders. The Court summarily stated that the

Fugitive Slave Act was constitutional, but asserted that point was unnecessary to the judgment: state courts simply had no authority to give orders to federal officials.

Modern-day lawyers find the state court's position in *Ableman* incomprehensible, and the result in the case strikes us as a clear application of federal supremacy. But it should be noted that the Taney Court itself had muddied the waters on the supremacy of federal law with respect to slavery: several pronouncements in Taney Court separate opinions had asserted that federal laws were ineffective to overcome states' rights of self-protection as expressed in their domestic race laws. So the Wisconsin court's ruling was not entirely far-fetched.

Ableman was at best a mixed victory for constitutional nationalism. *McCulloch* could easily have been cited for the proposition that states could not interfere with a federal official conducting federal business. But Taney again ignored *McCulloch*, disapproving its constitutional theory and placing the Court's pro-slavery nationalism on a compact-theory footing. The Constitution "was the voluntary act of the people of the several States, deliberately done, for their own protection and safety against injustice from one another," Taney wrote. It cannot "be inconsistent with the dignity of a sovereign State to observe faithfully, . . . the compact into which it voluntarily entered when it became a State of this Union."[94] Taney asserted that the purpose of federal supremacy was to empower the Supreme Court to act as "a common arbiter" between states whose "local interests, local passions or prejudices, incited and fostered by individuals for sinister purposes, would lead to acts of aggression and injustice by one State upon the rights of another. . . ." The Supreme Court was also charged with keeping peace between the "general government" and the states, which it could do only by functioning as a neutral arbiter between them: "for the States could hardly be expected to confide in the impartiality of a tribunal created exclusively by the General Government, without any participation on their part." The Court would fulfill its duty when "armed with power . . . by appropriate laws."[95] In context, "appropriate laws" could refer only to laws like the Fugitive Slave Act.

The surface impartiality of this language could thus not cover up its strong underlying bias toward the states' particular right to maintain slavery. Federal supremacy for Marshall meant the supremacy of the Constitution and of whatever federal policies were enacted into law. But Taney's *Ableman* opinion viewed federal law as supreme because the Union could be preserved only by ensuring that the constitutional compact balanced the competing and conflicting interests of the several states. Increasingly, this meant applying constitutional law to counterbalance the growing power of the northern states in federal electoral politics. In the 1840s, the Taney Court had (with the exception of *Prigg*) at least tried to gesture toward a neutral stance between state police powers in the southern states, which maintained slavery, and those in the northern states, which prohibited slavery. While in theory both sets of state policies should have been entitled to equal respect, the Taney Court increasingly tilted toward the states' right to maintain slavery rather than the right to exclude it. The Court increasingly read a pro-slavery spirit into the Constitution, asserting that the original southern slave states would never have agreed to the Constitution unless it was interpreted in a manner supportive of present slave-state demands.

The Taney Court's nationalism was pro-slavery first, and nationalism second. The justices in *Prigg* had emphasized the importance of a uniform national law of recapture of fugitive slaves. But Story's conclusion that states could not legislate in this area at all, whether to impede or promote fugitive slave capture, was quickly eroded. In *Moore v. Illinois* (1852),[96] for example, the Court upheld a state law making it a crime to harbor a fugitive slave. It was not necessary for the Court to distinguish *Prigg*, because even Story's opinion had included a significant loophole in his federal exclusivity ruling: he had acknowledged that states could apply their police powers "to arrest and restrain runaway slaves, and remove them from their borders," as they could "in cases of idlers, vagabonds, and paupers."[97] Uniform federal laws were unconstitutional, however, if they restrained slavery—as demonstrated by *Dred Scott* and the Taney Court's commerce-power cases.

Revisionist legal historians have made much of the extent to which the Taney Court's pro-slavery nationalism commanded considerable popular support, reflected mainstream constitutional ideas, and thus (they say) did not pervert the antebellum Constitution.[98] There is some truth in those claims. Perhaps the conventional criticism—the revulsion—that places *Dred Scott* in the constitutional "anti-canon" must primarily be based on reading an 1857 case through the lens of modern-day civil rights sensibilities. But only perhaps. Revisionism has a built-in tendency to overcorrect conventional wisdom, and we should not let partial truths lead us to unduly normalize the Taney Court's pro-slavery nationalism. The Taney Court was arguably the most ideological court in U.S. history. With the exception of Joseph Story, its entire membership represented one side—the states'-rights side— of the major debate over federalism. Taney Court justices all agreed that, as sectional division increased, preservation of the Union increasingly required making accommodations to southern interests in constitutional interpretation. In light of increasing southern demands that slavery not only be protected, but also expanded, these accommodations degenerated into appeasement.

Ableman confirmed what many critics of *Dred Scott* charged. The Court was demonstrating hubris in deciding that it alone could save the Union; that it alone had the wisdom and institutional capacity to balance the interests of North and South. Ultimately, of course, Taney and his colleagues were wrong in thinking that any amount of judicial appeasement would keep the South in the Union.

* * *

McCulloch had emphasized both the supremacy of federal power "within its sphere" and the need to view implied powers permissively to allow the "beneficial execution" of granted federal powers, irrespective of the states' reserved powers. The Taney Court reversed this emphasis. To the Jacksonian justices who dominated that Court, preservation of slave-state sovereignty—not the power of Congress to act for the benefit of the whole people—was the bedrock principle of the Constitution. Reserved state powers were sufficient to block implied federal powers. Moreover, sovereign state powers themselves radiated implied powers that could make inroads into the enumerated powers of Congress, absent conflict with federal statutes. States could regulate matters expressly delegated to the United States when it was conducive to exercising their reserved powers. By the early 1850s, the Taney Court had ignored *McCulloch* into oblivion, and reversed its thrust.

"The Various Crises of Human Affairs"

McCulloch in the Civil War

The Civil War confronted the United States with its greatest constitutional crisis ever. The secession of southern states in the winter and spring of 1860–61 raised the most basic question of Union itself: did states have the right to secede? That only began a seemingly unending cascade of constitutional problems regarding the Union's conduct of the war. Those which concern this chapter and Chapter 7 arose from uncertainties about the extent of the implied powers of Congress to run a civil war and reconstruct a divided nation. The Civil War raised the three issues for which *McCulloch* has been most celebrated: the nationalist Constitution, implied powers, and the capable Constitution. With *McCulloch* offering potential legal support for the Union cause, and the Taney Court's states'-rights jurisprudence in disrepute, circumstances seemed prime for *McCulloch* to re-emerge from its forty years of neglect.

* * *

The first and foremost constitutional question of the Civil War, both in time and importance, was whether the secession of a state was constitutional. Did the southern states have a constitutional right to secede? If they did, that would transform the nature of the Civil War from an effort to save the Union by putting down a rebellion into an extra-constitutional war of conquest by the northern states.

The myth of John Marshall as "nation-builder" began with the claim that *McCulloch* and his other nationalism decisions helped save the Union during the Civil War, presumably by answering this question in the minds of the northern public or their leaders. At the February 1901 John Marshall Day centennial celebration (which will be discussed in detail in Chapter 9), several speakers gave Marshall and *McCulloch* a prominent role in the Union victory. Speakers claimed that Lincoln "had been a deep student of [Marshall's] great opinions" and by following

Marshall's "chart of constitutional law for all future time" had "preserved [the] nation."[1] Some went as far as to cut out Lincoln and give direct credit to Marshall for winning the Civil War. The Civil War was the victory of the Constitution on the battlefield, said one speaker, "[a]nd to whom more than to John Marshall is due this glorious result?" As an "embodiment of political ideas," said another, "[t]he Southern Confederacy . . . surrendered not to Grant, not to Sherman, not to Thomas or to Sheridan, but to the statesman, the jurist and the sage—John Marshall."[2] Even Harvard law professor James Bradley Thayer, sophisticate though he was, joined this chorus. "Marshall's strong constitutional doctrine . . . was largely [what] saved the country from succumbing in the great struggle of 40 years ago, and kept our political fabric from going to pieces."[3] To this day, legal scholars reflecting on the constitutionality of secession find McCulloch highly relevant to the secession question, even if they tamp down the rhetoric.[4]

In the North in 1861, the popular answer to the secession question was clear: there was no constitutional right to secede. Overwhelming public sentiment, and Lincoln's conviction that it was his administration's role to save the Union at all costs, undoubtedly had more to do with the North's vigorous military response to secession than did constitutional argument. To the Confederate states, the northern effort to suppress a rebellion was an invasion of their sovereign soil. But constitutional answers were available in 1860 and 1861 as the secession crisis unfolded, and numerous constitutional interpreters came forward to offer them.

The constitutional theory of secession was an argument for the rights of states within, rather than outside the constitutional order. Nullifiers had claimed that a state had the right under the Constitution to declare a "palpably unconstitutional" law null and inoperative within the state's borders. Secessionists pushed this claim a step further by claiming a constitutional right to withdraw peaceably from the constitutional order—that is, from the Union. A constitutional right to secede implies that the remaining Union was constitutionally bound not to resist secession by force. This right differed crucially from a right of revolution, which is a unilateral declaration outside of and against the constitutional order. The right of revolution confers no rights limiting the majority from treating the revolution as rebellion or treason. It is the right to risk one's rights in a trial by force. Like the nullifiers, secessionists sometimes blurred the distinction. Webster and, later, Lincoln were careful to maintain this distinction, recognizing the majority's corresponding right to try to suppress the revolution by force.

The most famous writer or speaker against secession was, of course, Abraham Lincoln. Lincoln's acuity as a constitutional thinker has yet to be fully appreciated, perhaps because his writings were few and brief. But throughout the war, he repeated and refined a theme about the constitutional rightness of preserving the Union. Like any Whig and later Republican politician of his day, Lincoln probably held Marshall in high esteem, but he never referred to Marshall in his writings and barely mentions McCulloch—despite numerous speeches in the 1830s and 1840s arguing in favor of the constitutionality of chartering a third Bank of the United States.[5] In his 1858 Senate race, Lincoln frequently referred to "the Bank decision," but only in conjunction with Jackson's veto message to make the point that it was legitimate to politically overrule a Supreme Court decision—as he proposed to do with *Dred Scott*.[6] Although Lincoln was a great borrower, and his biographers are able to trace the literary influence of Daniel Webster and certain contemporary political figures, there is no evidence that he borrowed from Marshall.[7]

Given that the Court in 1861 was still the Court of Taney and *Dred Scott*, Lincoln might have undermined his position by bowing to the Court's authority as expounder of the Constitution. Accordingly, he leaned in the opposite direction. While Supreme Court decisions "must be binding in any case upon the parties to a suit," said Lincoln in his first inaugural address, and "entitled to very high respect," their authority went no further: "if the policy of the Government upon vital questions affecting the whole people is to be irrevocably fixed by decisions of the Supreme Court, . . . the people will have ceased to be their own rulers."[8] Even so, Lincoln might have drawn on *McCulloch's* arguments without attribution, were those adequate to the task. But they weren't.

Like Jackson, and in contrast to Marshall, Lincoln did not deem it essential to reject the idea of a compact of states to argue for perpetual Union. Even a contract could not be rescinded unilaterally, Lincoln argued. Borrowing from the anti-nullification arguments of Jackson, Webster, and others, Lincoln laid out two well-worn reasons why secession was unconstitutional. First, the Union was intended to be perpetual. National existence traced back to the first Continental Congress of 1774, which predated state independence, and was "matured and continued" by the Declaration of Independence and the Articles of Confederation, both of which adopted the style "United States of America." The Articles of Confederation was in fact a short title for the document called "Articles of Confederation *and perpetual Union*. . . ." Since the 1787 Constitution was designed "to form a more perfect Union," *a fortiori*, the constitutional Union must be at least as perpetual as the prior Confederation.[9] Perhaps this argument was a makeweight. Certainly, the bonds of Union strengthened at each step, but to claim that this in itself prohibited states' withdrawal from the Union begged the fundamental question. In any event, as noted in Chapter 5, this argument did not come from Marshall.

A second, better argument rested on the idea of an implied sovereign power against dissolution. "Perpetuity is implied, if not expressed, in the fundamental law of all national governments," Lincoln asserted, and "no government proper ever had a provision in its organic law for its own termination."[10] This gloss on anti-nullification arguments is plainly traceable to Webster and Jackson, even Hamilton, but not Marshall, who tiptoed around the idea of inherent sovereign powers.

Missing from these arguments was a compelling normative foundation. Why perpetuate a Union founded on consent in the face of deep disagreement between its constituents? The constitutional theories of Marshall, Webster, and Jackson offer a normative response stemming from a shared core idea. The sovereign authority of the Constitution derives from the will of the whole people, and cannot be controlled by a mere part. But "the people" who ratified the Constitution are something of a legal fiction. The deceased ratifiers offer an increasingly attenuated normative basis for republicanism over time. While this normative justification is static, the challenge of secession is dynamic: the secessionists claimed that a present legislative majority was oppressing a minority, and would continue to do so in the foreseeable future, without check by ordinary constitutional processes. *McCulloch* had little to say about this: resolving the Bank question did not require a republican theory incorporating the problem of masses of voters organized along sectional lines. Because Marshall was no democrat, it is doubtful that he could have conceived of a democratic republic in those terms. *McCulloch*'s representation-based theory—that the seceding states were attempting to "control" the others—was true in a technical and perhaps an economic sense. The Confederate states had indeed appropriated federal property within their borders and would be unilaterally deciding the nation's larger property rights, such as navigation on the lower Mississippi, on a strictly geographical basis. Yet these concerns could have been resolved by a post-dissolution accounting rather than enforcement of the original contract of Union. *McCulloch*'s structural theory of representation was not a fully satisfactory answer to the South's moral claim of oppression.

Lincoln offered a better answer. His was based on redefining the essence of republican government as majority rule within a framework of constitutional processes and limits. The framework by itself was static and could derive legitimacy from the fictive "people," but the majority-rule principle operating within that framework is dynamic. Secession was unacceptable in a democratic republic because it undermined majority rule. As Lincoln described it in the first inaugural, sovereignty was dynamic and extraconstitutional: "A majority held in restraint by constitutional checks and limitations, and always changing easily with deliberate changes of popular opinions and sentiments, is the only true sovereign of a free people." Because "[u]nanimity is impossible," there will always be a majority and a minority, and "[t]he rule of a minority, as a permanent arrangement, is wholly inadmissible." If the "minority will secede rather than acquiesce," Lincoln argued, it sets a precedent that at once destroys majority rule and the polity itself, as disgruntled minorities continue to secede from ever smaller confederacies. Thus, "rejecting the majority principle, anarchy or despotism in some form is all that is left."[11] It cannot be overlooked, of course, that Lincoln's clear electoral college majority in the 1860 presidential election was based on a plurality of the national popular vote, around 40% in a divided field of four major presidential candidates. But in the spring and summer of 1861, he spoke for a majority in strongly opposing secession.[12]

Lincoln continued to refine this idea during his presidency. Four months after his inaugural, he sent a written message to Congress at the start of its special session on July 4, 1861. The commencement of the armed rebellion clarified and raised the stakes of secession. "[T]his issue," Lincoln wrote,

> embraces more than the fate of these United States. It presents to the whole family of man, the question, whether a constitutional republic, or a democracy—a government of the people, by the same people—can, or cannot, maintain its territorial integrity, against its own domestic foes. It presents the question, whether discontented individuals, too few in numbers to control administration, according to organic law, in any case, can always, upon the pretences made in this case, or on any other pretences, or arbitrarily, without any pretence, break up their Government, and thus practically put an end to free government upon the earth. It forces us to ask: "Is there, in all republics, this inherent, and fatal weakness?" "Must a government, of necessity, be too strong for the liberties of its own people, or too weak to maintain its own existence?"[13]

Unlike Marshall and Webster, Lincoln envisioned "the people" as something beyond the static conception of the deceased ratifiers. The "same" people cannot be limited to the ratifiers, since they are not the ones now faced with the problem of maintaining their territorial integrity against domestic rebellion. "The people" at once comprise both a constitutional republic and a democracy.

Lincoln also reanimated the normative foundation of republicanism. Tying republicanism more closely to democratic majority rule suggested an ongoing renewal of consent rather than an eternally binding consent at the founding. Moreover, Lincoln asserted that the American people have a moral obligation to "the whole family of man" to undertake the sometimes arduous work of making democratic republicanism succeed. Lincoln's projection of the United States into the stream of world history was not grandiosity. Many observers in the monarchies of Europe viewed the expanding American Civil War in exactly these terms: to them, the Civil War was the inevitable outgrowth of the inherent flaws of republics and a vindication of long-held beliefs that the United States' experiment in democracy was bound to fail.[14] Lincoln continued,

> Our popular government has often been called an experiment. Two points in it, our people have already settled—the successful establishing, and the successful administering of it. One still remains—its successful maintenance against a formidable attempt to overthrow it. It is now for them to demonstrate to the world, that those who can fairly carry an election, can also suppress a rebellion—that ballots are the rightful, and peaceful, successors of bullets; and that when ballots have fairly, and constitutionally, decided, there can be no successful appeal, back to bullets; that there can be no successful appeal, except to ballots themselves, at succeeding

elections. Such will be a great lesson of peace; teaching men that what they cannot take by an election, neither can they take it by a war—teaching all, the folly of being the beginners of a war.[15]

Lincoln's constitutional theory was deceptively simple: a democratic republic based on majority rule cannot tolerate secession, which either disintegrates or makes war upon the very practice of majority rule.

Two years later, in November 1863, Lincoln crystalized this idea into a few simple lines in a speech dedicating a national cemetery for Union war dead. "Four score and seven years ago our fathers brought forth, upon this continent, a new nation, conceived in liberty, and dedicated to the proposition that 'all men are created equal.' Now we are engaged in a great civil war, testing whether that nation, or any nation so conceived and so dedicated, can long endure." The incorporation of the self-evident truth of the equality of all men from the Declaration of Independence, which Lincoln and fellow Republicans had long employed as a proof of the iniquity of slavery, was significant. On January 1 of that year, Lincoln had issued the final Emancipation Proclamation. The war aim of the North was no longer simply to preserve the democratic republican Union, but now extended to the abolition of slavery: "we here highly resolve that these dead shall not have died in vain—that this nation, under God, shall have a new birth of freedom—and that government of the people, by the people, for the people, shall not perish from the earth."[16] The liberty of the person, Lincoln implied, is uniquely able to be sustained in the democratic republic.

Lincoln's synthesis seems obvious to modern readers. But despite its simplicity, it advanced an argument for the Union that went beyond prior theories. Significant debts to earlier statesmen are observable. Lincoln borrowed Webster's cadences and built on Jackson's democratic presidentialism. He reinterpreted Jefferson's republicanism to link it, more closely than Jefferson ever did, with the liberty and equality of the Declaration. *McCulloch* can hardly be faulted because it didn't anticipate and solve the conundrum of secession. Still, contrary to subsequent myth making, Marshall's imprint is not apparent here.

* * *

Although *McCulloch*'s nationalist theory probably had no influence on Lincoln's views of his constitutional duty to save the Union, its theory of implied powers began to capture renewed interest in Congress. The two Congresses during the Civil War met almost entirely without representation from the eleven seceded states. With the bulk of states'-rights and pro-slavery votes in the House and Senate gone, Congress passed measures concerning slavery, the economy, and the conduct of the war that pushed the boundaries of federal power beyond what had been possible for the prior sixty years. The 37th Congress (1861–63) has been called one of the most productive congressional sessions in American history. It passed Homestead and Land Grant Colleges acts, which distributed public lands for settlers and agricultural colleges; established a Department of Agriculture to provide technical and material assistance to farmers; and incorporated the Union Pacific Railroad to build a rail line to the western border of Nevada. All of these enactments had been blocked in Congress or vetoed by Jacksonian presidents before the war, with objections that they exceeded the powers of Congress. But the constitutional arguments pro and con had been well worked out years before, and the thirty-seventh Congress tended to gloss over them.[17]

It was the waging of the Civil War itself that raised novel issues of implied powers. Suppressing the rebellion demanded unprecedented exertion of national power against states that claimed a constitutional right to rebel. Congress still had a fair number of conservatives who believed in constitutionally limited national power, even to suppress the rebellion, so the Civil War legislative agenda produced vigorous congressional debate over the limits of constitutional powers. Many of these issues involved questions of separation of powers; for example, whether the President could suspend habeas corpus or blockade the ports of the southern states on his own authority. But because the Constitution alluded to the powers to "declare war" and "suppress insurrections" only in the most general terms, many other war measures necessarily raised questions of implied powers that *McCulloch* might answer.

By the end of 1861, it was becoming increasingly clear that the war would be protracted and costly. In early January 1862, Lincoln bemoaned to an advisor, "General, what shall I do? The people are impatient; [the Treasury Secretary] has no money and he tells me he can raise no more; the General of the Army has typhoid fever. The bottom is out of the tub. What shall I do?"[18] The federal treasury was indeed running out of money, but a solution was in the works.

In December, Treasury Secretary Salmon P. Chase proposed an emergency borrowing plan to cover Union war expenses through uniform banknotes issued under a system of federally regulated state banks. Key members of Congress viewed this as insufficient. Congressman Elbridge Gerry Spaulding of New York, the Chairman of the House Ways and Means Committee, revamped Chase's proposal into a groundbreaking Legal Tender bill that would authorize the federal Treasury to issue $150 million in Treasury notes. This paper money would be legal tender, meaning that creditors would be required to accept the notes as payment at face value. The notes would become known as "greenbacks" for their color, and possibly also for the fact that they were not "backed" by gold dollars: they would be redeemable in gold only at some future time after the war.[19] The constitutional question was whether Congress had the power to make paper money a legal tender. Congress was authorized "to coin money [and] regulate the value thereof,"[20] and strict constructionists believed that this meant only gold and silver could be legal tender. Article I authorized Congress to issue "securities," which would of course be pieces of paper—Treasury notes or bonds.[21] Like banknotes, these could function as money, but not necessarily legal tender: they could be refused by creditors, or their value negotiated when tendered as payment, and were redeemable in gold on demand at par.[22] On the other hand, the Constitution expressly forbids the states to "coin money; emit bills of credit; [or] *make any thing but gold and silver coin a tender in payment of debts.*"[23] This last clause in particular shows that the Constitution's Framers knew how to articulate a clear prohibition on the issuance of paper money, and their failure to bar Congress in such plain terms suggests an intention not to deny a paper-money power to Congress.

The administration had offered no help with constitutional arguments in support of the bill. Chase's original proposal was based on a straightforward application of the borrowing power, and thus did not call for any constitutional argument. In early January, Spaulding wrote to Attorney General Edward Bates to ask for a legal opinion on the constitutionality of issuing federal legal tender notes. Bates lamely replied that he felt it inappropriate to advise Congress formally on the question, but "as a private man and a professed constitutional legist," he offered that "the Constitution contains no direct verbal prohibition" or implied prohibition against it.[24] That was all. Spaulding, a banking lawyer and former New York state treasurer whose legal studies consisted of an apprenticeship in a Buffalo law office, was left to his own devices for constitutional arguments.[25]

Spaulding opened the debate on his Legal Tender bill with a lengthy speech on January 28, 1862. After explaining the details of the bill and the practical need for it, he turned to "the question of constitutional power," and observed "we are not left without the recorded opinions of the ablest jurists in the country." Citing *McCulloch* and Hamilton's 1791 bank memorandum to Washington, Spaulding quoted a 600-word paraphrase of *McCulloch* from Kent's *Commentaries.*[26] Two other members joined Spaulding's argument based on *McCulloch*. Representative Thaddeus Stevens of Pennsylvania argued that the power to issue greenbacks followed directly from the long-established power to issue Treasury bills and notes. "The Supreme Court have settled certain principles with regard to the power of Congress over measures not expressly enumerated in the Constitution. The principle is, that where anything is necessary to carry into effect the granted power it is constitutional." He then summarized *McCulloch*, albeit imprecisely and without naming the case: "as Congress had power to regulate commerce, and to regulate the value of coin, and it deemed the establishment of a bank necessary to effectuate those powers, the Supreme Court pronounced it constitutional." More accurately, Stevens observed that "necessity need not be absolute, inevitable, and overwhelming—if it be useful, expedient, profitable, the necessity is within constitutional meaning. Whether such necessity exists is solely for the decision of Congress. Their judgment is absolute and conclusive."[27] Another congressman chimed in that the Supreme Court "decided, according to my recollection—though I have not read that decision latterly—that, under the power to regulate commerce, for the benefit of commerce, to aid commerce, Congress had the power to create a United States Bank. What was that for? . . . It was to make a currency for commerce. . . ."[28]

After relatively sparse opposition, the bill passed and was signed into law by Lincoln on February 25 as the Legal Tender Act of 1862. The Act proved to be a key piece of the Union's highly successful financial management of the Civil War, helping the United States government to absorb the cost of the war—about $1 million per day—without the ruinous inflation suffered by the Confederacy.[29] But the Legal Tender Act would become controversial after the war, both politically and constitutionally. It was wrapped up in the larger debate over paper money versus the gold standard, a controversy that would give rise to more than a dozen Supreme Court cases and not be fully resolved until 1935.

* * *

Despite voting a joint resolution in July 1861 stating that the North's war aim was to restore the Union and not to emancipate slaves, Congress quickly realized that slave labor was a major war asset to the Confederacy. This recognition raised the question of emancipation as a measure to help suppress the rebellion. Within days of the war-aim resolution, Congress passed its first Confiscation Act, which provided that property used in furtherance of the rebellion, including slaves, would be confiscated after judicial proceedings.[30] At the start of its second session, in early December 1861, Congress considered a more far-reaching bill that would dispense with the judicial proceedings and authorize Union armies to confiscate all property in rebellious areas, including slaves, regardless of whether the property was demonstrably being used to further the rebel war effort. The bill raised numerous constitutional objections, most notably its violation of the Constitution's Treason Clause, which prohibited forfeiture of property beyond the lifetime of the convicted traitor.[31] In its final form, the second Confiscation Act directed the president to seize slaves and other property of specified categories of rebels—primarily Confederate officers and high officials—for use in support of the Union war effort. The Act also provided that rebels convicted of treason or of a newly defined crime of engaging in or aiding insurrection would forfeit their slaves, among other punishments. Lincoln signed the bill into law in July 1862, but only after communicating his constitutional objections based on the Treason Clause and receiving an explanatory joint resolution from Congress that the bill would not be applied to forfeit real property beyond the lifetime of a rebel convicted of treason.[32]

Proponents of a more aggressive, wholesale approach to confiscation and emancipation of slaves were frustrated with the inefficient procedure of individualized prosecutions for treason or insurrection. They grounded their theory of confiscation on an argument based on the war powers that had first been advanced in Congress by John Quincy Adams in the 1840s.[33] A power to emancipate all slaves in the seceded states was implied in the war power, they argued, which was subject only to the limitations imposed by the international law of war. Specific constitutional protections did not apply even to "citizen enemies," it was now argued, and under the laws of war, property useful to the enemy in a war zone could be seized and appropriated, with no right of restitution to the owner. [34] Although *McCulloch* played relatively little role in the congressional debates, two speakers in the opening rounds of debate in January 1862 relied on *McCulloch* to argue that Congress had an implied power to confiscate slaves. "I adopt the strong words of Marshall," declared Congressman John Bingham of Ohio, who went on to quote *McCulloch's* assertion that "the government, which has a right to do an act, and has imposed on it the duty of performing that act, must, according to the dictates of reason, be allowed to select the means." Bingham cited a litany of powers, including the powers to provide for the common defense, declare war, and suppress insurrections. A week later, a first-term congressman from New York repeated the gist of Bingham's speech, cribbing these same quotations and authorities.[35]

The few references to *McCulloch* in the January 1862 debates on legal tender and confiscation were noteworthy, but are probably most accurately viewed as exceptional. It is possible that *McCulloch's* ideas could have been absorbed into the debate, but members of Congress on the whole seemed to prefer offering their own constructions of the Constitution, and did not need *McCulloch* to point them to the Necessary and Proper Clause, or define it for them. Most who discussed implied powers did so in a general way, without examining competing definitions of "necessary" or otherwise parsing the extent of implied powers. Others simply referred broadly to the war power, or to other enumerated powers without distinguishing exercises of enumerated and implied powers at all.[36] This is not to say that references to Marshall and Supreme Court decisions were unusual. But members were more likely to refer to Marshall's jurisprudence other than *McCulloch*. For example, Marshall's decision in *Brown v. United States*, regarding confiscation of enemy property, was cited as often in the Confiscation Act debates as *McCulloch* was.[37]

Lincoln had been pondering emancipation since March 1862, but was never persuaded that Congress had the constitutional authority to authorize it. Instead, he believed freeing slaves could be justified only as a presidential war power over the theater of military operations. He drafted his preliminary Emancipation Proclamation in late June and early July, and presented it to his cabinet. Secretary of State William Seward persuaded Lincoln not to issue the proclamation until the Union achieved a significant military victory, lest it be perceived internationally as an act of desperation. The battle of Antietam on September 16, 1862 sufficed for this purpose, and on September 22, Lincoln issued the preliminary Proclamation.[38] In it, Lincoln declared that on January 1, 1863, "all persons held as slaves within any state, or designated part of a state, the people whereof shall then be in rebellion against the United States shall be then, thenceforward, and forever free." The Proclamation offered no explanation of the constitutional source of his authority, but noted that "attention is hereby called" to two recent congressional enactments: a March 13,

1862 statute amending the Articles of War to prohibit Union officers from returning fugitive slaves to their masters; and section 9 of the second Confiscation Act, which emancipated all slaves escaping to Union lines or found in rebel areas captured by the Union Army. His doubts about congressional authority over emancipation are reflected in his failure to cite section 5 of the Second Confiscation Act, which authorized the president to direct the seizure of slaves.[39]

A noteworthy reference to *McCulloch* as authority for emancipation had cropped up in a book written by a Boston patent attorney and published probably in November 1862. It was entitled *War Powers of the President, and the Legislative Powers of Congress in Relation to Rebellion, Treason and Slavery*, and its author, William Whiting, argued that both Congress and the President had power to emancipate slaves in the United States. In a chapter entitled "The War Powers of Congress," Whiting cited *McCulloch* on implied powers and concluded, "Guided by these principles of interpretation, it is obvious that if the confiscation of property, or the liberation of slaves of rebels, be 'plainly adapted to the end,'—that is, to the suppression of rebellion,—it is within the power of Congress to pass laws for those purposes. Whether they are adapted to produce that result is for the legislature alone to decide."[40] Whiting's book was really a lengthy legal brief: neither particularly insightful nor scholarly, it relied heavily on lengthy extracts from legal authorities and even unattributed cribbing from congressional speeches in the early 1862 debates, including Spaulding's and Bingham's.[41] Whiting ultimately restated Adams's law-of-war argument, which he quoted (with attribution) at great length. Historians differ about the extent of the book's influence. It doesn't seem to have been noticed in Congress, and there is no evidence that Lincoln relied on it in drafting the final Proclamation at the end of 1862. But the book eventually came to Lincoln's attention, and he was sufficiently gratified by it to create a position of Solicitor of the War Department specifically for Whiting, who occupied the post from 1863 through 1865.[42]

On New Year's Day, 1863, Lincoln issued the final Emancipation Proclamation, in which he did, as promised, "order and declare that all persons held as slaves within said designated States, and parts of States, are, and henceforward shall be free." This time, he cited no acts of Congress, but instead based his action expressly on "the power in me vested as Commander-in-Chief, of the Army and Navy of the United States in time of actual armed rebellion against the authority and government of the United States, and as a fit and necessary war measure for suppressing said rebellion."[43] Throughout the war, Lincoln remained firmly committed to the belief that the federal government had no peacetime power to emancipate slaves. On that belief, he made it his reconstruction policy to require or cajole reconquered rebel states to adopt antislavery constitutions. Uncertain about even that approach, and unsure whether federal courts would recognize permanent freedom for those slaves freed under the Emancipation Proclamation, Lincoln would late in 1864 press for passage of the Thirteenth Amendment. By the time of the final Proclamation, Lincoln was convinced that whatever power the federal government had to liberate slaves extended no further than the *President's* war power. He thus had no particular use for *McCulloch*, which set out principles for the implied powers of *Congress*.

* * *

Even as *McCulloch* began to experience a revival in Congress, it still had an implacable foe on the Supreme Court. Chief Justice Taney remained an unapologetic southern sympathizer to his dying day, October 12, 1864. He very likely agreed with the Confederate position that the southern states had a constitutional right to secede and that, consequently, the North's war to preserve the Union was an unconstitutional coercion of sovereign states. In May 1861, Taney had challenged the Lincoln Administration by issuing a circuit opinion holding Lincoln's suspension of habeas corpus unconstitutional, but the White House ignored the ruling, and the case never reached the full Supreme Court.[44] Lincoln narrowly avoided a damaging judicial rebuke in the *Prize Cases* (1863),[45] a five-to-four decision upholding the constitutionality of his blockade of the southern ports. Taney joined the dissenters. Fortunately for the Union cause, the Supreme Court mostly stayed out of constitutional issues during the war.

Taney, though ailing, managed to draft two hypothetical decisions striking down important wartime legislation, to be used in suitable cases that he hoped would deal blows to the Union cause. In an opinion that would have invalidated the Legal Tender Act, Taney recapitulated the argument of congressional opponents that the power to coin money impliedly precluded a power to issue paper money, and further that the borrowing power did not authorize forcing creditors to accept Treasury notes as payment for private debts.[46] Taney also drafted an opinion striking down the 1863 act of Congress to create the first military draft. Prior to that time, all U.S. military forces had been raised either through volunteer regiments or by relying on state troop requisitions. Noting that conscription was at best a power implied from the enumerated power to "raise armies,"[47] Taney offered two arguments against the military draft law. First, conscription would unduly strip states of manpower needed for their own militias. In effect, Taney again asserted that a federal implied power could not overcome the states' reserved powers of sovereignty. Second, according to Taney, a lesser or more specific enumerated power necessarily negated a greater implied one. The express reference to one compulsory military force—the militia—negated any inference that another military force could rely on compulsory service by implication.[48] This argument was akin to Madison's failed argument against the first Bank in 1791, and the arguments against a legal tender power. Among the many problems with Taney's anti-draft argument is his reliance on dubious inferences from one power—here, that only the militia can draw on obligatory service—to negate an implied power. *McCulloch's* conception of implied powers would have virtually no room to exist under such an interpretive approach.

Neither a legal tender nor a conscription case arose in the Supreme Court, and Taney's opinions remained unpublished. But they are fitting monuments to Taney's lifelong antipathy toward *McCulloch* and implied powers. Not even the Civil War could bring him around to viewing the Constitution as adaptable to "crises of human affairs." Taney's implicit support for secession casts doubt even on whether he viewed the Constitution as "intended to endure for ages to come."[49] It is also fitting that *McCulloch* began to emerge as a symbol of the capable Constitution as Taney's life was ending.

* * *

Despite its potential relevance, *McCulloch*'s influence on constitutional argument during the Civil War was limited. Arguments against secession were developed without noticeable reliance on *McCulloch*, despite later claims to the contrary. In issuing the Emancipation Proclamation, Lincoln eschewed congressional powers and with them, *McCulloch*. Still, the few *McCulloch* references by leading congressmen on key implied-powers issues, if not a full-scale *McCulloch* revival in itself, prefigured things to come.

"The Government of All"

The Rise and Fall of Reconstruction, 1865–1883

A central tenet of Marshall's constitutionalism was that the Union was "the government of all." Congress sought to give this idea new and different meaning in reconstructing the nation after the Civil War. Black people would be participants in "the government of all," and rebellious states readmitted into the Union on the condition that they recognize that participation. *McCulloch*, whose principles of nationalism, implied powers, and the capable Constitution seemed to have triumphed in the Civil War, offered potentially useful guidance in this endeavor.

Given the centrality of slavery to U.S. constitutional politics, the dismantling of slavery held out the promise of revolutionizing American society. For a brief time, Reconstruction's great experiment in integrating black citizens into the constitutional order showed signs of success. But as Eric Foner has aptly said, Reconstruction was an "unfinished revolution." A process that began with the tragedy of Lincoln's assassination in 1865 ended with the slowly unfolding tragedy of abandonment of black Americans to their fate at the hands of white supremacist governments in the southern states.[1] While *McCulloch* did serve as a guidepost to a limited extent in Congress, the Supreme Court continued to disregard it, with unfortunate consequences for constitutional law.

The first seven months of Reconstruction (April to November 1865) were badly mismanaged by Lincoln's successor, Andrew Johnson. Congress in that era did not convene until the December following an election year, and soon after Johnson assumed the presidency, his deep-seated racist and states'-rights views came to the surface. Combined with his newfound interest in courting elites of the old South, Johnson handed out thousands of pardons to former rebels and permitted former Confederate states to enact "black codes" that effectively reduced newly freed black people to peonage. When Congress reconvened in December 1865, it reversed Johnson's policy and imposed military occupation on the southern states to enforce various new reconstruction and civil rights laws, all of which had to be enacted over Johnson's vetoes. After Ulysses Grant was sworn in as president in March 1869, Congress and the president acted more in concert. For a brief time, political mobilization of black people, united with a small minority of white Republicans, created genuine two-party democracy and biracial government throughout the South. Black men quickly occupied numerous state and local government posts, enacted state anti-discrimination laws, and sent a handful of black members to Congress. White racist resistance to these developments persisted throughout Reconstruction, often marked by mob violence and even paramilitary death squads in the heavily armed society where recently demobilized rebel soldiers had often been allowed to keep their weapons. While the violence ebbed and flowed in response to intermittent federal efforts to enforce civil and voting rights laws, it was never fully suppressed by the time the last federal occupation troops were withdrawn from the South in 1877. Worn down by intractable southern resistance, and preoccupied with economic issues following the Panic of 1873, northern Republicans increasingly reconciled themselves to accepting the so-called redemption of southern states by the late 1880s and early 1890s. This acquiescence meant single-party Democratic rule, suppression of black voting, and an oppressive racial caste system that would last for decades.[2]

* * *

The most significant development for constitutional law was the proposal by Congress, and ratification by the states, of three new amendments, all primarily aimed at abolishing slavery and guaranteeing political and civil rights to black Americans. The Thirteenth Amendment, proposed by Congress at Lincoln's strong urging in March 1865, and ratified in December, provides, "Neither slavery nor involuntary servitude, except as a punishment for crime whereof the party shall have been duly convicted, shall exist within the United States, or any place subject to their jurisdiction." The Fourteenth Amendment, proposed by Congress in June 1866 and ratified in July 1868, overrules *Dred Scott's* holding that African Americans were constitutionally barred from United States citizenship by providing, "All persons born or naturalized in the United States, and subject to the jurisdiction thereof, are citizens of the United States and of the state wherein they reside." It further provides, "No state shall make or enforce any law which shall abridge the privileges or immunities of citizens of the United States; nor shall any state deprive any person of life, liberty, or property, without due process of law; nor deny to any person within its jurisdiction the equal protection of the laws." And the Fifteenth Amendment, proposed in February 1869, and ratified in February 1870, declares, "The right of citizens of the United States to vote shall not be denied or abridged by the United States or by any state on account of race, color, or previous condition of servitude." Each of the three

Reconstruction Amendments contains a final section stating that Congress has the power to enforce the amendment "by appropriate legislation."[3]

Modern Supreme Court justices and constitutional scholars have assumed that the phrase "appropriate legislation" was intended to invoke "the *McCulloch* standard" for implied powers in each of these Reconstruction Amendments.[4] But the congressional debates on the Thirteenth Amendment appear to contain no reference to *McCulloch* or its conception of implied powers. If anything, supporters of the amendment sought to quell the implication that a power to enforce slavery abolition would authorize Congress to enact broad anti-discrimination laws.[5] In addition, speakers uttering the phrase "appropriate legislation" did not necessarily mean to invoke *McCulloch's* interpretation of the Necessary and Proper Clause. "Appropriate legislation" was a commonplace term meaning merely "suitable" or perhaps "constitutional" laws. It was frequently used by speakers who had no discernible intention to invoke *McCulloch* or in contexts that didn't call for it. For example, *McCulloch's* foremost judicial opponent, Taney, had described the 1850 Fugitive Slave Act as an "appropriate law" in *Ableman v. Booth*.[6] The phrase "appropriate legislation" reflects a type of redundancy to underscore a quality presumed to be inherent in the modified noun, common in both ordinary speech and legal language: consider "due regard," "fair notice," or "just compensation."

Although it may not have influenced the *wording* of the Thirteenth Amendment's enforcement clause, *McCulloch* emerged as a significant element in debates over Congress's powers to *enforce* the Thirteenth Amendment.[7] These debates figured prominently in the decision to propose the Fourteenth Amendment. The Thirty-ninth Congress convened on December 4, 1865. Ratification of the Thirteenth Amendment followed two days later, and Congress quickly went to work on a civil rights bill. The Civil Rights Act of 1866, a landmark law that remains on the books today, provided in its first section

> That all persons born in the United States and not subject to any foreign power, excluding Indians not taxed, are hereby declared to be citizens of the United States; and such citizens, of every race and color, without regard to any previous condition of slavery or involuntary servitude, ... shall have the same right, in every State and Territory in the United States, to make and enforce contracts, to sue, be parties, and give evidence, to inherit, purchase, lease, sell, hold, and convey real and personal property, and to full and equal benefit of all laws and proceedings for the security of person and property, as is enjoyed by white citizens. ...[8]

The second section of the act enforced the provisions of the first by making it a criminal misdemeanor for any person, "under color of any law, statute, ordinance, regulation, or custom," to deprive a person of the guaranteed civil rights. The law was enacted by Congress on April 9, 1866 after overriding President Johnson's veto.

Johnson's veto message had contended that the law violated the states' right to make racially discriminatory laws.[9] Significantly, the law did not specify any particular substantive rights within the states or nationally, only that whatever rights the states conferred on "white citizens" relating to contracts, property ownership, and so on, had to be conferred equally on "citizens of every race and color." That is, the law mandated equality in state-created rights, not the precise content of those rights. This limitation conformed to antebellum ideas about federalism and reserved state powers: that it was a matter of state sovereignty to supply the content of basic civil rights relating to free labor and "the security of person and property." Note, too, that civil rights as conceived in 1866 were limited to personal and property matters, and did not include the right to vote.[10] Finally, the citizenship clause of the law was a direct effort by statute to overrule *Dred Scott*, which had held that African Americans could never be citizens of the United States and that their state citizenship was a matter of state legislative grace.

The 1866 Civil Rights Act thus raised a vital question: was the Act appropriate legislation to enforce the Thirteenth Amendment's prohibition of slavery? *McCulloch* seemed perfectly tailored to address this question. Clearly, the enforcement clause in section 2 meant that the prohibition of slavery was not meant to be enforceable exclusively in court without implementing legislation. Given that congressional action was contemplated by the amendment, some aspects of the 1866 Civil Rights Act should have been straightforwardly constitutional. The law invalidated the 1865 state black codes, which had placed race-based restrictions on civil and free-labor rights of black people, restrictions that were designed to reintroduce slavery in substance if not in name. In theory, if abolishing slavery meant at the same time eliminating its "badges and incidents" (in the language of the time), might not any law equalizing the status of black and white people in society—even one going far beyond the 1866 Act—be "conducive" and "plainly adapted" to executing the granted Thirteenth Amendment power under *McCulloch*?

Congress never reached a consensus on how far it could go under the Thirteenth Amendment. While some radical Republicans like Charles Sumner read the Thirteenth Amendment as a constitutional guarantee of full equality, many did not.[11] But a sufficient number of congressmen believed the 1866 Civil Rights Act was indeed justified under the Thirteenth Amendment to pass the law. The case for constitutionality was put most succinctly by Congressman James F. Wilson of Iowa. "Who shall select the means" to enforce the abolition of slavery?, Wilson asked rhetorically. "Happily, sir, we are not without light on these questions from the Supreme Court," provided by "the celebrated case of *McCulloch vs. The State of Maryland. . . .*" Applying *McCulloch*, Wilson explained that the "end" of the Thirteen Amendment "is the maintenance of freedom to the citizen. . . . " Therefore, "[a] man who enjoys the civil rights mentioned in this bill cannot be reduced to slavery. Anything which protects him in the possession of these rights insures him against reduction to slavery. This settles the appropriateness of this measure, and that settles its constitutionality." Again citing *McCulloch*, Wilson asserted, "Of the necessity of the measure Congress is the sole judge."[12]

Justice Swayne, a Lincoln appointee, adopted the argument that *McCulloch* sustained the 1866 Civil Rights Act as appropriate legislation to enforce the Thirteenth Amendment. Sitting as circuit judge in *United States v. Rhodes* (1866),[13] Swayne held that the Amendment "reversed and annulled the original policy of the constitution which left it to each state to decide exclusively for itself whether slavery should or should not exist as a local institution, and what disabilities should attach to those of the servile race within its limits." Swayne "entertain[ed] no doubt of the of the constitutionality of the act in all its provisions," because *McCulloch's* definition of "necessary and proper," "show[ed] the spirit in which the [Thirteenth] amendment is to be interpreted."[14]

Nevertheless, even supporters of the 1866 Act were concerned that the full Supreme Court would take a restrictive view of Thirteenth Amendment enforcement powers. John Bingham, a leading radical Republican and champion of civil rights, argued vehemently that the Fourteenth Amendment was necessary in order to authorize Congress to enforce civil and political rights within the states. Although he had voted for the 1866 Act, he expressed reservations about its constitutionality, at least in the eyes of the Supreme Court. "Where is the express power to define and punish crimes committed in any State by its official officers in violation of the rights of citizens and persons as declared in the Constitution?" Bingham asked. "And from what expressly delegated power in the Constitution can any such power be implied?" Bingham wanted to see black citizens protected in express constitutional terms from state invasions of the rights guaranteed by the Bill of Rights. The same John Bingham who had prominently enlisted *McCulloch* in support of an implied federal power to confiscate slaves now cited *McCulloch* to argue against implied powers. "In McCullough vs. Maryland," Bingham asserted, "Marshall, C. J., says: 'The Constitution of the United States is one of limited and expressly delegated powers, which can only be exercised as granted or in cases enumerated.'"[15] Even allowing for paraphrasing, Bingham misquoted *McCulloch*, which said that Congress possessed "delegated," not "*expressly* delegated" powers. But the misstatement served Bingham's strategic purposes in trying to convince his colleagues of the need for the Fourteenth Amendment.

References to *McCulloch* gradually increased as the Reconstruction Congress debated and passed two military reconstruction acts, a bill significantly expanding the powers of the Freedman's Bureau, and three more civil rights enforcement acts, including the Civil Rights Act of 1871, which remains a cornerstone of civil rights law today.[16] A handful of speeches cited and quoted *McCulloch* both for and against Congress's power to enact these laws.[17] *McCulloch* was also increasingly cited on matters relating to federal corporate charters and internal improvements. To be sure, many members made assertions about the breadth of congressional powers without analyzing implied powers doctrine or using language redolent of

McCulloch.[18] Even those who did cite *McCulloch* may have gotten their ideas about the powers of Congress elsewhere, and may have cited *McCulloch* as a makeweight or to add erudition. Supporting his civil rights bill in 1872 debates, Charles Sumner cited *McCulloch* prominently—"When I assert that Congress has ample power over this question, I rely upon a well-known text often cited in this Chamber, often cited in our courts"—but just once in five lengthy speeches. To Sumner, the Thirteenth and Fourteenth Amendments were "each a fountain of power" on their own terms.[19] *McCulloch* was not on everyone's lips, but there were perhaps some thirty other references to *McCulloch* in the decade between 1865 and 1875, some in connection with various Reconstruction bills, others in connection with matters such as chartering corporations or funding internal improvements.[20]

The halls of the Reconstruction Congress were dominated by lawyers, who frequently cited legal authorities.[21] Many of the lawyers in Congress in the 1860s and 1870s would have received their legal training after the mid-1830s. That was a time when constitutional law, whether studied in law-office apprenticeships or in lecture halls at Harvard Law School, would have been conveyed largely through the treatises of James Kent and Joseph Story. These two treatises were often cited in Reconstruction Congress debates, and both summarized *McCulloch* at length. Representative Spaulding, as noted previously, quoted *McCulloch* indirectly through Kent's lengthy paraphrase when introducing the Legal Tender bill. Charles Sumner would have imbibed *McCulloch* at Harvard Law School, where he was a protégé of Story and later an instructor.[22] While it seems doubtful to suppose that Congress would have been incapable of enacting reconstruction legislation in the absence of ideas from *McCulloch*, it is certainly plausible that fence-sitting members might be swayed to vote one way or another on the basis of well-supported constitutional arguments.

Legal scholars tend to be interested in *McCulloch*'s direct influence on the framers of the Reconstruction Amendments for the light it sheds on the extent of Congress's enforcement powers today.[23] But that issue is academic. The Necessary and Proper Clause empowers congress make "necessary and proper" laws to execute powers granted anywhere in the Constitution, not just the "foregoing powers" in Article I, section 8.[24] It therefore applies to the enforcement provisions of the Reconstruction Amendments. Anyone who views *McCulloch* as the correct interpretation of implied powers under the Necessary and Proper Clause should therefore conclude that "the *McCulloch* standard" governs the enforcement clauses of the Reconstruction Amendments, whether or not the framers of those amendments had *McCulloch* in mind. The "appropriate legislation" tag is likewise immaterial, since the Necessary and Proper Clause calls for appropriate implementing legislation for all grants of legislative power. As an authoritative precedent interpreting the Constitution, *McCulloch* was already constitutionalized.

Or was it? The tradition of viewing congressional power as limited to enumerated powers had raised doubts that a mere grant of rights would authorize congressional

enforcement with sufficient clarity. The only direct precedent for an implied congressional power to enforce a right, as opposed to an express power, was *Prigg
v. Pennsylvania*, a Taney Court pro-slavery decision. Some members of Congress indeed cited *Prigg*, but that decision had been based on the antebellum Court's strong
pro-slavery presumption in interpreting congressional powers.[25] There was reason
to doubt that the current Court, or a future one with new Democratic appointees,
would indulge a presumption in favor of black civil rights. Accordingly, the enforcement clauses were deemed necessary to make clear that the amendments were
grants of legislative, as well as judicial power. If it was indeed Congress's intention
to build "the *McCulloch* standard" into the Reconstruction Amendments, the most
plausible reason for doing so would have been to bind the Supreme Court. With
hope, this would prevent the Court from backsliding into a narrow, Jacksonian
"strict necessity" test of implied powers. Had *McCulloch* truly been deemed a
binding precedent by the legal establishment, it would have been unnecessary to
write "the *McCulloch* standard" into the Constitution. Ironically, a perceived need
to do so only demonstrates *McCulloch*'s lack of influence on the Supreme Court at
that time. In any case, if the Reconstruction Congress indeed feared states'-rights
backsliding by the Court in reviewing Reconstruction enforcement legislation, that
fear was to prove well founded.

* * *

Congress had little reason for confidence that the Supreme Court in the early
Reconstruction period—the Chase Court—viewed *McCulloch* as a foundational
case. Salmon P. Chase, Lincoln's former Treasury secretary, was confirmed as chief
justice in December 1864, two months after Taney's death. From then until early
1870, the Chase Court comprised a five-to-three majority of Lincoln appointees.
McCulloch should have been back on the justices' constitutional map. Not only was
its nationalist constitutional theory ascendant in the Reconstruction period, but
also its theory of implied powers had received glimmerings of favorable notice in
Congress and in Justice Swayne's circuit opinion in *United States v. Rhodes*. Since
Marshall's stock would have risen with the bottoming out of Taney's postwar reputation, reaching back to Marshall Court precedents might seem a natural way to
rebuild the Court's prestige. Chase himself should have been inclined to revere
Marshall and to build up Marshall's "great" decisions. In his youth, Chase had
been a protégé of William Wirt—the longtime attorney general and co-counsel to
Webster in *McCulloch* and *Gibbons*. In law and politics, Chase had nationalist political commitments, having been an ardent abolitionist, Whig and later Republican.[26]
Nevertheless, throughout its first six years, the Chase Court disregarded *McCulloch*
in Reconstruction cases, despite the increasing attention to *McCulloch* in Congress.

When questions regarding the nature of the Union and the unconstitutionality
of secession arose in postwar litigation, Chase assigned the majority opinions to

himself. Perhaps consciously affecting the Grand Style of the Marshall Court, Chase expounded the Constitution as if writing on a clean slate, ignoring *McCulloch* and at times departing from it. In *Lane County v. Oregon* (1869),[27] for example, the Court unanimously decided that the Legal Tender Act was not intended to require states to accept greenbacks from state taxpayers, because the justices construed the term "debts" in the statute to refer to amounts owed under contracts and court judgments, but not to taxes. This plausible interpretation disposed of the case without raising constitutional issues, but Chase chose to discuss those anyway. Congress would not have tried to determine how state taxes should be paid, Chase reasoned, because it lacked the constitutional power to do so. Whatever might be said for that conclusion, Chase's summary statement was gratuitous: "The States disunited might continue to exist. Without the States in Union there could be no such political body as the United States."[28] Both claims are factually and legally debatable. More tellingly, Chase's point sounds much more like Andrew Jackson's unionism—the Constitution as an indissoluble compact of the states—than Marshall's nationalism in *McCulloch*.

Chase developed this neo-Jacksonian theme of the indissoluble compact in *Texas v. White* (1869),[29] which addressed the legal status of the rebellious states. During the Civil War, the rebel government of Texas used federal bonds held in its treasury to finance its military efforts, and the bonds circulated through various private hands. The postwar provisional government of Texas sued the various private bondholders to get the bonds back, on the theory that the contracts for war supplies in support of the rebellion were illegal and void. The defendant bondholders claimed that because Texas had not been readmitted into the Union, it was not a state and thus lacked the authority to sue in federal court. By a five-to-three majority, the Court ruled in favor of the provisional Texas government. Chase seemed determined to imprint his own constitutional theory on the Reconstruction debate regarding the place of the states in the Union, rather than drawing on precedents. "[U]nder the guidance of the Constitution alone," Chase set out to determine "what is the correct idea of a State" for constitutional purposes. Although at present a "provisional" government, Texas never stopped being a state in the Union, because the rebellion was unlawful and secession unconstitutional. Citing no authority other than his own opinion in *Lane*, Chase coined his famous assertion that "[t]he Constitution, in all its provisions, looks to an indestructible Union, composed of indestructible States." The admission of Texas into the Union "was something more than a compact; it was the incorporation of a new member into the political body. And it was final." But Chase seemed to suggest that the states as a collectivity were the relevant decision-maker: secession was unconstitutional absent the "consent of the [other] *states*."[30] Presumably that consent could be given only via constitutional amendment, and states do indeed ratify amendments through their legislatures. But those amendments must be proposed by Congress, meaning that the Constitution recognizes a pivotal role for the national government in giving any such consent.[31]

Under *McCulloch's* theory, the national government not only acts directly upon the whole people of Union, but also represents the interests of the whole people. A seceding state in effect tries to control the whole people by depriving them of access to the seceding state's territory, navigable waterways, and federally funded infrastructure. Chase's theory of *Texas v. White* is really a stronger form of the compact theory: the states came together to form a whole greater than the sum of the parts.

* * *

While Radical Republicans saw great potential in Congress's Reconstruction Amendment enforcement powers, the Court leaned heavily toward a return to the prewar norm of federalism. This spirit was captured at the very end of Chase's chief justiceship, in the *Slaughter-House Cases* (1873).[32] There, the Court upheld a New Orleans municipal law requiring all butcher shops to be located in a single market location controlled by a local monopoly.[33] Reaffirming the state's police powers over what it deemed a clear-cut health regulation, the Court gave its first extended interpretation of the recently enacted Fourteenth Amendment. The Court distinguished between the few skeletal rights guaranteed as the "privileges and immunities" of U.S. citizenship from those guaranteed by the states. The latter included "the right to acquire and possess property of every kind, and to pursue and obtain happiness and safety," and "embrace[d] nearly every civil right for the establishment and protection of which organized government is instituted."[34] Having identified these "fundamental" rights as state-protected, the Court asked rhetorically, "Was it the purpose of the fourteenth amendment . . . to transfer the security and protection of all the civil rights which we have mentioned, from the States to the Federal government?" Such an interpretation would authorize Congress to "pass laws in advance, limiting and restricting the exercise of legislative power by the States, in their most ordinary and usual functions, as in its judgment it may think proper on all such subjects" while making the Supreme Court "a perpetual censor upon all legislation of the States, on the civil rights of their own citizens, with authority to nullify such as it did not approve."[35] The Court found this interpretation unthinkable.

A robust application of the implied-powers principle of *McCulloch* to the Reconstruction Amendments held out the prospect for legislation to elevate freed slaves to full equality with whites. But the Court was unwilling to let constitutional interpretation go that far, even if Congress took the initiative. The prevailing understanding of constitutional politics melded black equality with continued white supremacy by distinguishing three categories of equality: civil, political, and social. Mainstream Republicans understood civil rights as guaranteeing their vision of free labor: the rights to free contract and protection of property. Some undoubtedly viewed these as basic rights of free persons that followed directly from the abolition of slavery. These were the rights identified in the 1866 Civil Rights Act. In contrast, political rights—to vote, hold office, organize and participate in electoral politics, and perhaps to sit on juries—were granted at the discretion of the body politic. As political scientist Pamela Brandwein has shown, this conception dominated the thinking of the Reconstruction-era Court.[36]

The Reconstruction Amendments guaranteed civil rights and granted political rights, but only in stages over the span of five years. It is today often forgotten that the Fourteenth Amendment intentionally preserved the power of states to deny black Americans the right to vote, which was only guaranteed two years later by the Fifteenth Amendment.[37] Even after recognizing black voting rights, the political mainstream balked at "social equality"—the idea that black and white people were social equals, mutually entitled to mingle freely in public social spaces, to educate their children together in integrated public schools, and to intermarry. White racial anxieties, the desire of whites to maintain superior social status over black people, pervaded politics and law to rule out social equality as a guaranteed right. White racial anxieties were most strongly expressed around the idea of interracial marriage: fear of "mixing of the races," "amalgamation," and the newly coined term "miscegenation" remained staples of Democratic Party rhetoric and offered potentially viable appeals to mainstream voters. There were advocates of full social equality for black Americans in the post–Civil War era, but like abolitionists before the war, these represented a radical minority element that lacked the voting strength to direct Republican Party policy.[38]

The Supreme Court positioned itself in the political center of the resulting constitutional controversies. On the one hand, the Court tended to enforce civil and political rights in clear-cut cases. It upheld the right of black men to sit on juries,[39] upheld core provisions of congressional statutes enforcing civil and voting rights,[40] and rejected challenges to Reconstruction laws when those challenges were based on Taney-era notions of state territorial sovereignty.[41]

On the other hand, the Court did little to promote and much to retard civil rights. The Court imposed strict limitations on the scope of congressional enforcement statutes and prosecutions under them. Indictments that did not meet high pleading standards to show clear evidence of racially discriminatory intent were routinely dismissed. Provisions in civil rights enforcement laws aimed at violence by Klansmen or white mobs were held unconstitutional.[42] The most infamous example was the judicial aftermath of the horrific Colfax Massacre, when a paramilitary mob of whites armed with rifles and a cannon attacked a large political meeting of mostly black freedmen, including some armed black militiamen, in the local courthouse. After a brief firefight, the surrounded and outgunned freedmen surrendered. In all, well over sixty and as many as eighty black men were murdered, many of them while they were disarmed prisoners.[43] The numerous initial indictments on conspiracy and civil-rights charges had been greatly whittled down by the lower courts, when the Supreme Court in *United States v. Cruikshank* (1876) dismissed the last three on the ground that the indictment had not made sufficiently clear that the white death squad had acted on account of race.[44]

The central theme of the Court's civil rights jurisprudence was that enforcement powers under the Reconstruction Amendments would be strictly construed to prevent federal law from entering traditional state legislative areas, the concern marked out in *Slaughter-House*. As demonstrated by *Cruikshank*, for example, Congress had no power to protect black Americans or white Republicans from violence in general, as opposed to violence specifically intended to deny a civil right on account of race. *Cruikshank* was also typical of a prevailing judicial attitude that interpreted the element "on account of race" with extreme narrowness, requiring something like proof of a specific and unalloyed racist motive. And as we will see, the Court refused to interpret the Reconstruction Amendments to allow Congress to legislate for social equality.

The Court's strong inclination to revert to the pre–Civil War norm of state control over race relations in the social sphere was truly reminiscent of the Taney era. The Taney Court viewed states' authority over race as a doctrine primarily to protect slavery, while strongly supporting federal powers mainly when those protected slavery. The Reconstruction-era Court likewise endorsed states' authority over race in the social sphere, except when federal power was necessary to permit racial subordination. This manipulation of federalism to promote segregation was evident in the Court's tortuous doctrine regarding segregated transportation. Common carriers represented an important area of conflict in the struggle for black equality. Accommodations on railroad cars and steamboats sent important signals of social status. For example, admission to the first class "ladies'" compartment signalled social respectability, while men were consigned to the fug and tobacco spit of the smoking car unless accompanying a lady. Conservative and some centrist Republicans believed that integrated transportation facilities would put law and society on a slippery slope to interracial marriage and biracial children.[45]

Since 1870, Senator Charles Sumner had led a radical Republican drive in Congress for a "public accommodations" bill that would integrate inns, theaters, and restaurants, as well as transportation and public schools. The bill was continually stalled in Congress, where it was not widely supported even within Republican ranks. The revered Sumner died in March 1874, having reportedly said on his deathbed, "take care of my civil rights bill." This apparently prompted the Senate to bring the bill up for renewed discussion. When the congressional elections of 1874–75 gave Democrats the majority in both houses of Congress for the first time since the Civil War, Republicans realized that any further civil rights legislation would be impossible once the current session of Congress ended. Thus, just days before the end of its lame duck session, the 42nd Congress passed Sumner's bill, stripped of the school desegregation provision, and President Grant signed it into law on March 1, 1875. It was widely understood that the bill was passed in homage to Sumner rather than because of any strong commitment to its principles.[46]

Nevertheless, Sumner's bill, the Civil Rights Act of 1875, was now the law of the land. It guaranteed "that all persons within the jurisdiction of the United States shall be entitled to the full and equal and enjoyment of the accommodations, advantages, facilities, and privileges of . . . public conveyances on land or water." The Act gave aggrieved persons a civil remedy of $500 and also subjected defendants to criminal prosecution for a misdemeanor.[47]

The landmark law was short lived. The Court struck down the law eight years later, in the *Civil Rights Cases* (1883).[48] In an eight-to-one decision by Justice Joseph P. Bradley, a staunch but centrist Republican appointed by Grant, the Court rejected the arguments of the statute's defenders that the Act was "appropriate legislation" to enforce the Thirteenth and Fourteenth Amendments. Because the Fourteenth Amendment specified that "no state" shall "deny to any person . . . the equal protection of the laws," Bradley reasoned, section 5 empowered Congress to regulate only "state action" that violated the equal protection guarantee. The Court distinguished between a "general" grant of legislative power (such as the Commerce Clause), which presumably could reach private conduct, and the purportedly more limited grant in the Fourteenth Amendment to issue only "corrective" legislation "such as may be necessary and proper for counteracting" offending state laws. The *Slaughter-House Cases* ten years earlier had prefigured this point. If the 1875 Civil Rights Act were deemed "appropriate for enforcing the prohibitions of the [Fourteenth] amendment," Bradley argued, "it is difficult to see where it is to stop. Why may not Congress with equal show of authority enact a code of laws for the enforcement and vindication of all rights of life, liberty, and property?" As for the Thirteenth Amendment argument, the Court was simply dismissive. "It would be running the slavery argument into the ground," Bradley asserted, "to make it apply to every act of discrimination which a person may see fit to make as to the guests he will entertain, or as to the people he will take into his coach or cab or car, or admit to his concert or theatre, or deal with in other matters of intercourse or business."[49]

The decision in the *Civil Rights Cases* is well-known, still taught in standard constitutional law courses, and in fact remains a valid precedent, establishing the "state action doctrine." According to this doctrine, the Fourteenth Amendment is deemed to apply only to acts or omissions that can be attributed to state and local governments. Thus, while race discrimination perpetrated by state legislatures or public officials violates the Fourteenth Amendment's Equal Protection Clause, private race discrimination does not. The *Civil Rights Cases* are understood as holding that the Civil Rights Act of 1875 was unconstitutional because Congress lacked power under the Fourteenth Amendment enforcement provision to prohibit race discrimination by privately owned businesses. That is certainly the case's core holding, in addition to a dismissal of a Thirteenth Amendment argument in support of the law. As such, the *Civil Rights Cases* represent a significant restriction of *McCulloch's* principle of implied powers as applied to the Reconstruction Amendments.

Notwithstanding its continued validity as precedent, the decision is poorly reasoned. The majority did not consider that privately owned businesses occupy the majority of public spaces, and that a business's decision to exclude black Americans thus differs greatly from that of the host of a private dinner party. The Court also ignored its own recent decision in *Munn v. Illinois* (1877),[50] which recognized that privately owned businesses could be deemed public entities for certain regulatory purposes. Justice Harlan, the lone dissenter in the case, did make that point. The law, he said, prohibited "discrimination practised by corporations and individuals in the exercise of their public or quasi-public functions."[51] Nor did the Court bother to consider how imposing a racial caste system through pervasive private ordering would undermine civil and political equality. This crabbed view of civil rights and the scope of the Thirteenth and Fourteenth Amendments was driven by a worldview that distinguished "social" from "civil" and "political" equality, one intended to leave the states in charge of ordering race relations in this social sphere with full knowledge that that ordering would enforce racial apartheid. Indeed, the Court ventured unnecessary dicta questioning whether "a right to enjoy equal accommodation and privileges in all inns, public conveyances, and places of public amusement, is one of the essential rights of the citizen which no State can abridge or interfere with"[52]— thereby prefiguring its decision in *Plessy v. Ferguson* (1896),[53] which would uphold even *state action* that segregated the "social" sphere. Despite flaws that are fully apparent to us today, the tragically misguided *Civil Rights Cases* remain "good law"— the decision was reaffirmed by the Supreme Court as recently as 2000.[54]

The decision in the *Civil Rights Cases* is another sign of the limited influence that *McCulloch* had on nineteenth-century jurisprudence. As Harlan argued in dissent, "the eradication" of slavery, "not simply of the institution, but of its badges and incidents," are appropriate subjects of legislation, and indeed, "[t]hey lie at the foundation of the Civil Rights Act of 1866," whose constitutionality was undisputed. Quoting *McCulloch* at length, Harlan expressly connected "appropriate legislation" in the enforcement clauses to Marshall's decision. "[I]t is for Congress, not the judiciary, to say that legislation is appropriate—that is—best adapted to the end to be attained," Harlan wrote. "The judiciary may not, with safety to our institutions, enter the domain of legislative discretion, and dictate the means which Congress shall employ in the exercise of its granted powers."[55]

As historian William Nelson has shown, the framers of the Fourteenth Amendment had no underlying consensus about questions surrounding social equality, and left those open for subsequent interpretation.[56] The 1875 Act was such an interpretation, only a few years removed from the Fourteenth Amendment's framing. But the Supreme Court majority ignored *McCulloch*'s principles of implied powers and deference to Congress. Not only did the Court give a stringent interpretation to concepts of "equal protection" and the prohibition of slavery, but the Court also narrowly construed the scope of implied powers. A conscious connection of "appropriate" legislation with *McCulloch* might have suggested a deferential approach to congressional choices about strategies and means for enforcing the constitutional guarantees.

And what about the Commerce Clause? The statute applied not only to "inns, . . . theaters, and other places of public amusement," but also to "public conveyances on land and water"—that is, transportation facilities. The Commerce Clause had no "state action" limitation; Congress had a recognized power to impose minute regulations on interstate navigation since early in the century. Congressional power over land-based interstate travel and transport was being recognized by the Supreme Court at this time (as we will see in the next chapter). Congress should have been authorized to prohibit race discrimination on interstate carriers of all kinds. Such regulatory power might even imply a power, were *McCulloch* applied to the Commerce Clause, to regulate *intra*state transportation if such legislation was conducive to effective implementation of an interstate policy of desegregated transportation. At a minimum, the commerce power would extend to intrastate segments on interstate lines—a principle that could find support even in *Gibbons v. Ogden*.

The 1875 Civil Rights Act's coverage of interstate transportation was not a trivial add-on to the law. As noted earlier, race discrimination on transportation facilities was a major civil rights issue, and upholding that aspect of the law would have been significant. Then as now, courts exercising judicial review were free to uphold constitutional portions of a law while striking down unconstitutional parts.[57] Four of the five cases consolidated into the *Civil Rights Cases* decision involved hotels and theaters, but the fifth, *Robinson v. Memphis & Charleston R. Co.*, was brought by a black woman who was subjected to race discrimination while traveling with her nephew on an interstate train journey.[58] Mrs. Robinson, who held a first-class ticket, was manhandled out of the ladies' car because of the conductor's racist belief that her nephew was white and that any black woman accompanying a younger white man must have been a prostitute. Robinson lost her trial for the $500 civil penalty after the judge instructed the jury that the conductor's "good faith" mistaken belief showed that his action was not *because of* her race. Robinson appealed the jury instruction, pointing out that the conductor reached his belief precisely because of her race. Before reaching this issue in the Supreme Court brief, plaintiff's counsel argued that "so far as the act of Congress applies" to interstate travel, "the power to pass it is beyond question" under the Commerce Clause. The defendant did not even try to contest that point, instead claiming the correctness of the jury instruction to dispose of the appeal.[59] The Commerce Clause issue was squarely before the Court, and offered a clear basis to uphold the Act as applied to interstate transportation.

Bradley's majority opinion admitted that, under the commerce power, Congress could "pass laws for regulating the subjects specified in every detail, and the conduct and transactions of individuals in respect thereof."[60] Yet earlier in the opinion, Bradley asserted, strangely, "Of course, no one will contend that the power to pass [the 1875 Act] was contained in the Constitution before the adoption of the last three amendments." But of course it was—in the Commerce Clause. Robinson's counsel had contended exactly that. What followed was one of the more epic evasions in Supreme Court history. Bradley asserted that the question of Congress's power to desegregate interstate transportation under the Commerce Clause "is not now before us." Why not? Because the power to enact the 1875 Civil Rights Act "is sought, first, in the Fourteenth Amendment, and the views and arguments of distinguished Senators, advanced whilst the law was under consideration, claiming authority to pass it by virtue of that amendment, are the principal arguments adduced in favor of the power."[61] In other words, the Court would simply refuse to consider the Commerce Clause as a foundation for the law because it had not been raised in congressional debate. This aberrational argument seems to have been conjured up for this case. The Court has not before or since suggested that Congress is required to identify the constitutional basis for its enactments, and Justice Harlan's dissent called out the majority for doing so.[62] While seeming to reserve decision on the commerce power issue, the Court nevertheless stated that its ruling disposed of all "of the cases now under consideration," including *Robinson*, and broadly concluded that the substantive provisions of the 1875 Act "are unconstitutional and void."[63] Whether intentionally or not, this passage obfuscated the Court's disregard of the Commerce Clause. Justice Harlan found it confusing, but the message was clear enough to later litigants: the 1875 Civil Rights Act was dead.[64]

* * *

The implied-powers doctrine of *McCulloch* was not sufficient to overcome a spirit of the post-Reconstruction Constitution that was determined to sustain social inequality between the races. This spirit is the only consistent through-line of the Court's jurisprudence involving the intersection of commerce and race. Five years earlier, in *Hall v. DeCuir* (1878),[65] a wealthy Louisiana plantation owner of mixed race, Josephine DeCuir, had been denied entry to a "whites only" cabin while traveling on a Mississippi River steamboat. Although the steamboat's route took it through several states, DeCuir was traveling only between two stops within Louisiana. DeCuir sued under an 1868 Louisiana law that prohibited segregated public accommodations, one of several equality laws enacted during the flowering of black political participation in the early Reconstruction era.[66] But the Court dismissed DeCuir's claim, striking down the Louisiana law for imposing "a direct burden upon inter-state commerce" in violation of "the exclusive power of Congress" to regulate interstate navigation. River navigation, Chief Justice Waite reasoned for the Court, required uniformity of legal regulations, for "[i]f each State was at liberty to regulate the conduct of carriers while within its jurisdiction, the confusion likely to follow could not but be productive of great inconvenience and unnecessary hardship . . ." The interstate carrier would be unable to operate "with satisfaction to himself, or comfort to those employing him, if on one side of a State line his passengers, both white and colored, must be permitted to occupy the same cabin, and on the other be kept separate." Congress had exclusive legislative power "untrammelled by

State lines" to secure the desirable "uniformity in the regulations . . . from one end to the other" of common carrier routes. Since Congress had not enacted regulations, its "inaction . . . is equivalent to a declaration that inter-state commerce shall remain free and untrammeled."[67]

This was half true. In the absence of regulation, private interstate carriers had begun experimenting with segregated facilities for the "comfort" of their passengers.[68] Though the practice of private race segregation was not uniform, the Court could still say that the freedom of interstate carriers to engage in race discrimination was a uniform rule of federal policy. Only it wasn't, because by 1878, Congress had enacted the 1875 Civil Rights Act. True, since DeCuir's incident occurred in 1872, the 1875 Act did not apply, but that was a technicality. The question for the Court was to interpret the principle of "free and untrammeled navigation" under the dormant Commerce Clause as of 1872. Why didn't that mean freedom from discrimination for the black traveler? The freedom of white travelers to move about the country, at least without state restriction, was recognized in *Crandall v. Nevada* in 1868.[69] Only by assuming that the unregulated status quo meant the carriers' freedom to segregate could the Court reach its conclusion. But the 1875 Civil Rights Act could easily have been understood to make explicit, rather than to change, a prior status quo of a national policy against segregated transportation. Instead, the Court spoke hypothetically, as if the 1875 Act had not existed: "If the public good requires such legislation, it must come from Congress and not from the States."[70] Even that statement required a doctrinal zigzag by a Court that, in other respects, believed that race regulation was a matter for the states. Ironically, counsel for the *steamboat owner* asserted the constitutionality of the Civil Rights Act of 1875 "so far as the Act relates to common carriers of passengers," arguing that that power demonstrated Congress's exclusive power to regulate interstate river traffic.[71]

Decided the way it was, *DeCuir* should nevertheless have established beyond doubt that states lacked the power to regulate the racial policies of interstate transportation facilities. But when southern states began doing just that by enacting their first round of Jim Crow laws in the late 1880s, the Court sustained them. In *Louisville, New Orleans & Tex. Ry. Co. v. Mississippi* (1890),[72] the Court upheld an 1888 Mississippi statute requiring separate rail cars "for the white and colored races." In *DeCuir*, the Court had disregarded the fact that the passenger was traveling purely within Louisiana, and found it dispositive that the statute purported to regulate interstate *carriers*. But in *Louisville*, the Court shifted its rationale and purported to distinguish *DeCuir* by (mis)interpreting the Mississippi law as applying only to the handling of *intra*state *passengers*, and not to the operations of *inter*state *carriers*. The distinction was nonsensical, not least of all because the laws in both cases were directed at the *carriers*. [73] By this sleight of hand, the Court was able to disregard the realities of travel, and the ways in which Jim Crow laws projected their effects beyond state borders. Jim Crow laws encouraged railroads to adopt segregation policies even for the interstate passengers, to avoid harassment once they reached Jim Crow states. Otherwise, interstate railroads would have to add cars for black passengers at state borders, and remove black passengers from integrated cars. These were the very kinds of disuniformities that underlay *DeCuir's* decision to hold interstate carriers immune from state laws respecting race discrimination in transportation. Justices Harlan and Bradley saw through the majority's ploy and dissented on the ground that *DeCuir* required striking down the state law.[74]

There is an ironic coda to these cases. In 1913, a civil rights lawyer brought a test case to the Supreme Court on behalf of a black woman who was relegated to second-class accommodations aboard a steamship traveling in U.S. coastal waters between Norfolk and Boston, despite having purchased a first-class ticket. The lawyer had closely read the *Civil Rights Cases* to notice the Court's failure to address another question. The statute applied "to all persons within the jurisdiction of the United States," but the Court had failed to consider whether the law could stand with respect to places under U.S. jurisdiction but outside the states: the District of Columbia, the territories, coastal waters, and ships at sea under U.S. registry. In *Butts v. Merchants & Miners Transportation Co.* (1913), the Court dismissed this claim, arguing unconvincingly that Congress would not have wanted its law to apply anywhere under its jurisdiction unless it could apply everywhere within the United States.[75]

* * *

Modern-day revisionist scholars point out either that the justices of the 1870s to 1890s were applying consistent doctrines or were following prevailing racial attitudes.[76] "In these formulations," writes historian Rebecca Scott, "'historical context' takes on an almost fatalistic explanatory value."[77] The revisionist implication is that the justices were simply men of their time, and should not be faulted for declining to take positions more congenial to our present attitudes against race discrimination, which would have required them to swim against the tide of public opinion. But that goes too easy on the justices. Life tenure for justices is legitimized by the expectation that they should be willing to make principled decisions that sometimes go against public opinion. Post–Reconstruction Supreme Court justices should be no more immune from criticism than justices of our own day when they manipulate principles to constitutionalize widespread opinions that they happen to share. Justices who ignore clearly presented issues (commerce, in the *Civil Rights Cases*) or misread the law to distinguish clear precedent (the state law in *Louisville*) know that they are stretching a point and give away their guilty legal consciences. Here, the effect of their rulings was to remit the race issue to the states, but only when doing so supported the majority preference for race discrimination.

A sympathetic revisionist reading of the *Civil Rights Cases* in particular is misplaced. Constitutional scholars have observed that the Supreme Court usually represents the views of the old regime, rather than the one just elected, due to the simple arithmetic of judges with life tenure, who serve through political realignments.[78] But the post-Reconstruction Court embraced the politics of the new regime and jettisoned the Republican civil rights agenda prematurely. The *Civil Rights Cases* struck down the Civil Rights Act of 1875 long before Democrats gained the power needed to repeal the law. The Democrats did not gain control of both Congress and the White House until 1894, at which point they did indeed repeal several Civil Rights Laws.[79] The Court anticipated this development with respect to the 1875 Civil Rights Act by eleven years. The fact that many congressional Republicans may have been lukewarm about the bill, or supported it only in deference to Senator Sumner's memory, is hardly the point. Congress did not establish a pro-segregation policy in law, but an anti-segregation policy. The 1875 Act garnered sufficient support to become the law of the land; judicial invalidation can't be justified by relying on legislators' underlying mixed emotions. Arguably, the Court didn't have to stretch a point to hold that barring segregation in the public space was not "appropriate legislation" under the Fourteenth Amendment. But just arguably. Adherence to *McCulloch* should have induced the Court to defer to Congress's judgment. Worse still, the Court went beyond its "state action" holding to hint gratuitously that even state-sponsored social segregation would be permissible under the Fourteenth Amendment. Finally, the Court bent over backward to stymie Congress's effort to desegregate transportation, ignoring the clear import of the Commerce Clause to block a significant step toward social equality. The *Civil Rights Cases* deserve much of the scorn heaped on *Plessy v. Ferguson*.

* * *

It would be an exaggeration to say that *McCulloch*'s influence on the Reconstruction Congress was pervasive. But it can be said that, after being buried by the late Marshall and Taney Courts, *McCulloch* was going through the beginnings of a revival. What is striking is that the revival was occurring in Congress, but not in the Supreme Court. While the Court did pay attention to *McCulloch* in one prominent post–Civil War episode—the *Legal Tender Cases* discussed in Chapter 8—that was the only occasion, and it involved Congress's implied powers over currency. When it came to the power to reconstruct the place of black Americans in the constitutional order, the Court ignored *McCulloch*, just as it had done under Marshall and Taney, and for much the same reason.

8

"Acting Directly on the People"

Post–Civil War Nationalism, 1868–1888

A key element of *McCulloch*'s nationalism was its confirmation of the Constitution's chief improvement over the Articles of Confederation: creating a government "possessing great and sovereign powers, and acting directly on the people," rather than governing indirectly through the states.[1] This point was so fundamental that it might have been taken for granted, but for the states'-rights theories that dominated the Taney Court and underlay nullification and secession.

Postbellum constitutional politics advanced the idea of reconfiguring governmental institutions to cement the Union victory in the Civil War. Constitutional commentary returned time and again to the theme of "nationalism." In a concurring opinion upholding the wartime Legal Tender Act, Justice Bradley linked the powers of Congress with what he took to be the central issue of the Civil War. The doctrines of compact theory and secession "should be regarded as definitely and forever overthrown," he wrote. "This has been finally effected by the National power, as it had often been before, by overwhelming argument."[2]

But this was not the nationalism of the New Deal or of modern-day interpreters of *McCulloch*. Rather, it was a more intensified version of the nationalism of the antebellum Whig party. Having had arisen in opposition to Andrew Jackson's 1832 re-election campaign, the Whigs dissolved a quarter century later as their northern and southern wings split irrevocably over slavery. Most northern Whigs had gravitated into the Republican Party, bringing with them a continuing belief in the nationalism of Henry Clay's American System and the agenda of internal improvements and tariffs. The Whig party had had an abolitionist wing, but by and large its opposition to slavery had been confined to a framework that viewed slavery as the price of Union. Slavery had been a matter of state sovereignty, and its accommodation had been a necessary compromise built into the Constitution.[3] Translated into post–Civil War Republican nationalism, this element of former

Whig nationalism was reflected in the increasing abandonment of a national civil rights agenda by Republicans noted in the previous chapter, as the Panic of 1873 led to a resurgence of the Democratic Party in congressional elections and economic issues began to displace racial equality on the political agenda. The former Whig brand of economic nationalism combined with a revived belief in reserved state powers, particularly over matters of race, seemed increasingly congenial to Republicans. While the Reconstruction Amendments mandated limited federal authority and attention to black equality, states regained a large and increasing measure of control over race relations. Post-Civil War nationalism thus meant a partial but significant reversion to prewar constitutionalism, while implementing the Whig nationalist economic agenda. The national bank was never restored, but the constitutional order recognized national control over the money supply along with the constitutionality of internal improvements and tariffs. The Supreme Court, after a fifty-year hiatus, began to embrace *McCulloch* as authoritative on a narrow subset of these issues.

* * *

McCulloch's revival in the Supreme Court began in 1870 and 1871, when the Court for the first time recognized *McCulloch* as an authoritative precedent for implied powers. In those two years, the Court issued two major decisions on the constitutionality of legal tender paper money. Because Congress's powers to regulate all aspects of national currency are now taken for granted, these legal tender decisions have fallen off the constitutional radar screen and out of memory. This is unfortunate, because the debate in those two cases goes to the heart of implied powers and our ideology of limited enumerated powers, as well as the role of the Supreme Court in a democratic society. The first case, *Hepburn v. Griswold* (1870),[4] struck down the Legal Tender Act of 1862. It marks the first time in U.S. constitutional history that the Court expressly rejected a congressional assertion of implied commerce powers, thereby anticipating *Lochner*-era laissez-faire jurisprudence by more than two decades.[5] The second of the two decisions, a consolidated set of cases known as the *Legal Tender Cases* (1871),[6] overruled *Hepburn*, the first time the Supreme Court overruled one of its own prior constitutional decisions. If the cases have a legacy, it is that they began to restore *McCulloch's* interpretation of implied powers to the judicial lexicon.

The 1862 Legal Tender Act gave rise to a host of legal challenges. Between 1862 and 1870, the gold value of greenbacks was never par (1:1), but fluctuated between $1.25 and $2.00 in greenbacks to $1 in gold coin.[7] This disparity created enormous potential for legal disputes over whether debts should be paid in paper or gold. Although the 1862 Act was a wartime measure, the controversy extended into peacetime. The Act had been vague about retiring greenbacks from circulation by redeeming them for gold, and the disparity between gold and paper dollars gave redemption such complex implications for politics and the economy that Congress did not settle on a policy until the late 1870s.[8]

Cases involving the Legal Tender Act began reaching the Supreme Court in 1867, and at least nine of these were docketed for 1869. The Court issued decisions on four of them, resolving each case on statutory interpretation grounds that avoided having to rule on the law's constitutionality. In one such case, the Court interpreted the Legal Tender Act to allow parties to provide expressly for payment in gold or silver coin, even though contracting around the law in that way could have undermined the law's effectiveness.[9]

The dispute in *Hepburn v. Griswold* arose out of a contract that was made prior to enactment of the Legal Tender Act and that did not specify the mode of repayment; the creditor refused the debtor's tendered greenbacks in satisfaction of the contract. The Court determined that the statute had to be read to apply to pre-enactment contracts, thus forcing a decision on the constitutional issue. Chief Justice Chase, who as Treasury Secretary had only reluctantly gone along with the expedient of making the Treasury notes a legal tender, wrote the opinion for the Court. Preparing the ground for his ruling striking down the Legal Tender Act, Chase gave an extended justification for judicial review in language reminiscent of *Marbury v. Madison*, but without citing that case. "It is the function of the judiciary to interpret and apply the law to cases between parties. . . . It can only declare what the law is."[10] Chase continued his citation-free, Grand Style exposition by controverting *McCulloch*, again without citation. While implied powers "are necessarily extensive," Chase contended, nevertheless "the extension of power by implication was regarded with some apprehension" by the Framers. They therefore included the Necessary and Proper Clause and the Tenth Amendment *as limitations* to preserve "the design of the Constitution" as a delegation of limited powers to Congress.[11]

After describing implied powers in a manner more congenial to Jacksonians than to adherents of Marshall, Chase curiously, and for the first time in any of his opinions, actually cited *McCulloch*. A power to issue legal tender paper money is not express, and "[t]he rule for determining whether a legislative enactment can be supported as an exercise of an implied power was stated by Chief Justice Marshall." Here, Chase quoted Marshall's narrow and ambiguous passages about judicial review, rather than his broad definitions of "necessary and proper": "Let the end be legitimate . . . ," and "the painful duty of this tribunal."[12] Chase grudgingly acknowledged that *McCulloch*'s rejection of the narrow "strictly necessary" test for implied powers under the Necessary and Proper Clause "must be taken then as finally settled, so far as judicial decisions can settle anything," but he then proceeded to apply this aspect of *McCulloch* in the narrowest possible way. It was not enough that legal tender paper money might "facilitate" government spending in wartime, Chase argued, because the same could be said about peacetime spending, and a peacetime legal tender power "carries the doctrine of implied powers very far beyond any extent hitherto given it." Chase thus seemed to suggest that novel uses of implied powers were presumptively unconstitutional. Moreover, Chase asserted, the government could have waged the Civil War by issuing Treasury notes as traditional banknotes without making them legal tender. Any benefit entailed in the legal tender aspect was "trifling," and was "outweighed" by its tendency to increase a "long train of [economic] evils."[13] In other words, the Legal Tender Act was bad policy: perhaps necessary to execute an enumerated power, but not necessary enough. Deference to congressional judgments about a law's necessity, Chase continued, would convert the national government into one "of unlimited powers," "confuse the boundaries" of separation of powers, and "obliterate every criterion" of judicial review established by Marshall ("the venerated Chief Justice") in *McCulloch*. Yet it was Chase who was obliterating every criterion of implied powers set out in *McCulloch*, which held that Congress had discretion to decide the degree of a law's necessity.

Chase then focused separately on the word "proper" and concluded that a law is not proper if it violates "the letter [or] spirit of the constitution," quoting *McCulloch*'s phrase. Because legal tender paper money depreciates, Chase explained, it deprives creditors of their property and undermines their legitimate contractual expectations of repayment in full.[14] To be sure, the prohibition against "impairing the obligation of contracts" applied only to the states. And the Chase Court was not quite willing to embrace the idea that the Due Process Clause could be applied to strike down an economic regulation.[15] Nevertheless, as Chase saw matters, these provisions infused the Constitution with a "spirit" that protected creditors against repayment in depreciated paper currency.[16]

Why would Chase turn to *McCulloch* now, when it tended to undermine rather than support his position? In prior cases, he had seemed almost to go out of his way to avoid *McCulloch*, even in cases involving banking and intergovernmental tax immunity. In *Veazie Bank v. Fenno* (1869),[17] for example, Chase wrote the unanimous opinion upholding the power of Congress to impose a prohibitive 10% tax on state banknotes. The law was plainly intended to drive state banknotes out of circulation, but this was an "appropriate" and "suitable" way for Congress to "restrain ... the circulation as money of any notes not issued under its own authority."[18] In *Bank v. Supervisors* (1869), the Court invalidated a state's attempt to tax state bank holdings of federal greenbacks. Chase wrote that it was "clearly within the discretion of Congress to determine whether . . . [the greenbacks'] usefulness, as a means of carrying on the government, would be enhanced" by the exemption from taxation. In neither case did Chase cite *McCulloch*, even though it was the standard citation for intergovernmental tax immunity. In the *License Tax Cases* (1867), Chase used the Jacksonian "strict necessity" formulation as the test for implied powers rather than *McCulloch*'s version.[19] And in *In re Turner* (1867),[20] sitting as circuit judge, Chase concluded that the Civil Rights Act of 1866 was "appropriate legislation" to enforce the Thirteenth Amendment. But whereas his colleague Swayne relied on *McCulloch* to decide the same issue in another circuit case, *United States v. Rhodes*, Chase did not.[21]

It is likely that Chase suddenly turned to *McCulloch* because he felt forced to, in order to rebut the dissenters, who relied heavily on it. The dissenters also rebuked Chase with an implicit invidious comparison between him and Marshall, which may have sharpened Chase's need himself to invoke "the venerated Chief Justice."[22] Chase was, after all, striking down a major Civil War measure in a politically charged decision by a close vote that depended on the assent of three Taney Court holdovers. It is of course possible that Chase sincerely believed *McCulloch* was controlling precedent, which would have been a novelty in itself. Whatever Chase's motivation, *Hepburn* would be the first of many times that the Court would invoke *McCulloch* to strike down an act of Congress.

Chase's *Hepburn* opinion, though badly reasoned and deeply flawed, is a watershed moment in constitutional history, in which Jacksonian ideas, emergent laissez-faire jurisprudence, and judicial supremacy began to merge. In 1870, Chase was eyeing the 1872 Democratic presidential nomination, giving him a strong incentive to appeal to that party's continuing Jacksonian ethos.[23] Chase artfully exploited *McCulloch*'s ambiguities and limitations to give it a Jacksonian gloss. By arguing that a law was not "necessary and proper" if it had undesirable consequences and "better" alternatives, Chase closely tracked the approach taken in Jackson's bank veto. Chase turned *McCulloch* on its head by contending that implied-powers claims are inherently suspect; that a novel extension of congressional power is presumptively unconstitutional; and that recognition of a new implied power leads inexorably to a consolidation of the national government and destruction of the states. These are Jacksonian themes, and they dress up Chase's discussion of the Due Process Clause, which anticipated the *Lochner* era's economic due process jurisprudence. Chase also asserted that a law with an unintended consequence of redistributing wealth from creditors to debtors violates an unspecified right found in the "spirit" of the Constitution. Although traditional Jacksonians might be queasy with *Hepburn*'s favoritism toward creditors, Chase managed to package these nascent laissez-faire ideas in Jacksonian states'-rights concepts.[24] *Hepburn* makes a bold and candid announcement, for the first time, of the Court's role as the enforcer of federalism by non-deferentially reviewing novel claims of congressional power, particularly the power to regulate the economy. This statement indelibly links what present-day constitutional scholars call "the judicial safeguards of federalism" with laissez faire, prefigures the rigid Commerce Clause jurisprudence of the *Lochner* era, and has echoes in the so-called federalism revival of the Rehnquist and Roberts Courts.[25]

The three-justice dissent by Justice Samuel Miller, Lincoln's first appointee to the Court in 1862, applied *McCulloch* as authority for expansive implied powers for the first time in a Supreme Court opinion. Miller's devastating critique began by lauding Marshall as "[t]hat eminent jurist and statesman, whose official career of over thirty years as Chief Justice commenced very soon after the Constitution was adopted, and whose opinions have done as much to fix its meaning as those of any man living or dead. . . . "[26] This praise was plainly intended not only to build up the authority of Marshall and *McCulloch*, but also to put the imperious Chase in his place.[27] In the "memorable" and "well known" case of *McCulloch*, said Miller, that "eminent expounder of the Constitution" gave the Necessary and Proper Clause its "most exhaustive discussion." Marshall's statements about the capable Constitution were to Miller, "almost prophetic," as if "he had had clearly before his mind the future history of his country." The majority's implicit use of a "strict necessity" test for implied powers, Miller said, had been given an "emphatic denial" and "satisfactory refutation" by *McCulloch*.[28]

The legal tender power, Miller argued, was necessary and proper to the powers to declare war, suppress rebellions, raise and support armies, and to spend and borrow for those purposes. Significantly, Miller did not mention the Commerce Clause or suggest that reserved state powers could be overcome by implied powers. Instead, the Constitution's various money clauses, while not "standing alone a sufficient warrant for the exercise of this power," did demonstrate that there would be no "invasion of any right reserved to the states" if Congress exercised an implied legal tender power. Miller easily refuted Chase's claim that the legal tender feature of the wartime Treasury notes was of limited utility. But its vital usefulness to the war effort was beside the point, because *McCulloch* had made clear that the Court was not at liberty "to declare the law void because the necessity for its enactment does not appear so strong to us as it did to Congress."[29]

Miller's rebuttal of Chase's "spirit" argument is particularly noteworthy as a manifesto against judicial review of economic regulation. It couldn't be against the spirit of the Constitution to favor debtors indirectly when the Constitution authorizes Congress to "directly destroy the creditor's contract" through bankruptcy laws, Miller argued. Declaring the law void would harm the property rights and reliance interests of debtors, and it was not for the Court to take sides in policy debates between debtor and creditor. The due process argument, Miller charged, was "too vague for my perception," since many constitutionally permissible acts "deprive" property by depreciating its value. As Miller observed, enacting or abolishing tariffs, borrowing money by increasing the supply of government bonds, or making war can all diminish significant property values. Moreover, the due process argument in general

> is too abstract and intangible for application to courts of justice, and is, above all, dangerous as a ground on which to declare the legislation of Congress void by the decision of a court. It would authorize this court to enforce theoretical views of the genius of the government, or vague notions of the spirit of the Constitution and of abstract justice, by declaring void laws which did not square with those views. It substitutes our ideas of policy for judicial construction, an undefined code of ethics for the Constitution, and a court of justice for the National legislature.[30]

Miller's rebuttal anticipated New Deal–era debates about economic due process. His statement about the proper role of the Court, to refrain from substituting its policy judgments for those of Congress, reflects a reading of *McCulloch* that would resonate today in debates about "judicial activism." As an interpretation of *McCulloch*, Miller's dissent was much more faithful to the original than Chase's.

* * *

Within a year, Miller's understanding of *McCulloch* became the majority view on the Court. President Grant's nominees, William Strong and Joseph Bradley, solid Republicans who believed in central government authority over matters of national sovereignty, were confirmed in February and March 1870, respectively. The new justices joined the three *Hepburn* dissenters to overcome efforts by the Chase bloc and various litigants to prevent reconsideration of the legal tender issue. A new set of legal tender cases was argued in early 1871, with a decision entered in May. In a decision known as the *Legal Tender Cases*,[31] the three *Hepburn* dissenters plus Strong and Bradley outvoted the remaining *Hepburn* majority justices five to four to overrule *Hepburn* and uphold the Legal Tender Act.*

Justice Strong's majority opinion began with a forceful statement of the Court's obligation, under *McCulloch*, to view assertions of congressional power with deference. To show "respect for a coordinate branch of the government," the Court will not strike down an act of Congress unless "unless the violation of the Constitution is so manifest as to leave no room for reasonable doubt."[32] No assertion of implied congressional power could be held unconstitutional unless the Court is convinced that it is "not appropriate means, or means conducive to the execution of any or all of the powers of Congress, or of the government, not appropriate in any degree (for we are not judges of the degree of appropriateness)," or else otherwise affirmatively prohibited. Where various means to accomplish a legitimate end are available, it is for Congress to make the choice: the degree of appropriateness and the judgment of what means are best are not judicial functions.[33]

Moreover, Strong argued, the boundary lines of constitutionality are far broader than suggested in *Hepburn*. Weaving together quotations from three great Marshall Court opinions—*McCulloch*, *Cohens*, and *Martin v. Hunters' Lessee*—Strong created an impression of precedential support for a description of legislative powers that went far beyond anything the Marshall Court ever decided. The enumerated powers were "but part of a system, a constituent of one whole" greater than the sum of its parts. The implied powers, said Strong, "reach beyond the mere execution of all powers definitely intrusted to Congress and mentioned in detail," and did not have

---

* The opinion is sometimes known by the caption of the lead case, *Knox v. Lee*, but subsequent Supreme Court opinions and legal treatises more commonly cite the case as the *Legal Tender Cases*, and I will follow that convention here.

to be connected to any specific enumerated power. Rather, the existence of an implied power "may be deduced fairly from more than one of the substantive powers expressly defined, or from them all combined. It is allowable to group together any number of them" to infer an implied power. In addition to powers implied by reading "an aggregate" of express powers together, Strong recognized that the Constitution creates unenumerated powers inherent in the nature of sovereignty, and suggested further that implied powers are those which serve and execute the purposes stated in the Preamble—the argument made by Pinkney in *McCulloch,* which Marshall steered clear of. [34]

To Strong, treating the enumerated powers as an exhaustive list made no logical sense and had not been followed in practice. Thus, for example, the express power to punish certain crimes (counterfeiting, piracy, treason) "was not regarded as an objection to deducing authority to punish other crimes from another substantive and defined grant of power." The argument that the power to "coin" money impliedly excluded the power to issue paper money as legal tender, Strong pointed out, left unexplained where Congress gets the power to make money of any kind a legal tender—including gold or silver coin. Strong was correct: no express legal tender power is conferred on Congress.[35] The Coinage Clause argument against legal tender paper money assumes that an *implied* power to make coins a legal tender excludes an implied power to make paper money a legal tender. "That argument," as legal scholar James Bradley Thayer would later put it, "is not a strong one."[36]

Justice Strong concluded with a capable Constitution argument. Given the Constitution's denial of money-issuing powers to the states, "[i]f the power to declare what is money is not in Congress, it is annihilated." But where the Constitution intends to "extinguish" "powers that usually belong to sovereignties," like the power to define its national currency, it does so expressly. Here, Strong echoed Hamilton's memorandum to Washington in support of the first Bank of the United States: implied sovereign powers are not withheld by implication.[37] At the same time, Strong anticipated Franklin Roosevelt's 1937 attack on the Court for creating a regulatory "no mans land" in which neither the states nor the federal government was capable of acting.

Having recognized these sovereign powers over the regulation of money, Strong easily brushed aside the *Hepburn* majority's claims that the Legal Tender Act violates some "spirit" of the constitution that protects creditors' contractual expectations. All property "in a state of civil society" is held "subject to the lawful demands of the sovereign," so that contracts cannot "defeat . . . legitimate government authority." The due process clause "has never been supposed" to apply to "laws that indirectly work harm and loss to individuals." These "spirit" arguments prove too much, because they would invalidate numerous acts of acknowledged governmental power. Incorporating but expanding on the examples in Miller's *Hepburn* dissent, Strong pointed out that Congress's reduction of the gold content of U.S. dollars had adversely affected creditors without raising any constitutional objections. It made no difference that some or even most of these acts of Congress diminishing contract expectancies were authorized by express rather than implied powers: there was "no warrant in the Constitution" to deem implied powers as weaker, or as more subject to affirmative constitutional prohibitions, than express ones.[38]

Justice Bradley concurred, boiling down his view of the controlling nationalism principles to two related points. First, he deemed it "a self-evident proposition" that the federal government was "invested with all those inherent and implied powers which, at the time of adopting the Constitution, were generally considered to belong to every government as such, and as being essential to the exercise of its functions." Second, Bradley deemed it "the prerogative of every government" to issue paper money on the credit of its anticipated revenues, unless there was an express constitutional prohibition. "Whether those issues shall or shall not be receivable in payment of private debts is an incidental matter in the discretion of such government unless restrained by constitutional prohibition." For his first and only time, Bradley paid homage to *McCulloch*'s discussion of implied powers: "A parade of authorities would serve but little purpose after Chief Justice Marshall's profound discussion of the powers of Congress in the great case of *McCulloch*. . . ." [39]

Four dissenting justices produced three opinions. Chase insisted that *Hepburn* had correctly followed "the rule" of *McCulloch*, that deciding whether a law is necessary and proper was "a judicial question."[40] All three dissents now argued that the words "coin money" in the coinage clause placed unwritten restrictions on Congress's currency powers. But this argument hardly fit *McCulloch*'s assertion that enumerated powers be given a "fair" rather than "strict" construction that would allow Congress to fulfill the national government's "great objects." Moreover, Marshall would have been loath to constitutionalize a highly contested substantive policy, such as the "hard money" policy advocated by the dissenters.[41]

While the *Legal Tender Cases*' majority interpretation of *McCulloch* was a far more faithful reading than *Hepburn*'s, Strong's broad claims of implied powers find only partial support in the language of *McCulloch*. Chase was undoubtedly correct in observing, in his dissent, that many of the ideas in the majority opinion were "advanced for the first time . . . in this court."[42] The *Legal Tender Cases*' assertion that the legislative powers of Congress were *not* limited to those enumerated was clearly stated for the first time. That doesn't make the assertion wrong, of course, but it would not be soon repeated.

Finally, the *Legal Tender Cases* contained elements that could limit its future application. It is unclear to what extent the majority justices were all on board with the entirety of Strong's analysis. Majority opinions in the Chase Court were not circulated among the justices for close editorial comment before issuance, and Strong's opinion included telltale passages that backtracked from some of his more sweeping claims. Strong "concede[d] that Congress is not authorized to enact laws in furtherance even of a legitimate end, merely because they are useful, or because they make the government stronger"—whatever that means. He ultimately rested the Legal Tender Act's necessity on the wartime emergency.[43] Most importantly, by emphasizing the lack of a state power over currency, the *Legal Tender Cases* refrained from reversing the Taney Court's principle that reserved state powers can block implied federal powers. The full potential of the *Legal Tender Cases* would not be realized for many decades.

* * *

Antebellum federalism had a strongly territorial quality. The states' "police power" over their "internal" affairs was thought to give states largely exclusive jurisdiction over most matters within the state's terrestrial borders. Marshall's suggestion in *Gibbons* that interstate commerce could reach into the state's interior may well have been consistent with this idea: federal authority could enter the states only abstractly, through trade goods, and concretely on navigable waterways. Significantly, most of the latter tended to skirt state borders. The resistance to internal improvements in the antebellum period was focused largely on the land and the interior, and the Marshall Court did not challenge that. Indeed, as late as 1871, in *The Daniel Ball*, the Chase Court noted this distinction, asserting that a case involving "transportation on the navigable waters of the United States" did not require deciding congressional power "over interstate commerce when carried on by land transportation."[44] To draw a protective cordon around slavery, the Taney Court had developed the idea that the reserved state powers of "police" and "self defense" could resist implied federal powers on dry land, an idea that extended to internal improvements. The resulting conception of federalism, contested by Whigs, treated the federal government almost as a sister state—a first among equals. perhaps—whose authority could enter state borders only with state consent.[45]

The "lesson" of the Civil War drawn by many constitutional commentators was that the idea of state territorial borders as a kind of bulwark against federal authority—always a controversial idea—was vanquished for good, along with the rebellion. This post-Reconstruction northern consensus was frequently expressed, and is well illustrated by an 1889 constitutional law treatise:

> the Civil War awakened the American people to a sense that their national existence was endangered by the laxity with which the Constitution was construed and administered, and that it could not be preserved without a vigorous exercise of the authority vested in the President and Congress. Above all, they were made to feel that the United States are a government of and for the people, acting directly on them, and having a paramount claim to their allegiance which may be enforced by arms as well as laws. The existence of such a right and duty is plainly written in the Constitution. Though long questioned in some quarters, it was vindicated by Hamilton

and Webster with unanswerable logic, and finally put at issue in the Civil War, and decided in favor of the United States.[46]

After the Civil War, the Supreme Court consistently decided cases in accordance with this consensus in areas regarding national territorial sovereignty: eminent domain, internal improvements, immigration law, and the capacity of federal law to reach the territorial interior of the states and bind all citizens. These cases raised *McCulloch*'s core issues of implied powers and the relation of the national government to "the people," yet *McCulloch* had scant perceptible influence on the Court's decisions.

A forerunner to this line of cases, *Crandall v. Nevada* (1868),[47] unanimously struck down a Nevada tax of $1 imposed on every person leaving the state, whether a resident or passer-through. "The people of these United States constitute one nation," the Court declared. As modern constitutional law scholar Charles Black observed, *Crandall* was thematically akin to *McCulloch* as an important case about the structure of the national Union.[48] Yet the justices passed over the opportunity to discuss *McCulloch* as a nationalism case in support of a right of citizens to travel freely throughout the states. Instead, *Crandall* cited *McCulloch* as "the leading case" on "the question of the taxing power of the States, as its exercise has affected the functions of the Federal government[.]"[49]

Kohl v. United States (1876) broke new ground by upholding a federal power of eminent domain.[50] No express provision in the Constitution authorizes Congress to condemn private property, but an eight-to-one majority of the Court concluded that there was an implied power to do so. "The powers vested by the Constitution in the general government demand for their exercise the acquisition of lands in all the States," the Court reasoned, and Congress couldn't be held hostage to private or state noncooperation. Moreover, the national government "is as sovereign within its sphere as the States are within theirs," and thus could use eminent domain as a means to executing its powers as much as states could. *McCulloch* could have offered an apt precedent for an implied power of eminent domain, since the latter was "convenient" and "conducive" to executing several enumerated powers. Moreover, *McCulloch* had emphatically disclaimed any intention in the Constitution "to create a dependence of the government of the Union on those of the States" for executing its powers. The *Kohl* opinion makes both of these points, but does not rely on *McCulloch*, instead citing assorted treatises and Taney's opinion in *Ableman v. Booth*.[51]

Claflin v. Houseman (1876) considered "the structure and true relations of the Federal and State governments" in order to hold that state courts had concurrent jurisdiction with federal courts over then-existing federal bankruptcy law.[52] Justice Bradley wrote for a unanimous court, "The laws of the United States are laws in the several States, and just as much binding on the citizens and courts thereof as the State laws are. The United States is not a foreign sovereignty as regards the several States, but is a concurrent, and, within its jurisdiction, paramount sovereignty."[53]

This language succinctly rejected Taney-era comparisons of the U.S. government to a sister state. *Claflin* thus broke down the territorialist approach to federalism, and powerfully reaffirmed the nationalist, anti-compact theory articulated in *McCulloch*. But it made no reference to *McCulloch*.

Kohl and *Claflin* implied that federal legislative jurisdiction was not hindered, let alone stopped, at state borders, and this view was emphatically asserted in the next few years in relation to internal improvements. *Pensacola Telegraph Co. v. Western Union Telegraph Co.* (1878)[54] was a striking analog to *Gibbons v. Ogden*, with telegraphs substituting for steamboats, and was decided the same way. The Court rejected a telegraph company's attempt to enforce its state-granted monopoly privileges against a competitor that was acting under a federal statute. The commerce and postal powers gave Congress an implied power to nullify state laws that would impede the interstate communications network. The Court asserted that when acting within the scope of these powers, the U.S. government "operates upon every foot of territory under its jurisdiction. . . . . Its peculiar duty is to protect one part of the country from encroachments by another upon the national rights which belong to all."[55] In *Ex parte Siebold* (1880), the Court offered a similar but more abstract version of this point, upholding federal criminal convictions of three local election officials for stuffing the ballot box in a congressional election.[56] Justice Bradley rejected the Taney-era argument that "the preservation of peace and good order," were reserved state police powers that could turn aside an implied federal power. "Here again we are met with the theory that the government of the United States does not rest upon the soil and territory of the country," Bradley observed, dismissively. "We hold it to be an incontrovertible principle, that the government of the United States may, by means of physical force, exercised through its official agents, execute on every foot of American soil the powers and functions that belong to it."[57]

The repeated assertion that the federal government had authority, within the scope of its powers, over "every foot of American soil," set the stage for a final, definitive ruling on the constitutionality of internal improvements. The antebellum compromise struck by President Monroe and followed more or less by his Democratic successors, maintained that the federal government could spend on internal improvements so long as the states retained jurisdiction over the thing built. In this worldview, roads in particular raised states'-rights concerns, since they went over land through the states, in contrast to navigable waters, which tended to skirt state boundaries. Even the Civil War Congress had balked at authorizing railroad companies to build lines through states.[58] But after the war, Congress granted the Central Pacific Railroad a franchise to build its rail line through California to Utah, where its linkup with the Union Pacific line completed the transcontinental railroad marked by the famous "Golden Spike" ceremony in 1869. In *California v. Central Pac. R. Co.* (1888),[59] the Court squarely upheld the power of Congress over land-based internal improvements. Rejecting California's argument that Congress lacked the power to grant the franchise to the Central Pacific within a state's borders, Justice Bradley proclaimed that "[t]he power to construct, or to authorize individuals or corporations to construct, national highways and bridges from State to State, is essential to the complete control and regulation of interstate commerce." The power "to establish ways of communication by land" such as "highways and bridges" was "one of the most important adjuncts" of commerce regulation. Any lingering constitutional doubts had to give way. "[I]n consequence of the expansion of the country" and the development of railroads, "a sounder consideration of the subject has prevailed and led to the conclusion that Congress has plenary power over the whole subject."[60] As historian Charles Warren observed, it was this "striking" language that "settled the great question of Internal Improvements, which, since the early years of the Nation, had been a topic of such sharp political division."[61]

Equally striking was Bradley's failure to rely on *McCulloch*'s conception of implied powers as the basis for this argument. Bradley came close to saying, but ultimately avoided saying, that internal improvements came within implied commerce powers. Instead, they were "essential to the complete control and regulation of interstate commerce." The omission of *McCulloch* here is all the more noteworthy, because the case so closely paralleled *McCulloch*. The state of California argued that the federal franchise to the railroad corporation exceeded Congress's enumerated powers; this was a predicate to California's right to collect state and county taxes on the railroad's property. Central Pacific claimed partial exemption from state taxation, for the value of its federal franchise and federally-granted rights of way. On that latter question, the Court did indeed rely on *McCulloch*: the federal franchises and rights were operations, rather than property, and immune from state taxation. It would seem that Justice Bradley and perhaps the majority of his colleagues viewed *McCulloch*, not as the leading case on constitutional nationalism and the implied powers of Congress, but as the leading case about intergovernmental tax immunity.

* * *

The post–Civil War Supreme Court recognized deep federal inroads into reserved state powers while confining them to narrow breadth. Thus, with the exception of the internal improvements cases described earlier, the Court continued to apply narrow constructions of the federal commerce power to protect reserved state powers. In *United States v. DeWitt* (1869),[62] the Court summarily rejected the government's argument that it possessed an implied power under the Commerce and Taxing clauses to regulate the storage of highly inflammable petroleum-based lighting oils. The government brief cited *McCulloch*; Chase's opinion for the Court did not.[63] In the *Trade-Mark Cases* (1879), the Court struck down the first federal trademark statute.[64] Rejecting the argument that the commerce power authorized Congress to protect interstate and foreign commerce from fraudulent use of trademarks, the Court declared that trademarks were a property right that must "rest on the laws of the States, and, like the great body of the rights of person and of property, depend on them for security." That a type of property "is the subject of commerce, or . . . is used or even essential in commerce," does not bring it "within the control of Congress" under the Commerce Clause.[65] Neither the Court nor the government cited *McCulloch* or considered an implied commerce power to regulate trademarks. And in *Kidd v. Pearson* (1888),[66] the Court upheld an Iowa law prohibiting in-state distillers from producing intoxicating liquors, even for sale on the interstate market. Applying principles unchanged from the Taney Court four decades earlier, the Court reaffirmed that the states' police powers "to provide for the safety and welfare of its people" "are not considered as an exercise of the power to regulate [interstate or foreign] commerce" and "not surrendered to the general government."[67]

* * *

As quickly as *McCulloch* appeared in the *Hepburn/Legal Tender Cases* episode, it fell out of view in Supreme Court jurisprudence. Why would the Court avoid embracing *McCulloch* and implied commerce powers in cases like *Pensacola Telegraph* and *Central Pacific*, where it resoundingly endorsed a federal power over internal improvements—a key element of nineteenth-century nationalism? We have seen this pattern before. As in *Gibbons*, where the Court was asked to extend the commerce power to include navigation, the Court in *Pensacola Telegraph* and *Central Pacific* was asked to extend the Commerce Clause to overland transportation and communications. Each time, the Court declined to treat the question as one of implied commerce powers or cite *McCulloch*, suggesting instead that the question involved the *definition* of interstate commerce as an enumerated power. The nationalism side of post–Civil War nationalism might have benefited from developing *McCulloch* as a precedent, but as we saw in the Chapter 7, confining the Reconstruction Amendments' enforcement powers required disregard of *McCulloch's* theory of implied powers. The Court seemed to want to confine *McCulloch* to taxation, banking, and currency matters. The decision in the *Legal Tender Cases* was a watershed in the history of implied powers, and was recognized as such at the time by many commentators. Yet the Supreme Court over the ensuing decade and a half seemed unwilling to follow through on its full implications.

9

"The Painful Duty of This Tribunal"

The Emergence of Judicial Supremacy, 1884–1901

Up to this point in the Supreme Court's history, *McCulloch* still did not appear destined to become a canonical case. The Court had yet to recognize it as a significant national powers precedent in any case that did not involve taxation, currency, or a national bank. This was about to change. But changes of any kind do not typically occur in causal or chronological straight lines. The emergence of *McCulloch* as a foundational case of constitutional law owed to several factors, each coming together on its own separate timeline, converging on the years 1895 to 1901.These factors included the personal interest in John Marshall's jurisprudence held by Supreme Court justices Harlan and Gray; the emergence of law as an autonomous profession; the related transition from the Grand Style to a common-law style in constitutional opinion writing; the publication of Harvard Professor James Bradley Thayer's first-ever constitutional law casebook; and the conservative reaction of the judiciary and legal elites to the Populist movement.

* * *

The Supreme Court appointments of John Marshall Harlan and Horace Gray were a key element in *McCulloch*'s path to canonization. Prior to 1884, the Court still largely adhered to the Grand Style in constitutional opinion-writing. The use of precedents was ever increasing, largely because there were simply more of them, but justices of the old school tended to construe precedents narrowly. For example, Justice Samuel Miller, who served on the Court from 1862 to 1890, called *McCulloch* "the most exhaustive discussion of [the Necessary and Proper] clause"[1] in his *Hepburn* dissent, yet he did not cite *McCulloch* as authority for implied powers in cases outside the banking and currency field. In Ex parte *Yarbrough* (1884), for example, he upheld an implied federal power to criminalize race-based violence against black voters in federal elections, based on the "universally applied" doctrine that implied powers are as much a part of the Constitution as express ones, and are "a necessity, by reason of the inherent inability to put into words all derivative powers—a difficulty which the instrument itself recognizes" in the Necessary and Proper Clause.[2] Whatever this language might owe to John Marshall, Miller based the argument directly on the text of the Constitution, and nowhere cited *McCulloch*. In an 1888–89 law school lecture course, Miller praised *McCulloch* as "one of the ablest of the opinions delivered by Chief Justice Marshall," that has "often been referred to and followed in subsequent cases." But he presented the case only as one leading example of implied powers, not as the doctrine itself, and he ultimately described *McCulloch's* contribution to constitutional law as empowering the government "to create a national currency" and "to provide for a national banking system."[3]

From its issuance in 1819 until 1883, *McCulloch* had been prominently cited in only one majority opinion in support of an assertion of congressional power—the *Legal Tender Cases*. But in the eleven years from the *Civil Rights Cases* in 1883 until the end of 1894, *McCulloch* would be cited as authority in support of an implied federal power in six majority opinions—all authored by either Gray or Harlan. Harlan also cited *McCulloch* in key dissents.[4]

Although they served together for over twenty years—Gray sat on the court from 1881 to 1902, and Harlan from 1877 until his death in 1911—the two were not personally close, and were as different as judicial colleagues could be. Harlan, a Kentucky lawyer and politician, began his career as a pro-slavery Democrat but evolved into an antislavery Republican following his Civil War service in the Union army. Gray, a Boston Brahmin and graduate of Harvard College and Harvard Law School, had sat on the Supreme Judicial Court of Massachusetts for eighteen years, the last nine of them as chief justice, before his appointment to the Supreme Court by President Chester Arthur. Oliver Wendell Holmes Jr., who succeeded Gray on the U.S. Supreme Court, later expressed disdain for their mutual colleague Harlan, saying that Harlan's "mind was like a powerful vise the jaws of which couldn't be got nearer than two inches to each other."[5] It is likely that Gray, known for a cold and highly formal demeanor, shared Holmes's opinion of the folksy Harlan.[6] In cases where the justices divided along conservative/progressive lines, Harlan usually took the progressive side and Gray the conservative. Harlan was plain spoken, direct, and not scholarly; Gray was deemed at the time as holding the "scholar's seat" on the Court. But Gray has left little impression on legal historians, and his jurisprudence has been regarded as pedestrian and forgettable. In contrast, Harlan is well remembered, and even lionized as the "Great Dissenter," most notably for his dissents in the *Civil Rights Cases* and *Plessy v. Ferguson*. While there are three full-length biographies of Harlan, there are none of Gray.

What the two justices had in common was a reverence for *McCulloch*. We have already seen that Harlan based his *Civil Rights Cases* dissent in large part on *McCulloch's* principle of deferring to congressional judgments of the appropriateness of legislation. For Gray, *McCulloch* seemed to stand for implied powers of national sovereignty. Both justices may have had a more personal sense of connection to Marshall's jurisprudence. When Harlan was born in Kentucky in 1833, Marshall was still alive and the Marshall family was still highly influential in the state. Harlan was named after John Marshall because his father "was an ardent admirer of John Marshall, and held to the views of constitutional construction which that great jurist embodied in [his] opinions."[7] After spending two years at a small liberal arts college in Kentucky, Harlan studied law at Transylvania College in Lexington, where one of his favorite instructors was Thomas A. Marshall, a cousin and protégé of John Marshall himself.[8]

Gray attended Harvard Law School in 1848, just two years after the death of Justice Story, who had greatly shaped the Harvard Law curriculum. Gray would almost certainly have studied Story's *Commentaries on the Constitution* as his assigned constitutional law text, and he likely absorbed some of Story's reverence for Marshall and *McCulloch*. From early in his legal career, Gray embraced an approach to legal analysis that relied heavily on case law. As reporter for the Massachusetts Supreme Judicial Court from 1854 through 1864, Gray supplemented the case reports with treatise-like digests that were "veritable textbooks," and he wrote a handful of legal historical articles. By the time of his appointment to the U.S. Supreme Court, Gray had a reputation as a scholarly judge with a penchant for legal research. As one of his eulogists put it, Gray "believed that an exhaustive collection of authorities should be the foundation of every judicial opinion on an important question."[9] To assist him in this task, Gray created the position of the judicial law clerk. As chief justice of Massachusetts, and subsequently as U.S. Supreme Court justice, Gray hired a top Harvard Law student each year as his "personal secretary," to serve as research assistant and intellectual sounding board, somewhat as judicial law clerks are used today. The students were handpicked by his half-brother, Harvard Law Professor John Chipman Gray, and one of his earliest clerks was Louis D. Brandeis, in 1875.[10]

* * *

McCulloch's revival in the Supreme Court began with Gray's majority opinion in *Julliard v. Greenman* (1884),[11] the third and final decision on the constitutionality of legal tender laws. A creditor refusing a tender of greenbacks challenged an 1878 act of Congress "to forbid the further retirement of United States legal tender notes."[12] The purpose of this act was in effect to extend greenbacks into peacetime on an indefinite basis. Since the *Legal Tender Cases* had upheld a wartime legal tender act, the argument was at least available that such a measure was not constitutional in the absence of a war emergency. All six justices appointed to the Court since 1871 joined Bradley and Miller, the two remaining justices from the *Legal Tender Cases* majority, to uphold the law; Field, who had dissented in 1871 was the sole dissenter now.

As a matter of strict legal doctrine, *Julliard* was essentially a rehash. All nine justices agreed that the case "cannot be distinguished in principle" from the *Legal*

Tender Cases. Reprising Strong's 1871 opinion, Gray mingled ideas of inherent sovereign power and implied powers from constitutional clauses read in the aggregate. As in the *Legal Tender Cases,* Gray insisted that *McCulloch's* "rule of interpretation . . . has been constantly adhered to and acted on by this court"—not true—and added, "No question of the scope and extent of the implied powers of Congress under the Constitution can be satisfactorily discussed without repeating much of the reasoning of Chief Justice Marshall in the great judgment in *McCulloch v. Maryland.*" Gray summarized *McCulloch* as teaching that "a constitution . . . is not to be interpreted with the strictness of a private contract," and added: "Chief Justice Marshall, after dwelling upon this view, as required by the very nature of the Constitution . . . added these emphatic words: 'In considering the question, then, we must never forget that *it is a constitution* we are *expounding.*'"[13] This was the first of many occasions in which the Court would quote the phrase that Felix Frankfurter would later call "the single most important utterance in the literature of constitutional law."[14]

Beyond its extension of the *Legal Tender Cases* into the peacetime context, Gray's opinion marked an important transition from the Grand Style to a common-law style in constitutional adjudication. The idea that constitutional interpretation is an edifice built up by the accretion of incremental decisions—that it is a judicial construction following the method of the common law—was clearly demonstrated in *Julliard's* conclusion that a legal tender power is an incremental step beyond Congress's "undoubted" implied power to issue a uniform national currency. Rather than deriving it exclusively from constitutional provisions, Gray argued that it arose out of a series of Marshall, Taney, and Chase Court opinions, from *McCulloch* to *Veazie Bank,* on matters of banking and currency.[15]

Gray made an additional move that is far more consistent with Supreme Court opinions of 130 years later than with its opinions of just fifteen years earlier. Parsing Marshall's opinions in *Craig v. Missouri*[16] and *Sturges v. Crowninshield,*[17] Gray concluded that "Chief Justice Marshall spoke very guardedly" about a legal tender power and that Marshall's decisions "contain nothing adverse to the power of Congress to issue legal tender notes." Gray then cited to records of the debates of the Constitutional Convention in an effort to uncover the Constitution's original meaning. While acknowledging that numerous Framers expressed opposition to a power to issue paper money as legal tender, others wished to preserve such a power, and the final text of the Constitution omitted an express prohibition. Thus, Gray concluded, "such reports as have come down to us of the debates in the Convention that framed the Constitution afford no proof of any general concurrence of opinion upon the subject before us."[18]

Why raise an inconclusive argument about the Constitutional Convention? Before *Julliard,* it was not customary to discuss original intent for purposes of showing it to be inconclusive. And why bring up Marshall Court opinions that were plainly not controlling? *Craig* had held that *state* treasury notes could not be legal tender, and *Sturges* dealt with the constitutionality of state bankruptcy laws. No one could or did argue that those cases were controlling precedents on the legal tender question.

In doing these things, Gray's *Julliard* opinion anticipated the analytical and rhetorical techniques used in modern judicial review. The Grand Style of constitutional analysis emphasized the language of the Constitution and its interpretation by congressional and executive branch precedents. The common-law style, in contrast, would emphasize *judicial* interpretation of both the Constitution's language and of the Court's own prior precedent. The Court would increasingly consider itself free to derive constitutional meaning without the mediating influence of past interpretations by the political branches, which could almost always be shown to be inconclusive. And unadorned interpretations of bare constitutional language would not suffice, for two reasons. First, the ability of a judge to read and understand a clause in the Constitution according to its plain English meaning is not necessarily superior to that of an elected official or even an ordinary citizen; the reference to printed authorities under the rubric of "legal research" would convert the interpretive enterprise into a matter of expertise. Second, reliance on the Framers' intent, or at least a good-faith effort to discern that intent even if it ultimately proved inconclusive, would demonstrate that the judges were relying on objective authority rather than their own subjectivity.

Gray's discussion of Marshall, too, differed from prior Court decisions, which tended to construe precedents narrowly. By treating *Sturges* and *Craig* as legal texts worthy of extended explanation, rather than dismissing them out of hand or ignoring them entirely, Gray's opinion suggested that the Court's *explanations* of its decisions, and not just case outcomes, *are constitutional law*. The interpretive techniques applied to constitutional text might now be extended to Supreme Court opinions. Only a few words of the Constitution are interpreted in a given constitutional case. But Gray's opinion in *Julliard* was 5,700 words. Roger Taney's opinion in *Dred Scott* was over 25,000 words. The invitation to mine these extensive documents for formulations of binding doctrine would make the meanings and intentions of judicial opinion writers an important source of legal argument.

But Gray's opinion also implied that not all constitutional cases are equal in authority. Marshall's opinions were worthy of mining for intentions, and Gray's placement of them *before* those of the Constitutional Convention subtly suggests that Marshall was himself a founder whose intentions are at least as important as those of the Constitution's Framers. This treatment of Marshall was a distinct departure from prior cases. Previously, Marshall's opinions were important when they were precisely on point. Here, Gray was essentially asking, "WWJMD?" ("What would John Marshall do?") Gray thus signaled, for the first time in a Supreme Court opinion, that the *spirit of Marshall Court opinions* is a significant element of constitutional interpretation.

* * *

Julliard's introduction of the modern common-law method in constitutional cases did not spring fully formed from Justice Gray's not terribly creative mind. Rather, it was part of a broader emergence of law as an autonomous "learned profession," a trend that had important consequences for the role of *McCulloch* in constitutional law.

The antebellum legal profession had been loosely regulated. Typically, lawyers were admitted to practice after a judge determined that the applicant possessed the rudiments of legal knowledge, based on a casual oral examination. There were no educational requirements, and few opportunities to obtain a formal legal education. Instead, most aspiring lawyers combined self-study with apprenticeship in a law office. The few university programs of legal study, such as at William & Mary or Harvard, had minimal entrance requirements and conferred no degrees. They had no established terms or courses of study: students essentially sat in on ongoing lecture series, beginning or ending their enrollment when they chose, for anywhere from a few months to a year or two. No exams or grades were given. Law teaching was a sidelight of active or retired judges or lawyers. Some instructors were distinguished jurists, like George Wythe at William and Mary or Joseph Story at Harvard, and these would often polish their lecture notes for publication as treatises, but there was no recognizable "legal academy" of full-time professors.[19]

All this began to change after the Civil War. In 1870, Harvard President Charles Eliot hired Christopher Columbus Langdell as Dean of the Harvard Law School. Eliot wanted to modernize Harvard by embracing the model of the German university, in which faculty produced scholarly research in their teaching fields. With Eliot's backing, Langdell embarked on an ambitious program to remake Harvard Law School along lines that eventually defined the modern law school. Prospective students would need to have a bachelor's degree and pass an entrance examination. They would then follow a set three-year course of classroom study, take exams, and receive grades. A degree would be conferred at the end. Full-time law professors would teach the courses and publish scholarship.[20]

The teaching method also changed. Traditionally, instructors taught by narrating digested legal principles in the expository style of legal treatises, and indeed they would often simply read aloud from a treatise, perhaps calling on students to recite rote passages. Langdell introduced the "case system" or "case method," in which each class hour would focus on post-mortem analysis of one or a few appellate decisions. The preferred style to deliver this material was the "Socratic method," in which professors interactively questioned students to supplement or entirely replace lectures. Compared to the stupefying boredom of hearing an instructor read aloud from a treatise, the case/Socratic method seemed like an exciting innovation. It brought forward some of the human conflict and drama underlying a lawsuit, and it generated potentially engaging, and certainly anxiety-producing, interactions between professor and student. [21]

By 1901, these innovations were well established at Harvard and were being actively imitated at the growing number of law schools nationwide.[22] And they played a significant role in the story of *McCulloch*'s climb to canonical status, for three overlapping reasons. First, the Harvard system institutionalized the pathway to elite employment and status for new lawyers after the 1870s, and raised the self-esteem of the bar as a prestigious, autonomous institution. The rigorous educational requirements reinforced the idea that law was a subject of professional expertise, inaccessible to the layman. The addition of constitutional law to the legal curriculum conveyed the idea that the Constitution was the special province of legal experts rather than a document to be read and interpreted by all. Second, the case method taught new generations of elite lawyers that the primary materials of legal interpretation and analysis were appellate court decisions, rather than statutes or, in the case of constitutional law, the text of the Constitution. And third, the creation of a legal academy of full-time faculty gave increasing influence to the scholarly work of law professors. Their thinking about law would naturally be influenced by the case method they practiced in the classroom, with the result that the parsing of appellate opinions would become a primary focus of their scholarship. The German university model placed primacy on "scientific" approaches to scholarship. "Social science" emerged as a field of inquiry contemporaneously with Langdell's reforms, and indeed several modern law schools began as university political science departments. Langdell and his followers promoted the idea that law was a science whose observable data consisted of appellate decisions; as with other scientific observations, general principles could be abstracted from these data. While Langdell did not invent this concept, his law school reforms certainly reinforced the idea that appellate decisions implied broad general principles that extended beyond their factual context.[23]

The modern interpretive approach would in time liberate *McCulloch* from its fact-bound context of banking and currency, but the two or three decades after Langdell launched the Harvard system were a transitional period in this trend. Established legal writers in the 1870s and 1880s had come to professional maturity under the older system, in which the Grand Style dominated judicial opinions on constitutional law. The idea that cases should be understood as conveying broad general principles rather than more specific results was emerging, but not dominant. *McCulloch*, for instance, might be understood to be a precedent for chartering a bank, or more generally a federal corporation; pushing it further, it could be understood as giving Congress an implied power to regulate the banking system or a national currency. But applying *McCulloch* to other implied-powers contexts, such as in internal improvements, required an additional level of abstraction and generalization.

Nineteenth-century constitutional-law treatise writers held a spectrum of views about the importance and meaning of *McCulloch*. Story's *Commentaries* remained highly influential and frequently cited in Supreme Court cases throughout the nineteenth century. It went through two postwar editions, a fourth in 1873, and a fifth and last in 1891. Given his admiration for Marshall and his participation in deciding the case, Story naturally placed great significance on *McCulloch*, citing it frequently throughout the treatise. As we have seen, Story's summary of *McCulloch* was often cited as a stand-in for *McCulloch* itself. While still sitting on the Supreme Court, Story taught constitutional law at Harvard Law School from 1829 until his death in 1845, using his treatise as a teaching text.[24] Undoubtedly, the exposure of sixteen years of Harvard Law students to Story and his treatise amplified *McCulloch*'s influence.

John Norton Pomeroy, the dean of the New York University Law School in the late 1860s and an influential treatise writer, published *An Introduction to Constitutional Law of the United States* in 1868. Plainly nationalist in his constitutional leanings, Pomeroy was one of a handful of treatise writers to identify *McCulloch* as an important landmark of implied federal powers. Pomeroy discussed *McCulloch* prominently to demonstrate his fanciful claim that the Supreme Court had "steadily adher[ed]" to a "liberal" rather than "strict" interpretation of the Constitution.[25] The treatise, written as a text for law students, went through ten editions by 1888.

Other treatise writers were less impressed with *McCulloch*'s importance. James Kent admired Marshall, but did not view judicial decisions as constitutional law itself, instead contending that the Constitution "furnishes essentially the means of its own interpretation. . . ."[26] Despite paraphrasing *McCulloch* at length as a leading example of implied powers, Kent was less than reverential, observing that the Marshall Court "thought" the implied-powers question "worthy of a renewed discussion" despite its having "been settled" by the two National Bank statutes in 1791 and 1816.[27] Kent's *Commentaries* went through numerous editions after his lifetime, and his posthumous editors retained his original text, reserving case updates and editors' commentary for the footnotes. Neither Kent nor any of his successive editors ever cited *McCulloch* as authority for internal improvements or any implied powers other than creation of the bank.[28] Oliver Wendell Holmes, Jr., editing the twelfth edition in 1873, kept the spirit of Kent's underwhelming appraisal of *McCulloch*. Holmes's editorial footnote identified the *Legal Tender Cases*, not *McCulloch*, as "the most important discussion of the implied powers of Congress that has ever taken place."[29]

The most influential constitutional-law treatise writer in the post–Civil War era, Thomas M. Cooley, was similarly unimpressed with *McCulloch*, despite the fact the he edited the fourth edition of Story's *Commentaries* in 1873.[30] In his renowned 1868 treatise *Constitutional Limitations*, Cooley reduced *McCulloch* to an unimportant "see also" citation in his discussion of implied powers.[31] In his 1880 law student textbook, *Principles of Constitutional Law*, Cooley joined Holmes in suggesting that the *Legal Tender Cases* were the leading judicial exposition of implied powers, and he played down the influence of *McCulloch*'s rejection of compact theory, stressing instead the importance of constitutional politics outside the courts.[32] Several other treatises, no longer well remembered but influential in their day, also gave *McCulloch* short shrift.[33]

McCulloch was beginning to be noticed in academic monographs about American institutions. In his *Congressional Government* (1885), political scientist Woodrow Wilson wrote a lengthy paean to "that puissant doctrine of the 'implied powers' of the Constitution which has ever since been the chief dynamic principle in our constitutional history." Implied powers "quickly constituted Congress the dominant, nay, the irresistible, power of the federal system," accounting for national growth. Wilson attributed the doctrine to Hamilton, but went on to say that it received "[i]ts final and most masterly exposition" in *McCulloch*.[34] Given his congressional dominance thesis, some hyperbole on this point is not surprising.

McCulloch's treatment in the legal academy remained decidedly mixed until the publication of Harvard law professor James Bradley Thayer's *Cases on Constitutional Law*, published in 1894 and 1895. Hired as Royall Professor at Harvard Law School in 1874, Thayer was probably the nation's most influential legal academic in constitutional law by the time of his death in 1902. In a 1963 reflection, Felix Frankfurter wrote that "Holmes and Brandeis influenced me in my constitutional outlook, but both of them derived theirs from the same source from which I derived mine, namely, James Bradley Thayer, with whom both had personal relations." Thayer's views "were in the air at the Law School while I was there and I undoubtedly imbibed that atmosphere."[35]

Thayer, though not prolific, made two significant written contributions as a constitutional law scholar.[36] His 1893 article *The Origin and Scope of the American Doctrine of Constitutional Law* has been called "the most influential essay ever written on American constitutional law."[37] The other was the *Cases*. This was the first-ever constitutional law "casebook"—that is, a Harvard "case method" textbook. Casebooks today are viewed somewhat dismissively as "mere" teaching materials, but Thayer's casebook was widely viewed as an important scholarly contribution: it was reviewed in *The Nation* and praised by such legal luminaries as Louis Brandeis.[38]

McCulloch appears prominently in Thayer's *Cases*. The third of its twelve chapters, entitled "The Jurisdiction of the United States," merges some general principles about the legislative powers of Congress with the Article III jurisdiction of the federal judiciary. Following three short excerpts about federalism, *McCulloch* is the first major case presented in the chapter. And while most other cases in the book are heavily edited—the universal practice of all casebook writers, who need to be concerned about the length of what is assigned to students—*McCulloch's* entire first section on the constitutionality of the bank is presented verbatim, all forty-six paragraphs. (The second main part of the opinion, dealing with Maryland's power to tax the bank, is split off and presented separately, in a chapter on taxation.)[39]

Thayer's *Cases* set the pattern for the dozens of constitutional law casebooks that have been published in the following 125-plus years: virtually all give *McCulloch* the same pride of place as the leading case on the powers of Congress, and most do so with far less cutting and excerpting than with other cases in the same book.[40] It is fair to assume that beginning with Thayer, generations of law students have been taught that *McCulloch* is the leading case that defines the implied powers of Congress and perhaps the proper approach to interpreting the scope of congressional power more generally.

Viewed in retrospect this seems obvious and inevitable. But it was neither to Thayer himself. In fact, the prominent placement of *McCulloch* in his casebook reflected a marked and very recent shift in Thayer's thinking about the meaning and importance of the case. As late as his spring 1893 Constitutional Law course, Thayer presented *McCulloch* to his students merely as a case about intergovernmental tax immunity, as he had done since he first taught constitutional law in 1880. In his printed syllabus for his Constitutional Law course in the 1892–93 academic year, Thayer listed *McCulloch* as case number 21 out of forty case excerpts under the heading "Taxation."[41] *McCulloch* did not appear elsewhere in the syllabus.

Thayer's relative lack of interest in *McCulloch* was also reflected in his pre-1894 scholarly work. In his 1887 *Harvard Law Review* article, *Legal Tender*, Thayer endorsed the reasoning of the *Legal Tender Cases* and *Julliard v. Greenman*. He refuted the argument, repeated by Holmes in an 1873 article, that an implied power from the Coinage Clause to make gold a legal tender impliedly deprived Congress of the power to make paper a legal tender. Thayer discussed numerous authorities, including Daniel Webster, Adam Smith, and Aristotle; Supreme Court Justices Strong, Bradley, Chase, and Bushrod Washington; and Marshall's obscure early implied-powers decision, *United States v. Fisher*. But he did not discuss, or even cite, *McCulloch*.[42] In his 1893 article, *Origin and Scope*, Thayer had still not fully discovered *McCulloch*. There, Thayer advocated congressional discretion to choose legislative means, and argued that laws should not be struck down unless their unconstitutionality is beyond reasonable doubt. Although *McCulloch* supports both these points, Thayer did not develop the connection at all. He quoted "it is a constitution we are expounding," but without attribution, as if he didn't know the source.[43]

But by 1894, in compiling his *Cases on Constitutional Law*, Thayer was a convert. The reasons for his change in thinking are unclear, though it is worth noting that Thayer's son, Ezra, served as law clerk to the Supreme Court's great *McCulloch* booster, Justice Gray, in the 1891–92 Supreme Court term.[44] Thayer was also in occasional correspondence with Gray.[45] Thayer went on to publish a short biography of John Marshall for the 1901 John Marshall Day centennial, in which he called *McCulloch* "probably [Marshall's] greatest opinion" and added, "If we regard at once the greatness of the questions at issue in the particular case, the influence of the opinion, and the large method and clear and skillful manner in which it is worked out, there is nothing so fine as the opinion in *McCulloch*."[46] But the short biography—fewer than 30,000 words, the length of a modern-day law review article—did not offer Thayer's analysis of the opinion. Thayer was gathering material for a full-length biography of Marshall, but he died in 1902 without having made much progress on it, and without giving us a fully matured understanding of the connection between *McCulloch* and his theory of judicial restraint.[47]

***

From the point of view of contemporaries, the appointment of Morrison Waite in 1874 marked the end of nearly a century of chief justices appointed from the first rank of statesmen. From John Jay, who had led the Confederation Congress as a de facto president before becoming first chief justice, to Salmon Chase, who had served as Ohio governor and Senator, a nationally reputed leader of the abolition movement, and wartime Treasury Secretary, the first six chief justices had significant records of public service. Waite's pre-Court public service was comparatively undistinguished.[48] The legal community had lobbied for the promotion of Samuel Miller, the senior associate justice, to the chief justiceship, but President Grant was apparently inclined to follow the tradition against promoting sitting members of the Court to the post. After five nominees either declined the position or ran into decisive Senate opposition, Grant settled on the uncontroversial Waite, in hopes of ending the increasingly embarrassing search. Waite's fourteen-year tenure as chief justice was jurisprudentially no more scintillating than his pre-judicial record.[49]

Waite died in March 1888, and filling the vacancy fell to Grover Cleveland, the first Democratic president since the Civil War. Recognizing that Cleveland would want to appoint a Democrat, the justices had asked him to promote the Court's sole Democrat, Stephen Field. But Cleveland selected Melville Fuller, a minor state politician who had turned down two previous offers of federal appointments by Cleveland and whose career was even less impressive than Waite's.[50] In a condoling letter to Field, Justice Bradley wrote that the justices were "greatly disappointed in the nomination" of Fuller, who "hardly fills the public's expectation" for a chief justice.[51] The second successive appointment of an undistinguished politico to the chief justiceship must have been viewed by many as an erosion of the Court's prestige, something to be offset by celebrating chief justices of the past. The justices, including ironically Fuller himself, would refer to Marshall as "*the* Chief Justice" when invoking Marshall's canonical authority.[52]

***

McCulloch's status received a major boost from the conservative reaction of the Supreme Court and legal elites against the Populist movement of the late nineteenth century. Populism was the agrarian and labor response to rapid industrialization and overreaching by large corporate interests. The Panic of 1873 and several waves of recessions over the next twenty years put severe economic stresses on farmers and workers. Farmers were hit by tight credit and price gouging by middlemen, grain elevators, and railroads in getting their produce to market. Industrial workers suffered long work hours under unhealthy conditions and oppressive anti-union practices of employers. The number of strikes increased throughout the 1880s, often becoming violent. The common thread of these issues was their nationwide extent and their source in unregulated behavior of multi-state corporations and monopolies. Various grass-roots protest movements of the 1870s rose and declined, eventually coalescing at the start of the 1890s into the Populist movement. Populists also reached out across racial lines in the South, where the African American vote was still significantly large in the early 1890's. Various groups who shared Populist ideals formed the People's Party, whose 1892 presidential candidate won over one million votes and carried five states, while several Populists won down-ticket races for Congress and state governorships. The People's Party platform called for several legislative reforms requiring broad national powers: the remonetization of silver, nationalization of railroads and the telegraph, nationwide postal savings banks, a graduated income tax, tariff reductions, direct election of senators, and an eight-hour workday, along with immigration restrictions.[53]

Although the Populists were not the socialist, communist, and anarchist threats as they were portrayed in the conservative press, conservative legal elites began to raise dire warnings even before the movement had coalesced.[54] Archconservative lawyer Christopher Tiedeman published a widely read 1886 legal treatise "to awaken the public mind to a full appreciation of the power of constitutional limitations to protect private rights against the radical experimentations" of the "great army of discontents" calling for social reform.[55] In an 1890 address to commemorate the centennial of the Supreme Court, Stephen Field warned that increasing popular demands to regulate "the enormous aggregations of wealth possessed by some corporations" had to be met by the Supreme Court "to enforce with a firm hand every guarantee of the Constitution" to protect property. Justice David J. Brewer gave a June 1891 commencement speech to Yale graduates that was entitled, "Protection to Private Property from Public Attack." Former judge and well-known treatise writer John F. Dillon, in his 1892 address as President of the American Bar Association, called the judiciary "the only breakwater against the haste and the passions of the people—against the tumultuous ocean of democracy."[56] Answering these calls, increasingly unsympathetic courts struck down protective labor laws and issued "labor injunctions" whose effect was to subject strikers to punishment without jury trial.[57]

Matters reached a crisis point following the Panic of 1893, the most severe depression in twenty years, with 13% unemployment in the non-agricultural workforce. In late spring of 1894, the Pullman railroad-car-manufacturing workers went out on strike after the company slashed their wages by more than 25%. The strike became nationwide when the newly organized American Railway Union, led by Eugene V. Debs, decided to join it on June 26. At the direction of U.S. Attorney General Richard Olney, a former railroad attorney and executive, government lawyers obtained a court injunction against the strike, and on July 4, President

Cleveland dispatched U.S. troops to enforce it. John Peter Altgeld, the Populist governor of Illinois, opposed using force to break the strike and claimed that the federal government had no authority to send troops unless requested to do so by the state government, pursuant to the Constitution's Guaranty Clause.[58] But Cleveland, on Olney's advice, asserted authority under the Commerce Clause to send troops because the railroad strike obstructed interstate commerce. After days of violence between federal troops and strikers, Debs was arrested, and his union collapsed.[59]

In the lingering haze of this crisis atmosphere during the winter and spring of 1895, the Supreme Court issued the three fateful decisions that would have lasting effects on U.S. constitutional law and politics. *United States v. E.C. Knight Co.,*[60] *In re Debs,*[61] and *Pollock v. Farmer's Loan & Trust Co.,*[62] differed in the technicalities of their doctrine and their results. But each was an example of conservative judicial activism, bending constitutional doctrines to protect (as they saw it) private property and assert the Supreme Court's role as a bulwark against radical political movements. As legal historian Gerard Magliocca has argued, a direct connection can be drawn between these decisions and reactive fears inspired by Populism.[63] *McCulloch* figured prominently in all three cases.

Debs, issued in May 1895, considered the constitutionality of the federal government's role in putting down the Pullman strike. Eugene Debs was cited for contempt for violating the anti-strike injunction, and appealed on the ground that there was no constitutional authority to issue it. The Supreme Court emphatically disagreed: "The strong arm of the national government may be put forth to brush away all obstructions to the freedom of interstate commerce or the transportation of the mails." The Court relied on *McCulloch,* quoting at length from Marshall's constitutional nationalism language.[64]

Debs made an interesting counterpoint with the first of the three decisions, *E.C. Knight* issued in January 1895. E.C. Knight Co. was owned by the American Sugar Refining Company, a massive trust that controlled 90% of the sugar refining business in the United States. Sued by the federal government for violating the Sherman Antitrust Act, the defendants claimed that Congress had no power under the Commerce Clause to regulate manufacturing. The Court decided for the defendants. While they did not strike down the Sherman Act, they held that it could not be construed to apply to manufacturing, which would be beyond Congress's constitutional powers. Even though manufactured products might be intended for the interstate market, "[c]ommerce succeeds to manufacture, and is not a part of it." Commerce regulation, the Court affirmed, cannot regulate any intrastate matter that "affects it only incidentally and indirectly."[65] Previously, the terms "direct" and "indirect" had been used in dormant Commerce Clause cases to identify whether police powers were constitutional: police powers were not excluded by the dormant Commerce Clause unless their effect on commerce was "direct."[66] The *E.C. Knight* Court for the first time made "direct" and "indirect effects" a limitation on the affirmative scope of the commerce power, holding that all productive activities, including manufacturing, were categorically related to commerce only indirectly and therefore not subject to federal regulation.

Here, moreover, the Court reaffirmed Taney Court principles of reserved state power in service of an emergent laissez-faire jurisprudence under the name of "dual federalism." "It is vital that the independence of the commercial power and of the police power, and the delimitation between them, however sometimes perplexing, should always be recognized and observed, for while the one furnishes the strongest bond of union, the other is essential to the preservation of the autonomy of the States as required by our dual form of government." The unbridgeable distinction between interstate commerce and intrastate productive activities, which the Taney Court had emphasized to protect slavery, was still in effect: "No distinction is more popular to the common mind, or more clearly expressed in economic and political literature, than that between manufacture and commerce." Commerce was restricted to "[t]he buying and selling and the transportation incidental thereto" of manufactured goods. The intention to sell the goods in interstate markets could not bring their production under the commerce power. Otherwise, "Congress would be invested, to the exclusion of the States, with the power to regulate, not only manufactures, but also agriculture, horticulture, stock raising, domestic fisheries, mining—in short, every branch of human industry."[67]

Justice Harlan's lone dissent applied *McCulloch's* theory of implied powers. "[T]he Constitution did not define the means that may be employed" to regulate interstate commerce. "[W]hether an act of Congress, passed to accomplish an object to which the general government is competent, is within the power granted, must be determined by the rule announced through Chief Justice Marshall three-quarters of a century ago. . . ."[68] The suggestion that Congress might be able to regulate manufacturing as an implied power of commerce, despite previous decisions placing it within the reserved state powers, had never previously been made by a Supreme Court justice and would not be again for decades.

In *Pollock,* the Court struck down the first peacetime federal income tax law. Enacted in 1894, the law taxed income "derived from any kind of property, rents, interest, dividends, or salaries, or from any profession, trade, employment, or vocation."[69] The challengers to the law argued that taxes on income derived from rents, real estate, and personal property (which included investments in securities) violated an arcane provision of the Constitution, that "[n]o capitation, or other direct, tax shall be laid, unless in proportion to the census. . . ."[70] The provision was designed to base "head" taxes—those imposed on the person's existence or the value of his real estate—on population rather than wealth. Since high-population and low-wealth states would always deem themselves unfairly taxed, their congressional representatives could be counted on to band together to defeat such taxes—perhaps that was the point. Because an income tax would be proportional to income, not population, it would be impermissible if it came within this clause.

The *Pollock* majority determined that taxing income from real property was a direct tax on property and therefore unconstitutional.[71]

Because the concept of a direct tax was never clearly understood, there was no compelling *constitutional* reason to treat a tax on property-derived income as indistinguishable from a tax on property values. But the decision was undoubtedly driven by the compelling *policy* reason that the income tax was, to the majority, an assault on property. Joseph Choate, an archconservative and one of the most successful lawyers to practice at the Supreme Court bar since Daniel Webster, argued the case against the tax. Leaving no doubt as to the political stakes raised by the case, Choate essentially asked the Court to check the Populist legislative agenda.

> I believe there are private rights of property here to be protected; that we have a right to come to this court and ask for their protection, and that this court has a right . . . to hear our plea. The act of Congress which we are impugning before you is communistic in its purposes and tendencies, and is defended here upon principles as communistic, socialistic—what shall I call them—populistic as ever have been addressed to any political assembly in the world.[72]

Choate spoke for the growing chorus of lawyers who viewed the Court as a bastion protecting the rights of property from redistribution, government regulation, and organized labor.

John Marshall was correspondingly becoming a symbol for the prestige of the Court and the legitimacy of assertive judicial review. Choate exhorted the Court to "courageously declare, as Marshall did, that it has the power to set aside an act of Congress violative of the Constitution, and that it will not hesitate in executing that power, no matter what the threatened consequences of popular or populistic wrath may be."[73] As if to shield the Court from the blow of hostile public opinion for invalidating the tax, Chief Justice Fuller began the *Pollock* opinion by citing *Marbury v. Madison* as establishing the Court's power to strike down unconstitutional laws. This was one of the first times that the Court cited *Marbury* to make that point, hoping to gain legitimacy from Marshall's coattails.[74]

But the story has a twist. There were actually two successive decisions in Pollock. Justice Howell Jackson, recuperating from an illness at home in Tennessee, did not participate in the first *Pollock* decision, argued in March and decided in April. The remaining eight justices split four to four on whether income from "invested personal property" (primarily securities investments) could be taxed, and whether the remaining constitutional portions of the law should stand by themselves, or the entire law struck down.[75] Leaving such important issues unresolved due to a four-to-four deadlock was deemed unacceptable, both to the Court and to public opinion. Chief Justice Fuller therefore set the case for re-argument before the full Court in early May, expecting that Justice Jackson would break the tie in favor of striking down the law. On May 20, the Court issued its revised *Pollock* decision, holding by a five-to-four vote that "personal property investment" income could not be taxed and that the entire law—including the taxes on income from work, which had not been challenged—must be struck down.[76] Surprisingly, Jackson dissented, which meant that one of the justices from the former four-to-four deadlock switched sides from upholding to striking down the law. The identities of the deadlocked justices were not disclosed in the original *Pollock* opinion. In the absence of direct evidence determining who switched, legal historians have debated whether the switch was made by Justices Gray or Shiras, with the weight of opinion leaning toward Gray.[77]

The suspicion of Gray is supported by a further clue—supplied by *McCulloch*. The reissued opinion was largely the same as before, except this time, the preface citing Marshall in support of judicial review dropped the quotation from *Marbury* and replaced it with one from *McCulloch*. Fuller's revised opinion began by reminding us "that it is a Constitution that we are expounding"—not to emphasize, as Marshall did, the adaptability of the capable Constitution, but to emphasize that the Constitution affords a basis to strike down an act of Congress.[78] Gray was the only member of the *Pollock* majority who made a habit of citing *McCulloch*, and the only justice who had ever quoted that particular sentence. Perhaps the change was an acknowledgment (or condition) for Gray's vote-switch to strike down the law.

These decisions were immensely unpopular, and produced a significant political backlash against the Court and the practice of judicial review. Although the *Pollock* decision did not prevent Congress from taxing income from work, the ruling seemed to protect income from sources typically held by corporations and the wealthiest Americans. In addition, dissatisfaction with lower courts for striking down protective labor laws, percolating before 1895, came fully to the surface. The 1892 People's Party platform had no plank attacking courts or judicial review. But when the Populist movement took control of the national Democratic party and nominated William Jennings Bryan for president in 1896, the Democratic platform attacked the *Pollock* decision and supported a bill granting a right to jury trial in labor injunction cases. More aggressive court-curbing measures were being advocated in public debate.[79] If conservative judges and lawyers were inclined to circle the wagons against Populist hostility before 1895, they were much more so after.

* * *

On February 4, 1901, the United States held its first and only national celebration to commemorate the appointment of a chief justice of the U.S. Supreme Court. "John Marshall Day," the one-hundredth anniversary of Marshall's accession to the chief justiceship, had been orchestrated with two years of planning by the American Bar Association (ABA). At the ABA's request, President McKinley mentioned the upcoming celebration in his December 1900 State of the Union address and conveyed the ABA's wish that Congress participate in the commemoration.[80] Federal and

state Courthouses closed for business as though it were the Fourth of July, and commemorative speeches and banquets were given in thirty-six states, the District of
Columbia, and the Territory of New Mexico. Speakers included Supreme Court
Justices Fuller, Gray, Brewer, and Brown; lower-court and state judges, including future justices Horace Lurton and Oliver Wendell Holmes, Jr.; U.S. Attorney General
Richard Olney; and legal scholars such as Thayer and Simeon Baldwin of Yale. The
archconservative John F. Dillon gave the main address at the New York celebration and later compiled and edited all the speeches in a three-volume collection
published in 1903.[81]

What was the point of all this? John Marshall Day was designed not to be a
mere intramural celebration for lawyers, but to provide a civics lesson for the general public. The idea had been proposed to the ABA at its 1899 annual meeting
by Adolph Moses, a Chicago corporate lawyer, "to elevate the spirit of both Bench
and Bar" and show that the legal profession was minding its "duty of guarding the
liberties and the rights of property of the people."[82]

Marshall Day speeches were on the whole conservative and backward looking,
using Marshall as a symbol to validate the constitutional developments of the previous three decades. Nationalism was a major theme, but it was not the legislative
nationalism of the emerging Progressive movement that in the ensuing decades
would latch onto *McCulloch*. It was rather the defensive nationalism that defeated
secession and confirmed federal sovereignty over "every inch of American soil." This
nationalism extended affirmatively only insofar as it validated federally chartered
railroads and telegraphs. Instead, speakers tried to transform Civil War nationalism
into laissez faire. Noting that most reformist legislation in 1901 was coming from
state legislatures, Dillon observed that "the plain lesson taught by our whole past
history is that whatever danger exists, . . . is to be found, not in the central power,
but in the States" who have always "passed many laws of a character that would
have broken up the Union" but for the continued enforcement of Marshall's nationalism principles.[83] If Marshall could save the Union from rebellious internal forces
by striking down laws attacking the constitutional order, the contemporary Court
could do so as well. Only now, the rebel forces were those of reformist regulation,
and the constitutional order was the protection of property.

The John Marshall Day celebration conveyed the conservative belief in judicial review as a bastion against populist "attacks" on property. The message was
encoded, to be sure, since the prestige of the judiciary depended on its seeming
impartiality in political debates. And a handful of speakers, such as Thayer, Holmes,
and Baldwin, offered more progressive messages of judicial restraint or the need to
regulate corporate wealth. But the conservative thrust was dominant. Speaker after
speaker praised Marshall as a protector of property. Future justice Horace Lurton
defended judicial review for counteracting "the disintegrating influences" of "extravagant political ideas." One speaker asserted that Marshall would have approved
the anti-strike injunction upheld in the *Debs* case, praising Marshall's jurisprudence

for establishing "Americans [as] essentially and emphatically a judge-ruled people; in the last resort we look to our courts to guard public order and tranquility, no less than individual safety and happiness."[84]

Marshall Day nationalism did not extend, via the Reconstruction Amendments, to congressional power to legislate race relations. On the contrary, Marshall Day speakers celebrated the post–Civil War reconciliation movement, whose point—largely achieved by 1901—was to bury the sectional divide, and deem the great wounds of the Civil War finally healed. The pragmatic and political aspects of the movement were to accept one-party Democratic rule in the South and abandon black southerners to their fate at the hands of "redeemed" white supremacist governments. In return, southern state representatives would make concessions on economic legislation desired by northern states. The legal aspect of North-South reconciliation was the constitutional acceptance of Jim Crow in cases like *Plessy v. Ferguson* (1896), which, as Gerard Magliocca has pointed out, assisted southern Democrats in breaking up the Populist effort to build a biracial coalition.[85] Ideologically, the nation embraced the southern "Lost Cause" mythology, one of the most massive and sustained domestic propaganda campaigns in U.S. history. Both popular literature and the historical scholarship of the Dunning School romanticized antebellum plantation life and southern military honor; falsely downplayed the extent of past and present white racial violence; and demonized and ridiculed Reconstruction and black political participation as corrupt, inept, and lawless.[86] On Marshall Day, Justice Gray, from Massachusetts, addressed the Virginia celebration, emphasizing that "the most cordial relations formerly existing between your State and my own" were "now happily restored."[87] A Georgia speaker praised the Supreme Court for striking down Reconstruction legislation "with un-shrinking courage and with immovable firmness" so as to defend "the peace and happiness of the homogeneous Anglo-Saxon population of these southern States."[88] As Dillon summarized in his introduction to the bound volumes, the event itself "shows that the results of the Civil War are everywhere loyally accepted, and that all sections and all parties rejoice in a re-united country." Therefore, everyone could indulge the handful of speeches in which "a soldier or a judge of the Confederacy heave a natural sigh or utter a tender lament over the 'Lost Cause.'"[89]

The hyperbole of commemorative speeches shouldn't divert us from a more serious underlying point. Marshall Day was above all an exercise in ideological myth making. The speeches extolled Marshall and paraded his decisions to demonstrate that great statesmanship emanates from the Supreme Court as much as from presidents, great generals, or Congress. Time and again, speakers strained rhetorically to elevate Marshall to the first rank of statesmen by equating him to Washington and Lincoln. We have already seen how several speakers credited Marshall with a crucial role in the Union victory in the Civil War. But most of all, John Marshall Day was a statement about the Supreme Court, whose statesmanship was of a particular, conservative type. The one Marshall Day speaker to recognize this was Holmes, whose speech was briefly mentioned in Chapter 1. "We live by symbols," noted Holmes, and "the setting aside of this day in honor of a great judge" made a symbol of Marshall. A symbol for what? "[F]or the fact that time has been on Marshall's side, and that the theory for which Hamilton argued, and [Marshall] decided, and Webster spoke, and Grant fought, and Lincoln died, is now our corner-stone." The theory in question was nationalism, but Holmes saw through the celebration of Marshall's exaggerated contribution to that theory "[t]o the more abstract but farther-reaching" point. To Holmes, the celebration of John Marshall "stands for the rise of a new body of jurisprudence, by which guiding principles are raised above the reach of a statute and State, and judges are entrusted with a solemn and hitherto unheard-of authority and duty."[90] By 1901, the Court had come into its own as the authoritative and final expounder of the Constitution. Marshall was above all a symbol of the judicial review that struck down the income tax and sharply restricted the antitrust laws.

* * *

Thayer's participation in John Marshall Day is fraught with irony, contradiction, and ultimately consensus. It is unsurprising that Thayer, as the nation's leading professor of constitutional law, entrenched at the nation's leading law school at a time when law school had become accepted by the bar as the main pathway to elite law practice, should have been invited to participate. His cordial relationships with such archconservatives as John F. Dillon and Joseph Choate, with whom he deeply disagreed over the question of judicial activism, reveal the importance of his Brahminical credentials relative to ideas. The irony of Thayer's all-in participation in John Marshall Day is that his interpretations of Marshall's jurisprudence, and particularly *McCulloch*, looked forward to Progressivism even as the dominant theme of the Day looked backward to shoring up institutional support for the judicial activism of the 1895 term. John Marshall Day marked an end and a beginning. The consensus of legal elites in celebrating John Marshall, from proto-Progressives like Thayer to archconservatives like Dillon and Choate, was that the Court was entitled to its role as final expounder of the constitution. Thayer was not a departmentalist, but rather believed that the Court should impose a doctrine of restraint on itself. Marshall was a hero to everyone involved. Going forward, constitutional interpretation would be the province of legal elites, and the question of how to interpret John Marshall's canonical cases would take on increasing rhetorical importance.

PART III

THE CANONICAL CASE

10

"Some Choice of Means"

The *Lochner* Era and Progressivism

Marshall wrote in *McCulloch* that Congress should "have some choice of means" so that it "might employ those which, in its judgment, would most advantageously effect the object to be accomplished."[1] The Progressive era was characterized by the growing belief that the problems of industrialization had to be solved by increasing governmental intervention in economic life. Opinions differed over whether the primary regulatory impetus should come from the federal or state governments, with Progressive Democrats tending more toward state and Progressive Republicans more toward federal regulation. Yet support for federal intervention could be found in both parties. At the same time, the extent of federal intervention was still relatively modest, compared to what would be pursued during the New Deal. Even so, the new concept of federal regulation required embracing the ideal of the capable Constitution.

The Progressive era was also the *Lochner* era, a period of conservative judicial activism conventionally identified as extending from about 1895 to 1936. The era is known for federal and state courts interposing significant constitutional obstacles to economic and social reform legislation, and it gets its name from the Supreme Court decision in *Lochner v. New York* (1905),[2] which invalidated a state law limiting the working hours of bakers. *Lochner* quickly became infamous for its high-handed disregard of the New York legislatures' stated concern for the health of employees in dangerous and unsanitary occupations, and for the Court's assumption that the core principles of laissez faire had constitutional status sufficient to block reform legislation.

By the early 1900s, after decades of neglect, *McCulloch's* status as a canonical case was established. It was cited both by advocates and the justices with increasing frequency.[3] These references were typically not bare citations, but tended to quote Marshall's language in ways indicating its authority and importance. Clearly, the turn-of-the-century Court had begun to treat *McCulloch* as somehow fundamental. But the question was, what did the case mean? In the first third of the twentieth century, the scope of this "choice of means" would become the center of constitutional dispute.

* * *

The debate over the meaning of *McCulloch* was a microcosm of the larger political debates over the role of the judiciary. In the early twentieth century, the two main political parties had become less ideologically opposed. Much of nineteenth-century party politics had been fought out by a Jeffersonian-Republican/Jacksonian-Democratic party of states' rights, slavery, and white supremacy against a Federalist-Whig-Republican party favoring a stronger national government promoting economic development. These ideological differences in party lines, always blurry around the edges and subject to crossover and interpenetration, blurred considerably as the Populist movement merged into the Democratic party in the 1896 and 1900 election cycles. Under the banner of their candidate William Jennings Bryan, the Populists committed the Democratic party to promoting national legislative solutions to the national economic problems facing their farmer and laborer constituents: exploitation by large interstate corporations as monopolists, employers, or shippers and processors of agriculture produce. After the failure of Bryan's second presidential campaign, the Populist movement petered out and its agenda was co-opted by the more elite-driven Progressive movement. Significantly, both the Democratic and Republican parties had conservative and Progressive wings, giving a bipartisan cast to the ideological conflicts of the era.[4]

For much of the nineteenth century, the Supreme Court was not a dominant player in establishing the limits of federal power. Constitutional controversies over federalism were predominantly fought out in Congress, in politics, and on the battlefields of the Civil War. The Court's effort to settle the most urgent federalism controversy of the antebellum period—its decision in the *Dred Scott* case—failed notoriously. In the late nineteenth century, however, the Court increasingly asserted a prominent role for itself in settling constitutional controversies, and achieved dominance by the end of the nineteenth century. Social scientist Charles Grove Haines could plausibly describe the Court's role by the title of his 1914 study, *The American Doctrine of Judicial Supremacy*.

In this political environment, the center of gravity of constitutional politics shifted from a conflict of Democrats versus Republicans to a conflict of legislatures versus courts. The fears of conservative legal elites who canonized Marshall to protect the judiciary proved justified. The period from the early 1900s to 1937 witnessed the most sustained and intensive attacks on the judiciary in U.S. constitutional history. Charges of "government by judiciary" were frequently heard in the political press. Proposals for court-curbing legislation and constitutional amendments were frequent and often high on the political agenda. Two serious third-party presidential bids—Theodore Roosevelt's Bull Moose campaign in 1912 and Robert LaFollette's 1924 Progressive Party candidacy—made "judicial reform" a centerpiece of the campaign. The judiciary's defenders were active as well. As Progressives continued the critique of judicial usurpation, conservative legal elites continued to develop their counter-narrative. Judicial supremacy, as Haines summarized, "was defended as the sole guaranty of national permanence and was lauded as 'the last and crowning political growth of our Anglo-Saxon civilization.'" Judicial supremacy was seen as protecting property and individual rights against the excesses of economic regulation; judicial conservatives of this era openly equated legislatures with majority tyranny.[5] The status of the judiciary in conservative circles was perhaps reflected by the fact that the Republican party nominated Charles Evans Hughes, a former (and future) Supreme Court justice, to oppose Woodrow Wilson's 1916 re-election campaign.

But the Progressive movement, too, had legal elites among its leaders and spokespersons. Far more elite-driven than the comparatively grass-roots Populist movement, Progressivism embraced a range of opinions about courts. Some leading Progressives tried to soften the edges of judicial reform and distinguish wrong-headed judges and legal doctrines from the judiciary and judicial review as an *institution*. For example, although Theodore Roosevelt made court-curbing a key plank of his 1912 presidential platform, his proposal to rein in "government by judiciary" was comparatively modest. He advocated popular referendums to confirm or reject court decisions invalidating legislative enactments, but this procedure would apply only to *state* courts striking down *state* laws under *state* constitutional provisions—a rather limited subset of the complained-of constitutional adjudications.[6] Despite his attacks on the Supreme Court's *Lochner* decision, Roosevelt expressed fundamental support for the institution of the courts, particularly the federal courts. Progressive legal elites were even more moderate. Harsh criticisms of particular decisions and doctrines by such leading lawyers, judges, and academics as Learned Hand, Roscoe Pound, and Felix Frankfurter emphasized the need for judicial *self*-restraint, implying that this was an adequate and preferred alternative to court-curbing laws and constitutional amendments.[7]

Many Progressives, particularly but not exclusively those in the Republican party, cast the current constitutional debate in the iconography of Jefferson versus Hamilton. Herbert Croly, the influential Progressive thinker and founding editor of *The New Republic*, captured this Manichean view in his influential book *The Promise of American Life* (1909). Croly argued that Jeffersonian "drift," in the form of states' rights and laissez-faire policies, had produced a "socially undesirable distribution of wealth." Instead, "Hamiltonian" nationalism and active legislative solutions to national problems were necessary to realize the American promise of "improving popular economic condition, guaranteed by democratic political institutions." Progressive Democratic theorist Claude Bowers presented a more pro-Jefferson view in his 1925 book *Jefferson and Hamilton*, writing, "The struggle of these two giants surpasses in importance any other waged in America because it related to elemental differences that . . . will continue to divide mankind far into the future."[8]

Marshall and his *McCulloch* decision were perfect symbols for this moderate Progressive position. For those advocating judicial restraint to reduce courts' interference with the Progressive agenda, it was completely natural to substitute Marshall for Hamilton. Marshall, not Hamilton, was the great expounder of the Constitution. Great legal mind though he was, Hamilton was never a judge; a passionate and polarizing figure who was brought down by a sex scandal and died in a duel, Hamilton could not be described as having a judicial temperament. A litigant could not count on persuading a judge by exhorting him to follow Hamilton's example; but Marshall's judicial example would appeal to judges' vanity. Aside from his admirable life and character, Marshall was perfectly cast as Hamilton's understudy, sharing many of Hamilton's nationalist virtues while personifying moderation. He had his own running feud with Jefferson, but it paled in comparison with Hamilton's. Marshall, like Hamilton, was closely linked with George Washington, though again less so than Hamilton. Marshall was a Federalist, though not a "high Federalist" like Hamilton. And of course, through *McCulloch*, Marshall was connected to the Bank, channeling Hamilton's constitutional arguments in order to sustain the constitutionality of the direct heir of Hamilton's original Bank of the United States. Even the most conservative judges were by 1901 already committed to Marshall as the iconic jurist. And the *McCulloch* opinion was full language supportive of liberally construed national legislative powers. For a Progressive lawyer, committed both to social and economic reform legislation and to constitutional review by an independent judiciary, the political contest between courts and legislatures could be calmed by recasting it as a debate over the correct interpretation of the Marshall symbol in general and his *McCulloch* opinion in particular.

Marshall's nationalism, translated into the new and different context of the early twentieth century, resonated with the peculiar linkage of imperialism and national problem-solving that characterized Republican party Progressives. In the 1890s, the United States entered its imperialist age. In April 1898, the United States went to war against Spain for the ostensible purposes of avenging the sinking of the battleship *Maine* and of liberating Cuba from Spanish rule. But the sprawling naval war extended across the Pacific to the Philippines, leading Congress to annex Hawaii as a useful naval base. By the treaty ending the short and successful war, signed in December 1898 and ratified by the Senate in April 1899, the United States acquired the Spanish colonies of the Philippines, Puerto Rico, and Guam.

These territorial acquisitions, and the prospect of future ones, touched off a major political debate with constitutional dimensions. Support for the war with Spain had been bipartisan, as both parties sympathized ideologically with the Cuban liberation movement. But opposition to imperial territorial acquisition largely followed party lines. The Democrats were opposed, making anti-imperialism a major issue in the presidential campaign of 1900. The basis of opposition combined racism and high principle. The Democratic party platform of 1900 declared "that any government not based upon the consent of the governed is a tyranny; and that to impose upon any people a government of force is to substitute the methods of imperialism for those of a republic." The nub of the constitutional objection was captured in the phrase "the Constitution follows the flag,"[9] meaning that full constitutional rights should apply everywhere under the jurisdiction of the United States. This argument was intended to be a poison pill: the anti-imperialism argument maintained that territories could be acquired only for the purpose of eventual admission as states, and the notion that people of color in the new territorial possessions could be citizens, vote in U.S. elections, and send representatives to Congress was anathema to many.[10] But the Supreme Court rejected the anti-imperialism argument in *Downes v. Bidwell* (1901), citing *McCulloch* for the proposition that Congress has an implied power to govern its territories "without limitation," and therefore need not treat them as destined for statehood or as fully integrated into the constitutional order.[11]

In public debates surrounding the new territorial acquisitions, advocates of imperialism asserted arguments based on the capable Constitution, that the Constitution was sufficiently expansive and adaptable to accommodate permanent colonies. These arguments would soon be transformed into arguments about the Constitution's capability to accommodate Progressive legislation. This curious relationship between *McCulloch*'s theme of the capable Constitution, imperialism, and Progressivism can be seen in the ideas of three important figures of the era: James Bradley Thayer, Theodore Roosevelt, and Albert Beveridge.

Although Thayer died in 1902, as the Progressive movement was just beginning to come into self-consciousness, his ideas prefigured and influenced the thinking of Progressive legal elites. His 1893 essay, *The Origin and Scope of the American Doctrine of Constitutional Law*, argued that judicial review, properly conducted, should and did uphold legislative acts unless their unconstitutionality was clear "beyond a reasonable doubt."[12] This principle of judicial review, if applied, would curb the power of judges to interfere with social and economic legislation through a voluntary and self-imposed norm of judicial restraint rather than by means of an external check on judicial power. It encapsulated the moderate Progressive view of the problem of judicial activism: defective judicial doctrines rather than a defective constitutional structure.

Thayer's view was embraced by Progressives throughout this period, and the *Origin and Scope* essay itself became a sacred text. Felix Frankfurter, who enrolled at Harvard Law School a year after Thayer's death, noted that Thayer's ideas were "in the air" at the law school, where Thayer's surviving colleagues expounded his ideas and encouraged or required students to read *Origin and Scope*. As legal historian and Frankfurter biographer Brad Snyder sums up, "Any discussion of Frankfurter's jurisprudence must begin with Thayer," whose influence on Frankfurter was "profound."[13] Justice Frankfurter acknowledged this later in life: "One brought up in the traditions of James Bradley Thayer, echoes of whom were still resounding in this very building [Harvard Law School] in my student days, is committed to Thayer's statesmanlike conception of the limits within which the Supreme Court should move."[14] A generation of Harvard Law graduates would thus have carried Thayer's influence into government and politics throughout the Progressive era and into the New Deal. Thayer's influence on Progressive and later New Deal constitutional thought would have been great even had its direct influence been limited to Frankfurter. Among his many career accomplishments, Frankfurter would graduate from Harvard Law School to become the greatest professional networker and one-man career placement service in the history of American law.[15]

As noted in Chapter 9, Thayer was still working out his thoughts about *McCulloch* at the end of his life. His short 1901 biography of Marshall identified *McCulloch* as Marshall's greatest opinion, but Thayer summarized its substance in two short, unremarkable paragraphs. Thayer, who was not prolific, published his last law review article in the *Harvard Law Review* in 1899, entitled *Our New Possessions*. In it, Thayer applauded the end of Spanish colonial "misrule" in the recently acquired territories, but he considered U.S. acquisition of them "discreditable" and an ill-judged entanglement "with the politics of other continents."[16] But Thayer's main focus was "constitutional law," rather than policy, politics, or morals. Thayer dismissed narrow constitutional construction as "loose thinking which is vaguely called the 'spirit' of the Constitution." The unconstitutionality of buying Louisiana and Florida, chartering a bank, issuing legal tender paper money, enacting a protective tariff, "and a hundred other things" have been "solemnly and passionately asserted by statesmen and lawyers." The arguments against acquiring and governing colonies were more of the same. The United States had inherent sovereign power—"the same power that other nations have"—to acquire and govern colonies. "The trouble has been, then as now, that men imputed to our fundamental law their own too narrow construction of it, their own theory of its purposes and its spirit, and sought thus, when the question was one of mere power, to restrict its great liberty." The judiciary was no more immune from such interpretations than the most opportunistic politician: "few indeed are the [judges] who have not, now and again, signally failed to appreciate the large scope of this great charter of our national life. Petty judicial interpretations have always been, are now, and always will be, a very serious danger to the country." But properly interpreted, the Constitution "is forever dwarfing its commentators, both statesmen and judges, by disclosing its own greatness." Echoing Marshall, Thayer asserted that the Constitution is "astonishingly well adapted for the purposes of a great, developing nation," and "shows its wisdom mainly in the shortness and generality of its provisions, in its silence, and its abstinence from petty limitations. . . . Men have found, as they are finding now, when new and unlooked-for situations have presented themselves, that they were left with liberty to handle them."[17] Although the article did not cite *McCulloch*, Thayer apparently told his Constitutional Law class that the two-page passage containing most of the foregoing language summarized his thoughts on *McCulloch*.[18]

Theodore Roosevelt was the most famous Progressive of the age, and a strong believer in the capable Constitution. His views, which he eventually branded under the label "the New Nationalism," combined a recognition of broad congressional powers to manage the effects of large corporations and mass labor domestically, with a pro-imperialist stance abroad.[19] Roosevelt explicitly connected these views with the jurisprudence of John Marshall. In a book review of Albert Beveridge's *Life of Marshall* for *The Outlook* magazine in 1917, Roosevelt called Marshall "one of the six or eight foremost figures of American statesmanship" who "actually did the constructive work of building a coherent National fabric out of the loose jumble of exhausted and squabbling little commonwealths. . . ."[20]

Roosevelt's admiration for Marshall was such that it nearly caused him to pass over Oliver Wendell Holmes Jr. to fill the Supreme Court vacancy created by the resignation of Justice Gray in 1902. It was still the custom to designate Supreme Court seats by state or region, and Holmes, then chief justice of the Massachusetts Supreme Judicial Court, had been recommended by Henry Cabot Lodge, the junior Senator from Massachusetts and Roosevelt's close friend. In a letter to Lodge mulling over the Holmes nomination, Roosevelt expressed reservations, which stemmed from his reaction to Holmes's John Marshall Day speech of 1901. Roosevelt found it "not really a small matter that his speech on Marshall should be unworthy of the subject, and above all show a total incapacity to grasp what Marshall did." Holmes would "not in my judgment [be] fitted for the position unless he is a party man, a constructive statesman, constantly keeping in mind his adherence to the principles and policies under which this nation has been built up and in accordance with which it must go on. . . ." Marshall, according to Roosevelt, had "rendered such invaluable service because he was a statesman of the national type, like Adams who appointed him, like Washington whose mantle fell upon him." In contrast, Taney had been "a curse to our national life because he belonged to the wrong party and faithfully carried out the criminal and foolish views of the party which stood for such a construction of the Constitution as would have rendered it impossible even to preserve the national life." Roosevelt's primary concern was that the Court might decide against the constitutionality of the recent territorial acquisitions, and he fretted that the current appointment would tip the balance either way. Roosevelt concluded that he "should like to know that Judge Holmes was in entire sympathy with our views, that is with your views and mine and Judge Gray, for instance . . . before I would feel justified in appointing him."[21] Justice Gray, as we saw in the previous chapter, linked *McCulloch*'s concept of implied powers with the notion of implied sovereign powers—the idea that national powers could be implied from the unwritten concept of sovereignty itself in addition to those implied from the enumerated powers. These powers could be used to justify colonial acquisitions. Roosevelt saw his own Progressive nationalism as a more democratic version of Marshall's federalism, which combined "devoted Nationalism, . . . advocacy of military preparedness, . . . and insistence upon a wide application of the powers of the Government under the National Constitution. . . ."[22]

Roosevelt's transition from imperialist to Progressive domestic reformer was far from unique. Another important figure in the *McCulloch* story, and a Roosevelt ally, followed the same path. Albert Beveridge, a two-term Republican Senator from Indiana from 1898 to 1910, began his political career as an ardent imperialist and near the end of his life wrote the first serious full-length biography of Marshall. Born in 1862 to an impoverished farm family, Beveridge worked his way through college at Depauw University, studied law through the old method of apprenticeship rather than law school, working around his law firm clerical duties to read law books and receive tutoring from the Indianapolis law firm's senior lawyers. In an unpublished autobiography, Beveridge recalled having been deeply moved by reading *McCulloch*. The opinion's nationalism and "soldierly" style resonated with Beveridge's own pro-Union, anti-secession upbringing. After building a successful Indianapolis law practice, in 1898, at age thirty-six, he was elected by the Indiana legislature to the U.S. Senate. By then, Beveridge was an outspoken believer in imperialism, both as an outlet for surplus American production and as a means to spread American "Anglo-saxon" governance to peoples he believed racially inferior and thus incapable of salutary self-government.[23]

Beveridge's first Senate speech was devoted to his racialist and economic policy arguments, but he also addressed the constitutional objections raised in the imperialism debate. Congress had the power to acquire and govern new territories whether or not "written in the Constitution" because "not all powers of the national government are expressed." Moreover, "if the constitution had not had the capacity for growth corresponding with the growth of the nation, the constitution would and should have been abandoned." This "golden rule of constitutional interpretation" was incorporated by Hamilton "when he formulated the doctrine of implied powers. Marshall recognized that when he applied that doctrine into constitutional interpretation in McCulloch vs. Maryland." Beveridge then referred to historical and judicial precedents for implied powers: the issuance of legal-tender paper money; the use of federal troops to suppress rebellions by Washington and Lincoln, and strikers by Cleveland; and the charter of a national bank. By these actions, "The legislative, the executive, and the judiciary departments of our government have recognized and confirmed the doctrine of implied powers by which alone the constitution lives, the people make progress, and the republic marches forward to its imperial destiny. . . ."[24]

By 1910, the imperialism issue had receded from atop the political agenda, and Beveridge was increasingly concerned with the domestic agenda of Progressivism: the public health and welfare issues raised by "muckraking" journalists, corruption, and the control of business trusts. He had become a full-fledged Progressive. But in the 1910 election, the Democrats gained control of the Indiana legislature, and

Beveridge was defeated in his re-election bid. In 1912, he campaigned for Theodore Roosevelt's unsuccessful third-party presidential bid, and then lost his own race for the Senate in 1914, the first Senate election based on direct popular vote pursuant to the Populist/Progressive-inspired Seventeenth Amendment. At that point, at age fifty-two, Beveridge retired from politics and turned to his long-standing ambition to write the authoritative biography of Marshall. Although not a trained historian, Beveridge immersed himself in original documents and by 1919 completed the four-volume work.[25]

Beveridge's *Life of Marshall* filled a literary and historical void, since there was as yet no full-length professional biography of Marshall.[26] His ultimate intention was to explain and highlight Marshall's judicial work, which "has been of supreme importance in the development of the Nation, and its influence grows as time passes." But this influence, he believed, required him to fill in the sketchy myth-like portrait of Marshall with a more factual account and supply detailed historical context for Marshall's opinions.[27] Beveridge's *Marshall* received critical acclaim, both in the popular press and from professional historians, and won the 1920 Pulitzer Prize for biography. Influential legal elites, including Holmes and Frankfurter, praised the work, as did Edward Corwin, the Princeton political scientist who himself published a book on Marshall in 1920 and who would do much to connect Marshall and *McCulloch* to New Deal constitutionalism in the 1930s.[28]

Beveridge, according to his own biographer Claude Bowers, approached the *Life of Marshall* with the interpretive biases of an early-twentieth-century Progressive and "Hamiltonian": a believer in the American nation state and in the power of the national government to address national problems. Beveridge devoted a chapter to *McCulloch*, entitled "Vitalizing the Constitution." For Beveridge, *McCulloch* was "a major treatise on constitutional government," and stood alone among Marshall's great opinions as having "so decisively influenced the growth of the Nation that, by many, it is considered as only second in importance to the Constitution itself." Much of the chapter wove together frequent and lengthy quotations with Beveridge's uncritical, often fawning summaries. For instance, Marshall's "let the end be legitimate" passage was "that celebrated passage—one of the most famous ever delivered by a jurist." The passage describing the United States as "this vast republic, from the St. Croix to the Gulf of Mexico" was "language . . . as exalted as that of the prophets."[29]

But Beveridge made some notable interpretive points that reveal *McCulloch*'s influence on Progressive legal thought. First, where Marshall criticized the narrow "strict necessity" interpretation of the Necessary and Proper Clause, Beveridge substituted "The State Rights theory" as the doctrine that Marshall had called "capable of arresting all the measures of the government, and of prostrating it at the foot of the states." In truth, there are many more elements to "State Rights theory" than the strict necessity interpretation of implied powers, and Marshall did not reject all of them, either in *McCulloch* or later. But for Beveridge, the "State Rights theory" in all its parts was indistinguishable from secession. Second, Beveridge misread

Marshall's general reference to the Commerce Clause as though it were *McCulloch's* constitutional basis for the Bank. Congress's power to establish a bank, Beveridge said, "flows from 'the great powers to lay and collect taxes; to borrow money; to regulate commerce; to declare and conduct a war; and to raise and support armies and navies.'"[30] Recall that Marshall instead opted somewhat weakly to base the Bank on the government's power to manage its "fiscal operations." Third, Beveridge's summary of *McCulloch* offered a broad interpretation of the spirit of the opinion: "In effect John Marshall thus rewrote the fundamental law of the Nation; or, perhaps it may be more accurate to say that he made a written instrument a living thing, capable of growth, capable of keeping pace with the advancement of the American people and ministering to their changing necessities."[31]

Whether Beveridge's broad readings of *McCulloch* influenced subsequent readers, or whether instead Beveridge simply crystallized an interpretation that was widely shared, is hard to say. What is clear is that Beveridge's interpretation of *McCulloch* would have been attractive to Progressives and later New Dealers, that his *Life of Marshall* was widely read by those audiences, and that many subsequent interpreters of *McCulloch* have said much the same thing. A twenty-first-century constitutional law professor characterizes *McCulloch's* "St. Croix to the Gulf of Mexico" as Marshall "engag[ing] in prophesy."[32] That this author used essentially the same terms as Beveridge without attribution shows how Beveridge's neo-Hamiltonian reading of *McCulloch* has been replicated through many retellings to become common wisdom.

But Beveridge's interpretation of *McCulloch* differed significantly from the Supreme Court's. When *The Life of Marshall* was being published, the Court had not yet let go its embrace of reserved state powers, a core element of "the State Rights theory." Nor had it applied *McCulloch's* doctrine of implied powers in a way that was "vitalizing the Constitution" or "keeping pace with the advancement of the American people." Beveridge's interpretation was admonitory, and the Court was not yet listening.

* * *

The *Lochner* era is best known for the frequent invalidation of state-law social and economic reforms by federal and state courts. Using the Fourteenth Amendment Due Process Clause, or state-law analogs, such laws were held to violate substantive economic and property rights, such as "freedom of contract." In a much smaller number of cases, the Supreme Court ruled on federal laws, and frequently cited *McCulloch* in doing so. The Court struck down only a few federal laws in this era, but sent Congress a clear message. *E.C. Knight* (1895), discussed in Chapter 9, established parameters that the Court maintained with a depressing consistency. The constitutional power to regulate labor and productive activities was extremely limited and, notwithstanding *McCulloch*, was generally impermissible even if necessary and proper to the effective implementation of a regulation of commerce. The Court did not strike down many federal laws in the Progressive era, but it didn't have to. As Felix Frankfurter reflected on this period, "a single decision may decide the fate of many measures."[33]

Moreover, a small number of restrictive Court decisions seemed effective to narrow the constitutional imagination of Progressive-era members of Congress. However one characterizes the volume of Progressive-era legislation, most of those laws hewed closely to a narrow conception of federal powers. With the notable exception of child labor laws, discussed later, Congress's attempts to regulate labor were restricted to interstate transportation workers. Other notable Progressive-era federal laws included the Clayton Act (a major antitrust amendment), new regulation of railroad rates and routes, progressive taxes on incomes and estates following ratification of the Sixteenth Amendment, regulation of agricultural middlemen, new infrastructure projects, and a consumer-friendly postal savings-bank system.[34] New laws regulating food and drugs were structured as regulations of interstate sales.[35] Although *McCulloch* was frequently cited in congressional hearings and debates on these laws—one congressmen quoted *McCulloch*, "the greatest case ever decided in the history of the world," in support of the implied power to create the postal savings bank—the legislation stayed close to the traditionally narrow understandings of the enumerated powers.[36] In short, the Progressive-era Congress simply did not test the limits of its constitutional powers, making it unnecessary for the Court to strike down numerous federal statutes. Even when the Court upheld federal Progressive-era laws, it made clear that Congress had a narrow scope to legislate under the Commerce Clause. This can be seen in three areas of federal commerce regulation: antitrust, police powers, and interstate transportation.

The Court never struck down the federal antitrust laws wholesale, examining instead whether particular applications of the law were constitutionally permissible. In *Northern Securities Co. v. United States* (1904),[37] for example, the Court sustained the application of the Sherman Antitrust Act to a railroad monopoly engineered by the financier J.P. Morgan. The defendant, a holding company that had bought up controlling interests in competing railroad lines, argued that its mere purchase and holding of shares was an intrastate transaction, notwithstanding that the railroad monopoly operated across several states. Justice Harlan's plurality opinion relied heavily on *McCulloch* to hold that Congress had an implied power to reach the stock purchase, even if that were deemed merely an intrastate contract, because that regulation was "appropriate" and "plainly adapted" to its power to regulate interstate restraints on trade.[38]

Northern Securities foreshadowed how the Court would limit *McCulloch*'s reach in Commerce Clause doctrine, even while respecting *McCulloch*'s authority. The dispute between the majority and dissent turned on their respective characterizations of the purpose of the law. The majority said the regulation sought to remove the obstruction of monopoly from interstate commerce, and focused on the *purchase* of the railroad stock, not its mere ownership. The four dissenters, who included Holmes, argued that the law was being used to regulate stock ownership, which was not commerce, under *Gibbons*'s definition. And despite a nod to *McCulloch*, the dissenters argued that there was no implied commerce power to regulate something that was not commerce.[39] Holmes wrote an additional dissent. Aside from his now-famous quip that "great cases like hard cases make bad law," this was not one of his better moments on the Court. He endorsed *E.C. Knight*'s "direct/indirect effects" distinction that dominated *Lochner*-era commerce jurisprudence: that the commerce power did not reach regulatory subjects that affected interstate commerce only indirectly.[40] Despite their disagreements, neither the majority nor dissent suggested that *McCulloch* allowed regulation of something that was not at least *intrastate commerce*. In this way, the entire Court adhered to the direct/indirect distinction: regulations of intrastate things that were not themselves commerce were connected to interstate commerce only *indirectly*, and could not be regulated by Congress.[41]

The Court continued to adhere to the restrictive *E.C. Knight* doctrine in antitrust cases throughout the *Lochner* era. The Court outraged Progressives by maintaining the double standard, begun in *Debs*, that labor unrest could be regulated as a direct obstruction of interstate commerce, thus applying the antitrust laws to continue issuing anti-strike injunctions.[42] But the Court's only significant application of antitrust laws to *businesses* involved interstate price fixing, whether by collusion of several firms or through monopolization by a single firm.[43] Best known are the cases involving price fixing in the packing and stockyard operations of the meat industry. The Court developed the idea that federal regulation could not be defeated "by a nice and technical inquiry into the non-interstate character of some of [the] necessary incidents and facilities" of an interstate "stream of commerce" by viewing them in isolation.[44] But this so-called "stream of commerce" doctrine was not a significant expansion of commerce authority: it merely continued the doctrine of allowing Congress to regulate interstate price-fixing agreements, recognizing that the monopolistic activity could occur at a key instrastate point in the interstate "stream." Notably, price fixing involves buying and selling.

The second line of cases involved transportation, which had been recognized as part of the definition of commerce since *Gibbons v. Ogden*. This definition was applied to railroads and other land transportation in the post-Reconstruction era. So it was hardly surprising that the Court would uphold various efforts by the Interstate Commerce Commission to regulate railroad rates. In the Progressive era, the Court narrowly extended this regulatory field. The modern-day Court has grandly labelled this line of cases as the power to regulate "the instrumentalities" of commerce,[45] but it really boils down to trains and other modes of transportation. The leading case in this line was the *Shreveport Rate Cases* (1914),[46] in which the Court upheld the power of the Commission to override intrastate railroad rates that discriminated against interstate shippers. While some constitutional scholars view the case as a significant signal of the Court's openness to Progressive-era commerce regulation,[47] the holding was really quite limited. The setting of prices falls within the narrow nineteenth-century definition of commerce, and by deciding that Congress could regulate intrastate railroad pricing as part of its comprehensive regulation of interstate railroad rates, *Shreveport* simply applied the core holding of *Gibbons* to a different form of transportation.

Recognizing that transportation involves more than the buying and selling of passenger tickets and cargo space, the Court upheld federal regulations of other aspects of interstate carriers' operations, such as safety.[48] But the Court drew strict lines when it came to regulating employment. In the *Employers Liability Cases* (1908),[49] the Court struck down a statute liberalizing the rules for railroad and other transportation employees to sue their employers for workplace injuries. The Court held that Congress could regulate employment relations of workers only while they were actually engaged in interstate transportation activities. Since the law purported to regulate all employees of interstate carriers without regard to their specific job duties, the Court ruled it unconstitutional in its entirety.[50] Three justices concurring in the result hinted that employment relations were excluded from commerce power, period.[51] Only Justice Moody, a recent Roosevelt appointee, suggested that Congress had "wide discretion" under *McCulloch* to cover all interstate transportation employees as a means to promote the federal interest in transportation safety.[52] In April 1908, Congress responded to the *Employers' Liability Cases* by amending the law to apply only to workers injured while engaging in interstate commerce.[53] When the challenge to the new law reached the Court in the *Second Employers' Liability Cases* (1912),[54] the three justices who opposed any commerce regulation of employment relations were gone, replaced by slightly more progressive Taft appointees. This time, a unanimous Court upheld the law. Implied commerce powers extended to regulation of safety and accidents on interstate transportation, and to workers engaged in interstate operations.

But commerce power did not extend to other aspects of employment law. In *Adair v. United States* (1908),[55] the Court struck down a federal law prohibiting railroads and other interstate carriers from imposing "yellow dog" employment contracts, which forbid the employee from joining a union. Justice Harlan, whose far-sightedness on social policy questions was regrettably inconsistent, wrote for the majority that union membership lacked any "real or substantial relation to or connection with the commerce regulated." Harlan gave a nod (uncited) to *McCulloch*, noting that Congress has "a large discretion" in the choice of the means, but nevertheless concluded that a railroad worker's "fitness" for the job and "diligence" in performing it were unrelated to "his being or not being a member of a labor organization."[56] Despite some later vacillation around the margins of these doctrines—the Court would eventually uphold the 1926 Railway Labor Act, which permitted railroad worker unionizing[57]— the Court made clear that the general rule placed most employment relations off limits to commerce regulation.

In the third line of cases, the Court developed the doctrine that "Congress has ample power. . . . to keep the channels of [interstate] commerce free from the transportation of illicit or harmful articles, to make such as are injurious to the public health outlaws of such commerce and to bar them from the facilities and privileges thereof."[58] The first decision embracing this "outlaws-of-commerce" theory was *Champion v. Ames* (1903),[59] also known as the *Lottery Case*, in which the Court upheld an 1895 federal act making it a crime to ship lottery tickets across state lines. The five-to-four decision written by Justice Harlan concluded that Congress could rightly consider lottery gambling to be a noxious form of commerce and could therefore prohibit that interstate traffic as "a fit or appropriate mode" of regulation. Harlan found support in *McCulloch* for giving "to Congress a large discretion as to the means that may be employed in executing a given power." Legislation to protect health, safety, or morals was deemed to be a matter of "police power," which traditionally was considered by many jurists to fall within the reserved powers of the states. But the *Champion* majority wholeheartedly embraced the conclusion that the federal government could use commerce regulation to safeguard the health, safety, and morals of the American people—what else was regulation for?[60] The dissenters, citing *McCulloch*, argued that the purported commerce regulation was a mere pretext to execute a power it did not have: "doubtless an act prohibiting the carriage of lottery matter would be necessary and proper to the execution of a power to suppress lotteries; but that power belongs to the States and not to Congress."[61]

The majority and dissent also engaged in a debate over the capable Constitution that anticipated the New Deal Court-crisis thirty years later. "We should hesitate long before adjudging that an evil of such appalling character, carried on through interstate commerce, cannot be met and crushed by the only power competent to that end," wrote Justice Harlan. Only Congress could regulate interstate commerce, he reasoned, and the Framers "never intended that the legislative power of the Nation should find itself incapable of disposing of a subject matter specifically committed to its charge."[62] The dissent joined issue: "It will not do to say . . . that state laws have been found to be ineffective for the suppression of lotteries, and therefore Congress should interfere. The scope of the commerce clause of the Constitution cannot be enlarged because of present views of public interest."[63] The dissenters' views lost vitality over the ensuing years, as the Court went on to apply the outlaws-of-commerce theory to uphold several federal statutes, regulating impure or mislabeled food and drugs, prostitution and sex trafficking, and stolen vehicles, among other things.[64]

Congress tried to take advantage of the Court's acceptance of the outlaws-of-commerce theory to restrict child labor, the farthest-reaching assertion of its legislative power in the Progressive era. Senator Beveridge introduced the first child labor bill in the Senate in December 1906. Modeled after the previously upheld lottery prohibition, the bill would prohibit interstate shipment of child-made goods violating specified standards. In a debate over the bill's constitutionality, Beveridge argued that the "phrase 'interests of the Nation,'" used by the Court in *Champion v. Ames,* "was first used by Chief Justice Marshall in *McCulloch v. Maryland,*" and "has been the most powerful phrase in the interpretation of the Constitution. The 'interests of the Nation' are more greatly imperiled by the products of child labor than even by diseased meat or adulterated food." The debate strikingly illustrated the degree to which Congress had acceded to the Court's supremacy in constitutional interpretation as representatives grappled with the fine points of judicial doctrine governing congressional powers. Beveridge's bill did not pass in that or the next few sessions of Congress, but it was finally enacted as the Child Labor Act of 1916. [65] The Act's structure as a prohibition of shipping child-made goods in interstate commerce confirmed the connection between *McCulloch* and the outlaws-of-commerce theory.

But in *Hammer v. Dagenhart* (1918),[66] the Court struck down the law. Recognizing that the law must be deemed constitutional under an outlaws–of–commerce theory, the five-to-four majority opinion distinguished the Child Labor Act by announcing that child-made goods "were harmless in themselves," compared to rotten eggs and debauched women. The Court seemed to be saying that it made a constitutional difference whether the regulatory target was something that occurred before or after shipment of the thing in interstate commerce. If after, then "the use of interstate transportation was necessary to the accomplishment of harmful results," and Congress could deny that use, because it was exercising its "ample" authority "over interstate transportation." But if the "harmful results" occurred *before* shipment, then Congress was regulating an intrastate matter that did not depend on interstate transportation to become harmful.[67]

This reasoning is as unconvincing as it sounds. If Congress couldn't regulate intrastate harms, it shouldn't have mattered whether the harm occurred before or after transportation across state lines. But if Congress could declare items to be "outlaws of commerce," it should have had the authority to decide that child-made goods are an evil that should not be bought and sold on the interstate market. The Court's suggestion that manufacturers' access to interstate markets had no impact on their practice of using child labor was nonsense: Manufacturers were using child labor on the assumption that the child-made goods would be shipped interstate. Indeed, the Court contradicted itself on that point by acknowledging that the real impact of the law was to discourage factory employment of children.

The point of the Court's tortured reasoning was to characterize the law as having an invalid purpose. The outlaws-of-commerce cases had upheld the laws in question on the theory that Congress could protect the integrity of the channels of interstate commerce, while the discouragement of prostitution or gambling was deemed an incidental benefit. Here, asserting that "[a] statute must be judged by its natural and reasonable effect," the Court followed the *Lottery Case* dissent by focusing on regulation of employment and manufacturing as the goal of the law. That goal was impermissible, according to the *Hammer* majority. Not only was it not commerce; it was barred by the Tenth Amendment, which reserved such matters to the states. To hold otherwise would mean that "all manufacture intended for interstate shipment would be brought under federal control to the practical exclusion of the authority of the States," which would "destroy the local power always existing and carefully reserved to the States in the Tenth Amendment to the Constitution."[68]

In its brief in support of the Child Labor Act, the government argued the need for a uniform, nationwide law to prevent unfair competition. States permitting cheap child labor would put their resident industries at a competitive advantage, creating a state legislative incentive to loosen child labor restrictions. This "race to the bottom" is a form of collective action problem endemic to the federal system. The Court brushed aside this argument, saying "The Commerce Clause was not intended to give to Congress a general authority to equalize such conditions." But that too was plainly wrong. Perhaps the Framers had not thought specifically about labor laws, but they certainly intended the Commerce Clause to control unfair economic competition between states. As for *McCulloch*, the Court quoted Marshall out of context for the assertion that "our federal government is one of enumerated powers"—conveniently forgetting that the gist of the case was to recognize the government's implied powers.[69]

Critics both at the time and in later years would contend that *Hammer* was an aberration, out of step with the Progressive direction of the Court's own doctrine.[70] But in refusing to apply *McCulloch* to the Commerce Clause to authorize federal regulation of employment and production, *Hammer* was entirely consistent with *E.C. Knight* twenty-three years before and with its 1935–36 decisions striking down New Deal legislation. Certainly, the Court could have applied its relatively new outlaws-of-commerce theory to uphold the Child Labor Act, but a longer line of cases held that employment and production fell outside the commerce power. Significantly, neither *Champion* nor any other outlaws-of-commerce case suggested that Congress could regulate things that were not commerce as means to an end of making interstate commerce regulation more effective. Upholding the Child Labor Act would have effectively overruled *E.C. Knight*, something the outlaws-of-commerce cases had not done.

* * *

The *Lochner* era began before the Progressive era and lasted long after. The Court was not progressive during this time, in any lasting sense. Its consistent refusal to recognize implied commerce powers by itself justifies the conventional characterization of this era of jurisprudence as one of conservative judicial activism. Some revisionist historians, echoing the Courts' defenders during the *Lochner* era itself, claim that the judicial record was not particularly conservative. They support these arguments with tallies of decisions upholding Progressive laws versus those striking them down.[71] Undoubtedly, the truth about the *Lochner* era's conservative judicial activism is more mixed and complex than the conventional portrayal—as is the case with any broad-brush summary, however useful. But relying on balance sheets of laws struck down and upheld as evidence tending to disprove the conventional interpretation of the *Lochner* era is itself problematic. Given the centrality of the ongoing dispute between labor and capital, denial to Congress of a power to regulate employment left a major hole in Progressive-era legislative power. The Court remained on the whole a conservative judicial-activist Court, and as late as 1924, its conservatism remained a sufficient irritant in public policy that court-curbing once again became a presidential campaign issue. The economic boom of the late 1920s quieted this for a time. But then the nation was plunged into the Great Depression.

11

"Withholding the Most Appropriate Means"

The New Deal and Judicial Crisis, 1932–1936

The Great Depression was the longest and most-entrenched economic downturn in U.S. history. Following the stock market crash in October 1929, a deflationary spiral sent prices, profits, and businesses' net worth to record lows. Incomes fell by 20–50%, while debts remained fixed, resulting in record high bankruptcies, bank runs, hoarding, and suicides. Unemployment reached a previously unimaginable 25% in 1933, and over 9,000 banks failed in the 1930s, 744 in the first ten months of 1930 alone. Unlike the Civil War, the Depression did not divide the nation into sharply opposed sectional interests. If anything, it unified the nation, delivering massive electoral victories in 1932 and 1936 to a Democratic regime determined to use unprecedented federal government intervention to restore the economy. But like the Civil War, the Great Depression shook the nation to its constitutional foundations. And as in the Civil War, the government would need to push the boundaries of constitutionally permissible federal action to save the nation.

The Civil War had tested whether democratic-republican government could survive, and this was no less true—and perhaps more true—during the Depression, which again raised Lincoln's question of 1861: "Must a government, of necessity, be too strong for the liberties of its own people, or too weak to maintain its own existence?"[1] The parliamentary and representative structures of the major democracies—Britain, France, and the United States—seemed dithering and incapable of solving the economic collapse. Focused on their domestic woes, and unwilling or unable to lead in international affairs, the democracies' systems looked increasingly weak and passé. Fascism and communism were on the march in Europe, and even gaining popularity in the United States, offering what appeared deceptively to be aggressive, forward-looking solutions to the failures of capitalism.[2] *McCulloch* asserted that the

Framers would not have intended for the Constitution to obstruct beneficial government action by "withholding the most appropriate means."[3] Would the government follow that injunction to address the crisis now?

The federal government's initial answer was discouraging. Constrained by a combination of laissez-faire ideology and "dual sovereignty" constitutional thinking, the Hoover administration responded weakly and inadequately. Under these views, regulation of labor and production needed to come from the states. But the Court seemed ready to stymie even state-level legislative solutions by adhering to its *Lochner*-era jurisprudence. In an early test case decided before the 1932 elections, *New State Ice Co. v. Liebmann* (1932),[4] the Court struck down a state law restricting entry into the ice-selling business under substantive due-process principles. The law was intended to test the hypothesis that overproduction and cutthroat price competition were significant causal factors in the Depression, but the majority saw only "a regulation which has the effect of denying or unreasonably curtailing the common right to engage in a lawful private business."[5]

The majority seemed oblivious to the ongoing economic crisis, prompting a memorable dissent from Justice Louis Brandeis. The Depression, wrote Brandeis, was "an emergency more serious than war." Noting that "[m]isery is wide-spread, in a time, not of scarcity, but of over-abundance," and that experts and businessmen alike were "searching for the causes" and "seeking possible remedies" for the "unprecedented" economic collapse, Brandeis argued that governments must be allowed to test hypotheses and try out economic solutions. "Denial of the right to experiment may be fraught with serious consequences to the Nation. It is one of the happy incidents of the federal system that a single courageous State may, if its citizens choose, serve as a laboratory; and try novel social and economic experiments without risk to the rest of the country." In exercising judicial review, the Court "has the power to prevent an experiment" but must not "erect our prejudices into legal principles. If we would guide by the light of reason, we must let our minds be bold."[6] Brandeis was no Hamiltonian—as a Progressive Wilsonian Democrat, he leaned in a states'-rights direction—but his dissent could be read as an impassioned plea for the capable Constitution. The American voters implicitly but decisively chose bold-minded leadership in the 1932 elections, in a landslide that elected Franklin Delano Roosevelt to the White House and put Democratic majorities in both houses of Congress.

* * *

FDR was inaugurated on March 4, 1933 (as the Constitution then dictated) and immediately initiated key programs of the New Deal to revitalize the economy. During the "the first 100 days" of his administration—a term he coined to emphasize the speed and productivity of the response to the Depression—Roosevelt and Congress calmed the public runs on the banks; created deposit insurance under the Emergency Banking Act; passed the Emergency Conservation Work program, which eventually employed almost 2.5 million men; and enacted the Agricultural Adjustment Act of 1933, which paid subsidies to reduce farm surpluses and raise agricultural prices. They also created the Tennessee Valley Authority to spur economic development, gave relief grants to states under the Federal Emergency Relief Act, and passed the Emergency Farm Mortgage Act to relieve farmers facing foreclosures. The signature law of the first hundred days was the National Industrial Recovery Act (NIRA), which funded infrastructure projects, set minimum wages, protected workers' right to unionize, and created boards of "fair competition" to try to control deflationary overproduction.[7]

The Court's initial reaction was to give at least a grudging benefit of the doubt to emergency-inspired government intervention in the "private" affairs of the market, as signaled by two decisions in early 1934. In *Nebbia v. New York*, the Court upheld a state legislative scheme of milk price supports to boost the hard-hit dairy industry.[8] And in *Home Bldg. & Loan Assoc. v. Blaisdell*, the Court upheld a state's emergency moratorium on mortgage foreclosures. Chief Justice Hughes, a moderate Republican, wrote for a bare five-to-four majority that "[w]hile emergency does not create power, emergency may furnish the occasion for the exercise of power."[9] Both cases involved state, not federal, laws, but many at the time read *Nebbia* as a signal that the Court would disavow the substantive due-process jurisprudence of the *Lochner* era. In retrospect, that hope proved premature—two years later the Court would strike down a state wage and hour law as a violation of "freedom of contract."[10] Perhaps contemporary observers should have paid closer attention to *Nebbia*'s backward-looking, nineteenth-century doctrinal reasoning, which relied heavily on Taney Court police-powers cases such as *Miln* (1837), and on the hoary precedent for states' power to regulate businesses infused with the public interest, *Munn v. Illinois* (1877).[11]

Blaisdell was more promising, in its direct and forward-looking acknowledgment of the need for constitutional adaptation. Chief Justice Hughes proclaimed that

> there has been a growing appreciation of public needs and of the necessity of finding ground for a rational compromise between individual rights and public welfare.... [T]he question is no longer merely that of one party to a contract as against another, but of the use of reasonable means to safeguard the economic structure upon which the good of all depends....
>
> [If] it is intended to say that the great clauses of the Constitution must be confined to the interpretation which the framers, with the conditions and outlook of their time, would have placed upon them, the statement carries its own refutation. It was to guard against such a narrow conception that Chief Justice Marshall uttered the memorable warning—"We must never forget that it is a constitution we are expounding" (McCulloch

v. Maryland)—"a constitution intended to endure for ages to come, and consequently, to be adapted to the various crises of human affairs."[12]

This resounding endorsement of the capable Constitution was added by Hughes at the insistence of Justices Cardozo and Stone, who believed Hughes's original opinion too weak; they had circulated a concurring opinion under Cardozo's name that opened with that exact *McCulloch* quotation.[13] In its final form, *Blaisdell* marked the first instance in which the Court relied on *McCulloch* to affirm radical government intervention in the economy.

The first judicial test for *federal* intervention into the depressed U.S. economy came up in February 1935, in the Gold Clause cases. In June 1933, at President Roosevelt's urging, Congress passed a joint resolution to cancel all "gold clauses" in private contracts and government bonds. A gold clause was a contractual provision requiring repayment of a debt in gold rather than paper money, and with gold valued at $1.69 in paper currency in 1933, continued enforcement of gold clauses would bring a windfall to creditors and crushing debt onto farmers and homeowners, as well as a huge burden on cash-strapped taxpayers and public treasuries already pressed to provide economic relief. The joint resolution would be a major step toward taking the United States permanently "off the gold standard"—that is, the dollar would no longer be "backed" (i.e., redeemable) by gold coin in domestic transactions.[14] As the cases wound their way to the Supreme Court, the Roosevelt Administration became extremely worried that the Court would strike down the gold-clause cancellation, with disastrous economic consequences. To forestall that, Roosevelt quietly decided that he would defy such a Supreme Court ruling, and he prepared to announce that intention in his next Fireside Chat after such a Court decision.[15]

The Court sustained the nation's policy—barely. In *Norman v. Baltimore & O. R. Co.* (1935), the Court upheld the cancellation of gold clauses in private contracts. Reaffirming *McCulloch*—or more specifically, *Julliard*'s interpretation of *McCulloch*—Chief Justice Hughes wrote for the Court that "the broad and comprehensive national authority over the subjects of revenue, finance and currency ... derived from the aggregate of the powers granted to the Congress" gave Congress the power to demonetize gold.[16] While *Julliard* and the *Legal Tender Cases* had not applied to express gold clauses, the power of the government to declare public policies that could override contracts would make abolition of gold clauses a natural and logical step from Congress's power to require creditors to accept "greenbacks." As the *Norman* Court reasoned, gold clauses were, after all, contracts for repayment in valid money rather than for repayment in a commodity, such as gold bullion.[17] But the *Norman* decision was five to four, and the government's victory was even narrower in the companion case, *Perry v. United States*.[18] There, the Court said that cancelling gold clauses in Treasury bonds was unconstitutional. However, the Court held that bondholders could not win monetary compensation for the violation of the gold clauses in their bonds, because the true value of gold coins at the time the bond was issued could not be adequately proven.[19] With this finesse, the Court narrowly avoided the constitutional crisis of a president defying the Court's ruling.

Despite narrowly upholding the Roosevelt Administration's gold-clause policy, the Court soured on the New Deal by early 1935. The four conservatives who dissented in the Gold Clause cases remained implacable opponents. Nicknamed "the Four Horsemen of the Apocalypse," they were convinced that Roosevelt was setting himself up as dictator, and they voted against every state and federal New Deal law that came before the Court. The swing voters on the Court, Hughes and Owen Roberts, shared concerns that Congress was legislating in too slapdash a manner. Over the next year the Court ruled against the Roosevelt administration in seven of eight cases that came up for decision. Three of these cases involved separation-of-powers issues, in which the court unanimously agreed to limit the scope of presidential power.[20] The Court also invalidated a federal mortgage relief law that was somewhat more ambitious than the state law upheld in *Blaisdell*, on the ground that it deprived creditors of their property in violation of the Fifth Amendment Due Process Clause.[21] On federalism questions, involving the powers of Congress, the Court struck down four major New Deal laws.

The first two of these came in May 1935 and demonstrated the continuation of the Court's narrow, *Lochner*-era interpretation of the commerce power. In *Railroad Retirement Board v. Alton R. Co.*,[22] a five-to-four majority struck down a law requiring railroads to develop pension plans for their retired employees. The ruling reaffirmed the Court's narrow limits on federal employment regulations, holding that the authority to regulate railroad workers under the Commerce Clause was limited to matters "directly affecting" the interstate operations of the railroad: safety, hours of work, and labor regulations designed to control work stoppages.

Three weeks later, in *A. L. A. Schechter Poultry Corp. v. United States*,[23] a unanimous Court invalidated the National Industrial Recovery Act of 1933. The precise issue before the Court was a challenge to the indictment of a chicken supplier to Kosher butchers in New York City for allegedly selling diseased chickens in violation of the NIRA's "live poultry code." This was one of many "codes of fair competition" created by ad hoc commissions authorized to issue commercial rules under the NIRA to regulate health, wages, prices, and competitive practices. The immediate result of the decision was not a heavy blow to the economic recovery effort. The NIRA was due to expire in just a few weeks, and since it was increasingly viewed by experts as unsuccessful, the law had dim chances of renewal by Congress. But aside from the symbolic implications of striking down the Administration's signature economic recovery law of the first hundred days, the reasoning of the decision portended further invalidations of more vital New Deal laws.

Primarily, the *Schechter* Court reaffirmed its narrow view of the Commerce Clause. While earlier cases had allowed Congress to regulate seemingly local transactions if they could be said to be within the "stream" or "current" of interstate commerce, Chief Justice Hughes's opinion for the Court flatly refused to extend this doctrine to transactions occurring, in the Court's view, after the end point of the "current" of commerce. Such transactions were categorically beyond the power of Congress because they did not "directly affect" interstate commerce.[24] A concurring opinion by Justice Cardozo, joined by Stone, offered cold comfort by suggesting obliquely that the majority's "direct/indirect effects" test was not categorical: "The law is not indifferent to considerations of degree" and "[w]hat is near and what is distant may at times be uncertain." Perhaps local production or employment could directly affect interstate commerce, but not in this particular case: "To find immediacy or directness here is to find it almost everywhere," and "would obliterate the distinction between what is national and what is local in the activities of commerce."[25] The *Schechter* ruling, along with the *Railroad Retirement* case, cast doubt on the ability of New Deal legislation to restrain deflationary overproduction and to regulate wages and working conditions of labor. The National Labor Relations Act, the nation's first comprehensive labor law, was then working its way through Congress, and its constitutionality was thrown into doubt.

The constitutional outlook for the New Deal did not improve the following year. In *Ashwander v. Tennessee Valley Authority* (1936), the only decision favorable to a New Deal program in this period, the Court upheld Congress's Commerce Clause power to build a dam and sell the electric power it generated. But even there, Chief Justice Hughes ominously warned, quoting *McCulloch*, "The Congress may not, 'under the pretext of executing its powers, pass laws for the accomplishment of objects not entrusted to the government.'"[26]

The Court's most devastating blow yet to the New Deal came in *United States v. Butler* (1936),[27] which involved a challenge to the Agricultural Adjustment Act of 1933, another vital law from Roosevelt's first hundred days in office. The Act created a comprehensive price support system for agricultural products, for the relief of farmers whose incomes plummeted as a result of a deflationary overproduction spiral. A key feature of the Act was the imposition of a tax on middlemen for farm products—wholesalers and grain elevator operators—which would in turn be used to pay subsidies to encourage farmers to restrict their production.

The law could be upheld under two potential powers of Congress: the spending power or the commerce power. Spending power doctrine had remained somewhat unsettled for the previous century. Strict constructionists had long argued that Congress's authority to spend under Article I, section 8, clause 1—the "Taxing and Spending Clause"—was limited to subject matter falling within the other enumerated powers. If Congress could not regulate agriculture directly—for example, under its commerce power—it could not spend federal money to promote or regulate agriculture, either. This view, prominently espoused by Jefferson and Madison, became known as the Madisonian interpretation. Opposed to it, naturally, was the Hamiltonian interpretation. Both interpretations agreed that the word "provide" in this clause means "spend." But the Hamiltonian view construed the language of the clause, to "provide for the common defense and general welfare of the United States," to authorize Congress to spend for any national purpose. While advocates of the Madisonian interpretation piped up through the nineteenth and early twentieth centuries, the federal government more often than not embraced the Hamiltonian view, going all the way back to the Monroe administration. *Butler* finally settled this question in favor of the Hamiltonian interpretation: Congress could spend for any national purpose. And at least in principle, conditions could be placed on the spending: "you may take our money as long as you use it for X."[28]

That was the good news, but the *Butler* decision was ultimately bad news. The conditions placed on receiving federal money would count as regulation, not spending, if they were "coercive" in nature. In that event, the spending could be undertaken only under one of the other enumerated powers after all. And the *Butler* Court took a very broad view of what was coercive: coercion meant anything less than complete freedom to decline the government offer of largesse. Under the Act, any farmers who took the subsidies would gain a competitive advantage over those who declined it. This benefit would pressure all farmers to take the subsidy, making it coercive, and therefore regulatory. It thus could pass constitutional muster only if it was valid regulation of interstate commerce. And here the Court reasserted its long-held, narrow view going all the way back to Jefferson and the slave owners, that agriculture was not commerce but was a regulatory matter reserved to the states, and not reachable under the commerce power.[29]

Butler was a six-to-three decision with the moderate conservatives Hughes and Roberts joining the Four Horsemen. Roberts's majority opinion followed what was becoming standard procedure in controversial decisions to strike down a law. First, the justices asserted that they were just following the commands of the Constitution, rather than imposing their own views. The Court simply "lay[s] the article of the Constitution which is invoked beside the statute which is challenged . . . to decide whether the latter squares with the former. . . . This court neither approves nor condemns any legislative policy." Second, they summoned Chief Justice Marshall for help. Because Congress had "under the pretext of executing its powers, pass[ed] laws for the accomplishment of objects not intrusted to the government," Roberts wrote, quoting *McCulloch*, it was therefore "the painful duty of this tribunal . . . to say that such an act was not the law of the land."[30]

* * *

In retrospect, *Butler* can be seen as a turning point in the history of *McCulloch*, because it galvanized the thinking of Justice Harlan Fiske Stone, who did as much as any other justice, and perhaps more, to establish *McCulloch* as a precedent for broad congressional powers. Stone, a Republican appointed to the Court by President Coolidge in 1926 after briefly serving as Attorney General, was arguably the Hughes Court's most progressive member. In late 1920s, during Taft Court, he had been pigeonholed as one of the Progressive "Three Musketeers," along with Holmes and Brandeis, and was proud of the appellation.[31] Before 1936, Stone had given limited thought to the impact of *McCulloch* on New Deal legislation. Though he, along with Cardozo, had insisted that Hughes revise the *Blaisdell* majority opinion to add the *McCulloch* quotation on constitutional adaptability, Stone had not yet seen how a broad and flexible approach to implied powers might be relied on to sustain New Deal legislation. He was content in early 1935 to sign onto the Cardozo's case-by-case application of the direct-indirect effects test for commerce powers in the *Schechter* case.

But Stone began to change his views in response to the *Butler* majority opinion. Stone was dismayed at how little analysis was given to the spending-power justification for the statute during conference, and he issued a vigorous dissent, joined by Brandeis and Cardozo. Stone opened his dissent by chiding the majority for disregarding "two guiding principles of decision which ought never to be absent from judicial consciousness." First, "courts are concerned only with the power to enact statutes, not with their wisdom." And second, "the only check upon our own exercise of [judicial review] power is our own sense of self-restraint." Stone did not challenge the majority's assertion that crop production fell outside Congress's regulatory powers. Instead, he attacked the conclusion that the imposition of conditions in the statute made the use of the spending power coercive and therefore regulatory. "The power of Congress to spend is inseparable from persuasion to action over which Congress has no legislative control."[32] Had he ended there, his dissent would not be particularly noteworthy. But he went on to argue that the effectiveness of the subsidy to direct the productive activities of farmers was the very thing that made it an appropriate implied power under the Spending Clause. It was paradoxical, wrote Stone, that the majority found this very quality to be the coercion that made the law *unconstitutional*. Thus, *McCulloch's* "time-honored principle of constitutional interpretation that the granted power includes all those which are incident to it is reversed" by the majority. Moreover, the majority's belief that agriculture was "within the sphere of state government" effectively limited Congress's enumerated powers, because it blunted the use of implied powers needed to effectuate the enumerated power. "It is a contradiction in terms to say that there is power to spend for the national welfare, while rejecting any power to impose conditions reasonably adapted to the attainment of the end which alone would justify the expenditure."[33]

Stone was beginning to understand that the doctrine of reserved state powers, which dated all the way back to the Taney Court, reversed the principle of *McCulloch* by creating implied limitations on federal powers. No prior Supreme Court justice had made this connection. Interestingly, nothing in Stone's prior formal writing or correspondence indicates where he got these ideas. Stone had been a professor and dean of Columbia Law School, though he did not teach or write about constitutional law. Yet he seems to have been an admirer of Marshall, having named his first son "Marshall," and himself claimed (probably apocryphally) to have been named after one of Marshall's other great admirers, John Marshall Harlan.[34] The most plausible explanation is that his thinking on this point was stimulated by the government's lengthy (280 page!) brief in *Butler*. The government's brief, which cited *McCulloch* eight times, had argued that *McCulloch*'s conception of implied powers should be applied to the Spending Clause to sustain the statute. The spending provisions of the law were "an exercise of the broad powers vested in Congress to stabilize and preserve the credit structure of the nation, to protect the banks and other credit agencies which it had already established or sponsored, and to protect the credit of the Government itself."[35] While Stone did not incorporate that argument exactly, he did embrace the suggestion of analyzing the case as one involving implied powers. The government brief also addressed the conflict between implied federal powers and reserved state powers. In a section entitled "The Act Does Not Violate the Tenth Amendment," the Justice Department attorneys argued that "the Tenth Amendment requires only that the Act be a proper exercise of a power granted to Congress by the Constitution," and that "[w]here the means adopted are properly within the power of Congress, their validity is not destroyed by the fact that results may be brought about which Congress could not have directly compelled or required."[36]

Although this Tenth Amendment argument was not developed at length or with great clarity, it was enough to put Stone is a state of intellectual ferment. He was dissatisfied with his dissent, despite receiving praise for it. The day after the opinions were announced, Felix Frankfurter cabled Stone: "Despite all, history remains the ultimate tribunal. Their votes are not counted but argument weighed and so your dissent will take its place with the great moral pronouncements of your court."[37] But Stone complained privately that the majority's rush to get the decision out left him with inadequate time to research and think the case through.[38] That winter Stone apparently read an article by Thomas Reed Powell, a constitutional law professor then at Harvard who had been a colleague of Stone's at Columbia, asserting "that the words of the commerce clause and of the Tenth Amendment fix no limit to national power. They merely assert that there is a limit. The necessary and proper clause allows any expansion that judges think is justified."[39] Shortly afterward, Stone began a brief correspondence with another former Columbia colleague, the Progressive constitutional historian Charles Beard, author of the famous *An Economic History of the Constitution* (1913) and a student of the Founding era. Stone asked Beard whether the Framers thought there were implied limitations on federal powers under the Tenth Amendment. Stone believed that the Framers "would have been surprised, even after the Tenth Amendment, to learn that the Constitution reserved an exclusive legislative field to the states. It granted powers to the national government and, in the vernacular of the farmer, 'the tail goes with the hide.'" In reply, Beard told Stone about the first Congress's defeat of the attempt in what became the Tenth Amendment to limit the federal government to "*expressly* delegated" powers: "Madison said that no gov[ernmen]t could endure on express powers, and the proposal was defeated, leaving the Constitution really unamended, for no person in his right mind contended that the Fed[eral] Gov[ernmen]t had any powers not given to it." Beard concluded by wishing "that sometime you could write the true and simple story of federal power into one of your ma[s]terly opinions, to fix the nature of that power firmly in the minds of lawyers and the public." Stone promised to take "the first opportunity to do something of the kind."[40]

* * *

The last straw in the Supreme Court's reaction against the New Deal came a few months after *Butler*, at the end of the Court's 1935–36 term. *Butler* had dealt a serious blow to the New Deal. Not only did the agricultural sector represent close to 20% of the domestic workforce,[41] but the reasoning of the case cast serious doubt on the constitutionality of the Social Security Act, whose structure of collecting taxes to fund a social insurance program closely paralleled the taxing-spending structure of the Agricultural Adjustment Act. In May and June 1936, the Court issued decisions in *Carter v. Carter Coal Co.*,[42] invalidating the Bituminous Coal Conservation Act, and *Morehead v. New York ex rel. Tipaldo*,[43] signaling that the *Lochner* decision was alive and well by striking down a state minimum-wage law as a violation of the Fourteenth Amendment Due Process Clause.

    Carter Coal was a manifesto, laying out a judicial philosophy that was the antithesis of implied commerce powers under a broad reading of *McCulloch*. The Bituminous Coal Conservation Act was an omnibus New Deal regulation attempting to cope with labor unrest, cutthroat competition, and deflationary wage and price spirals in the hard-hit coal industry. The Act included provisions for wages and hours, collective bargaining, and controls over prices and production. Hughes and Roberts once again joined the "Four Horseman" to make a six-to-three majority striking down the law.[44] The regulation of employment and production (here, mining) fell within the reserved powers of the states and had only an "indirect" affect on interstate commerce. The majority expressed utter indifference to the problem of disempowering the federal government from addressing a massive interstate industrial problem that could not be legally or practically addressed by individual states. Once again, "[t]he proposition, often advanced and as often discredited, that the power of the federal government inherently extends to purposes affecting the nation as a whole with which the states severally cannot deal. . . . [has] never been accepted but always definitely rejected by this court." The only "constitutional way" to address such problems was through "preparing and securing the passage by the several states of uniform laws," as was done with state laws "with respect to marriage and divorce."[45] This time Cardozo dissented, joined by Brandeis and Stone. In his characteristic literary and elliptical style, Cardozo observed that "a great principle of constitutional law is not susceptible of comprehensive statement in an adjective." His point was that the statute in this case met his case-by-case, "I know it when I see it" standard for intrastate activities having a "direct" effect on interstate commerce.[46]

The constitutionality of the Coal Act depended on Congress's power to regulate interstate commerce, and the Court defined commerce in the narrow terms of the nineteenth century: "the word 'commerce' is the equivalent of the phrase 'intercourse for the purposes of trade,' and includes transportation, purchase, sale, and exchange of commodities between the citizens of the different states."[47] By itself, that narrow definition did not necessarily spell doom for the statute. Congress was attempting a comprehensive regulation of the interstate coal market, to ensure an uninterrupted supply of coal against work stoppages while at the same time controlling overproduction, price-gouging competition, and unlivable wage cuts. If Congress could regulate the interstate buying and selling of coal, Congress should have the implied power under McCulloch to regulate matters incidental to that which were not themselves interstate commerce—at least according to Justice Stone's Butler dissent. But the majority rejected this theory, arguing that Congress had discretion over means, but not ends. Quoting McCulloch's "let the end be legitimate" language, the majority flatly stated that mining and employment were illegitimate ends of legislation. "Thus, it may be said that to a constitutional end many ways are open; but to an end not within the terms of the Constitution, all ways are closed." Poetry aside, this was willfully bad logic. The interstate coal trade was a legitimate regulatory goal, to which "many ways" should have been "open"—including regulation of labor and mine operations. Instead, as in Hammer v. Dagenhart, the Court flipped the means and ends: since production (mining) and employment were reserved state powers and were not commerce, these were deemed illegitimate ends, and not means.

*　*　*

The debate between the New Dealers and conservative constitutionalists reignited the interpretive debate over McCulloch. Conservative lawyers and judges arguing to strike down New Deal laws drew on three passages in Marshall's opinion to support anti–New Deal judicial activism. They quoted the famous "let the end be legitimate" passage to suggest either that the law under review fell outside the enumerated powers—hence the end was not legitimate—or that the law was not "consistent with the letter and spirit of the Constitution." To the conservatives, the spirit of the Constitution, its unspecified values, included the "implied limitations" inherent in the Tenth Amendment. The conservatives pointed to Marshall's acknowledgment that the federal government is "one of enumerated powers," to contest the suggestion that Congress's powers should be interpreted broadly enough to approach a general police power. And they reminded their readers of the Court's "painful duty" to strike down laws enacted by Congress "under the pretext of executing its powers"— particularly when Congress tried to use its taxing or spending powers to regulate presumed intrastate matters like production or employment.[48] Conservatives frequently called these passages the "doctrine" of *McCulloch*, but it was not in any formal sense judicial doctrine. Rather, the quotations from *McCulloch* restated the principles of judicial review and of federalism at extremely high levels of generality, providing symbolic reassurance that the justices could claim the mantle of John Marshall in striking down New Deal laws.

New Dealers had three potential approaches to contest the conservative interpretations. One would be to argue that *McCulloch's* spacious concept of implied powers should permit Congress to exercise a wide choice of means to address the nation's economic crisis. In particular, *McCulloch* could be applied to the Commerce Clause to recognize the legitimacy of implied commerce powers. Since the economy hinges on interstate and foreign trade, it should be logically straightforward to see that intrastate behavior of any kind affecting interstate markets could potentially come within implied commerce powers. A second potential use of *McCulloch* in support of the New Deal would have been "Thayerism"—the idea of judicial self-restraint embodied in Thayer's 1893 maxim that laws should be upheld unless their unconstitutionality is clear beyond a reasonable doubt. In *McCulloch*, Marshall had written that "to inquire into the degree of [a law's] necessity, would be to tread on legislative ground," and the Court "disclaims all pretensions to such a power."[49] Both of these theoretical approaches would treat *McCulloch* as binding doctrine that dictated upholding particular New Deal laws.

Yet New Dealers for the most part declined to pursue either of these theories during the early New Deal. Their legal briefs and scholarly publications through 1939 do not draw on *McCulloch* to suggest deferential review or implied commerce powers. In litigation before the Supreme Court, *McCulloch* was far more likely to be cited in briefs and arguments *against* the constitutionality of New Deal legislation than for it. For example, in *Schechter Poultry*, where the district court had relied on *McCulloch* to sustain parts of the NIRA, the government did not cite *McCulloch* at all; the challengers to the law did.[50]

In academia, numerous books and law review articles of the 1930s discussed *McCulloch* and Marshall's jurisprudence at great length. But New Deal scholarship failed to develop the specific argument about implied commerce powers.[51] Instead, New Deal scholars referred to implied powers, if at all, to make a more general point about the breadth of federal constitutional powers to meet the New Deal crisis. Following *McCulloch's* lead, wrote one typical author, "the Supreme Court more than once has permitted the national legislature to stretch out a very long arm to reach the means desired for the exercise of a given power."[52] The author, a political science professor at Northwestern, had nothing more to say about *McCulloch*. Some New Dealers emphasized the Commerce Clause without reference to *McCulloch* or implied powers at all, arguing that *Gibbons v. Ogden* defined commerce with sufficient breadth to accommodate New Deal legislation.[53]

Pro–New Deal academics were no more likely to develop Thayerism. Felix Frankfurter's April 1936 lecture series, "The Commerce Clause under Marshall,

Taney, and Waite," offers a striking example of this omission, given that Frankfurter would later become the apostle of Thayerism.[54] Frankfurter concluded the lectures with an extended quotation, not from Thayer's *Judicial Review* article, but from Thayer's *Our New Possessions*. The quoted passage is the one summarized in Chapter 10, in which Thayer connected *McCulloch* with a theory of the capable Constitution and an attack on the small-mindedness of narrow constitutional interpretations. Frankfurter said of that passage, "Nowhere has the meaning of the Constitution, as it has fulfilled itself in the life of our people, been more luminously expressed according to the traditions of its greatest expounders."[55] But Thayer hadn't been discussing judicial self-restraint ("Thayerism") in that passage. Frankfurter again omitted Thayerism when referring to Thayer in a 1931 article apparently written to encourage Brandeis's support for federal legislative responses to the Depression, which he many have anticipated would be grudging.

> Rich experience at the bar confirmed the teachings which Mr. Brandeis had received from James Bradley Thayer, the great master of constitutional law, that the Constitution had ample resources within itself to meet the changing needs of successive generations. . . . The work of Mr. Justice Brandeis is in the tradition of Marshall, for, underlying his opinions, is the realization "that it is a constitution we are expounding." . . . This general point of view has led Mr. Justice Brandeis to give free play to the States and the Nation within their respective spheres. For him, the Constitution affords the country, whether at war or at peace, the powers necessary to the life of a great nation.[56]

Quite apparently, Frankfurter in the 1930s was more concerned to develop the idea of the capable Constitution than the related but different concept of judicial self-restraint.

The capable Constitution idea was, in fact, the third potential approach to using *McCulloch* in support of the New Deal, and it was the one almost universally pursued by legal academics. Here the focal point was Marshall's evocative pair of statements on the Constitution's longevity and adaptability. That the Constitution was "intended to endure for ages to come, and, consequently, to be adapted to the various crises of human affairs," seemed particularly apt for the New Deal crisis. The Constitution's endurance depended on judicial interpretations keeping up with changing times and circumstances. Brandeis had made this point before the Depression, in *Olmstead v. United States* (1928).[57] A five-to-four majority of the Court had reached the wrong-headed, shortsighted conclusion that government wiretapping of a private telephone could not be an unreasonable search because the Fourth Amendment applied only to searches of "persons, houses, papers and effects." In his famous dissent, Brandeis used the other of the well-known *McCulloch* quotations on constitutional adaptability. Brandeis wrote, " 'We must never forget,' said Mr. Chief Justice Marshall in *McCulloch* v. Maryland, 'that it is a constitution we are expounding.' Since then, this Court has repeatedly sustained the exercise of power by Congress, under various clauses of that instrument, over objects of which the Fathers could not have dreamed." Just as regulatory power of government had expanded under the Court's adaptive approach to constitutional limits, Brandeis continued, so "[c]lauses guaranteeing to the individual protection against specific abuses of power, must have a similar capacity of adaptation to a changing world."[58]

Brandeis might have again referred to *McCulloch* when he returned to this theme during the Depression, in his *New State Ice* dissent. He didn't explicitly, but his academic acolytes drew the connection for him. Writing shortly after the *New State Ice* decision, Alpheus T. Mason asserted that "Mr. Justice Brandeis understands that the Constitution must be given liberal construction, if it is, as John Marshall once said, 'to endure for all ages to come, and, consequently, to be adapted to the various crises in human affairs.'"[59]

The emphasis on emergency powers in Brandeis's *New State Ice Dissent* and the Court's *Blaisdell* decision offered a shaky foundation for New Deal legislation, however. "There are emergencies and emergencies," wrote Edward Corwin. "An earthquake, a riot, a war, a housing shortage can perhaps be authenticated by a court without a too great strain on the normal judicial function; but what of a nationwide depression—and just how depressed does it have to be?" Corwin argued that the constitutionality of New Deal laws was permanent, not based on temporary emergencies; among other things, Congress should have power to prevent crises, not just react to them. Constitutional interpretation necessarily had to change over time: "the Constitution must mean different things at different times if it is to mean what is sensible, applicable, feasible."[60] Indeed, the New Deal tested "the capacity of the Constitution to absorb a revolution."[61] A more permanent foundation to sustain the New Deal would have to resort to history.

Edward S. Corwin was the leading academic advocate of the New Deal. With prominence and intellect comparable to Frankfurter, Corwin wrote far more frequently and assertively in support of the New Deal than any other legal scholar. Corwin had joined the political science faculty at Princeton in 1905, becoming a protégé of Princeton's then-president Woodrow Wilson, and eventually succeeded Wilson as the McCormick Professor of Jurisprudence. Though Corwin had no law degree, he became a highly respected and accomplished legal scholar and helped establish a tradition of political science professors studying constitutional law and history. During the early New Deal, Corwin published dozens of articles in law reviews and the popular press, lectured frequently, gave radio addresses, and even published three books, all supporting the constitutionality of New Deal programs. Corwin supported Roosevelt's re-election campaign in 1936, and then went out on a limb by speaking publicly and testifying in Congress in support of Roosevelt's ill-fated 1937 plan to expand—and pack—the Supreme Court. Corwin attained sufficient public profile that his name was frequently mentioned as a potential nominee for the next opening on the Supreme Court. But Corwin did not get the nomination when that occurred in 1937—possibly in part due to the taint of his association with the Court-packing plan—and he became somewhat embittered toward the Administration, eventually becoming a critic of excessive presidential power. But in the early New Deal, Corwin was well positioned to develop a New Deal version of legal history drawing on Marshall Court jurisprudence.

Corwin presented his historical approach to the New Deal in his 1936 book, *The Commerce Power and States Rights*. On the first page of his Preface, he explained the book's subtitle, "Back to the Constitution," as "the motto of this small volume, and by the 'Constitution' is meant the Constitution of George Washington, Alexander Hamilton, James Madison (the Madison of 1787, not of 1798, nor of 1829), and of John Marshall."[62] Most of the book was framed as a set of extended, historically grounded rebuttals to "six propositions" that had been asserted against the constitutionality of commerce regulation over the years. The most important for New Deal constitutional arguments were his rebuttals of propositions 4 and 5. These propositions asserted that reserved state powers under the Tenth Amendment "withdraw certain matters" from interstate commerce regulation, particularly the matter of "production." Recognizing that the commerce power is "[t]he most important source of national power touching private conduct," Corwin argued that the scope of federal commerce power should have grown commensurately with the growth of "the factual subject-matter . . . brought within" the originally intended terms of the Commerce Clause. But it hadn't: the lag between the recognition of congressional authority and the much larger growth of interstate commerce as a practical field of regulation meant that the regulatory power of Congress was effectively "today far less than it was" during the Constitution's first century.[63] Significantly, Corwin never developed a concept of implied commerce powers, instead basing the scope of congressional regulatory discretion on *Gibbons v. Ogden* and a broad understanding of the Commerce Clause itself.

While Corwin barely mentioned *McCulloch* in his Commerce Clause book, giving the starring role to *Gibbons*, many pro–New Deal legal scholars made significant use of *McCulloch* as their historical point of departure. They went off in two diverging, even contradictory directions. Some scholars emphasized that the Constitution was "intended to endure for ages to come," and therefore had to change with the times—or at least interpretations of it did. This view suggested that the Court's error in 1936 was not that it failed to apply a long-established doctrine, but that it failed to create a new one. Alpheus T. Mason disparaged the interpretive theory "that the Constitution embodies provisions of definite and unchanging meaning to be found only by historical inquiry into the framers' intentions." That theory should give way to *McCulloch*'s view "that the Constitution is a Constitution, not an ephemeral enactment," and "must be construed broadly" and "remoulded from time to time to meet new and unforeseen demands."[64] But others took the opposite tack, arguing that *McCulloch* itself established once and for all the doctrine that the national government was fully empowered to address national problems. Charles Grove Haines argued that the Court's 1935 decisions striking down the Railroad Retirement Act and the NIRA erroneously applied "the Jefferson-Madison doctrine" of reserved state powers that had only recently been revived, when it should have applied the "Hamiltonian-Marshall principle" of implied powers that had been confirmed through "nation building" practice for "more than a century."[65]

Haines's version of legal history was highly contentious and slanted. But it was the standard story developed by pro–New Deal legal scholars, who pushed matters even further in hopes of giving Marshall's nation-building jurisprudence a more bipartisan cast. This task meant enlisting Marshall's successor, Roger Taney, to their side, and indeed the 1930s saw an increased interest in the Taney Court and an effort to rehabilitate the author of the infamous *Dred Scott* opinion. Political scientist Carl Brent Swisher published a sympathetic biography of Taney in 1935, arguing in reference to *Dred Scott* that "[i]t is inconsistent to denounce Taney for deciding questions broadly in hope of benefiting the country, while praising others, Marshall for instance, for doing the same thing."[66] Louis Boudin, a socialist lawyer who had published celebrated attacks on "Government by Judiciary," wrote a 1936 article on Marshall and Taney that offered a revisionist view of the latter.[67] After describing Marshall in pro–New Deal terms as a nationalist who "decided that the government of the United States has ample power" to legislate for the public good, Boudin surprisingly characterized Taney as a sort of Wilson Progressive: "Taney comes closest to Marshall: He, like Marshall, favored that interpretation of the Constitution which would permit the government to do things, instead of an interpretation which would hamper it." Boudin read Taney's opinions favoring new forms of property against old monopolies as evidence that "Taney had an evolutionary view of our great charter of government, for the reason that if this charter was to endure for ages, and therefore cover the institution of property as it evolves from age to age, the meaning of the Constitution had to be taken as of the time when it was being applied rather than as of the time when it was adopted." Boudin concluded, "Needless to say, had this view of the Constitution been followed consistently by Taney's successors, the entire course of our constitutional development would probably have been different from its actual historical course."[68]

This startling appraisal of Taney might have been good advocacy, but it was poor history. As we have seen, Taney fundamentally rejected *McCulloch*'s "ample power" jurisprudence. But even sophisticated legal scholars like Corwin and Frankfurter pursued this line, although they added nuance by acknowledging more and longer periods of Taney's departure into states'-rights dogma.[69] Frankfurter did so by playing down Taney's pro-slavery judicial attitude while playing up his resistance to monopoly. In his 1936 Commerce Clause lectures, Frankfurter wrote, "The mists of prejudice are only gradually lifting from Taney's reputation," which was unduly damaged by those who overstated "his share in the responsibility of the whole Court for the tragic Dred Scott affair." It was "not slavery, but Taney's fear of the growing power of finance [that] was most clearly reflected in his opinions." The dominant theme of his commerce jurisprudence was to empower states "to avoid the evils of financial monopoly."[70] The states'-rights "political tradition represented by Taney and his colleagues is definitely not that of Shays' Rebellion, the Kentucky Relief Laws, and the later Populists," but rather that of "the Insurgency of the elder LaFollette, the Progressivism of Theodore Roosevelt, and the New Freedom of Woodrow Wilson." Taney was "second only to Marshall in the constitutional history of our country."[71]

Corwin was too good a historian to suggest, like Boudin, that Taney's jurisprudence was consistent with Marshall's. On the contrary, he recognized that the Taney Court's opinions were "pervade[d]" by a "theory" of reserved state powers that had been rejected by Marshall in both *McCulloch* and *Gibbons*. Nor could Corwin bring himself to agree with Frankfurter's claim that Taney prefigured the Progressive movement. Instead, Corwin tried to finesse the Taney era by a sort of technicality, emphasizing the Taney Court's tendency to issue seriatim opinions in its major Commerce Clause cases. On this thin reed, Corwin offered the spurious conclusion that the "States-Rightism" of the Taney era "never received the sanction of an authoritative opinion of the Court until after the Civil War."[72]

Like the legal scholars, New Deal litigators were reluctant to put forward either the implied commerce powers or judicial restraint interpretations of *McCulloch*. With the notable exception of *Butler*, the federal government's Supreme Court briefs before the 1937 "Switch in Time" either omitted *McCulloch* entirely or cited it to make a general point urging broad and permissive constitutional interpretation. In *Carter Coal*, for example, the government cited *McCulloch* to suggest that the Court approach the Coal Act broad-mindedly, citing Marshall's language that the Constitution was written in "broad outlines" and "intended to endure for ages to come."[73]

This hesitancy of litigators to use *McCulloch* is understandable. The deference-to-Congress argument would in effect fling the justices' own judicial activism back in their faces, and would not likely win many cases. And a full application of *McCulloch* to the Commerce Clause to recognize an implied power to regulate employment and production would require a direct confrontation with established reserved-powers/Tenth Amendment doctrine and ask the Court to take a novel step. Better, from the litigators' point of view, to argue that long-established lines of precedent authorized the New Deal law in question. Litigators know that Courts are inherently reluctant to change and even resentful about acknowledging prior mistakes.

But academics are free to suggest new lines of doctrine without risk of losing a specific court case. Why, then, did pro–New Deal academics neglect the implied commerce and judicial restraint interpretations of *McCulloch*? The question becomes more pointed when we consider that these theories offered clear doctrinal pathways to sustaining New Deal laws, while the historical approach was fuzzy and factually dubious. Perhaps the *McCulloch* commerce theory struck them as so far out of the doctrinal mainstream that the argument would make its advocate look like a crank. And maybe they believed that Thayerism would simply not sway the pre-1937 Court. Academics are free to dream, but they also want their ideas to be taken seriously. Litigators may have encouraged academics to pursue slanted historical arguments. When New Deal lawyer Thurman Arnold, a sometime Yale Law School professor then serving in the Department of Justice, sought outside help for arguments to support the Social Security Act, he turned to Corwin to ask specifically for historical arguments.[74] Another answer, at least for the failure to develop a *McCulloch*-commerce theory, is that it may simply have been beyond the legal imagination of the 1930s. Either way, the failure of litigators and academics to produce this theory demonstrates the powerful habit of mind that dominated *Lochner*-era thinking about the Commerce Clause and lingered into New Deal thought.

* * *

New Deal thought boiled down to a set of arguments for the Constitution's capability to sustain unprecedented federal legislative programs. This agenda was at once revolutionary and conservative: dramatic change had to be accommodated within the framework of the Constitution and the forms of tradition. While many supporters of the New Deal pursued the idea of constitutional amendment, the official position of the Roosevelt administration was that the existing Constitution was capable, if properly interpreted.[75] This position was as much a pragmatic acknowledgment as an interpretive principle. The amendment process was slow and uncertain, and history had shown that the Court was able to undermine amendments designed to overrule their constitutional decisions.[76]

McCulloch was not deployed in either of the two usefully available doctrinal approaches: as a precedent for broad implied commerce powers, or for a principle of judicial restraint in reviewing Congress's interpretation of its powers under the Necessary and Proper Clause. Instead, New Deal litigators and scholars relied on an ideological-history approach to make New Deal legislation seem consistent with constitutional tradition. The New Deal was said to be following fundamental principles laid down by Marshall, particularly *McCulloch*'s idea of the capable, adaptable Constitution. New Dealers claimed that the Court's anti–New Deal decisions were aberrations from the traditions established by Marshall.

By the time *Carter Coal* was decided, *McCulloch* had plainly become the canonical case. But its meaning was disputed. The ambiguities of its famous "let the end be legitimate" passage were exploited by arguments attacking and defending the constitutionality of New Deal laws. Both the majority and dissent in *Butler* quoted that passage. And advocates on both sides of the constitutional issues felt it necessary to argue that *McCulloch* supported their side.

In doctrinal terms, the New Deal judicial crisis can be summarized as the Court's continued refusal to recognize implied commerce powers—its refusal to apply

McCulloch to the Commerce Clause. A single, arresting sentence in *Carter Coal* captured the essence of the Court's early–New Deal jurisprudence, and indeed the essence of over a century of Supreme Court Commerce Clause doctrine. "In exercising the authority conferred by this clause of the Constitution, Congress is powerless to regulate anything which is not commerce."[77]

"It Is a Constitution We Are Expounding"

The Triumph of Implied Powers, 1937–1968

The aggressive nationalism interpretation maintains that *McCulloch* "laid the foundations for the modern welfare state." This may not reflect the intentions of the Marshall Court, but there is little doubt that *McCulloch* came to be interpreted this way. The post–New Deal expansion of federal power in our constitutional order proceeded along two lines. First, the Court recognized Congress's authority to regulate virtually all aspects of the national economy. Second, the Court acknowledged Congress as having broad powers to regulate civil rights—race relations and other issues of civil and political equality. After decades in which the Court ignored or restrained it, *McCulloch*'s concept of implied powers finally earned its triumph. The Court for the first time fully applied *McCulloch* to the Commerce Clause and the Reconstruction Amendments, and removed the concept of reserved state powers as a barrier to implied powers under these constitutional provisions.

* * *

In his March 4, 1937 Victory Dinner speech, the day after his second inaugural, Franklin Roosevelt took the Supreme Court to task for striking down key New Deal legislation the previous year. Roosevelt said that a majority of the Supreme Court had determined "that we live in a Nation where there is no legal power anywhere to deal with its most difficult practical problems—a No Man's Land of final futility." The reference to the desolate, uninhabitable strip of war-torn ground between the opposing trenches of World War I just twenty years earlier would have been particularly compelling to a 1937 audience. Roosevelt explicitly blamed the *Carter Coal* case, among others, as creating that regulatory No Man's Land. If some problems couldn't be addressed by either the states or the federal government, the *Carter*

Coal opinion had suggested, well that was just too bad.[1] In his peroration, Roosevelt picked up the gauntlet thrown down by the Court and demanded federal legislative solutions to the litany of problems facing the country: "Here is one third of a nation ill-nourished, ill-clad, ill-housed—now! Here are thousands upon thousands of farmers wondering whether next year's prices will meet their mortgage interest—now!" The list concluded, "If we would keep faith with those who had faith in us, if we would make democracy succeed, I say we must act—now!"[2]

A month before this speech, the Roosevelt Administration's Judicial Procedures Reform Bill was introduced in Congress. Known ever since as Roosevelt's "Court-packing plan," the bill would create a new seat on the Supreme Court for each justice who retained his seat beyond the age of seventy.[3] A few days after his second inaugural, Roosevelt explained the plan to the public in one of his Fireside Chats. Against advice, Roosevelt couched the plan in terms of the inefficiency of superannuated judges to handle the Court's workload. No one was fooled.[4] In his 1941 book *The Struggle for Judicial Supremacy*, Robert Jackson, then Roosevelt's Attorney General and soon to be appointed by Roosevelt to the Court, acutely summed up the truth of the situation. "The operation of life tenure in the judicial Department, as against elections at short intervals of the Congress, usually keeps the average viewpoint of the two institutions a generation apart," Jackson wrote. "The judiciary is thus the check of a preceding generation on the present one; a check of conservative legal philosophy upon a dynamic people, and nearly always the check of a rejected regime on the one in being."[5] In retrospect, Roosevelt might have been better off by frankly basing the plan on the need to overcome old-guard judicial opposition. But as Roosevelt formulated it, the Court-packing plan met powerful opposition, and the blowback hurt other policy initiatives of the Administration. Even so, Roosevelt's popularity was such that the proposal did not die in Congress until after it was overtaken by events on the Court.

The events were the famous "switch in time that saved the nine." The "switch" of two crucial votes, Hughes and Roberts, sustained two key pieces of New Deal legislation, saving a nine-member Court rather than Roosevelt's proposed eleven to fifteen justices. In two five-to-four decisions, the Court removed its obstacles to both federal and state regulation of the economy. State economic regulation had been inhibited by the use of substantive due process under *Lochner* and its progeny. The reaffirmation of *Lochner* in *Morehead* in 1936 was reversed by *West Coast Hotel v. Parrish*[6] in late March 1937. Two weeks later, the Court upheld the National Labor Relations Act under the Commerce Clause in *National Labor Relations Board v. Jones & Laughlin Steel Corp.*[7] These decisions took the remaining wind out of the sails of the Court-packing plan in Congress. While historians have debated the extent to which Hughes and Roberts were cowed by the Court-packing plan, the two never again voted to strike down New Deal economic legislation before their respective retirements in 1941 and 1945. As Jackson archly summarized the result,

"The President's enemies defeated the court reform bill—the President achieved court reform."[8]

* * *

The New Deal turnaround required the Court to change course by close to 180 degrees, shifting from narrow to broad interpretations of congressional powers and from relatively strict to comparatively deferential judicial review of social welfare legislation. Most of the expansion of federal power involved the reinterpretation of the Commerce Clause. As a result of these changes, regulation of virtually all economic matters is today held to fall within Congress's commerce power. Former categories of reserved state powers over the economy, such as production and employment, have essentially been eliminated. So firmly have these principles been established in constitutional law that reverting to pre-1937 doctrine is unthinkable. Contentious debates still occur at the margins, but the core of this doctrine has remained settled for eighty years. Even the staunchest states'-rights conservatives on the modern Supreme Court grudgingly acknowledge this historical reality.[9] This New Deal "constitutional settlement" occurred without formal constitutional amendments, leading many modern-day commentators to realize that constitutional change can occur through political realignment rather than the formal amendment process, and that social reality has more impact on constitutional law than the other way around.[10]

The aggressive nationalism claim that *McCulloch* "laid the foundation for the modern welfare state" can be tested by observing its influence on these developments. Did *McCulloch* provide impetus, or at least doctrinal direction and explanation, for the New Deal's breakthrough to modern commerce-power doctrine? The doctrinal logic is clear enough. Were the Court to apply *McCulloch* to the Commerce Clause, it would understand Congress to have the power to employ any means that it believed "conducive" to regulating interstate commerce, irrespective of purportedly limiting categories of reserved state powers under the Tenth Amendment. Even if "commerce" were construed in the narrow sense given by Marshall in *Gibbons*—commercial intercourse, including trade and navigation—implied commerce powers under *McCulloch* would permit regulation of most productive activity and uphold all New Deal legislation against Commerce Clause challenges. It would certainly mandate the reversal of decisions like *Carter Coal, Hammer v. Dagenhart,* and *E.C. Knight.*

McCulloch played a key role in this breakthrough, though not as clearly as the aggressive nationalism thesis suggests. As we will see, the breakthrough decisions that relied on *McCulloch* were bookended by decisions that did not. To see this point requires first that we understand that the New Deal transformation did not occur all at once. The drama of the 1937 "switch in time" has tended to create the false impression that modern Commerce Clause doctrine burst forward in the

Jones & Laughlin Steel case. Even Supreme Court justices have been taken in by this misperception, giving undue precedential weight to *Jones & Laughlin Steel*'s statement of Commerce Clause doctrine. But the truth is that the transition to modern commerce-power doctrine occurred incrementally through several cases over five years, from 1937 to 1942.

In *NLRB v. Jones & Laughlin Steel Corp.* (1937),[11] the Court was not yet ready to embrace the general notion of applying *McCulloch*'s implied-powers analysis to the Commerce Clause. The Court upheld the constitutionality of the National Labor Relations Act of 1935 (NLRA), which established the framework for labor-management relations that exists to the present day—union organizing, collective bargaining, strikes, arbitration, and so forth. Recognizing that the Court's decisions going back from *Carter Coal* to *Hammer v. Dagenhart* (1918) to *E.C. Knight* (1895) had held general labor regulation off limits to Congress, the NLRA's drafters emphasized that its provisions were meant to apply to workers "involved in" or "directly affecting" interstate commerce. The drafters hoped to stretch the meaning of these terms to break out of the previous confines limiting federal labor laws to interstate transportation workers. *Jones & Laughlin Steel* presented the best possible facts to make this case. The company was part of a massive steel conglomerate operating nineteen steel plants across numerous states, with vertically integrated businesses involving mining, oil and gas production, steam and rail transportation, and distribution and warehousing. If this company did not sufficiently link production and employment with interstate commerce, then nothing could.[12]

Chief Justice Hughes, writing for the Court, announced a "fundamental principle . . . that the power to regulate commerce is the power to enact 'all appropriate legislation' for 'its protection or advancement.'"[13] While this sounds like broad new doctrine and a clear reference to *McCulloch*, it was neither. Hughes did not cite *McCulloch* anywhere in the opinion, and he derived the "appropriate legislation" quotation from *The Daniel Ball* (1871),[14] a Chase Court decision about dormant commerce power over navigable waterways that did not itself cite *McCulloch*. This strongly suggests that Hughes's omission of *McCulloch* was intentional, and we can see why. Hughes stopped well short of stating that Congress had full power to execute its commerce power by "appropriate legislation." Instead, "activities [that] may be intrastate in character when separately considered" can be regulated by Congress "if they have *such a close and substantial relation to interstate commerce* that their control is essential or appropriate to protect that commerce from burdens and obstructions[.]"[15] Hughes must have known that only a dubiously narrow reading of *McCulloch* would lend support to his requirements that the means-ends connection be "close and substantial."

Further, Hughes reserved the "close and substantial relation" inquiry to the Court. The scope of the commerce power, Hughes wrote, "must be considered in the light of our dual system of government and may not be extended so as to embrace effects upon interstate commerce so indirect and remote" as to "obliterate the distinction between what is national and what is local and create a completely centralized government. The question is necessarily one of degree."[16] This passage, which cited *Schechter* without page references, combined language from Hughes's own *Schechter* majority opinion ("completely centralized government") with an unattributed borrowing from Cardozo's *Schechter* concurrence ("obliterate the distinction"). Hughes was plainly signaling an intention to retain the *Schechter-Carter Coal* direct/indirect effects test for regulation of matters relating to commerce, but modifying it to allow regulation of formerly off-limits subject matter, such as employment or production, in appropriate cases. But making the question "one of degree" for judicial determination signaled a burdensome, case-by-case judicial scrutiny that would generate ongoing uncertainty about whether any given statute would meet the Court's "I know it when I see it" test.[17] *Jones & Laughlin Steel* was significant for its result, but its grudging incrementalism was no revolution.[18] Perceptive commentators recognized this at the time: Irving Brant, the pro–New Deal journalist, behind-the-scenes advisor, and Madison biographer wrote to Stone that Hughes showed "a combination of foxiness and stubbornness" by "exerting his prerogative" to write unduly narrow opinions "in all the key cases," including *Jones & Laughlin*.[19] Indeed, as doctrine, *Jones & Laughlin Steel* was far closer to *Schechter* than to the later New Deal decisions of 1941–42. And by keeping judicial control over determining the appropriateness of commerce regulations, Hughes contradicted *McCulloch's* statement that the "degree of necessity" was a congressional determination. For Hughes, it was better not to cite *McCulloch* at all.

As late as 1940, the Court still had not completed its transition to the modern understanding of the commerce power. In *Sunshine Anthracite Coal Co. v. Adkins* (1940),[20] the Court upheld the 1937 Bituminous Coal Act, a narrowly drafted successor to the Coal Act that had been struck down in *Carter Coal* in 1936. The Court found the 1937 law to be "clearly within the power of Congress under the commerce clause" because it regulated only "sales or transactions in, or directly or intimately affecting, interstate commerce."[21] This ruling didn't break new ground: Congress's power to regulate intrastate prices as part of the regulation of an interstate market had been recognized as far back as the *Shreveport Rate Cases* (1914), and the phrase "directly or intimately" showed that the Court was still applying the pre-1937 test for commerce regulation.[22]

The doctrinal obstacle to breaking out of *Lochner*-era restrictions was the conception that the Tenth Amendment reserved identifiable subject matter for exclusive state regulation. If regulation of employment and production were reserved to the states, then they could not be regulated by federal law even if helpful to a national market regulation. These limitations were necessarily implied—*McCulloch* in reverse. It was clear that the Tenth Amendment would have to be reinterpreted in conjunction with any recognition of implied commerce powers.

As we saw in Chapter 11, this point—the direct conflict between *McCulloch* and the Tenth Amendment—had largely escaped the notice of New Deal scholars, as well as Supreme Court justices with the exception of Harlan Fiske Stone. Justice Stone had already taken significant notice of *McCulloch* in his unpublished concurring opinion in *Blaisdell* and his *Butler* dissent, and he did so again in his famous "footnote 4" in *United States v. Carolene Products Co.* (1938), the case which established the modern doctrine of deferential "rational basis" review for substantive due-process challenges to economic regulation.[23] It was Stone who made the analytical breakthrough on the Tenth Amendment problem, in *United States v. Darby Lumber Co.* (1941).[24] *Darby* involved a challenge to a criminal conviction under the Fair Labor Standards Act of 1938, which prohibited the employment of workers in violation of the Act's minimum wage and maximum hours requirements, and also prohibited shipment of goods produced in violation of those requirements. The former provision ran up directly against the Supreme Court's long-standing doctrine that employment relations were local and not interstate. The latter provision was included in the Act in the hope that its interstate shipment requirement might stand a better chance of meeting the narrow outlaws-of-commerce theory of regulation that the Court had sometimes upheld. The defendant, a local lumber manufacturer criminally charged with violating provisions of the Act, relied heavily on *Hammer v. Dagenhart* and *Carter Coal* to argue that the Act's regulation of employment exceeded Congress's power under the Commerce Clause.[25]

The government defended the law by advancing an implied commerce theory for the first time before the Court. Starting from the premise that Congress could keep "goods produced under substandard labor conditions" out of the channels of interstate commerce, the government argued that prohibiting substandard labor conditions at the source "is a reasonable and appropriate method" of achieving that end. *McCulloch's* "maxim that Congress may choose the means by which its powers are to be exercised has frequently found expression in statutes applicable to transactions not in themselves within any of the granted powers" and "has frequently been applied to statutes enacted under the commerce clause."[26] The government was stretching the historical point, but its bigger problem was *Hammer v. Dagenhart* and the Court's prior view of the Tenth Amendment. The government had to take on both. "The effect of the decision in *Hammer v. Dagenhart* was to establish a limitation upon the commerce power which is contained nowhere in the Constitution, and which is contrary to the scope of that grant of power as defined in cases running from *Gibbons v. Ogden* to the most recent decisions." *Hammer* should be overruled, the government argued. As for the Tenth Amendment, it "offers no independent limitation upon the powers granted to the United States," the government argued, citing *McCulloch*, "but merely states the unquestioned principle that the central government is one of enumerated powers."[27]

The transition from *Jones & Laughlin's* incremental expansion of the pre-1937 doctrines to the New Deal Court's embrace of broad commerce powers played out in the case conference on *Darby*. According to conference notes of Justices Frank Murphy and William O. Douglas, a vigorous debate unfolded between Hughes and

Stone. Hughes opened the conference with a summary of the issues that was so lengthy it put Justice McReynolds and even, briefly, Stone to sleep.[28] Hughes felt that the Act's prohibition of shipment of goods could be sustained as having a sufficiently direct connection to Congress's commerce power to regulate transportation. Presumably, Hughes was prepared to go so far as to overrule *Hammer v. Dagenhart*, perhaps on a Progressive-era outlaws-of-commerce theory. But he expressed serious doubts about the direct regulation of production and employment, which were "not part of interstate commerce," and could come within the commerce power only if they had a "close and immediate" or "close and substantial relation to the interstate commerce."[29] For Hughes, that relation was still a case-by-case determination, and Hughes believed that the statute was constitutionally infirm because it "provides no machinery" allowing an allegedly covered employer to disprove that his business had a close and substantial relation to commerce in a particular case. Instead, the Act categorically found that substandard wages sufficiently affected interstate commerce in any business fulfilling "outside [interstate] orders." As a result, the Act would impose a minimum wage requirement on "some little man with a mill." If the Court extended permissible commerce regulation to such "remote relationships," Hughes warned, "our dual system [of federalism] would be at an end." To Hughes, "[t]his is the most important case we have had by far in connection with the commerce power."[30]

Stone responded that both the shipment and production provisions of the Act should be upheld. Admitting that the Court was "dealing with a new situation," and even an "extraordinary" one, Stone argued that Congress appropriately found "that [a] sub-standard wage in any state does have a profound effect on commerce." Implying that the Court need not revive the old outlaws-of-commerce theory, Stone emphasized that in protecting interstate commerce, "Congress could stop [the evil] at its source." Further, the problem of substandard wages was such that case-by-case findings were unnecessary: "no textile manufacturer would say that substandard wages did not affect commerce. . . ." Surprisingly, Justice Roberts echoed Stone, saying. "I think we have to give credence to what Congress says." Congress found the Act necessary to "stop discrimination"—unfair competition—"between states." When the vote was taken, Stone's position held a commanding seven-vote majority, with Hughes and McReynolds passing. The justices joining Stone seemed entirely untroubled by the implications of upholding the law.[31]

The opinion was assigned to Stone as the senior justice in the majority. To Hughes, nearly seventy-nine years old and already contemplating retirement,[32] it must have been evident that the Court was now Roosevelt's New Deal Court and would take the law in a new direction. "Even with the best possible test, the statute is a highly unsatisfactory one," Hughes complained in a note to Stone, and he "should prefer not to write" an opinion.[33] The justices recognized that upholding the Act would produce a result significantly different from the outcomes of prior cases— Hughes and Stone both acknowledged that the Act presented a "new" or "unique" situation—yet nothing in the written record suggests that the justices anticipated that Stone's opinion would expressly work a major doctrinal shift. At conference, the justices still spoke in terms of older doctrinal tests. Roberts saw wages as having a "direct effect on commerce," while Frankfurter noted that the products in question "have to go into [the] stream of commerce." Stone at most hinted at doctrinal change by speaking in terms of a "substantial effect" on commerce, dropping the restrictive adjectives "close" and "direct."[34]

Nevertheless, over the following month Stone crafted the opinion that truly launched the New Deal's "constitutional revolution."[35] The Court's decision to uphold the Act and overrule *Hammer* was unanimous. Hughes joined reluctantly, stating, "I will go along with this."[36] The crusty James McReynolds, the lone holdout from the conservative Four Horsemen, saw the *Darby* decision as his impetus to retire, grumbling privately that "any country that elects Roosevelt three times deserves no protection."[37]

Stone's opinion first addressed the shipment prohibition. Taking up the government's invitation to adopt a *McCulloch* approach to commerce regulation, Stone acknowledged that "manufacture is not of itself interstate commerce," but argued that "the shipment of manufactured goods interstate is such commerce and the prohibition of such shipment by Congress is indubitably a regulation of the commerce."[38] This conclusion brought the Tenth Amendment to the forefront, and here Stone fulfilled his 1936 promise to Professor Beard to "fix the nature" of the relationship of implied federal powers and the Tenth Amendment. Stone denied that there were any implied exclusions from the commerce power, because that power (cherry-picking broad language from *Gibbons*), "is complete in itself, may be exercised to its utmost extent, and acknowledges no limitations other than are prescribed in the Constitution." That is to say, the commerce power is limited only by express ("prescribed") and not implied (Tenth Amendment/reserved state powers) limitations. Thus, "[i]t is no objection" to the commerce power that it overlaps with "the police power of the states." Indeed, the Tenth Amendment was not, despite long contrary belief, the repository of implied exclusions from the commerce or other powers under the label "reserved state sovereignty." "The [Tenth] amendment states but a truism that all is retained which has not been surrendered."[39] Stone then pressed further, explaining ideas that must have emerged from his correspondence with Beard. "From the beginning and for many years," he asserted, "the [Tenth] amendment has been construed as not depriving the national government of authority to resort to all means for the exercise of a granted power which are appropriate and plainly adapted to the permitted end." Here he cited *McCulloch* and another Marshall Court classic, *Martin v. Hunter's Lessee*, along with a slew of more recent cases. The point was clear: the doctrine of reserved state powers could not be used to defeat a genuine claim of implied federal powers.

Stone next turned to the direct regulation of employment and manufacturing, though the analytical work was largely in place from the shipment discussion. If manufacturing is not interstate commerce, how could it be regulated under the commerce clause? *McCulloch* provided the answer. "The power of Congress over interstate commerce is not confined to the regulation of commerce among the states," Stone announced. "It extends to those activities intrastate which so affect interstate commerce or the exercise of the power of Congress over it as to make regulation of them appropriate means to the attainment of a legitimate end, the exercise of the granted power of Congress to regulate interstate commerce." Stone cited *McCulloch* as direct authority for this proposition. Because the power to regulate interstate commerce permits Congress to "adopt[] the policy of excluding from interstate commerce all goods produced" in violation "of the specified labor standards, it may choose the means reasonably adapted to the attainment of the permitted end, even though they involve control of intrastate activities."[40] And because there was no practical way to distinguish between a manufacturer's goods intended for the interstate market and those intended to be sold intrastate, it was reasonable for Congress to regulate the entirety of the product.

Darby was thus the first case to recognize that *McCulloch*'s doctrine of implied powers applied fully to the Commerce Clause and that implied federal powers could not be blocked by a notion of regulatory areas exclusively reserved to the states under the Tenth Amendment. The clarity of these ideas was muddied a bit by Stone's references to an alternative theory, that Congress could regulate "activities intrastate which have a substantial effect on the commerce or the exercise of the Congressional power over it."[41] Under either test, *Darby* was revolutionary, and the Court's Roosevelt appointees embraced the revolution. Justices Hugo Black and Douglas "heartily agree[d]" with Stone's opinion, Douglas adding that the opinion "has the master's real touch!" Justice Stanley Reed noted, "It has been a long journey, but the end is here. We should have overturned Hammer years ago." Justice Frankfurter's join memo called the opinion "a grand plum pudding" with "so many luscious plums in it that it's invidious to select. But I especially rejoice over (1) the way you buried Hammer v. Dagenhart and (2) your definitive exposure of the empty hobgoblins of the 10th amend[men]t."[42]

Strictly speaking, *Darby*'s analysis extended the commerce power only as far as manufacturers who sold at least some of their products on the interstate market. It remained to be seen whether the Commerce Clause could regulate producers who operated only within a single state but who produced goods *of a type* that was sold by others in interstate markets. The Court addressed this question the following year in *United States v. Wrightwood Diary Co.* (1942).[43] There, the defendant challenged the application of federal milk price supports to its "entirely intrastate" dairy business. Now, with the *Darby* case in its arsenal, the government argued aggressively "that the commerce power extends to the regulation of intrastate *acts* when necessary to make the control of interstate commerce effective." This implied-commerce theory followed directly from "the basic constitutional doctrine" of *McCulloch*, which permits Congress to choose means that fall outside the scope of the enumerated power.[44] Significantly, the government's argument extended implied commerce powers to intrastate *acts* rather than, as in *Gibbons* and former times, to intrastate *commerce* (buying, selling, and transportation) only.

The Court was convinced, and upheld the law. By 1942, ten years into Roosevelt's presidency, the Court consisted of eight Roosevelt appointees plus the pro–New Deal Stone, whom Roosevelt had just elevated to the chief justiceship to replace Hughes. This was a New Deal Supreme Court, packed as effectively through the normal process of retirements as it could have been through Roosevelt's Court-packing plan. Writing for a unanimous Court, Chief Justice Stone referred to evidence suggesting that the federal milk price supports would be undermined if intrastate milk sellers could escape the regulation, since their activity affected the interstate price. "It is the effect upon interstate commerce or upon the exercise of the power to regulate it, not the source of the injury which is the criterion of Congressional power," Stone reasoned.[45] Because "Congress plainly has power to regulate the price of milk distributed through the medium of interstate commerce," it therefore "possesses every power needed to make that regulation effective." The commerce power "extends to those activities intrastate which so affect interstate commerce, or the exertion of the power of Congress over it, as to make regulation of them appropriate means to the attainment of a legitimate end." Stone cited *McCulloch* as the leading case establishing this principle, and *Darby* as the most recent precedent.[46]

The very next sentence, however, outlined a subtly different approach, based on *Gibbons*. "The power of Congress over interstate commerce is plenary and complete in itself, may be exercised to its utmost extent, and acknowledges no limitations other than are prescribed in the Constitution." After citing *Gibbons*, Stone continued, "the reach of that power extends to those intrastate activities which in a substantial way interfere with or obstruct the exercise of the granted power."[47] The two approaches together produced something of a muddle: can Congress regulate all intrastate activities whose regulation is "appropriate" to making an interstate commerce regulation effective? Or only those intrastate activities "which *in a substantial way* interfere with or obstruct" the interstate regulation? Though the two can be harmonized, the *Gibbons* formulation reads more naturally as an alternative to the *McCulloch* formulation of the federal commerce power over intrastate activities— and possibly a narrower one.

Nor could the Court fully bring itself to overrule *Schechter* and *Carter Coal* and dispense with the "direct/indirect" effects test. This language from *Schechter* posed a problem, Stone had said in conference, because it had been incorporated into the statute, which gave the Secretary of Agriculture authority to regulate products "directly affecting" interstate commerce.[48] But the regulation of intrastate milk selling would not fit the *Schechter* understanding of direct effects, even though it met the more recent test of *Darby*. Stone finessed this problem by interpreting the statute as intended to exert the commerce power to the fullest extent permitted by the Court, whatever that might be.[49] This maneuver delighted Frankfurter, who told Stone. "Your disquisition on *Schechter* . . . ought to delight every chess-player." Frankfurter saved his highest praise for Stone's articulation of the new test for commerce power: "Marshall and Holmes would like your first four pages on [the] Commerce Clause."[50]

* * *

McCulloch's triumph as the guiding spirit of the new commerce-power doctrine was short lived. In November 1942, just nine months after *Wrightwood Dairy*, the Court decided *Wickard v. Filburn*,[51] the case now generally regarded as fully establishing the controlling interpretation of the Commerce Clause to this day. *Wickard* considered a Commerce Clause challenge to the Agricultural Adjustment Act of 1938, a modified version of the law struck down in *Butler*. Filburn, an Ohio farmer, had exceeded his wheat quota in the course of growing a wheat crop that was intended to feed his livestock or be milled into flour for his home consumption. The Agriculture department imposed a $117 penalty on Filburn for his excess production under the terms of the Act, and Filburn challenged the statute's application to his wheat crop. The district court sided with Filburn and issued an injunction blocking the fine against him. In the Supreme Court, Filburn's lawyers argued that the Commerce Clause could not reach produce that "has not yet moved into any channel of trade" so that "the relationship to interstate commerce . . . has not yet been called into existence."[52] But the slightly different point that most concerned the Court was that Filburn's home-consumed wheat crop was small potatoes—not intended for any market, and too insignificant to affect the interstate market. This argument had not been directly addressed in *Wrightwood Dairy*, where the dairy had sold its milk within the state.

The government's brief did not cite *McCulloch*, but relied heavily on Stone's incorporation of *McCulloch's* key conceptual terminology in *Darby* and *Wrightwood Dairy*. "The power of Congress extends to intrastate activities 'which so affect interstate commerce, or the exertion of the power of Congress over it, as to make regulation of them appropriate means of' protection, or effective regulation, of interstate commerce," the government argued. It was reasonable for Congress to conclude that "the beneficial purposes of the statute could best be achieved if the quota system applied to all wheat available for marketing and not merely to that which was actually sold." The government brief concluded, again citing *Darby* and *Wrightwood Dairy*, "It has repeatedly been recognized that the Constitution allows Congress to choose the means which it deems most appropriate for the carrying out of the powers entrusted to the Federal government."[53]

Wickard is famous for applying the Commerce Clause to small-scale local activities that are neither interstate nor commerce, and doing so with a unanimous Court. Yet, as Barry Cushman has shown, the underlying decision was surprisingly fraught, causing Justice Jackson, the opinion's author, to agonize over the issue for months.[54]

Wickard was initially argued on May 4, 1942, and Chief Justice Stone opened the May 7 conference by suggesting reversal, to uphold the statute. According to Stone, the case was controlled by *Darby* and *Wrightwood Dairy*. Congress could regulate intrastate matters that were not commerce if they had "a fair relation to commerce," and the regulation of homegrown wheat was a permissible "means"—"perhaps indispensable" means—of regulating commerce "as a matter of logic and economics."[55] Stone's allusion to *McCulloch's* terminology of implied powers seems clear, and the justices' initial vote appeared to favor upholding the statute by seven to zero.[56]

But over the next two weeks, some of the justices seemed to waver, especially Jackson, to whom the opinion had been assigned. On May 22, Jackson circulated a draft opinion that expressed doubts about Congress's commerce power. "We cannot blink the fact that if this Act . . . is to be sustained it regulates intrastate, in fact intra-farm, activities beyond any statute sustained by any former decision of this Court. . . . The regulation appears to extend to matters which would not be thought of as commerce at all. . . ." Jackson cautioned, "To establish the power of Congress over intrastate activity it is of course not sufficient simply to spell out some plausible relationship between such activity and interstate commerce."[57] That sentence could have been lifted out of *Carter Coal*. The same could be said for the conclusion. Congress had "plenary" power over interstate commerce such that "it may exercise it to the fullest extent regardless of reasonableness," Jackson admitted. But a statute "reaching into the reserved power of the states" could be "justified only by a state of facts showing that the intrastate activities sought to be reached are of such quality and substantiality that what would otherwise be an intrusion is proper for the protection and effective exercise of a granted federal power." Because those facts were "far from clear on the record and the legislative history presented," Jackson proposed to remand the case, noting in a Parthian shot that "[a] mere finding of convenience will not sustain federal invasion of an intrastate field."[58] Justices James Byrnes and Frankfurter immediately signed onto this opinion. But Stone, Black, and Douglas wanted to decide the merits of the case, presumably to uphold the statute, and at a conference the next day, the other six justices, including Jackson, shifted to a middle ground favoring re-argument the next term. The Court issued an order for a rehearing on October 12, 1942 to discuss the constitutionality of the Act "so far as it deals with wheat consumed on the farm of the producer."[59]

Over the summer, Jackson agonized over the decision, setting out his thoughts in June and July in two lengthy memos to his law clerk. Jackson found it "a good deal of a problem to me" to extend the commerce power to "a regulation of production and of production not for commerce." The gist of the problem for Jackson was that the *Shreveport Rate Cases* had made "economic relationships" determinative of the scope of the commerce power, transforming a judicial question into a matter of economics and policy. The Court "felt that there must be some standards of economic effects," such as the direct/indirect effects test "made by Chief Justice Hughes in the *Schechter* case and referred to again by him in the *Jones & Laughlin* case." But these

formulations "have not been clear," and even the *Darby* test that "Congress may regulate what is 'appropriate' for regulation in connection with interstate commerce"
"has no real value, as this case amply demonstrates." Jackson seemed certain that
the Court would vote to uphold the Act, but noted, "If we sustain the present Act,
I don't see how we can ever sustain states' rights again as against a Congressional
exercise of the commerce power." This would be merely "the shadow of judicial review," and would disserve both the Court and Congress: "To keep up the pretense
means that we must more and more engage in pure quibbling as to what is appropriate, making the judicial process disrespectable . . ." while "the necessity of waiting
for a quibbling judicial review leads to the framing of legislation in a disrespectably
indirect and inefficient manner, as witness the present scheme."[60] In the end, Jackson
was inclined to throw his hands up in resignation. "Our years of experience have
proved that legal phrases of limitation have almost no value in weighing economic
effects. . . . In such a state of affairs the determination of the limit is not a matter . . . of
constitutional law, but one of economic policy." Better "[t]o place responsibility for
the intelligent and moderate use of the powers of Congress upon the Congress itself" than to "keep up a pretense" of meaningful judicial review. Jackson concluded
that in the *Wickard* case, "[w]e cannot say that there is no economic relationship
between the growth of wheat for home consumption and interstate commerce in
wheat. . . . [We] have no legal standards by which to set our own judgment against
the policy judgment of Congress."[61]

The government's brief for the October re-argument invoked *McCulloch* in
presenting a lengthier elaboration of implied commerce powers. "Congress has the
power to choose any means reasonably adapted to the attainment of a legitimate
end under the commerce clause," the government brief argued. "The exercise of
control over interstate flow and prices . . . is a legitimate object of legislation under
the commerce clause," and "Congress has the power to choose the means to achieve
such a legitimate end." This included the power "to control intrastate transactions,"
a power that "ultimately stems from the doctrine of implied powers and the 'necessary and proper clause." The brief proceeded to cite three pages of excerpts from
McCulloch in support of this "basic rule."[62] The brief was coauthored by Assistant
Attorney General Robert L. Stern, one of the few commentators in the 1930s to
notice (albeit briefly in a footnote) that *McCulloch* could give rise to a theory of implied commerce powers. Interestingly, Jackson had read, and indeed "dog-eared and
underlined," the article in which Stern made this observation.[63]

In his new opinion following re-argument, Jackson upheld the statute in a positive and confident register, shedding the frustrated, downbeat, almost nihilistic
tones of his internal memos. He brushed aside the problem of small-scale local
activity. *Wickard*'s "contribution to the demand for wheat may be trivial by itself,"
but that did not "remove him from the scope of federal regulation," because "his
contribution, taken together with that of many others similarly situated, is far from
trivial."[64] In this case, even home consumption of wheat would affect supply and

demand on the interstate market, since homegrown wheat substitutes for wheat purchased on the open market. The bigger question was under what circumstances Congress could regulate purely local activity in regulating interstate commerce. In *Gibbons*, as read by Jackson, "Marshall described the federal commerce power with a breadth never yet exceeded. He made emphatic the embracing and penetrating nature of this power by warning that effective restraints on its exercise must proceed from political rather than from judicial processes."[65] In the key part of the opinion, Jackson teased out the present-day "substantial effects test" for commerce regulation from language found in *Gibbons*:

> Whether the subject of the regulation in question was "production," "consumption," or "marketing" is, therefore, not material for purposes of deciding the question of federal power before us. . . . [E]ven if appellee's activity be local and though it may not be regarded as commerce, it may still, whatever its nature, be reached by Congress if it exerts a substantial economic effect on interstate commerce, and this irrespective of whether such effect is what might at some earlier time have been defined as "direct" or "indirect."[66]

Jackson was certainly on solid ground in arguing that the *Lochner*-era tests and implied limitations on the commerce power lacked any basis in the language of the Constitution. But nothing in *Gibbons* had suggested that commerce extended beyond trade and navigation (or "intercourse") to include local production. Marshall had said that "completely internal" commerce *does not* fall within the commerce power; he had not said that things "not . . . regarded as commerce" *do*. Bridging this gap between *Gibbons* and the *Wickard* substantial effects test requires abandoning a precise definition of commerce. For Jackson, the scope of the Commerce Clause did not hinge on resolving a debate over whether the linguistic definition of "commerce" included "manufacturing," "agriculture," or "production." Rather, the reach of the commerce power was based on "economic effects."[67] *Wickard* relied less on Marshall's analysis in *Gibbons* than on the idea, as Webster had put it, that "[i]t was in vain to look for a precise and exact definition of the powers of Congress."[68]

But if it was important to connect this new commerce-power doctrine with Marshall, why not rely on *McCulloch*, which tells us that implied powers can extend to matters falling outside the definition of the enumerated power? *Wickard* was unanimous, and in his note to Jackson joining the opinion, Stone professed, "I like very much what you say about 'direct' and 'indirect.' I had hoped for something like that when I remained silent and left it to Cardozo to write the concurring opinion in the *Schechter* Case. But he did not see the matter as you and I do."[69] Yet the opinion lacked the doctrinal refinement of Stone's own opinions in *Darby* and *Wrightwood Dairy*, and one wonders whether Stone noticed the absence of a *McCulloch*-based implied-commerce-powers theory. At the October 13 conference following oral argument, Stone had suggested resolving the case on the basis of such a theory: regulation of interstate shipments in wheat "without including farm consumption was ineffective," and therefore the Act was "appropriate regulation of something which affects commerce."[70] Jackson acknowledged that "if we had to go back to direct & indirect effect doctrines this statute would have to go down," whereas upholding the statute "pushes us one step beyond [the] Darby case."[71] Yet he did not cite *McCulloch*'s test of implied powers, or analyze the case as involving implied powers, perhaps because he found the "appropriate" standard, as he said in the law clerk memo, to have "no real value."

Jackson's intellectual struggle to reach the result he did in *Wickard* was, as Barry Cushman observes, "not without irony." A New Deal partisan and FDR's Attorney General, Jackson had vigorously attacked the Court's undue solicitude for states' rights that now gave him pause.[72] It is remarkable that a justice of Jackson's keenness and ability was unable to break out of the traditional constitutional habit of mind that refused to comprehend implied commerce powers: this, despite the fact that he was self-consciously casting aside traditional doctrine and reaching rhetorically to early constitutional history and Marshall Court opinions. Rather than seeing that the logic of implied powers allowed Congress to regulate things that were not commerce, he took a more blunt-edged approach that the Court could not judge economic matters. He was stuck on the notion that the connection of intrastate activity to interstate commerce was necessarily an economic fact that the Court could not judge. In any event, Jackson did not cite *McCulloch* in his Commerce Clause analysis, and *Wickard*'s substantial effects test is not formulated in *McCulloch*'s terms. *Wrightwood Dairy* stated that Congress "possesses every power needed to make [commerce] regulation effective,"[73] permitting regulation of intrastate matters meeting *McCulloch*'s standard for appropriateness. Jackson's substantial effects test requires regulation of intrastate matters to have a "substantial effect" on interstate commerce, implying vaguely that such regulation falls within the meaning of the Commerce Clause.

Wickard is a foundational case that, in marked contrast to *McCulloch*, established an important doctrinal test that has been more or less followed to this day: Congress has the power to regulate intrastate activities that substantially affect interstate commerce. But *Wickard*'s success as the leading precedent makes the extent of *McCulloch*'s influence on the New Deal transformation uncertain. Stone's opinions in *Darby* and *Wrightwood Dairy* relied directly on *McCulloch* to articulate a theory of implied commerce powers. *Jones & Laughlin Steel* decided before, and *Wickard* decided after Stone's opinions, did not. *McCulloch* had some influence on *Wickard*, however. It is noteworthy that both Stone and Jackson bought into the ideological history offered by New Deal academics. In *Darby*, Stone asserted that *Hammer v. Dagenhart* was a temporary and wrong-headed "departure" from the principles of *McCulloch* and *Gibbons* that "have been so long and repeatedly recognized by this Court" for "more than a century."[74] Jackson likewise dismissed the century of reserved-powers jurisprudence as "a few dicta and decisions of this Court" that were inconsistent with "the course of decision under the Commerce Clause."[75] Jackson did cite *McCulloch* in *Wickard*, not for implied commerce powers, but for judicial restraint. "The conflicts of economic interest between the regulated and those who advantage by it are wisely left under our system to resolution by the Congress under its more flexible and responsible legislative process."[76]

Wickard thus steered the understanding of *McCulloch* away from implied commerce powers and toward a variant of Thayerism that would be developed in the mid-twentieth century by the so-called Process School of constitutional interpretation. Fields of government activity primarily assigned to one branch raise a presumption of interbranch deference—here, deferential judicial review—and assignment to a branch can be inferred from that branch's procedural qualities. In this instance, regulation of the economy requires "flexibility" and "responsibility." The former term refers to the fact that a legislature's range of remedial options far exceeds that of courts; the latter term refers to the democratic representativeness of legislatures relative to courts.[77]

Does *Wickard*'s adoption of a *Gibbons*/definitional approach to the commerce power rather than the *McCulloch*/implied-commerce approach make a difference? In most cases, the two analyses undoubtedly produce the same result. But not in all. We will return to this question in Chapter 13.

* * *

The popular history of the mid-twentieth-century Civil Rights era is dominated by the Supreme Court's decision in *Brown v. Board of Education* (1954), the famous case that struck down state laws mandating racial segregation in their public schools. So powerful is the symbol of *Brown* as a statement of our constitutional value of racial equality that the case tends to overshadow legislative developments that were arguably more important to the progress of civil rights. *Brown*'s importance is undeniable, but its myth has contributed to a misleading portrait of judicial leadership and supremacy in the interpretation of racial equality under the Constitution. Books have been written attempting to appraise the relative contributions of *Brown* in comparison to the grass-roots civil rights movement and legislation responding to it, and that complex task can't be undertaken here.

My focus is on the important role played by *McCulloch* in the evolving constitutional law of racial equality, and that focus emphasizes congressional powers. As seen throughout the previous chapters, the two sources of power by which Congress might regulate race under the doctrine of limited enumerated powers are the Commerce Clause and the Reconstruction Amendments. Congress's constitutional authority to regulate race would depend on the Court's view of implied powers under either or both of these parts of the Constitution. In the mid-twentieth century, the New Deal revolution in federal intervention in the economy would come together with the mid-century Civil Rights movement to give *McCulloch* new meaning, as the Court reconsidered Congress's implied powers to regulate race relations.

In August 1954, three months after *Brown* was decided, Congress designated September 1955 as John Marshall Bicentennial Month to observe the 200th anniversary of Marshall's birth on September 24, 1755. Congress created a commission chaired by Chief Justice Earl Warren to oversee the bicentennial, and President Eisenhower followed up with a proclamation endorsing the tribute and urging citizens to study the Constitution "for a better understanding and appreciation of our country and John Marshall."[78] The timing was opportune. By 1954, iconographic appeals to Chief Justice Marshall had become a source of comfort and confidence to Supreme Court justices anxious about public criticism. The Court was feeling the expected political backlash from its ruling in *Brown* and the follow-up ruling the next year on the desegregation remedy. If John Marshall stood for anything, it was for the supremacy of the Constitution over *state* laws, and that was the same legal posture presented in *Brown* and the anticipated federal judicial intervention into state-mandated southern racial apartheid.

The Marshall Bicentennial was even more widely observed than the 1901 John Marshall Day, with a media campaign and events around the country not limited to lawyers and courthouses.[79] Eisenhower and Warren both spoke at the American Bar Association ceremony in Philadelphia, on August 24, 1955, to kick off the month-long tribute. Although the President's speech was apparently focused on the burgeoning Cold War, he lauded Marshall for showing Americans "that the independence and integrity and capacity of the judiciary are vital to our nation's continued existence."[80] Warren similarly stressed, "Without an independent judiciary, there can be no freedom." Marshall's "[i]nsistence upon the independence of the judiciary" was his "greatest contribution to constitutional law." Marshall, said Warren, "never sought to enlarge the judicial power beyond its proper bounds, nor feared to carry it to the fullest extent that duty required."[81] Ironically, the Commission's final report opened with Holmes's observation that Marshall was the only conceivable icon for American law, completely ignoring the ironic critique in Holmes's message.[82]

Justice Frankfurter spoke at a related event at Harvard, and his lecture, published in the Harvard Law Review under the title *John Marshall and the Judicial Function*, was the source of the most often-quoted assessment of *McCulloch*:

> Unashamedly I recall the familiar phrase in which he expressed the core of his constitutional philosophy: "it is a constitution we are expounding." M'Culloch v. Maryland, 4 Wheat. 316, 407 (1819). It bears repeating because it is, I believe, the single most important utterance in the literature of constitutional law—most important because most comprehensive and comprehending.[83]

"Unashamedly." That word is defensive, and no doubt reflects Frankfurter's sheepish sense that he had in fact quoted the familiar phrase too much already, having inserted it into four of his judicial opinions in the previous few years, and not always to mean the same thing. In *Kovacs v. Cooper* (1949), a First Amendment case, he quoted it to caution his brethren to avoid the "doctrinaire attitude" that "any law touching communication is infected with presumptive invalidity."[84] A few months later, he chastised the majority for forgetting that it was expounding a constitution by "tak[ing] liberties" with the Constitution's narrow grant of Article III jurisdiction to the federal courts.[85] Concurring in the famous *Steel Seizure Case* (1952), he explained that the phrase—which he dubbed "[t]he pole-star for constitutional adjudications"—meant that the Constitution should be given a "spacious" view of government powers, but also "as narrow a delimitation of the constitutional issues as the circumstances permit."[86] Two years after the Harvard lecture, Frankfurter gave the reminder for a fifth time, to argue that the Fifth Amendment should not be read so literally as to allow the military trial of civilian wives of active military personnel: "It may be tiresome, but it is nonetheless vital, to keep our judicial minds fixed on the injunction that 'it is a *constitution* we are expounding.' "[87]

While the great quotation was subject to varying interpretations, Frankfurter used it in the 1955 Harvard lecture to promote the capable Constitution, and to suggest that constitutional adjudication required adaptation to change. I say "suggest" because the essay was a typical Frankfurter performance: elliptical, using historical gloss and rhetorical denial to hit a point close to but not dead on his target, so that he could avoid saying something controversial while letting the reader make the ultimate connection. While lionizing Marshall, Frankfurter was nevertheless not "an adherent of the hero theory of history."[88] And while never mentioning *Brown* or racial justice, he plainly wanted his listeners to understand that the Court was not engaging in judicial activism by adapting the Equal Protection Clause to changing norms of equality. Frankfurter was channeling, if not devising, an indelible connection between *McCulloch*'s theme of the capable Constitution and the Court's desegregation decision.

* * *

The crucial twenty-year period from the end of World War II to the landmark Voting Rights Act of 1965 saw civil rights rise to the top of the political agenda. In the preceding decades, the legislative impetus for civil rights had been limited to federal anti-lynching proposals, which had been repeatedly blocked by southern members of Congress. But in the 1940s and 1950s, members of Congress proposed increasing numbers of civil rights bills, including not only anti-lynching laws, but also federal prohibitions of racially disenfranchising state "poll taxes," school desegregation laws, and public accommodations laws. These political developments were aided by a major shift in thinking about Congress's legislative power under the Reconstruction Amendments, in which revisionist legal scholars argued that the Fourteenth Amendment was intended to confer broad enforcement powers on Congress.[89]

The New Deal constitutional transformation ushered in a new Supreme Court that readily accepted a broad federal power to regulate most or all aspects of the national economy, and thereby reach matters that had for over a century been viewed as exclusively of state legislative concern. The lesson of this for civil rights legislation was not lost on Congress. The practices of race discrimination and segregation in America took place to a large degree in the privately owned public space: business enterprises offering jobs to workers, and goods and services to the public. New Deal constitutionalism could bring these practices within reach of commerce regulation. Thus, a 1946 Federal Fair Employment Practice Bill backed by the Truman administration contained a preface of congressional findings that race discrimination in employment substantially affected the national economy, contributing to "industrial strife," "substandard conditions of living," and depressed wages.[90]

The Fourteenth Amendment and the Commerce Clause figured prominently in these legislative developments. Because civil rights enforcement legislation depended on implied powers, *McCulloch* played a significant role. On December 5, 1946, President Truman announced the formation of a President's Committee on Civil Rights to make recommendations for new legislation. Referring to the last of Franklin Roosevelt's wartime "Four Freedoms," Truman contended that "Freedom from Fear" was "under attack" by racially motivated violence and that the federal government had "a duty to act when state or local authorities abridge or fail to protect" the constitutional guarantees of individual liberties and equal protection of the laws.[91] The Committee's report, written for the general public and published in 1947 as the book *To Secure These Rights*, laid out a program of civil rights legislation with detailed factual and legal justifications. In a section addressing the question of congressional power to enact civil rights laws, the report began with *McCulloch* and "John Marshall's doctrine of liberal construction":

> Our constitution has long been recognized by the Supreme Court itself as a flexible document, subject to varying interpretations and capable of being adapted to the different needs of changing times. Chief Justice Marshall in his great opinion in *McCulloch v. Maryland* called it "a constitution intended to endure for ages to come, and consequently, to be adapted to the various crises of human affairs."
>
> The American people, by and large, have accepted John Marshall's view for more than a century and a quarter. Again and again, the Constitution and its clauses have been construed to authorize positive governmental programs designed to solve the nation's changing problems . . .[92]

The report then listed several constitutional powers, from which civil rights enforcement powers could be implied, including the Commerce Clause "as a basis for fair employment legislation."[93]

Invariably, Congress blocked the several bills proposed in the wake of this report. Even as majority support coalesced for civil rights legislation of various kinds, the structure of Congress worked against passage. Southern members, enjoying long-term incumbency as a benefit of virtual one-party rule in the South, held a disproportionate share of key committee chairmanships in both houses, and southern members could employ the filibuster to hamstring legislation in the Senate.[94]

This gridlock in Congress elevated the potential role of the Court. Legal historian Christopher Schmidt details how several of the justices in the early 1950s expressed strong preferences for congressional rather than judicial action against school segregation. In their conferences and at oral argument in the *Brown* case, several justices suggested that Congress should prohibit school segregation under its Fourteenth Amendment section 5 enforcement powers rather than leaving it to the Court to overrule *Plessy v. Ferguson* (1896), which had held that state-mandated segregation did not violate the Equal Protection Clause. Their assumption was that Congress could go further than mandated by judicial doctrine to promote racial equality. According to this view, Congress could mandate nationwide school desegregation even though "separate but equal" schools remained consistent with the Fourteenth Amendment under *Plessy*. In an unpublished draft concurrence in *Brown*, Justice Jackson argued that the Court was being imposed upon "to supervise transition . . . from segregated to desegregated schools" simply "because our representative system has failed." Jackson along with several leading academics believed that congressional leadership in school desegregation was preferable as a constitutional matter and likely to be more effective to change social norms. Even segregationists who attacked the *Brown* decision argued, strategically, that Congress and not the Court had power to desegregate the nation's schools.[95]

It took Congress ten more years to push through the long-awaited national civil rights law. This landmark legislation, the Civil Rights Act of 1964, prohibited discrimination on account of race, sex, and other grounds in public accommodations, employment, and education. The act greatly extended the ground covered by the Civil Rights Act of 1875, which had been limited to "inns, public conveyances [and] . . . places of public amusement." Its effect is to outlaw race discrimination in private-sector institutions where such discrimination could effectively maintain a social caste system that would make racial equality impossible. So important is this law, and so entrenched is its core principle extending equal protection to the societal domain, that many scholars view it as of quasi-constitutional dimension.[96]

The 1964 Civil Rights Act was signed into law on July 2 and was immediately challenged in federal court by local businesses in the South. By the fall, a pair of cases reached the Court, which upheld the law. In *Heart of Atlanta Motel v. United States* (1964),[97] the Act was challenged by a small motel that refused to rent rooms to black customers. In *Katzenbach v. McClung* (1964),[98] the challenge was brought by the owner of Ollie's Barbecue, a local restaurant that refused to serve black patrons in its dining area. The parties and lower courts assumed without much discussion that the *Civil Rights Cases* (1883) meant that private businesses could not be regulated under the Fourteenth Amendment, so the arguments there and in the Supreme Court focused on the Commerce Clause. The challengers argued that their businesses did not involve interstate commerce under *Wickard*.[99] But the Supreme Court upheld the Act as a valid regulation of interstate commerce. Even if the businesses were "purely local," Congress's power "to promote interstate commerce also includes the power to regulate the local incidents thereof, including local activities in both the States of origin and destination, which might have a substantial and harmful effect upon that commerce." Race discrimination by businesses was "an obstruction to interstate commerce" that Congress could prohibit, "however 'local' their operations may appear."[100] *Wickard's* holding that purely local activities could be regulated if, in the aggregate, they substantially affected interstate commerce, was plainly adequate to sustain the law. Nevertheless, the Court took pains to add that the two businesses had interstate connections. The motel served interstate travelers, and thus participated in a system of exclusion that made interstate travel a potential nightmare for black people. The restaurant "either serves or offers to serve interstate travelers or serves food a substantial portion of which has moved in interstate commerce," and thus contributed to the imposition of "burdens both upon the interstate flow of food and upon the movement of products generally."[101]

The majority opinions began a trend of the Court to blur the distinction between the *Gibbons*/definitional approach to commerce-power cases marked by *Wickard*, and the *McCulloch*/implied-powers approach marked by *Darby* and *Wrightwood Dairy*. The *Heart of Atlanta Motel* opinion cited *McCulloch*, though only once, at the tail end of a lengthy quotation from *Darby* to the effect that Congress may regulate intrastate activities as "appropriate means" of regulating interstate commerce. Yet the Court began its commerce discussion with lengthy quotations from *Gibbons*, from which it derived the "determinative test" as "simply whether the activity sought to be regulated is 'commerce which concerns more States than one' and has a real and substantial relation to the national interest"—not whether the activity was an appropriate means of commerce regulation.[102] The *McClung* opinion did not cite *McCulloch* at all, yet nevertheless suggested *McCulloch's* influence by making the now-axiomatic statement that congressional conclusions about the extent of the effects on interstate commerce should be reviewed deferentially by the Court: "where we find that the legislators, in light of the facts and testimony before them, have a rational basis for finding a chosen regulatory scheme necessary to the protection of commerce, our investigation is at an end."[103]

By underutilizing *McCulloch* in these cases, the Court missed the chance to place the 1964 Civil Rights Act on a more solid constitutional footing, or at least a more weighty and dignified principle. To forestall the objection that race discrimination is not "commerce," the Court in *McClung* found it necessary to rely on picayune transactional details. Ollie's Barbecue purchased out-of-state supplies, the Court observed, and its discriminatory actions involved selling food. More importantly, the Court bypassed its opportunity to base Congress's landmark civil rights law squarely on the legislative power to enforce the Fourteenth Amendment Equal Protection Clause. Under *McCulloch*'s view of implied powers, the Court could have acknowledged Congress's power to prohibit "private" discrimination in the social space as necessary and proper to enforcing the Fourteenth Amendment guarantee of "public" racial equality. Such a decision would have required overruling the *Civil Rights Cases*. Justices Hugo Black, William O. Douglas, and Arthur Goldberg each wrote concurring opinions arguing that the majority should have done exactly that.[104] Instead, the majority distinguished the *Civil Rights Cases* as inapplicable, since that precedent had not considered whether the commerce power could be used to prohibit race discrimination. As previously noted, the *Civil Rights Cases* remains good law, reaffirmed by the Rehnquist Court as recently as 2000. The result is not inconsequential.[105]

The Supreme Court's 1964 decisions on the Civil Rights Act, together with the 1883 *Civil Rights Cases* create a painful irony. In our commercial nation, where the private sector owns and operates most of our social space, the Supreme Court understands Congress's power to prohibit race discrimination in the social space as a function of its power to regulate "the interstate flow of food and . . . of products generally." The landmark 1964 Civil Rights Act is constitutional, not because of Congress's power to enforce "the equal protection of the laws," but because Congress has the power to regulate the sale of a barbecue sandwich.

* * *

Before 1965, the Court had not connected the enforcement language of the Reconstruction Amendments with *McCulloch*. Only two dissenting opinions more than eighty years previously had done so.[106] The Black and Douglas concurrences in *Heart of Atlanta Motel* were thus significant in relying on *McCulloch* to argue that the Civil Rights Act of 1964 was "'appropriate' and 'plainly adapted' to the end of enforcing" rights under the Reconstruction Amendments.[107] This connection was soon turned into doctrine by a majority of the Court, though not so far as to overrule the *Civil Rights Cases*.

The occasion for doing so arose out of constitutional challenges to another major piece of mid-twentieth-century civil rights legislation, the Voting Rights Act of 1965. The Act outlawed racially discriminatory voting practices and created powerful new federal enforcement mechanisms to crack down on state laws restricting minority rights. Of particular concern was the state use of subterfuges to evade the Fourteenth and Fifteenth Amendments with laws that seemed race neutral on their face but that were designed to disenfranchise black and other racial minority voters.

Among other provisions, states and localities with a history of discriminatory voting practices would have to submit any change in voting laws to the U.S. Department of Justice for approval before they could go into effect.

Two Supreme Court cases decided in the 1965–66 term considered constitutional challenges to the Voting Rights Act. The state of South Carolina led a broad attack on the core provisions of the Act, sections 4 through 6, which require suspension of voting procedures with racially discriminatory impact, and federal review and approval of changes to voting laws for jurisdictions with abnormally low rates of minority voting. In *South Carolina v. Katzenbach* (1966),[108] the state challengers argued that those provisions encroached on the states' traditional powers to determine voting procedures, and exceeded the enforcement powers of Congress under the Fifteenth Amendment. Those enforcement powers, the challengers argued, merely authorized Congress to lay out general principles of voting rights, and not to implement specific preventive measures. The Court swept away these arguments by imposing "clear" "ground rules" in interpreting the scope of congressional enforcement powers: "The basic test to be applied in a case involving § 2 of the Fifteenth Amendment is the same as in all cases concerning the express powers of Congress *with relation to the reserved powers of the States.* Chief Justice Marshall laid down the classic formulation, 50 years before the Fifteenth Amendment was ratified." The "the task of fashioning specific remedies" was precisely what is entailed by the power to adopt means to execute its powers as expressed by *McCulloch.*[109] The phrase "with relation to the reserved powers of the States" emphasized the eradication at long last of the Taney-era doctrine that reserved state powers could create implied limitations on the implied powers of Congress.

The Court took this principle a step further a few months later in *Katzenbach v. Morgan* (1966).[110] New York state challenged § 4(e) of the Voting Rights Act, which barred the use of English language proficiency as a requirement for voting. In enacting this provision, Congress specifically had intended to overrule New York's disenfranchisement of citizens who had relocated to New York from Puerto Rico. The difficulty, and the difference with the *South Carolina* case, was that the Supreme Court had recently decided that an English literacy requirement was not prohibited by the Fourteenth and Fifteenth Amendments. Nevertheless, the Court now concluded that § 4(e) was constitutional. Although the English literacy requirement was not itself a violation of the Fourteenth Amendment's Equal Protection Clause, prohibiting it was "appropriate legislation" under section 5 of the Fourteenth Amendment because Congress could view the measure as a reasonable prophylactic to prevent violations of equal protection of the laws. This conclusion seems to follow naturally from the application of *McCulloch's* implied-powers principle to the Fourteenth Amendment's enforcement clause. Just as *McCulloch* was read in *Darby* and *Wrightwood Dairy* to permit regulation of activities that are not interstate commerce where necessary and proper to effectuate a regulation of interstate commerce, so Congress could prohibit practices that did not themselves violate equal protection where it deemed such a prohibition "conducive" to protecting against equal protection violations. Justice William Brennan, the liberal icon who served on the Court from 1956 to 1990, wrote for the seven-to-two majority, making this exact point. The "*McCulloch v. Maryland* standard is the measure of what constitutes 'appropriate legislation' under § 5 of the Fourteenth Amendment," Brennan wrote. "Correctly viewed, § 5 is a positive grant of legislative power authorizing Congress to exercise its discretion in determining whether and what legislation is needed to secure the guarantees of the Fourteenth Amendment." The question for the Court, then, was simply whether § 4(e) of the Voting Rights Act was " 'appropriate legisla- tion' to enforce the Equal Protection Clause, that is, . . . whether it is 'plainly adapted to that end' and whether it is not prohibited by but is consistent with 'the letter and spirit of the constitution.' "[111] To require a judicial determination that a state law violated the Fourteenth Amendment before Congress could prohibit it "would depreciate both congressional resourcefulness and congressional responsibility for implementing the Amendment" and "would confine the legislative power" to an "insignificant role."[112]

Katzenbach v. Morgan was a case whose far-reaching potential was never fully understood or realized, as we will see. By reading a "*McCulloch* standard" into the enforcement provisions of the Reconstruction Amendments, *Katzenbach* might have been seen to overrule the *Civil Rights Cases*, which had been premised on the idea that Congress's enforcement powers were strictly limited to the scope of the rights granted by the amendments. As Justice Brennan had written a few months previously in a separate opinion in *United States v. Guest* (1966), by "adopting the *McCulloch v. Maryland* formulation for each of the [Reconstruction] Amendments," the Court would henceforth view section 5 of the Fourteenth Amendment "as a positive grant of legislative power, authorizing Congress to exercise its discretion in fashioning remedies to achieve civil and political equality for all citizens."[113]

* * *

The thirty-odd years from the New Deal turnaround to the late 1960s represented a high-water mark for *McCulloch*. For the first time, the Court treated *McCulloch*'s test for implied powers as binding authority fully applicable to all constitutional grants of power to Congress. Prior to 1941, the Court had virtually denied *McCulloch*'s ap- plicability to the Commerce Clause and the Reconstruction Amendments in order to prevent Congress from broadly regulating race relations or the national economy. The Court had never come out and said *McCulloch* was so limited. Instead, the Court had refused to recognize most such implied powers, subjecting the legisla- tive powers of Congress to implied limitations arising out of the Tenth Amendment doctrine of reserved state powers. The pre-1941 Court simply failed or refused to see that *McCulloch* might require otherwise. Now, with the Tenth Amendment con- straint removed by the Court in *Darby*, *McCulloch* for the first time was being ap- plied to something like its full potential. But this was not to last.

13

"A Splendid Bauble"

McCulloch in the Long Conservative Court, 1969–2018

Since 1969, *McCulloch's* canonical status has only increased. Since 1985, the Supreme Court has cited *McCulloch* with greater frequency than ever before—on average, about two to three times in its fewer than eighty published opinions each year.[1] The bulk of academic scholarship canonizing *McCulloch* as the aggressively nationalistic decision that established the constitutionality of broad federal powers has also been written during this period. But this time frame has also seen the advent of a long conservative Court, which—as we will see in this chapter—has retreated from implied commerce powers and broad Reconstruction Amendment enforcement powers. The Court has certainly not retreated all the way back to 1936, but it has done so notably. Marshall had warned against restrictive interpretations of implied powers that would "impair the right of the legislature to exercise its best judgment in the selection of measures to carry into execution the constitutional powers of the government." To do so would reduce the Constitution to "a splendid bauble."[2] It is fair to say that the Civil Rights–era decisions of the 1960s represented a high-water mark for *McCulloch* as a precedent, and that *McCulloch* has since reverted to a largely symbolic role—"a splendid bauble." Why would scholarship about *McCulloch* become so insistent that it has established the foundations of the modern welfare state during the same period of time that the Supreme Court is creating uncertainty about that very thing?

* * *

The Warren Court ended in June 1969, *McCulloch's* sesquicentennial, when Warren Burger assumed the chief justiceship on the day of Earl Warren's retirement. While "liberal"/"conservative" labels applied to the Supreme Court are broad-brush characterizations that admit exceptions, the post–New Deal and Warren Courts can be characterized as fairly liberal for the thirty-two years from mid-1937 to mid-1969. President Richard Nixon set out to reverse the Warren Court's liberalism with his judicial appointments, and by the end of his first term, 1969–72, he had appointed four justices. The Court has held conservative majorities of five to four or six to three ever since. The impression of a "long conservative Court" is heightened by the unprecedented stability (or stasis) in the actual composition of the Supreme Court. The rate of turnover of Court personnel from 1970 to 2018 was about half that of the turnover rate from 1937 to 1969.[3] Moreover, in the twenty-four years from Stephen Breyer's appointment in 1994 through the end of 2018, there were only six changes in Court personnel, and each new appointment involved replacing a retired justice with someone of the same general ideological stance.[4]

The doctrinal impact of this conservative majority has been profound. While the results have not been uniform across the board of social and political issues reaching the Court, constitutional law has taken a decided conservative turn in this time period. The Court has severely restricted the rights of criminal defendants and of individuals to sue states for damages. The Court has presided over the erosion of the right to obtain an abortion. It has blocked the ability of government to attack the lingering effects of race discrimination by almost completely outlawing race-based affirmative action programs. It has gutted the Voting Rights Act, blocked government attempts to control gun violence, and made it virtually impossible to regulate of the outsized role of money in electoral politics. In the name of states rights, it struck down the Medicaid expansion provision of the Affordable Care Act, leaving several million of the nation's poor without viable health insurance. This is a partial list.

* * *

McCulloch rarely does any real doctrinal work in modern Supreme Court decisions, despite the fact that it has been cited in over 130 opinions since 1969. Most of the time, the justices used *McCulloch* as a symbol for a very abstract point or to signal the importance of the constitutional issue it was deciding. In *INS v. Chadha* (1983),[5] for example, the Court cited *McCulloch* to point out that acts of Congress are constitutional if they do "not offend some . . . constitutional restriction." The majority in *New York v. United States* (1992) cited *McCulloch* as authority for the proposition that the Necessary and Proper Clause authorizes Congress to make laws necessary and proper to execute its powers: the Court quoted the Clause itself, but apparently deemed that authority insufficient.[6] The Court has more recently cited *McCulloch* for the proposition that "all political power flows from the people," that the Constitution should be read "as a unified, coherent whole," that federal legislation must "be consistent with the letter and spirit of the constitution," and that as a "general principle," the "federal government has a wide choice of . . . mechanisms and means."[7]

Two exceptions to this largely symbolic use of *McCulloch* show what doctrinal treatment of the case might look like. In *United States Term Limits v. Thornton* (1995),[8] a five-justice majority opinion by Justice Stevens relied heavily on *McCulloch's* structural principles to conclude that states lacked the power to impose term limits on their federal congressional representatives. More recently, *United States v. Comstock* (2010) parsed *McCulloch* closely in an extensive analysis of the meaning of the Necessary and Proper Clause.[9] The Court upheld a federal law that authorized continued "civil" detention of federal prisoners who were found to be dangerous sexual predators as of the expected date of their release. The basis for the congressional power was challenged, and the Court held that it was necessary and proper to executing Congress's power to maintain a federal prison system, which itself was necessary and proper to its power to enact and enforce criminal laws (many of which are themselves implied from other particular enumerated powers). The majority based its decision on "five considerations, taken together":

> (1) the breadth of the Necessary and Proper Clause, (2) the long history of federal involvement in this arena, (3) the sound reasons for the statute's enactment in light of the Government's custodial interest in safeguarding the public from dangers posed by those in federal custody, (4) the statute's accommodation of state interests, and (5) the statute's narrow scope.[10]

The two dissenters (Scalia and Thomas) questioned whether legislative powers could be implied from other implied powers. At some point, doesn't congressional power go too far afield? But despite its superficial appeal, this argument can't be put into practice without embracing an unworkable, case-by-case test of "directness." Implied powers can always be sliced thinly to make it look as though there were multiple levels of implication. At the same time, the constitutionality of implied powers to execute implied powers has long been settled. To take just one example: the power to raise and support armies implies the power to implement a military draft, which implies a power to issue draft cards, which implies a power to criminalize burning a draft card.[11] The most famous example, of course, is found in *McCulloch* itself: the power to charter the Second Bank was implied from the implied power of the government to conduct fiscal operations through a treasury department. (The power to create a treasury is not enumerated in the Constitution.) It seems a bit late in the day to raise constitutional eyebrows about this issue now.

Comstock re-raises an unanswered ambiguity at the heart of *McCulloch's* implied-powers analysis. As seen in Chapter 3, *McCulloch* suggested that Congress has broad discretion to determine the extent of its own implied powers, but Marshall walked back from that position with hints about the Court's authority to second-guess that discretion. It remains to be seen whether *Comstock's* "five factors" harden into an elaborate, non-deferential test. If a *"Comstock* test" becomes the norm for all challenges to congressional exercises of implied powers, the Court will be generating a lot of work for itself, while eroding the deference-to-Congress reading of *McCulloch*.[12]

* * *

Starting in the early 1990s, constitutional law commentators watched with alarm as the Court's conservative majority began to strike down increasing numbers of federal laws on various federalism grounds. Of particular interest here, the Court rediscovered—or clarified, depending on one's viewpoint—limitations on the extent of Congress's powers under the Reconstruction Amendments and the Commerce Clause, and thus renewed the debate over how *McCulloch* should be interpreted.

In two Rehnquist Court cases, the five-to-four conservative majority imposed limitations on Congress's section 5 power to enforce the Fourteenth Amendment "by appropriate legislation." *City of Boerne v. Flores* (1997),[13] involved the Religious Freedom Restoration Act (RFRA), a 1993 federal law intended to impose a restrictive judicial test of "strict scrutiny" on state and federal laws that incidentally affect religious practices. The law purported to overrule a 1990 Supreme Court decision, *Oregon Division of Employment v. Smith*,[14] that applied the far more permissive "rational basis" test to such laws. In *Smith*, the Court had decided that Oregon's drug laws did not impermissibly restrict religion even though they interfered with a Native American's ritual ingestion of peyote. In *Boerne*, the Court held that a municipal historic-landmark law that happened to bar the renovation of a historic church likewise did not impermissibly interfere with religious exercise. While these results are plausible and even sensible, the reasoning of *Boerne* was ominous for congressional enforcement of civil rights. Congress's power to enforce the Fourteenth Amendment did not permit it to define the constitutional right, the Court reasoned. Therefore, laws that protected constitutional rights more broadly than the Court defined them had to meet a test much more stringent than the deferential *McCulloch* test for "appropriate legislation." Congress can cast a remedial net that is wider than the Court's definition of the scope of a Fourteenth Amendment right, but only if the remedy is "congruent and proportional" to some historic or ongoing violation by state or local government. In *Boerne*, there was no history or current practice of curtailing religious exercise, so RFRA was held unconstitutional as applied to state and local governments.[15]

This principle was applied to strike down a key provision of the Violence Against Women Act (VAWA) in *United States v. Morrison* (2000).[16] The law offered a civil damages remedy to women who were victimized by crimes motivated by gender animus, and *Morrison* involved such a suit stemming from a rape. As with the 1875 and 1964 Civil Rights Acts, the law challenged in *Morrison* was potentially sustainable under either the Fourteenth Amendment or the Commerce Clause. The problem with the Fourteenth Amendment theory (the Commerce Clause issue will be discussed later) was that the rape was "private" conduct, and the Court made clear that the state action requirement from the *Civil Rights Cases* remained good law. While recognizing that state neglect might meet this requirement and justify federal enforcement, a five-to-four majority found insufficient evidence of states failing to protect women against acts of violence. The Court thus applied *Boerne* to invalidate the law as an impermissible attempt by Congress to broaden the Fourteenth Amendment right to equal protection of the laws.[17]

A striking and explicit limitation of *McCulloch* in modern civil rights jurisprudence occurred in *Shelby County v. Holder* (2015).[18] There, the Court invalidated the "preclearance" provision in section 4 of the Voting Rights Act of 1965, which required state or local jurisdictions to submit any changes in their voting rights laws for prior approval by the Civil Rights Division of the U.S. Department of Justice. The preclearance requirement was intended to prevent states from holding elections under racially discriminatory voting laws while those laws were being challenged in protracted court cases. Because preclearance was recognized as a stringent remedy, jurisdictions would be subject to it only if they had an egregious prior record of voting discrimination. The preclearance requirement had prevented implementation of hundreds of racially discriminatory voting schemes, and had been reaffirmed by an overwhelming bipartisan majority of Congress in its 2006 amendments to the Voting Rights Act.[19]

Nevertheless, a five-to-four majority struck down the preclearance provision. Brushing aside arguments that the *McCulloch* standard gave Congress broad discretion to select appropriate means to enforce the Fifteenth Amendment's guarantee, Chief Justice Roberts's opinion maintained that the law violated two principles of federalism: the states' traditional role in regulating elections, and a "fundamental principle of equal [state] sovereignty."[20] Once again, as in the nineteenth century, an unwritten principle of state sovereignty, drawn from the "spirit" of the Constitution, blocked implied federal powers under *McCulloch*. The dissenters pointed this out.[21]

* * *

The "federalism revival" first caught the attention of commentators in 1995, when the Court struck down a federal law as exceeding Congress's commerce powers for the first time in nearly sixty years. *United States v. Lopez* (1995)[22] invalidated the Gun Free School Zones Act, which made it a federal crime to possess a gun within 1,000 feet of a school. The law was duplicative of state laws and appeared at the time to add little to school safety. Of greater concern than the immediate result was the majority's reasoning, that the regulated activity was neither itself "economic" in nature nor sufficiently connected with economic activity to qualify as commerce regulation.[23] These concerns surfaced again in 2000 in *Morrison*, where the same five-to-four majority struck down VAWA's civil damages remedy for gender-motivated violence. In addition to rejecting the Fourteenth Amendment argument, as discussed earlier, the Court also dismissed the Commerce Clause argument by following *Lopez*. The regulated conduct—a sexual assault—was neither economic activity in itself nor, despite the manifest economic consequences of violence against women, sufficiently connected to economic activity to qualify as commerce regulation.[24] In both cases, the dissenters warned that this sort of reasoning harkened back to the *Lochner* era, which struck down laws regulating purportedly noncommercial activity, such as employment or production, based on categorical tests of "direct" relatedness to interstate commerce.[25]

Was the *Lochner* era concept, that reserved state powers could defeat implied commerce powers, making a comeback? Critics seemed to think so. *Lopez* and *Morrison* suggested that there must be some subject matter that Congress cannot regulate under the commerce power, because otherwise the commerce power would be unlimited and "obliterate the distinction between what is national and what is local and create a completely centralized government."[26] This need to preserve a national/local regulatory distinction based on defined categories is indeed a pre–New Deal idea. Although the *Lopez* and *Morrison* opinions cited *Jones & Laughlin Steel* for the quotation, as if to give it post–New Deal legitimacy, we have seen that the quotation actually originated with Justice Cardozo's 1935 concurrence in *Schechter Poultry*.[27] The idea that there "must be something" Congress cannot regulate—what I have elsewhere called the "mustbesomething rule"—stands in tension with *Darby's* principle that the Tenth Amendment is a "truism" rather than a repository of definable regulatory fields denied to Congress. *Lopez* and *Morrison* fail to tell us what that "something" is, but only that it exists, as if it were a kind of constitutional dark matter that is known without being fully identifiable.[28]

During the years *Lopez* and *Morrison* were decided, the first few states began to enact medical-marijuana legalization laws. The first such law was California's, and it came up for review before the Supreme Court in *Gonzales v. Raich* (2005).[29] A cancer patient sued federal officials for seizing her homegrown marijuana plants, which she possessed legally under state law. The federal officers had acted pursuant to the federal Controlled Substances Act (CSA),[30] a sprawling federal criminal statute that regulates the massive national black market in illegal drugs along with the abusive distribution of prescription drugs. The question for the Court was whether the federal law could constitutionally regulate simple possession of marijuana; if so, it would preempt the state legalization law under the Supremacy Clause. Conservative libertarians hoped that the conservative justices' rediscovered interest in states' rights would lead them to trim back the coverage of the CSA and uphold the state legalization law. But the four liberals now acceded to the *Lopez-Morrison* "economic activity" qualification on the commerce power, and joined by the conservative Anthony Kennedy ruled in favor of the federal law. "Consumption" of marijuana was indeed economic activity, they reasoned. Because legal "medical" marijuana could easily slip into the black market for illegal marijuana, the aggregate impact of all marijuana consumption could substantially affect interstate commerce, and therefore be subject to Commerce Clause regulation by the CSA. The five-justice majority opinion thus relied on the *Wickard-Gibbons*-definitional approach to the Commerce Clause.

The majority glossed over one small but important point: Raich's plants were seized pursuant to the CSA's prohibition of "simple possession" of marijuana, and simple possession of a commodity is not "economic activity" under *Lopez*.[31] Undoubtedly, Raich intended to consume her marijuana, but the statute in question did not make "intent to consume" an element of the crime of possession. The majority finessed this difficulty by asserting, "Prohibiting the intrastate possession or manufacture of an article of commerce is a rational (and commonly utilized) means of regulating commerce in that product."[32] The rationality of the means is undoubted, but since simple possession is not commerce, it can be swept into a commerce regulation only by virtue of a *McCulloch*/implied-powers argument, not by reliance on the definition of commerce. The majority did not acknowledge this problem or cite *McCulloch*.

Justice Antonin Scalia saw this issue. In providing an interesting sixth vote to sustain the federal law and invalidate the state legalization of medical marijuana, he issued a concurrence in the judgment, relying on a *McCulloch*/implied-commerce theory. Quoting *Wrightwood Dairy's* statement that Congress "possesses every power needed to make [interstate commerce] regulation effective," Scalia carefully distinguished the *McCulloch* and *Gibbons* approaches, in the only Supreme Court opinion ever to do so. "The regulation of an intrastate activity may be essential to a comprehensive regulation of interstate commerce even though the intrastate activity does not itself 'substantially affect' interstate commerce," Scalia explained. "Congress may regulate even noneconomic local activity if that regulation is a necessary part of a more general regulation of interstate commerce. The relevant question is simply whether the means chosen are 'reasonably adapted' to the attainment of a legitimate end under the commerce power. . . ." Citing *McCulloch*, Scalia concluded that "the Necessary and Proper Clause . . . empowers Congress to enact laws in effectuation of its enumerated powers that are not within its authority to enact in isolation." Simple possession, homegrowing, and consumption of marijuana, were not "economic activities" within the definition of commerce, but that was "immaterial." Congress could regulate them as implied commerce powers under *McCulloch*, because their prohibition was reasonably adapted to the regulation of an interstate black market in marijuana.[33]

Scalia offered a cogent theory of implied commerce powers that helped make sense of *Lopez* and *Morrison*. Both the Gun Free School Zones Act and VAWA were regulations of crime, not of interstate markets. If the overall target of a law is not itself an economic activity, perhaps it was reasonable to require that the immediately regulated conduct be economic activity, at least if one adhered to the doctrine of limited enumerated powers. That is to say, there must be regulation of economic activity somewhere in a law enacted under the Commerce Clause. But where, as in the CSA, the law regulates an interstate market, the implied-powers concept allows Congress to regulate even non-economic, intrastate things, so long as doing so is reasonably believed to make the interstate market regulation more effective.

These issues came up again in *National Federation of Independent Business (NFIB) v. Sebelius* (2012),[34] the case challenging the Affordable Care Act with which this book began. There, the question was whether Congress could impose an "individual mandate" that required all Americans to have health insurance or else pay a penalty with their income taxes. It was widely understood that the individual mandate was critical to the functioning of the law: the uninsured population tended to be overrepresented by younger and healthier people, and their absence from the insurance pool would drive insurance rates to prohibitively expensive levels. The fate of the mandate was thus critical to the survival of the entire program. The argument made by the challengers to the law was that the commerce power could only regulate "economic *activity*," under *Lopez* and *Morrison*. But the uninsured population was engaged in "*in*activity"—opting out of participation in the market for health care. The Court's five conservative justices agreed that the individual mandate was an unconstitutional attempt to regulate "inactivity." Four (Scalia, Kennedy, Thomas, and Alito) issued a "joint dissent" arguing that the entire law should be struck down. Chief Justice Roberts issued his own opinion, agreeing with the joint dissent that the federal commerce power could not reach "economic *in*activity" but upholding the mandate under the taxing power—because a person could pay a tax in lieu of buying unwanted health insurance.

Although the Affordable Care Act survived a close call, it is worth considering the reasoning and implications of the ruling that "inactivity" can't be regulated under the commerce power. On its face, the reasoning is bad. To define the refusal to buy health insurance as "inactivity" is mere semantics. Uninsured people could easily be characterized as engaged in the economic activities of "free-riding," "market-timing," or even "gambling" on continued good health. Either they would get their health care needs met at the emergency room, where hospitals would be morally or legally obligated to treat them; or they would jump into the insurance pool later in life, at a stage when they would be using the health care system more regularly. Moreover, the five conservatives were making something of a fetish of the word "activity" as it had appeared in prior cases. The Court in cases like *Wickard*, *Morrison*, and *Lopez* did say that the commerce power could extend to "intrastate activities."[35] But the Court in former cases clearly meant that Congress could employ the substantial effects test to regulate things that *are not* interstate commerce. There is no constitutional basis for insisting that those noncommercial things constitute "action" rather than "inaction." The word "activity" was a mere placeholder that meant "subject of regulation," and could easily have been replaced with words like "behavior," "matter," or "thing." Had the Court used one of those words in

Wickard or *Lopez*, the almost absurd fussiness of the activity/inactivity distinction in *NFIB* would have been more plainly exposed.

The "inactivity" argument is even more dubious if we apply the *McCulloch*/ implied-commerce theory so cogently explained by Scalia in his *Raich* concurrence. The concept of implied powers, established in *McCulloch*, tells us that Congress may assert a power not expressly granted (in *NFIB*, regulation of "inactivity") that is convenient, plainly adapted, or conducive to executing its enumerated powers (here, regulation of interstate commerce). Saying that "inactivity" is not "commerce" merely tells us that regulating inactivity is not an exercise of the express power of regulating commerce. But implied powers do not depend on *definitions* of express ones. Rather, they flow from the practical relationship between the regulatory object and the express power. Was regulating "inactivity" reasonably adapted to the effectiveness of the Affordable Care Act's regulation of the health care market? Plainly it was. Chief Justice Roberts and the *NFIB* joint dissenters recognized this. Indeed, the joint dissenters argued that the entire statute had to be struck down because the individual mandate was so integral—not just reasonably adapted—that the Affordable Care Act could not function without it.[36]

Scalia's *McCulloch*/implied-powers argument in *Raich* irrefutably supported the individual mandate. That presented no problem to Scalia himself. As Professor Randy Barnett quipped, Scalia "would not even have to break a sweat" to distinguish away his *Raich* concurrence in order to rule against the individual mandate.[37] Scalia may not have broken a sweat, but that was only because he was not one to sweat when contradicting himself: he signed onto an opinion that simply ignored his opinion in *Raich*.

Chief Justice Roberts made a token effort to address *McCulloch*. He first offered a circular argument that however "necessary" the individual mandate was, it was not "proper"—*because it was not within the definition of commerce.* "The individual mandate . . . vests Congress with the extraordinary ability to create the necessary predicate to the exercise of an enumerated power."[38] That is to say, the mandate impermissibly requires a purchase of health insurance in order to bring uninsured people within the commerce power, where it can regulate them. But the claim that the individual mandate creates the "necessary predicate" for commerce power regulation simply assumes away *McCulloch* and implied commerce powers, which allow regulation to extend beyond the definitions of enumerated powers. Roberts then adapted James Madison's failed argument to Congress in opposition to the Bank of the United States in 1791. The Necessary and Proper Clause, Roberts argued, "does not license the exercise of any 'great substantive and independent power[s]' beyond those specifically enumerated."[39] But Roberts offered no further insight into what a "great power" is, or why requiring the purchase of health insurance is the exercise of a "great power" rather than merely an implied commerce power. He would have been extremely challenged to do so, because there is no sensible rule that could tell us that making someone buy health insurance is "greater" than chartering a Bank of the United States, exercising eminent domain, making paper money a legal tender, deporting or excluding aliens, acquiring territories, or drafting civilians into military service. Yet all those other implied powers have been recognized by the Supreme Court.[40]

It is undoubtedly naive to suggest that doctrinal fine points dictate the results of close or highly contested constitutional cases. The five conservative justices in *NFIB* had sufficient motivation, whether in judicial philosophy or political preference, to mold existing doctrine to reach a particular result. Moreover, the *Gibbons/McCulloch* distinction would not change the outcome in most cases. But by making the inquiry "one of definition," to quote Marshall's original phrase, the *Gibbons* approach gave the *NFIB* conservatives cover to ask whether sitting out of the health insurance market fell within the definition of "activity" and therefore within the purported definition of "commerce." The *McCulloch* approach would have made that argument beside the point.

Once again, the Court's unwillingness to apply *McCulloch* to recognize implied commerce powers has led to a decision that Congress lacks the authority to enact an important law under the Commerce Clause. While the Affordable Care Act was ultimately sustained under the taxing power, that was due to the happenstance that the regulation was ultimately a question of who would pay for health care—it was in some sense an accounting measure that could be handled through the tax system. That will not always be the case, especially where what is needed is not simply money, but cooperation. The *NFIB* precedent could stand as an obstacle to important federal mandates in the future.

* * *

Let's recall the moment, quoted in Chapter 3, during the *NFIB* oral argument, when attorney Paul Clement reminded Justice Breyer that "*McCulloch* was not a commerce power case."[41] Clement was right in one important sense. It is true that Marshall avoided basing the constitutionality of the Second Bank of the United States on the Commerce Clause. But *McCulloch should be a commerce power case*. As a general statement of the principle of implied powers, *McCulloch* should be viewed as a commerce power case, a taxing power case, a borrowing power case, a bankruptcy power case, and a war power case. It should apply to all the powers of the national government.

It is easy to argue that the Commerce Clause is in some sense unique among the enumerated powers. It is now, hands down, the broadest regulatory power Congress has, and it has undoubtedly undergone the most transformative expansion in how our constitutional order interprets it. These features of the Commerce Clause are well known. What has flown beneath the radar is a kind of "Commerce Clause exceptionalism" with respect to *McCulloch* and implied powers. Five justices in *NFIB* refused to apply the doctrine of implied powers to the Commerce Clause.

And in *Raich*, eight justices ignored *McCulloch*, appearing to believe that the concept of implied commerce powers was irrelevant to their Commerce Clause analysis. Those who fail or refuse to acknowledge implied commerce powers in cases like *Raich* and *NFIB* do not explain why. Perhaps they don't even realize that they have ignored *McCulloch*.

The three themes for which *McCulloch* is celebrated—the nationalist constitution, implied powers, and the capable Constitution—were finally realized in Supreme Court doctrine in the late New Deal and Civil Rights eras. *McCulloch* was finally treated as a precedent rather than a symbol or an iconic statement of broad ideas. Yet the treatment of *McCulloch* as a binding precedent for implied commerce powers, a precedent doing doctrinal work in deciding cases, was short lived. *Darby* and *Wrightwood Dairy* were almost immediately displaced by *Wickard*. And the "*McCulloch* test" for Reconstruction Amendment enforcement powers has, since the late 1960s, been followed more in the breach than the observance.

Conclusion

"As Long as Our System Shall Exist"

Revisionist arguments are easily caricatured as mirror images of oversimplified statements of the conventional wisdom. The conventional wisdom says *McCulloch* was a nationalist decision and very important; therefore, the revisionist argument must be saying that *McCulloch* was not a nationalist decision, and was unimportant. That of course hasn't been my argument. *McCulloch* was undeniably a nationalist decision, and a hugely important one. But its nationalism has been oversimplified and its importance misunderstood.

McCulloch's nationalizing potential has never been fully realized, having been reined in by the Supreme Court for most of the past two centuries. This reining-in started with Marshall himself, in the *McCulloch* opinion itself. Had *McCulloch*'s logic of implied powers been applied fully to the Commerce Clause, it would have been difficult to deny recognition of congressional powers to pursue internal improvements, to restrict slavery and child labor, and to regulate the areas of economic life now deemed within Congress's authority under the Commerce Clause. *McCulloch* is undeniably an important opinion, certainly one of the most important in U.S. constitutional history. But the claims that it made law, built the nation, or shaped constitutional politics have little basis in U.S. constitutional history, and can all be traced to identifiable eras or moments when participants in constitutional politics felt the need to give a historical gloss to a contemporary argument.

McCulloch's nationalist constitutionalism is an important element of the opinion. In theory, *McCulloch* might have contributed to nation-building by asserting the supremacy of federal law, but that principle was already established by clear constitutional text in the Supremacy Clause. Most antebellum constitutionalists other than Virginia Republicans believed in federal supremacy within the "sphere" of federal power, and mainstream thinkers debated not the supremacy principle, but the extent of the federal sphere. *McCulloch* was just one in a long string of cases asserting federal supremacy, including Taney Court precedents like *Prigg* and

Ableman, Reconstruction precedents like *Veazie Bank* and *Pensacola Telegraph*, and even Marshall Court landmarks like *Cohens* and *Gibbons*. None of those cases cited *McCulloch*, let alone described it as the leading Supremacy Clause precedent. *McCulloch's* concise presentation of a structural, representation-based theory— that a national government representing the whole people cannot be controlled by the people of a state—was smartly done. But when that type of theory was of greatest use, the statesmen who rejected nullification or secession did not draw on *McCulloch*. In any event, *McCulloch's* constitutional theory is predominantly defensive in its nationalism, seeking to preserve the Union against state efforts to dominate the general government, rather than to expand federal nation-building powers. This element of *McCulloch* did not do much to make constitutional law or politics, or build the nation.

McCulloch's broad theory of the implied powers of Congress undoubtedly held the greatest potential to contribute to nation-building. In the antebellum period, as Henry Clay made clear, nation-building meant developing the nation's internal markets and communications. The Bank of the United States was a significant contributor to the American System, but so were internal improvements. As we saw, *McCulloch* was cagey and guarded about whether the national government possessed an implied internal-improvement power at all, let alone under the Commerce Clause. Marshall appears to have been concerned that expressly recognizing implied commerce and internal-improvements powers would alarm the slave-owning Virginia Republicans among whom he lived. (A large-scale owner of slaves himself, Marshall may even have shared this anxiety.) He thus eschewed the opportunity to endorse internal improvements or implied commerce powers, both in *McCulloch* and again in *Gibbons*. Far from giving the impetus to Congress to build roads and canals, Marshall confined his opinions to private letters suggesting that Congress could build roads under its war and postal powers, but not its commerce power. After an initial effort to defend *McCulloch* in the press, Marshall let the case quietly fade into the background, declining to use his opportunities to reaffirm its implied powers or constitutional nationalism elements in several subsequent opinions.

The Taney Court ignored *McCulloch* into oblivion, simply declining to cite it while adopting something close to the Jeffersonian "strict necessity" test for implied powers. At the same time, the Taney Court hailed *Gibbons* as the leading case on the scope of the Commerce Clause, inflating *Gibbons'* solicitude for state police powers into an anti-*McCulloch* theory of reserved state powers. In the Taney Court, reserved state powers could defeat arguments for implied federal powers and gave *states* implied powers to regulate matters within the delegated powers of Congress. To protect slavery from federal interference on the off-chance that northern anti-slavery sentiment should ever gain control of Congress and the presidency, the Taney Court embraced aspects of Virginia Republicanism: that states controlled their own soil, that land-based internal improvements could not be built without state consent, and that productive activities were enclosed within the protective cordon of reserved state powers.

These limitations on *McCulloch*'s theory of implied powers by the both the Marshall and Taney Courts set a pattern that would persist for more than 120 years. Marshall did not openly reject implied commerce powers, but his failure to confirm their existence in *McCulloch*, together with *Gibbons*'s insistence that navigation was part of the definition of commerce, encouraged subsequent Supreme Courts to treat implied commerce powers as nonexistent. Careful readers of *Gibbons* might notice Marshall's cautious indication that the Commerce Clause could extend to regulation of intrastate *commerce*. The *Lochner*-era Court took this indication as a cue, when it finally exhumed *McCulloch*'s implied-powers holding from its decades'-long interment, to limit implied commerce powers to intrastate buying, selling, and navigation. But through the entire nineteenth and early-twentieth centuries until 1936, the Court held that, under the commerce power, "Congress is powerless to regulate anything which is not commerce."[1] Had *McCulloch* expressly recognized implied commerce powers, it would have been difficult for later Marshall-worshipping justices to say this.

These facts put a significant dent in the argument for Marshall as a nation-builder and *McCulloch* as a nation-building case. Only the *Legal Tender Cases* and *Julliard v. Greenman* built on *McCulloch* in any nation-building sense before 1941, but both of those opinions were careful to point out that the implied power they recognized made no inroad into reserved state powers—because the Constitution expressly denied the states any power over the nation's currency. The post–Civil War Court extended national sovereignty to "every foot of soil" without reference to *McCulloch*, perhaps because the justices also wished to ignore *McCulloch* in order to impose narrow limits on the Reconstruction Amendments' enforcement clauses. The doctrinal frontier from the early 1800s was reserved state powers: could implied commerce powers make an inroad into reserved state powers and thereby regulate "[some]thing which is not commerce"? Neither the *Legal Tender Cases* nor *Julliard* pushed *McCulloch* across that frontier. Nor did any other case before 1941, despite increasingly frequent citations to *McCulloch* after 1890.

The nineteenth-century revival of *McCulloch*'s theory of implied powers, such as it was, occurred in Congress during the Civil War and Reconstruction. *McCulloch* was invoked by a handful of congressmen in support of implied powers to issue legal tender paper money and confiscate slaves. After the war, more members of Congress invoked *McCulloch* in support of civil rights legislation under the enforcement clauses of the Reconstruction Amendments. These handful of speeches provide the best case for *McCulloch* as influencing constitutional debate and contributing to nation building. It is a case, but not a strong one. References to *McCulloch* did not pervade the debate or seem to structure members' ideas about the extent or limits of congressional powers. Did *McCulloch* form people's ideas? Charles Sumner, who studied under Joseph Story and taught at Harvard Law School, viewed the

Reconstruction Amendments as "fountains of power," but not necessarily because they incorporated a *"McCulloch* standard" for implied powers. Nevertheless, *McCulloch* references cropped up again in twentieth-century Congresses as they weighed legislation that would break across the barrier of reserved state powers: the child labor bill in the Progressive era, New Deal economic measures, and mid-century civil rights legislation.

McCulloch re-emerged and was hailed as an important case at the end of the nineteenth century. Several factors contributed to this revival, but the most important may have been the John Marshall revival movement motivated largely by conservative legal elites hoping to use Marshall as a positive symbol of judicial review in the face of Populist and Progressive attacks. This revival relied on the first of two early-twentieth-century waves of ideologically motivated, inaccurate history. In 1901, no broad consensus could be built around Marshall's protection of property or around deference to congressional interpretations of implied powers, but wide agreement could be obtained in support of the Union's victory in the Civil War and national unity in the face of the war with Spain. Marshall Day speakers connected *McCulloch* to those themes, going so far as to suggest that Marshall's ideas guided Lincoln and helped save the Union.

The second wave of ideologically motivated history occurred in the early New Deal. Constitutional scholars paid great attention to *Gibbons* and the Commerce Clause, and they paid great attention to *McCulloch* as well, but they did not connect the two to develop a theory of implied commerce powers. Instead, they interpreted *McCulloch* as a hazy, general statement about the capable Constitution, that Congress should have the power to address new and unforeseen national problems. New Deal constitutional history was an advocacy project designed to convince the Court that its *Lochner*-era jurisprudence was a wrongheaded innovation that deviated from the long-standing, original, and correct principles laid down by Marshall and adhered to by Taney and his successors up to 1890 or so. That history is very wrong. As I have argued, the *Lochner* era's denial of implied commerce powers reflected a remarkably consistent and tenacious continuation of Taney Court reserved-powers doctrine, for which Marshall himself regrettably sowed the seeds.[2]

McCulloch's heyday lasted one generation, from 1941 to about 1966. In that period, the Court treated it as a binding doctrinal precedent for implied commerce powers to regulate the economy in *Darby* and *Wrightwood Dairy*. *McCulloch* was then relied upon to uphold the 1964 Civil Rights Act as an implied commerce power. The Court extended *McCulloch*'s implied-powers theory to the Reconstruction Amendments in 1966 in *Katzenbach v. Morgan*. These triumphs for full recognition of implied powers, both of commerce and of civil rights enforcement, were incomplete. *Wickard* quickly replaced the *McCulloch*/implied-powers approach with a slightly narrower *Gibbons*/definitional one. And the Court, after deciding *Katzenbach v. Morgan*, was never able to circle back to overrule the *Civil Rights*

Cases. This unfinished business left a clear path for the long conservative Court to reaffirm the *Civil Rights Cases,* rein in *Katzenbach,* and put the Affordable Care Act individual mandate outside the reach of the Commerce Clause without overruling any precedents.

The ambiguity of *McCulloch* gives rise to interpretive debates about the meaning of Marshall's opinion and, more broadly, over the Constitution's distribution of powers between the federal government and the states, and between Congress and the Supreme Court. The meaning of *McCulloch* would not matter so much if we were to acknowledge the idea that the Constitution creates a capable national government, one empowered to address all national problems. Despite more than a century of judicial resistance, the Supreme Court since 1941 has by and large yielded to the idea of the capable Constitution. The Court has tacitly acknowledged that it makes little sense to disable the federal government from addressing a truly national problem because of some fictitious or unwritten "spirit" of the Constitution, whether in the form of crabbed interpretations of granted powers or of reading the Tenth Amendment as placing regulatory areas off limits to the federal government. Yet the Court has done so while continuing to pay lip service to enumerationism, maintaining the form but not the substance of a federal government of limited enumerated powers. That ideology gives *McCulloch* ongoing doctrinal importance, because *McCulloch's* recognition of implied powers becomes necessary to make the Constitution capable. Even under a theory of limited enumerated powers, *McCulloch's* logic of implied powers applied to the Commerce Clause allows Congress to legislate about most things that "we the people" need it to. This is the case even if we interpreted "commerce" narrowly, as perhaps in *Gibbons v. Ogden.* The Commerce Clause, even narrowly construed, authorizes the regulation of national markets—the buying and selling of goods and services across state lines. Since most of the nation's problems are filtered through such national markets, implied powers under *McCulloch* reach anything that affects them. Properly understood, *McCulloch* thus makes contemporary (academic) debates about the "original meaning" of the Commerce Clause immaterial.[3]

* * *

At the beginning of this book, I set out to examine the present-day appraisal of *McCulloch* as the most important case in American constitutional law and as an aggressively nationalistic, nation-building case. In Chapter 13, I asked why these appraisals of *McCulloch* have occurred around the same time as the long conservative Court has receded from the full recognition of implied commerce and civil rights powers. The answer may be that the present-day appraisal of *McCulloch* represents a third wave of ideological history. In the New Deal, the specific doctrinal emphasis was placed on *Gibbons,* with *McCulloch* viewed as an amorphous statement of the capable Constitution. Today, *McCulloch's* doctrine of implied powers gets greater emphasis. But in both periods, the argument is that today's Supreme Court decisions would come out right, if only the Court would understand and apply Marshall Court cases correctly. Once again, commentators with liberal leanings hope to outflank judicial conservatives with an appeal to history, by claiming a direct doctrinal link to the Great Chief Justice, the original Expounder of the Constitution.

Why bother to question the present-day ideological history of *McCulloch*? Viewed one way, my revisionist argument can be denigrated as an academic exercise. Worse, my argument might be seen as undercutting arguments for liberal constitutional values I agree with. To me, the restrictions placed on implied commerce and Reconstruction Amendment powers are mostly wrong. Doesn't mythologizing *McCulloch* at least aim to set things right? Perhaps so. But there is a value in questioning historical myths that goes beyond demystification for its own sake.

The New Deal and present-day enterprise of outflanking a conservative Court by making a direct appeal to John Marshall embraces a conservative methodology. It strikes me as ineffectual, for two fundamental and closely related reasons. First, it exaggerates the power of Marshall Court precedents to bind Courts, or more specifically to convince conservative justices to change their minds. That is not what changed minds in 1937. Politics did. Once the Court had been remade with the appointment of several New Dealers by 1941–42, the *Lochner*-era jurisprudence was bound to be overruled. The New Deal historical gloss was not necessary to convince anyone, but merely gave the justices convenient cover to write off *Lochner*-era cases as a historical aberration while perpetuating the myth of a precedent-bound Court. As Justice Scalia demonstrated with his about-face in *Raich* and *NFIB*, a correct understanding of *McCulloch* is not enough to make a Supreme Court justice overcome his or her strongly held judicial views.

Second, *McCulloch* is simply too ambiguous to mandate a particular result in most contested cases about congressional power. Marshall ambiguated *McCulloch*'s substantive import by hedging on the extent of implied powers, and particularly in failing to establish implied commerce powers. Perhaps more important is *McCulloch*'s ambiguity about judicial supremacy and judicial review. *McCulloch* is as much a case about judicial power as it is about congressional power. It is no accident that Congress has nearly always been more apt than the Court to rely on *McCulloch* as expansive authority for implied congressional powers. In cases involving the scope of congressional power before 1941, the Court more often than not omitted mention of *McCulloch*, interpreted it relatively narrowly, or cited its language about congressional "pretext" and a "spirit of the Constitution" to strike down laws. Congress asserts its power by legislating, and hence is apt to cite *McCulloch*'s language about broad legislative powers and deference to Congress. The Court asserts its power by striking down legislation. *McCulloch* is at best an exhortation to future Courts to use their power sparingly. But institutions rarely give up powers, and *McCulloch* itself lays claim to a power of judicial review even as it calls for deference to Congress. These ambiguities have enabled the Court to resist *McCulloch*'s broader implications for decades even while purporting to follow it. As Chief Justice Roberts demonstrated in *NFIB*, even the plainest application of *McCulloch* can be avoided while paying lip service to the great case's authority.

The canonizing and mythologizing of *McCulloch* thus produces dubious benefits, and it comes at a cost. Although elements of the *McCulloch* opinion mandate deference to the discretion of Congress, the insistent appeal to *McCulloch*'s authority paradoxically emphasizes judicial supremacy. Elected officials acting under the Constitution, and interpreting it, have proven far more adaptable to crises in our national affairs than have the justices of the Supreme Court. Constitutional scholars who extol Marshall's pronouncements about the Constitution's adaptability are trying to exhort the justices to exercise their judicial supremacy adaptably; the basis for this exhortation, paradoxically, is to insist on the binding authority of a 200-year-old judicial precedent. If a precedential argument is called for, we should ask ourselves why resort is made to *McCulloch* rather than to the legislative precedent of the 1791 charter of the original Bank of the United States. If a sacred text is needed, why not use Hamilton's memorandum to Washington in support of that Bank? The chartering of the Bank of the United States is an astounding precedent—for implied powers, for national sovereign powers, for the power to create a major administrative agency to conduct the business of government. The *McCulloch* opinion was merely a pale echo of that precedent. The fact that constitutional lawyers have substituted *McCulloch* for the original Bank charter as the defining statement of constitutional law speaks volumes about our acceptance of judicial supremacy.

The appeal to Marshall has similar consequences. Holmes recognized as much on John Marshall Day in 1901, when he told his audience that Marshall-worship "stands for the rise of a new body of jurisprudence, by which guiding principles are raised above the reach of a statute and State, and judges are entrusted with a solemn and hitherto unheard-of authority and duty."[4] It would also be useful for constitutional scholars to inquire into the connection between the canonization of Marshall Court precedents and the largely conservative project of "originalism." Arguments from history and precedent are not necessarily the same thing as present-day originalist methodology, but they are not unrelated. A methodology of WWJMD—"what would John Marshall do?"—certainly tracks with a version of originalism by claiming that the "original meaning" of the Constitution binds us today, simply substituting Marshall's interpretations for other evidence of the Framers' or ratifiers' intentions.

McCulloch is an exceedingly important case in American constitutional law, not because it shaped the course of American constitutional history, but because important interpreters of the Constitution have said *McCulloch* is important. At the start of this book, I observed that American constitutionalism has been shaped by debates about the extent to which our Constitution mandates a strong central government and a Supreme Court with interpretive supremacy. These questions, to borrow Marshall's words, are "perpetually arising, and will probably continue to arise, as long as our system shall exist." Because *McCulloch* deals centrally with both these questions, it has been used as a focal point for discussing them. As a result, the interpretation given to *McCulloch* through successive generations tells us much about each generation's spirit of the Constitution. The truth is that *McCulloch* did not make great constitutional law. Rather, constitutional law made *McCulloch* great.

Appendix 1

SUPREME COURT CITATIONS TO *McCULLOCH* (IMPLIED POWERS AND CAPABLE CONSTITUTION)

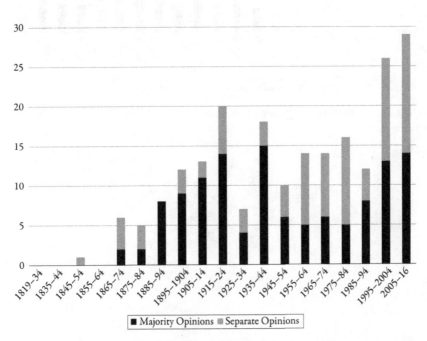

Figure 1.1 Total citations to *McCulloch*, in majority and separate opinions

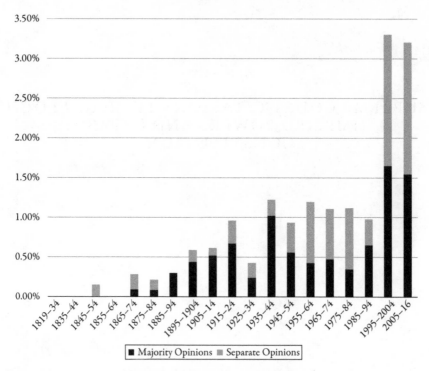

Figure 1.2. Percentage of Supreme Court cases citing *McCulloch* (in either majority or separate opinions)

McCULLOCH'S TERMINOLOGY FOR THE
CONTESTED INTERPRETATIONS
OF "NECESSARY AND PROPER"

(Numbers are cites to pages at 17 U.S. Reports)

Marshall's Interpretation		*Maryland's Interpretation*	
Ample means	408	Indispensable	413
Appropriate means, the most appropriate means, appropriate mode	408, 415, 421, 422, 423	Without which the power would be nugatory	413, 415
Choice of means, selection of measures	408, 409, 413, 420	Most direct and simple [means]	413
Ordinary means, usual means, not less usual than other means	409, 421	Absolute physical necessity	413
Most convenient means	409	Necessity so strong that one thing cannot exist without the other	413
[allowed to] select the means, select any appropriate means	410	Those single means without which the end would be entirely unattainable	414
Calculated to subserve legitimate objects	411	Indispensably necessary	416, 417, 418
The best means	411, 415		
Direct mode of executing [enumerated powers]	411		
Necessary means	411		

Marshall's Interpretation	Maryland's Interpretation	
[Laws which] may have relation to the powers conferred	413	
Convenient	414, 422	
Useful, utility	414, 422	
essential	414, 417, 418, 422	
Calculated to produce the end, really calculated	413, 423	
Conducive [to the end, to the beneficial exercise, to the complete accomplishment]	415, 417, 418, 424	
Needful	418	
Requisite, required	418, 422	
Means which facilitate the execution of [granted powers]	418	
Those which in [Congress's] judgment would most advantageously effect the object	419	
Adapted, plainly adapted [to the end]	419, 421	
Means which tended directly to the execution [of enumerated powers]	419	
Free use of means	420	
Importan[t]	423	

NOTES

Introduction

1. McCulloch v. Maryland, 17 U.S. (4 Wheat.) 316, 421 (1819).
2. 17 U.S. at 405.
3. McCloskey, *Supreme Court*, 66.
4. Levinson, "Close Reading."
5. Magliocca, "Legal Tender Cases," 125.
6. Ellis, *Aggressive Nationalism*, 3–4.
7. Email from Sanford Levinson to author (Jul. 20, 2018).
8. Steffel v. Thompson, 415 U.S. 452, 464 n. 13 (1974).
9. Michael Klarman's excellent 2001 study asking "How Great Were the 'Great' Marshall Court Decisions?" summarizes and critiques the conventional view of Marshall's influence.

Chapter 1

1. McCulloch v. Maryland, 17 U.S. (4 Wheat.) 316, 400–401 (1819).
2. U.S. Const., art. I, § 8, cl. 18; *McCulloch*, 17 U.S. at 422.
3. 6 U.S. 358 (1805).
4. *McCulloch*, 17 U.S. at 405.
5. Levinson, "Close Reading."
6. Holmes, "John Marshall," in *Collected Legal Papers* 266, 270. Historian G. Edward White explores the psychological underpinnings of Holmes's double-edged comments about Marshall in his beautifully written essay, "Looking at Holmes Looking at Marshall."
7. Jean Edward Smith's excellent *John Marshall: Definer of a Nation* (1996) is the authoritative modern biography. The first comprehensive biography of Marshall, still an important work, is Albert Beveridge's Pulitzer Prize–winning *The Life of John Marshall* (1919).
8. Story the sculptor was the son of Marshall's dear friend and colleague, Joseph Story. Another copy of the statue sits outside the Philadelphia Museum of Art.
9. Frankfurter, "John Marshall," 219.
10. Newmyer, "Southern Constitutional Tradition," 108; Balkin and Levinson, "Canons," 1008.
11. Schwartz, "Misreading," at 8–9 n. 21.
12. Karst, *Belonging to America*, 198.
13. Frankfurter, "John Marshall," 217; Fallon, "Constitutional Theory," 579; Sunstein, *Radicals in Robes*, 35; Newmyer, *Heroic Age*, 302; Weinberg, "Fear and Federalism," 1296–97.
14. Frankfurter, "John Marshall," 217–19; Jackson, "Federalism and the Court," 148–49; Whittington, *Judicial Supremacy*, 111; Killenbeck, *McCulloch*, 7–8; see also Balkin and Levinson, "Canons," 973.

15. White, *Marshall Court*, 486; Hobson, *Great Chief Justice*, 123; Nelson, "Eighteenth-Century Background," 898; McCloskey, *American Supreme Court*, 27–28, 37–38, 50–52.

16. Howe, *What Hath God Wrought*, 144–45; Smith, *Marshall*; Newmyer, *Heroic Age*.

17. Gunther, *Marshall's Defense*, 7–8; Newmyer, *Heroic Age*, 301–2.

18. Gillman, "Fuller Court's Jurisprudence," 419.

19. Klarman, "How Great?," 1141–42, 1126–27.

20. Since the day *Brown* was decided, May 17, 1954, it has been cited in 182 Supreme Court opinions, compared to 152 for *McCulloch*. The counts are based on LEXIS/Shepard's database searches on June 2, 2018. The statement in the text should be qualified to note that the handful of cases rooted in constitutional law but cited as "tests" for civil or criminal procedural law, such as *Terry v. Ohio*, 392 U.S. 1 (1968), or *Erie R. Co. v. Tompkins*, 304 U.S. 64 (1938), are cited with greater frequency.

21. See Home Sav. Bank v. Des Moines, 205 U.S. 503, 517 (1907).

22. U.S. Const. art. VI.

23. 17 U.S. at 405.

24. 17 U.S. at 428–36.

25. 17 U.S. at 405.

26. Brockenbrough, "Amphictyon," in Gunther, *Marshall's Defense*, 76. As William Nelson observed, "the Supremacy Clause . . . mandated the supremacy of federal law over conflicting state law . . . as clearly as any legal text requires a specific result." Nelson, "Eighteenth Century Backgrounds," 896.

27. See Dobbins v. Commissioners of Erie County 41 U.S. 435, 449 (1842).

28. Frankfurter, "John Marshall," 219.

29. Ellis, *Aggressive Nationalism*, 3–4.

30. Hobson, *Great Chief Justice*, 123, 149. See White, *Marshall Court*, 594; Newmyer, "States' Rights Tradition," 886; Frankfurter, *Commerce Clause*, 38–39.

31. 17 U.S. at 403.

32. 17 U.S. at 403–5; see James Madison, *Federalist* No. 37 in *The Federalist Papers*, ed. Clinton Rossiter (New York: New American Library, 1961), 227. ("The genius of republican liberty seems to demand . . . that all power should be derived from the people").

33. Schwartz, "A Question Perpetually Arising," 575–76 (coining term "capable federalism").

34. Vermeule, "Living It Up."

35. 17 U.S. at 406–7 (emphasis added).

36. Frankfurter, "John Marshall," 219.

37. 17 U.S. at 415.

38. 17 U.S. at 408; see id. at 409, 415, 417, 418, 421.

39. 17 U.S. at 407, 431.

40. Newmyer, *Heroic Age*, 302; Fallon, "Constitutional Theory," 569 n. 188; Ellis, *Aggressive Nationalism*, 3–4; Balkin and Levinson, "Canons," 973; Gunther, *Marshall's Defense*, 7–8; see also Chemerinsky, *Constitutional Law*, 242 (*McCulloch* "thus establishes several crucial aspects of constitutional law"); Tribe, *American Constitutional Law*, 799–800 (*McCulloch* "authoritatively constru[ed] the Necessary and Proper clause); Farber and Sherry, *American Constitution*, 358 (*McCulloch* put "in place" "the basic framework of the Constitution").

41. Stone et al., *Constitutional Law*, 62.

42. Compare Gillman, Graber, and Whittington, *American Constitutionalism*, 25 (constitutions "constrain," "construct," or "constitute" politics).

43. See Chapter 2.

44. Newmyer, *Heroic Age*, 301–2; Gunther, *Marshall's Defense*, 7–8; Klarman, "How Great?," 1126–27; Gillman, "Fuller Court's Jurisprudence," 419.

45. 109 U.S. 3 (1883).

46. Heart of Atlanta Motel v. United States, 379 U.S. 241 (1964); United States v. Morrison, 529 U.S. 598 (2000). See Chapters 12 and 13.

47. Balkin and Levinson, "Canons."

Chapter 2

1. McCulloch v. Maryland, 17 U.S. (4 Wheat.) 316, 405 (1819).
2. LaCroix, "Interbellum Constitution," 400. This point is exemplified throughout David Currie's valuable four-volume work, *The Constitution in Congress*.
3. Marshall, *Life of Washington*, 5:261–62.
4. Gillman, Graber, and Whittington, *American Constitutionalism*, 25–26; Graber, *American Constitutionalism*, 212–15; Graber, "New Deal Conceptual Universe," 117, 125 and n. 93.
5. U.S. Const., preamble and art. I. § 8 cl. 1. See Mikhail, "Fixing the Constitution's Implied Powers"; Primus, "Essential Characteristic."
6. Schwartz, "A Question Perpetually Arising."
7. 17 U.S. at 407.
8. CIC 1:3, 62–65, 70, 81.
9. AHP, 8:98. (Italics omitted.)
10. Livingston v. Van Ingen, 9 Johns. 507, 574 (1812).
11. *Papers of Jefferson*, 19:278.
12. 6 U.S. (2 Cranch) 358, 396 (1805).
13. 6 U.S. at 396.
14. Articles of Confederation, art. II: "Each State retains its sovereignty, freedom, and independence, and every power, jurisdiction, and right, which is not by this confederation, expressly delegated to the United States, in Congress assembled." See Johnson, "Dubious Enumerated Power Doctrine," 27 (rejection of "expressly" from Tenth Amendment).
15. Act of July 14, 1798, 1 Stat. 596 (Sedition Act); Act of July 6, 1798, 1 Stat. 577 (Alien Act); Elkins and McKitrick, *Age of Federalism*, 590–93, 710–16.
16. Virginia and Kentucky Resolutions, in Urofsky, *Documents* 1:158–63; Elkins and McKitrick, *Age of Federalism*, 700–701, 719–20; Neely, *Triumph of the Nation*, 5–8.
17. See, e.g., Gibbons v. Ogden, 22 U.S. (9 Wheat.) 1, 188, 222 (1824) ("powerful and ingenious minds" argue for "narrow [constitutional] construction, which would cripple the government"). For letters expressing these concerns late in his life, see, e.g., Marshall to Richard Peters, Dec. 3, 1832; Marshall to Peter S. Du Ponceau, Dec. 9, 1832; Marshall to Story, Dec. 25, 1832; PJM 12:241–43, 248–49. Newmyer, *Heroic Age*, 386–414, 456–58.
18. 17 U.S. at 405.
19. Novak, *The People's Welfare*.
20. James Kent argued that commerce powers were concurrent in *Livingston v. Van Ingen*, 9 Johns. 507, 574 (1812). Henry Clay's speeches advocating internal improvements repeatedly argued that states would have concurrent jurisdiction over federal roads. HCP, 2:453; 3:585, 587.
21. Houston v. Moore, 18 U.S. (5 Wheat.) 1 (1820) (involving overlapping state and federal powers over the militia).
22. U.S. Const. amend. 10.
23. Articles of Confederation, art. II.
24. See, e.g., Chisholm v. Georgia, 2 U.S. (2 Dall.) 419 (1793) (Iredell, J.) ("the United States have no claim to any authority but such as the States have surrendered to them"); Martin v. Hunter's Lessee, 14 U.S. 304, 325 (1816) ("the sovereign powers vested in the state governments, by their respective constitutions, remained unaltered and unimpaired, except so far as they were granted to the government of the United States"); Brown v. Maryland, 25 U.S. (12 Wheat.) 419, 452 (1827) (Thompson, J., dissenting) ("the power of Congress to regulate commerce . . . was a power possessed by the States respectively before the adoption of the constitution, and. . . . is to be viewed, therefore, as the surrender of a power antecedently possessed by the States").
25. See, e.g., Sturges v. Crowninshield, 17 U.S. (4 Wheat.) 122 (1819); Houston v. Moore, 18 U.S. (5 Wheat.) 1 (1820).
26. James Madison, *Federalist* No. 45 in *The Federalist Papers*, ed. Clinton Rossiter (New York: New American Library, 1961), 237.

27. E.g., Clay, "Speech on Internal Improvements," HCP, 2:460 (rebutting this argument). See Corwin, *Commerce Power*, 23–31.

28. HCP, 2:460, 3:585.

29. Gibbons v. Ogden, 22 U.S. (9 Wheat.) 1, 9–10 (1824) (argument of Webster).

30. Hammond, *Banks and Politics*, 89.

31. U.S. Const. art. I, § 10, cl. 2.

32. Gibbons v. Ogden, 22 U.S. (9 Wheat.) 1 (1824), 10–14, 17 (argument of Webster); id. at 231 (Johnson, J., concurring); New York v. Miln, 36 U.S. 102, 158 (1837) (Story, J., dissenting).

33. 9 Johns. R. 507 (N.Y. 1812).

34. 9 Johns. R. at 580.

35. Hall, "Reframing the Fathers' Constitution," 267; Howe, *What Hath God Wrought*, 202–84; CIC, 2:250, 258–59; Peterson, *Great Triumvirate*, 81; LaCroix, "Interbellum Constitution," 400.

36. MPP, 1:576; CIC, 2:117–18, 258–60; Peterson, *Great Triumvirate*, 48–49.

37. MPP, 2:18; CIC, 2:267–70, 335 and n. 111. For example, in an 1817 debate on such an amendment, Henry St. George Tucker cogently argued that "every unnecessary amendment only serves to narrow and circumscribe the construction of the instrument, and, whilst it gives one power, furnishes a weapon by which ten more may be wrested from us." Henry Clay called on "those who believed that the constitution . . . already conveys the power" to join with "those who think that Congress have not, and ought not to have it" to defeat the measure.

38. 32 Annals of Cong. 89 (1818); CIC, 2:271–78.

39. Marshall to Story, Sep. 26, 1823; JMP 9:338.

40. 31 Annals of Cong. 1139–51 (1818) (Rep. Smyth); 1151–64 (1818) (Rep. Barbour); 1201–17 (1818) (Rep. Austin); 1224–35 (1818) (Rep. Johnson). Monroe, "Internal Improvements," in MPP, 2:555–57; 41 Annals of Cong. 1297 (1824) (Rep. Randolph). Madison vetoed the Bonus Bill on March 3, 1817, his last day in office. MPP, 1:584. Monroe vetoed the Cumberland Road bill in 1822. See also Searight v. Stokes, 44 U.S. 151, 166 (1845) (declining to decide that Congress has a power to build post roads).

41. Clay, "Speeches on Internal Improvements," Mar. 7 and 13, 1818, Jan. 14, 1824; HCP 2:453, 469; 3:585.

42. HCP, 3:574–75, 583 (Clay's House speech describing state disincentives); Veazie v. Moor, 55 U.S. 568 (1853) (affirming state police power over internal improvements); Howe, *What Hath God Wrought*, 117–20 (Erie Canal).

43. Marshall to Charles Hammond, Dec. 28, 1823, JMP, 9:367–68. Clay's Supreme Court arguments included *Osborn v. Bank of the United States*, 22 U.S. (9 Wheat.) 738 (1824), *Green v. Biddle*, 21 U.S. (8 Wheat.) 1 (1823); *Ogden v. Saunders*, 25 U.S. (12 Wheat.) 213 (1827), and *Groves v. Slaughter*, 40 U.S. 449 (1841). Clay represented the Second Bank of the United States in several litigation matters. Peterson, *Great Triumvirate*, 66–67.

44. HCP 2:448–50, 458–59.

45. HCP, 2:455, 463.

46. HCP, 2:473–74.

47. U.S. Const. art. I., § 9, cl. 1. Fehrenbacher, *Slaveholding Republic*, 33–37.

48. Slave Trade Act of 1794, 1 Stat. 347. Lightner, *Slavery and Commerce Power*, 17–19, 102.

49. Prohibition on Slave Importations Act of 1807, 2 Stat. 426.

50. Veazie v. Moor, 55 U.S. 568, 574 (1853).

51. McPherson, *Battle Cry*, 54–55.

52. "House Resolution on Quaker Memorials," in Van Cleve, *Slaveholders' Union*, 290–291.

53. Van Cleve, 61; Lightner, *Slavery and Commerce Power*, 90–112.

54. Scott v. Sandford, 60 U.S. 393, 407 (1857) (Taney, C.J.) (under the Constitution, African Americans "had no rights which the white man was bound to respect"); Neely, *Triumph*, 114–18.

55. See Lightner, *Slavery and Commerce Power*, 57.

56. Jefferson to William Giles, Dec. 26, 1825, quoted in Warren, *Supreme Court*, 80–81.

57. 31 Annals of Cong. 1139–40 (1818) (Rep. Smyth) ("If reasons like these will justify the exercise of power, then Congress may regulate agriculture . . .").

58. 41 Annals of Cong. 1306–8 (Jan. 30, 1824) (Rep. Randolph) (emphasis in original). The same result could be obtained, Randolph said, by applying the doctrine of implied powers to the war power.

59. McPherson, *Battle Cry*, 52–58.

60. McPherson, 54–55; Neely, *Triumph*, 116–20.

61. See U.S. Const. art. I, § 2, cl. 3.

62. Howe, *What Hath God Wrought*, 147–54.

63. White, *Marshall Court*, 158.

64. The Missouri debate centered on the Territories and New States clauses. See U.S. Const. art. IV, § 3, cl. 1 ("New states may be admitted by the Congress into this union"); cl. 2 (granting Congress the power to "make all needful rules and regulations respecting the territory or other property belonging to the United States"). CIC 2:235–45. Application of these clauses did not raise issues of implied powers or the scope of the Necessary and Proper Clause.

65. A series of Supreme Court decisions established federal money power in stages between the *Legal Tender Cases*, 79 U.S. 457 (1871), upholding Congress's power to issue paper money, *First Nat'l Bank v. Fellows*, 244 U.S. 416, 418–20 (1917), upholding the Federal Reserve system, and *Norman v. Baltimore and O. R. Co.*, 294 U.S. 240 (1935), upholding Congress's power to take U.S. money off the gold standard. Each of these decisions relied on *McCulloch*. See Chapters 8–11.

66. U.S. Const. art. I, § 8, cls. 2, 5, and 6; § 10, cl. 1.

67. Hurst, *Legal History of Money*, 8.

68. Hamilton, "Bank Report," AHP 7:305, 350; CIC, 1:78. Hamilton's third report was his Report on Manufactures.

69. AHP, 7:307–10, 322–23, 331.

70. Hammond, *Banks and Politics*, 105–116, 123; Chernow, *Hamilton*, 357–61.

71. 2 Annals of Cong. 1894–1902, 1956–59 (1791).

72. 2 Annals of Cong. 1896 (Rep. Madison) (listing Taxing, Borrowing, and "Necessary and Proper" Clauses); 1912 (Rep. Sedgewick) (arguing for commerce power); 1957 (Madison's Feb. 8 reply).

73. Primus, "Essential Characteristic" 454–62 see also CIC, 1:121, 79–80; Hammond, *Banks and Politics*, 115; Lomazoff, *Bank Controversy*, 19-26.

74. 2 Annals of Cong. 1962 (1791) (Rep. Sedgwick).

75. U.S. Const. art. I., §7, cl. 2.

76. Hammond, *Banks and Politics*, 116–17; CIC, 1:80.

77. *Papers of Jefferson*, 19:276–78.

78. Chernow, *Hamilton*, 352–53.

79. AHP, 8:104–5, 121–22.

80. AHP, 8:124.

81. AHP, 8:126–27, 131–32.

82. Hammond, *Banks and Politics*, 139, 205–8, 258; CIC, 2:250–251; Hurst, *Legal History of Money*, 77–78.

83. Hammond, *Banks and Politics*, 146, 188–89, 198–99; Lomazoff, *National Bank Controversy*, 47, 59–67, 70–76. The First Bank, as the agent for collection of federal taxes, would inevitably become the creditor of the state banks, whose customers would pay their federal taxes with state banknotes and checks written against their state bank deposits. The First Bank could at any time demand these state bank notes and credits be redeemed in specie, and refuse to accept non-redeemable notes. This would in turn limit the state banks' ability to issue loans and banknotes, which had to be in proportion to their specie reserves.

84. CIC, 2:252–53; Hammond, *Banks and Politics*, 223; Killenbeck, *M'Culloch*, 49–51. Vice President George Clinton cast the tie-breaking vote in the Senate to defeat the Bank.

85. Hammond, *Banks and Politics*, 227–32; Killenbeck, *M'Culloch*, 54; Lomazoff, *National Bank Controversy*, 108–18.
86. Madison, "Seventh Annual Message," MPP 565.
87. Lomazoff, *National Bank Controversy*, 94–120. The Coinage Clause art. I., § 8, cl. 5 authorizes Congress "To coin money, regulate the value thereof, and of foreign coin, and fix the standard of weights and measures." See Chapter 8.
88. 29 Annals of Cong. 1061–62,1064–65 (1816).
89. 29 Annals of Cong. 1061–62 (1816).
90. See Hurst, *Legal History of Money*, 57, 159–63 (explaining central banking function). Hurst suggested that U.S. policymakers did not comprehend the nature of a central banking function before Nicholas Biddle's assumption of the presidency of the Second Bank in 1823. But clearly, many, including Calhoun, did understand it. See Lomazoff, *National Bank Controversy*, 59–67, 108–16.
91. Hammond, *Banks and Politics*, 240, 244; Ellis, *Aggressive Nationalism*, 42.
92. Hammond, 208; Killenbeck, *M'Culloch*, 64–72.

Chapter 3

1. John Jay to John Adams, Jan. 2, 1801, in Marcus and Perry, *Documentary History*, 1:146–47; Haskins and Johnson, *Foundations of Power*, 87, 103–4.
2. The number of Supreme Court justices is set by statute, rather than Constitutional provision, see U.S. Const., art. III, § 1, and Congress has changed the number over time. See Judiciary Act of 1789, 1 Stat. 73 (six); Judiciary Act of 1807, 2 Stat. 421 (seven); Judiciary Act of 1837, 5 Stat. 176 (nine); Judiciary Act of 1863, 12 Stat. 794 (ten); Judiciary Act of 1866, 14 Stat. 209 (attrition down to seven). The 1863 law was intended to give Lincoln an extra appointment to balance the Court, while the 1866 law was intended to prevent Andrew Johnson from appointing any justices. After Grant's election in 1868, Congress raised the number of seats back to nine. Judiciary Act of 1869, 16 Stat. 44.
3. White, *Marshall Court*, 181–95; Smith, *Marshall*, 282–84, 286–87, 295; Finkelman, *Supreme Injustice*, 34.
4. White, 190–95.
5. Marshall, *Life of Washington*, 5:251, 251–62.
6. Killenbeck, *M'Culloch*, 90–91.
7. Killenbeck, "Maryland and the Second Bank."
8. McCulloch v. Maryland, 17 U.S. (4 Wheat.) 316, 317 (1819); Ellis, *Aggressive Nationalism*, xx; Killenbeck, *M'Culloch*, 90–95.
9. White, *Marshall Court*, 230–37 (Martin); 289 (Jones); 255–66 (Wirt); 267–88 (Webster); 220, 244–50 (Pinkney); Peterson, *Great Triumvirate*, 98 (Webster); http://bioguide.congress.gov/scripts/biodisplay.pl?index=H000784 (Hopkinson)
10. *McCulloch*, 17 U.S. at 362–66, 372–74, 402–6.
11. 17 U.S. at 389 (Pinkney); 325 (Webster); 353–54 (Wirt).
12. 17 U.S. at 365, 368 (Jones).
13. E.g., 17 U.S. at 401, 402, 404, 414; White, *Marshall Court*, 290, 543; Killenbeck, *M'Culloch*, 95–96, 109, 122.
14. The Affordable Care Act Cases, Oral Argument, Mar. 27, 2012, https://www.oyez.org/cases/2011/11-393.
15. *McCulloch*, 17 U.S. at 422–23.
16. CIC, 1:80; White, *Marshall Court*, 549; Magliocca, "Legal Tender Cases," 126 n. 31.
17. Roane, "Hampden Essays," in Gunther, *Marshall's Defense*, 133.
18. *McCulloch*, 17 U.S. at 422; see Lomazoff, *National Bank Controversy*, 96–98.
19. 17 U.S. at 411.
20. 17 U.S. at 407–8.
21. 17 U.S. at 417.

22. 17 U.S. at 405.
23. U.S. Const. art. I, § 8, cl. 18.
24. Schwartz, "A Question Perpetually Arising," 629–31.
25. John Mikhail's meticulous research has begun to uncover persuasive support of this interpretation of *McCulloch*. Mikhail, "*McCulloch's* Strategic Ambiguity."
26. See Marshall, *Washington,* 5:252 (emphasis added).
27. Killenbeck, *M'Culloch,* 64–72; Hammond, *Banks and Politics,* 208.
28. *McCulloch,* 17 U.S. at 406.
29. 17 U.S. at 408. Jack Balkin suggests that this language shows Marshall peering into the future and outlining a prophetic image of the continental republic that would not be realized for decades. Balkin, "Marshall's Greatness," 1336–37. But Marshall was merely referring to the existing territorial claims of the United States as of 1819, as he explained in his editorial defense of *McCulloch.* Marshall, "Friend of the Constitution," in Gunther, *Marshall's Defense,* 182.
30. *McCulloch,* 17 U.S. at 417 (emphasis added).
31. Gunther, *Marshall's Defense,* 7–8; see also Newmyer, "States' Rights Tradition," 880 (*McCulloch* "overrode" Madison's Bonus Bill veto).
32. 17 U.S. at 416–18.
33. 17 U.S. at 407.
34. 17 U.S. at 414–15 (citing U.S. Const. art. I, § 10, cl. 2 ["No state shall, without the consent of the Congress, lay any imposts or duties on imports or exports, except what may be absolutely necessary for executing it's inspection laws"]).
35. 17 U.S. at 413–15, 419–20 ("The clause is placed among the powers of Congress, not among the limitations on those powers").
36. 17 U.S. at 415.
37. 17 U.S. at 407–8 (italics added). Note that the Constitution nowhere actually enumerates the power "to conduct" a war. Schwartz, "A Question Perpetually Arising," 624–29.
38. AHP, 8:105; HCP, 2:450.
39. 17 U.S. at 386 (Pinkney).
40. 17 U.S. at 406, 415.
41. 17 U.S. at 381–85.
42. 17 U.S. at 405.
43. See Appendix 2.
44. 17 U.S. at 409, 413, 415, 419, 420.
45. 17 U.S. at 411, 418. Today, essential means "1. Absolutely necessary . . . 2. Relating to the essence of a thing." See Essential, http://www.wordreference.com. This order of usage may have been reversed in Marshall's time; obviously, he did not use "essential" to mean "absolutely necessary." But see definition 1 in Samuel Johnson's Dictionary, 721 (defining essential as "1. Necessary to the constitution or existence of any thing").
46. 17 U.S. at 408, 409, 411, 419.
47. 17 U.S. at 408, 409, 421, 423.
48. 17 U.S. at 352 (Wirt); 326 (Webster); 380, 387 (Pinkney).
49. 17 U.S. at 400–402.
50. 17 U.S. at 421 (emphasis added).
51. 17 U.S. at 423.
52. See, e.g., National Federation of Independent Business v. Sebelius, 567 U.S. 519 (2012) (opinion of Roberts, C.J.) (holding the individual mandate is not sustained by the commerce power); Carter v. Carter Coal Co., 298 U.S. 238, 291 (1936) (striking down Bituminous Coal Act); Bailey v. Drexel Furniture Co. (Child Labor Tax Case), 259 U.S. 20, 40 (1922) (striking down the child labor tax); Hepburn v. Griswold, 75 U.S. 603, 625 (1870) (holding that Congress has no power to issue paper money).
53. For arguments that the deferential quality of *McCulloch's* test broadens national power, see Caminker, "Appropriate Means-Ends Constraints," 1134–43. For arguments that

Marshall meant to show a willingness to rein in broad assertions of national power, see White, *Marshall Court*, 550; Whittington, "Judicial Review before the Civil War," 1294 and n. 228.

Chapter 4

1. 22 U.S. (9 Wheat.) 1 (1824).
2. Newmyer, *Heroic Age*, 269.
3. *McCulloch v. Maryland*, 17 U.S. (4 Wheat.) 316, 415 (1819).
4. 22 U.S. (9 Wheat.) 738 (1824).
5. Brown v. Maryland, 25 U.S. (12 Wheat.) 419 (1827); Weston v. Charleston, 27 U.S. (2 Pet.) 449 (1829); Providence Bank v. Billings, 29 U.S. (4 Pet.) 514, 563 (1832).
6. The fifth citation was to a technical point of appellate procedure, that Supreme Court review is not precluded by the trial judge's failure personally to sign the court record. See Worcester v. Georgia, 31 U.S. (6 Pet.) 515, 537 (1832). The sixth and final citation is in United States v. Arredondo, 31 U.S. (6 Pet.) 691 (1832), a suit over a land claim in the Florida territory. The opinion, authored by Justice Baldwin, included a curious citation to *McCulloch*, omitting its name and citing only a page number ("4 Wh. 423") in a long string of citations, apparently for the proposition that certain legislative acts are not judicially reviewable. 31 U.S. at 729–30 ("All other questions are settled by the decision made or the act done by the tribunal or officer; whether executive, [1 Cr. 170–171]—legislative, [4 Wh. 423; 2 Peters, 412; 4 Peters, 563]—judicial, [11 Mass. 227; 11 S. and R. 429; adopted in 2 Peters, 167, 168], or, special, 20 J.R. 739, 740; 2 Dow. P. Cas. 521, &c. unless an appeal is provided for, or other revision, by some appellate or supervisory tribunal, is prescribed by law") (emphasis added).
7. E.g., Hobson, *Great Chief Justice*, 181–82.
8. 27 U.S. (2 Pet.) 245, 251 (1829).
9. Magruder, *Marshall*, 166; LCJS, v. 1, at 160, 304, 433, 477; v. 2, 116, 207.
10. Newmyer, *Heroic Age*, 295 (*McCulloch* "was a magisterial performance . . . that displayed Marshall's 'grand style' at its grandest"); Hobson, "Defining the Office," 1423 ("the 'grand style' that became Marshall's hallmark"); Mikhail, "Necessary and Proper Clauses," 1065 ("grand style" might have been inhibited by a norm of strict construction); Currie, "Powers of the Federal Courts," 646–47 ("the grand style we have come to associate with Marshall"). Karl Llewellyn coined the term "grand style" to describe Marshall's commercial decisions, and he seems to have used the term somewhat differently from the way commentators did on Marshall's constitutional decisions. Llewellyn, *Common Law Tradition*, 77–91.
11. Kent, *Commentaries* 1:242 n. "a" (3rd ed. 1836). See also Hobson, *Great Chief Justice*, 182 (arguing that Marshall resolved many constitutional cases "by applying rules for construing written instruments").
12. Marshall to Monroe, Feb. 4, 1824, JMP, 10:3–4. The Supreme Court apparently did not have its own law library for many years. When Congress eventually funded a law library with its book list to be "furnished . . . by the Chief Justice," Marshall asked Story to provide the list. Marshall to Story, Aug. 2, 1832, JMP, 12:225–26. David Currie observed that "[i]t was typical of Marshall not to cite even his own opinions although they squarely supported him." Currie, "Constitution in the Supreme Court," 931. Currie speculated that this may have had something to do with forgetfulness as well as the lack of case indexing in Marshall's day.
13. 25 U.S. 419, 449 (1827).
14. 27 U.S. 449 (1829).
15. 29 U.S. 514, 563 (1832).
16. 19 U.S. (4 Wheat.) 264 (1821).
17. 14 U.S. (1 Wheat.) 304 (1816).
18. *Cohens*, 19 U.S. at 394, 423.
19. 19 U.S. at 380–381, 387, 414.

20. 19 U.S. at 424–25, 429. See art I. § 8, cl. 17, authorizing Congress "[t]o exercise exclusive legislation in all cases whatsoever, over such District (not exceeding ten miles square) as may, by cession of particular states, and the acceptance of Congress, become the seat of the government of the United States. . . ."

21. Marshall, "Friend of the Constitution," in Gunther, *Marshall's Defense*, 155.

22. Smith, *Marshall*, 11.

23. Newmyer, "Southern States' Rights Tradition"; Beach, "Roane and the Richmond Junto," 2; Heubner, "Consolidation of State Judicial Power," 47, 67–68; Thornton, "Marshall versus Roane," 297; Gutzman, *Virginia's American Revolution*, 120–29; Ammon, "Richmond Junto," 395, 399–400; Howe, *What Hath God Wrought*, 359 ("Old Republicans"); Peterson, *Great Triumvirate*, 75 ("Virginia Old Republicans").

24. http://www.virginiaplaces.org/population/pop1820numbers.html   (Henrico   County population).

25. Gunther, *Marshall's Defense*, 15.

26. Marshall to Story, Apr. 28, 1819; Marshall to Bushrod Washington, Apr. 28, 1819; Marshall to Story, May 28, 1819; JMP, 309–15.

27. Gunther, *Marshall's Defense*, 15–16, 78, 155. The April "Union" essays were originally published in the *Philadelphia Union*, where they were badly garbled.

28. Gunther, 172–73 (emphasis added).

29. Gunther, 173.

30. Roane, "Hampden," in Gunther, 129.

31. Taylor, *Constructions Construed*, 294–300.

32. 41 Annals of Cong. 1306–8 (Jan. 30, 1824). On their relationship, see Marshall to Randolph, May 5, 1826, JMP, 10:288–89.

33. Morgan, *Justice William Johnson*.

34. 8 F. Cas. 493 (C.C.S.C. 1823).

35. Marshall to Story, Sep. 26, 1823, JMP 9:338.

36. 30 F. Cas. 239, 244 (1820).

37. JMP 9:338.

38. Finkelman, *Supreme Injustice*. That much of the evidence for this bias has been hiding in plain sight, in the well-edited and easily accessed Marshall Papers, demonstrates the tenacity of the Marshall myth. See, e.g., JMP, 12:130 (describing free black people as "pests" and criminals); 11:6–8 (disposing of slaves in his will).

39. Monroe, "Internal Improvements," in MPP, 2:144; see also id. 2:142 (shorter veto message).

40. MPP, 2:157–62.

41. MPP, 2:164–67; Howe, *What Hath God Wrought*, 360–366 (noting Jackson's frequent approval of internal-improvements spending projects); Searight v. Stokes, 44 U.S. 151 (1845).

42. Story to Monroe, Jun. 24, 1822, in Warren, *Supreme Court*, 2:56.

43. Johnson to Monroe (undated) in Warren, *Supreme Court*, 2:56–57.

44. Without any additional evidence, Warren credited Johnson's claim to have "obtained the views of his associates," by assuming Johnson's letter—though undated—to have been written after the Marshall and Story letters. Warren, 2:56 and n. 1. Historians have described the incident as an unprecedented Supreme Court advisory opinion. Morgan, *Justice Johnson*, 122–25; Howe, *What Hath God Wrought*, 213.

45. [Sic]. " . . . . [I]n *all* that you have expressed"? The meaning is the same either way. Marshall to Monroe (Jun. 13, 1822), JMP, 9:236.

46. JMP, 9:236 (emphasis added).

47. Marshall was known for his affability and for bridging political differences. He and Monroe were old friends, having spent a year together in boarding school in their early teens and later carousing together as fellow officers during the Revolutionary War. Smith, *Marshall*, 35, 98. Plainly, both Johnson and Marshall agreed with less of Monroe's pamphlet than their general blandishments suggested. Two years later, in *Gibbons v. Ogden*, they implicitly rejected

Monroe's narrow interpretation of the Commerce Clause as conferring no express power over domestic commerce. But it is hard to believe that Marshall would misstate his own constitutional views, knowing that they might, coming from the Chief Justice, encourage the President to issue an unwarranted veto of some future bill.

48. Pickering was a high Federalist and Hamilton acolyte who had served as Washington's last and Adams's first Secretary of State. He had been removed from office in John Adams's purge of Hamilton loyalists from his cabinet—and replaced by Marshall. It was Pickering, as Secretary of State, to whom Marshall sent his famous XYZ dispatches from France. Chernow, *Hamilton*, 611–16; Smith, *Marshall*, 197, 266–67.

49. Marshall to Pickering, Mar. 18, 1828, JMP 11:87.

50. Finkelman, *Supreme Injustice*, 45. Marshall was personally strongly in favor of internal improvements as a policy matter, and editorialized (anonymously) in favor of Virginia's pursuit of a major canal project. Marshall, "Address of 'A Subscriber,'" JMP, 12:228–31.

51. Herbert Johnson, *Gibbons v. Ogden*, 72, 104.

52. 4 Stat. 22 (Apr. 29, 1824).

53. For Virginia Republican opponents, see 41 Annals of Cong. 1244 (Jan. 28, 1824) (Rep. Archer) (Necessary and Proper Clause served "to confine" incidental powers); 1285–86 (Jan. 29, 1824) (Rep. Stevenson) (implied powers must be "necessary to the fair execution of" enumerated ones pursuant to the "universal law" of "nature, nations, of the common law, and of reason"); 1327 (Feb. 3, 1824) (Rep. Barbour) (implied powers must "necessarily be the result of legislative discretion, limited by the terms of the Constitution"); 1352–54 (Feb. 4, 1824) (Rep. Rives) (implied power must be more than "useful" or "tend[ing] to promote," but have an "immediate . . . relation" to enumerated power).

54. 41 Annals of Cong. 1407 (Feb. 6, 1824) (Rep. Smyth).

55. Rep. Henry Storrs, a New York Federalist, said that the postal power "includes all the means which are adapted to that end." 41 Annals of Cong 1287 (Jan. 29, 1824). Rep. McDuffie of South Carolina paraphrased *McCulloch* in saying, "We must look to the great objects which [the Constitution] was designed to accomplish, and give it such an interpretation as will most effectually promote them." Id. at 1379 (Feb. 5, 1824).

56. HCP, 3:573, 592.

57. Clay derived implied powers from "the utter impossibility of forseeing all the turns and vicissitudes in human affairs," and referred to the "Mexican Gulf" rather than "the river Del Norte" as the southern territorial boundary of the United States. HCP 3:580, 584. Compare *McCulloch*, 17 U.S. at 407 ("this vast republic, from the St. Croix to the Gulph of Mexico"), 415 ("the various crises of human affairs").

58. HCP, 3:585.

59. HCP, 3:587.

60. Herbert Johnson, *Gibbons v. Ogden*, 27–37; Primus, "*Gibbons* Fallacy," 579–82.

61. *Gibbons*, 22 U.S. at 132 (argument of Emmet) ("The license . . . only gives some privileges as to payment of tonnage duties); Herbert Johnson, 90–91; Primus, 607–14.

62. 22 U.S. at 189–90.

63. 317 U.S. 111, 120 (1942). See, e.g., Williams, "Dormant Commerce Clause," 820 (*Gibbons*'s "description [of the commerce power] was striking in its breadth"); Stern, "Commerce Clause," 648 (*Gibbons*'s "sweeping interpretation of the clause"); Corwin, *Commerce Power*, 9 (*Gibbons* defined commerce power in "sweeping terms").

64. 22 U.S. at 194–97.

65. 22 U.S. at 33, 38 (argument of Oakley), 91 (argument of Emmett).

66. 22 U.S. at 187 (emphasis added).

67. 17 U.S. at 419–20.

68. 22 U.S. at 189.

69. 22 U.S. at 10–14, 16–17 (argument of Webster).

70. E.g., John Adams to Abigail Adams, May 12, 1780 in Butterfield et al. *Adams Family Correspondence*, 3:342 (hoping his sons would study "mathematicks and philosophy, geography, natural history, naval architecture, navigation, commerce and agriculture").

71. 41 Annals of Cong. 1015 (Jan. 13, 1824) (Rep. Holcombe); HCP, 2:463 (Clay's Mar. 13, 1818 speech).

72. United States v. The William, 1808 U.S. Dist. Lexis 5, 30–31 (D. Mass. 1808).

73. Elkison v. Deliesseline, 8 F. Cas. 493, 495 (C.C.S.C. 1823) (per Johnson, J., on circuit) (emphasis added).

74. See, e.g., *McCulloch*, 17 U.S. at 418 ("the power of punishment appertains to sovereignty, and may be exercised whenever the sovereign has a right to act, as incidental to his constitutional powers"); Marshall, "Friend to the Union," in Gunther, *Marshall's Defense*, 171–72 ("An 'incident,' Hampden tells us, 'is defined, in the common law, to be a thing appertaining to, or following another, as being more worthy or principal'").

75. 30 F. Cas. 239, 243 (C.C. Va. 1820) (per Marshall, C.J., on circuit) (emphasis added).

76. 30 F. Cas. 239, 243; *McCulloch*, 17 U.S. at 406.

77. 30 F. Cas. at 243.

78. 22 U.S. at 117 (argument of Emmett).

79. See Hamilton and Adair, *The Power to Govern*, 14–15, 57–63; Balkin, "Commerce," 5, 15–16.

80. 22 U.S. at 189–90.

81. See The Passenger Cases, 48 U.S. 283, 401 (1849) (McLean, J.); Carter v. Carter Coal Co., 298 U.S. 238, 298 (1936).

82. 22 U.S. at 190.

83. 22 U.S. at 20 (argument of Webster) ("generally speaking, roads, and bridges, and ferries, though, of course, they affect commerce and intercourse, do not obtain that importance and elevation, as to be deemed commercial regulations").

84. 22 U.S. at 194–95. This language is clear as can be that Marshall was not making a broad, general reference to limitations on federal power. As Richard Primus has persuasively argued, Marshall's point was that states had a residual commerce power, not that the federal government lacked a general police power. Yet Rehnquist and Roberts Court decisions have mistakenly quoted Marshall out of context in support of the latter interpretation. See Primus, "*Gibbons* Fallacy," 586–95.

85. Primus, "*Gibbons* Fallacy," 584 n. 77, 597.

86. 22 U.S. at 195.

87. 22 U.S. at 194–95.

88. 22 U.S. at 203–4.

89. 22 U.S. at 203–4.

90. 22 U.S. at 203–4.

91. 22 U.S. at 22, 19 (argument of Webster).

92. 22 U.S. at 190.

93. Klarman, "'Great' Marshall Court Decisions?," 1144.

94. 22 U.S. at 209–10, 210–21.

95. See, e.g., Frankfurter, *Commerce Clause*, 16–17; Williams, "*Gibbons*."

96. 22 U.S. at 37 (argument of Oakley). While there is some support in the text of *Gibbons* for such a distinction between express and implied powers, Marshall does not clarify whether or not federal statutes enacted under implied commerce powers would be field-preemptive.

97. 9 Johns 507, 576 (1812) (Kent, J.).

98. 22 U.S. at 91 (argument of Emmett).

99. 22 U.S. (9 Wheat.) 738 (1824).

100. Newmyer, *Heroic Age*, 299–300; Warren, 1:528–38.

101. 17 U.S. at 390 (argument of Pinkney); AHP, 7:331.

102. *Osborn*, 22 U.S. at 864–65, 866–67. Marshall apparently understood the national Bank's ability to control the nation's money supply. Marshall to Story, Aug. 2, 1832, JMP 12:226 (noting that

elimination of the Second Bank would leave powerful New York and Philadelphia banks in "a commanding control over the currency and the exchanges of the country").

103. *Osborn*, 22 U.S. at 872–73 (Johnson, J., dissenting).

104. 36 U.S. (11 Pet.) 257, 349 (1837) (Story, J., dissenting).

105. 25 U.S. 419 (1827).

106. 25 U.S. at 449. U.S. Const. art. I, § 10, cl. 2 provides, "No state shall, without the consent of the Congress, lay any imposts or duties on imports or exports, except what may be absolutely necessary for executing it's inspection laws[.]"

107. A Shepard's citation search conducted on October 21, 2018, shows that *Brown* was cited eighty-one times in Supreme Court opinions up to the year 1900, compared to eighty-four citations to *McCulloch*.

108. 27 U.S. 245 (1829).

109. Newmyer, *Heroic Age*, 403, 408–9.

110. Story, *Commentaries* (1833 ed.), 3:150–53.

111. Marshall to Story, Jul. 31, 1833, JMP, 12:291; Story, *Commentaries* (1833 ed.), 1:iii–iv. Story wrote his *Commentaries* primarily as lectures to be delivered to Harvard law students. His reference to *McCulloch* as a source of implied commerce powers—an idea studiously avoided by Marshall—would plant the seeds for a revival of the case that the Supreme Court had already laid to rest.

112. *Gibbons'* primary holdings were cited seventeen times in support of the judgment in Taney Court decisions. *McCulloch* was cited but once for a proposition relating to implied powers, in an opinion by Justice Thompson. See United States v. Gratiot, 39 U.S. 526, 537 (1840). Thompson had served with Marshall and was a great admirer. See Briscoe v. Directors of the Bank of Kentucky, 36 U.S. 257, 328 (1837) (Thompson, J., dissenting) (referring to "the late Mr. Chief Justice Marshall; a name never to be pronounced without reverence").

Chapter 5

1. *McCulloch v. Maryland*, 17 U.S. (4 Wheat.) 316, 417–18 (1819).

2. AHP, 8:97.

3. 31 U.S. 515 (1832).

4. *Worcester*, 31 U.S. at 561; see *McCulloch*, 17 U.S. at 426, 436.

5. He cited *McCulloch* for the picayune point that the Court could consider an appeal even when the lower-court judge had not affixed his signature to the court record. 31 U.S. at 537.

6. 31 U.S. at 569 (McLean, J., concurring).

7. *Gibbons v. Ogden*, 22 U.S. (9 Wheat.) 1, 187 (1824).

8. Magliocca, *Andrew Jackson*, 50; Howe, *What Hath God Wrought*, 384.

9. See, e.g., S. Rep. No. 283, at 8–9 (Feb. 9, 1832) (Bank upheld by "the solemn and unanimous decision of the Supreme Court, in a case which fully and distinctly submitted the constitutional question to their cognizance"); id. at 53 (Minority Report) (suggesting *McCulloch* was contrary to intent of framers); 8 Reg. Deb. 1004 (Jun. 1, 1832) (Sen. Sprague) ("agree[s] perfectly with the decision of the Supreme Court"); 997 (Sen. Bibb) (*McCulloch* wrongly decided); 1001 (Sen. Benton) ("principles and premises" of *McCulloch* "were erroneous").

10. Howe, *What Hath God Wrought*, 376–77; Hammond, *Banks and Politics*, 369–450.

11. Veto Message, Jul. 10, 1832; MPP, 3:1145–46. Jackson accurately quoted various synonyms for "necessary and proper" found in *McCulloch*.

12. Among other policy matters, Jackson objected to the bank's immunity from state taxes, foreign ownership of bank stock, capitalizing the bank without a public stock offering, selling monopoly privileges at less than market value, and permitting state banks but not individuals to redeem national bank notes at any location. Above all, Jackson believed the bill would further enrich wealthy financial interests. MPP, 3:1140–42, 1151–53. Jackson raised purported constitutional objections to an implied power to grant monopoly privileges and to authorize the

purchase of lands within the states. MPP, 3:1147–48. Jackson also sought to constitutionalize his policy objections by saying that unnecessary features of the Bank were ipso facto unconstitutional. This seems to have been more of a rhetorical ploy than a serious constitutional argument. MPP, 3:1146.

13. Gillman, Graber, and Whittington, *American Constitutionalism*, 19.

14. Magliocca, "Veto!," 214–19.

15. Remini, *Bank War*, 63, 83; Magliocca, *Andrew Jackson*, 55–58. The day after Jackson's Veto message was sent to the Senate, Daniel Webster attacked the veto as the abnegation of the president's duty to faithfully execute the law: "It is no bank to be created, it is no law proposed to be passed, which he denounces; it is the law now existing, passed by Congress, approved by Madison, and sanctioned by a solemn judgment of the Supreme Court, which he now declares unconstitutional, and which, of course, so far as it may depend on him, cannot be executed." Webster, *Speeches*, 1:518.

16. Swisher, *Taney*, 193–97.

17. Graber, "Naked Land Transfers," 112–13.

18. Magliocca, "Legal Tender," 132–33. The 1840 election put Whig candidate William Henry Harrison in the presidency and gave the pro-Bank Whigs in control of both houses of Congress. But by the time Congress passed a bill to charter a Third Bank, Harrison had died. His successor, the imperious states'-righter John Tyler, vetoed it. Had Tyler instead signed the bill, a constitutional challenge to the Bank would probably have reached the Court, but there is no guarantee the Court would have overruled *McCulloch*, for the reasons stated in the text.

19. Howe, *What Hath God Wrought*, 404–8.

20. Howe, 397–400.

21. Calhoun, *Works* 6:73–74.

22. Marshall likened the Nullification Crisis to the 1794 Whiskey Rebellion, which "would have been equally fatal had it not been quelled by the well timed vigor of General Washington. We are now gathering the bitter fruits of the tree even before that time planted by Mr. Jefferson, and so industriously and perseveringly cultivated by Virginia." Marshall to Story, Dec. 25, 1832, JMP 12:248–49. See also Marshall to Richard Peters, Dec. 3, 1832, JMP 12:241–42 (nullification's "pernicious consequences to our country"); Marshall to Peter S. Du Ponceau, Dec. 9, 1832, JMP 12:243 ("the dangers which now threaten [our nation's] future"). Marshall had also presided over Aaron Burr's treason trial for an alleged conspiracy to lead western states to break away from the Union; and he had lived through the Hartford Convention of December 1814, which involved some serious discussion of secession by New England states.

23. Jackson, Proclamation Regarding Nullification, Dec. 10, 1832, MPP, 3:1211.

24. Jackson, Proclamation, MPP 3:1210; Webster, *Speeches*, 1:600–601.

25. Marshall to J.Q. Adams, Aug. 9, 1831; JMP, 12:96.

26. Webster made this claim as to *Dartmouth College* and *Gibbons*, at least. White, *Marshall Court*, 285–88; Johnson, *Gibbons*, 100–101.

27. Quoted in Smith, *Marshall*, 523–24. Marshall died of a diseased and enlarged liver. Id. Interestingly, his biographers are too respectful to speculate that this might have had some connection to his legendary fondness for wine and his noted tipsiness at gatherings of the Richmond Quoits Club.

28. Simon, *Lincoln and Taney*, 1, 5–25.

29. Although the 1837 Judiciary Act did specify a *residency* requirement, it stated, "The allotment of their chief justice and the associate justices of the said Supreme Court to the several circuits shall be made as heretofore." 5 Stat. 176. This was understood to codify the previous custom of appointing justices who resided in the circuit in which they would hear cases. Hoffer, Hoffer and Hull, *Federal Courts*, 109–10; Frankfurter and Landis, "Business of the Supreme Court," 1036, 1052–53.

30. Graber, "Overruling McCulloch?" The Whig appointee was Benjamin Curtis of Massachusetts, appointed by President Fillmore.

31. 36 U.S. 102 (1837).

32. 36 U.S. at 142, 132.

33. 36 U.S. at 139 (emphasis added).

34. The License Cases, 46 U.S. 504, 608 (1847) (Catron, J.) (a state's internal trade was "beyond the reach of Congress"); id. at 619–20 (Woodbury, J.) ("the subject of buying and selling within a State is one . . . exclusively belonging to the power of the State").

35. *Miln*, 36 U.S. at 133 ("we hold that both the end and the means here used, are within the competency of the states"); id. at 137 (state police power laws are constitutional, "[a]lthough the means used in their execution may sometimes approach [federal legislative means], so nearly as to be confounded").

36. 40 U.S. 449 (1841).

37. 46 U.S. 504 (1847).

38. 48 U.S. 283 (1849).

39. The License Cases, 46 U.S. at 631 (Grier, J.).

40. The License Cases, 46 U.S. at 576 (Taney, C.J.).

41. 48 U.S. at 457 (Grier, J.).

42. The License Cases, 46 U.S. at 589–90 (McLean, J., from Ohio); see also id at 613 (Daniel, J., from Virginia).

43. The Passenger Cases, 48 U.S. at 396–97 (McLean, J.).

44. These Taney Court pronouncements that an overriding state's right to self-defense gave a paramount status to a state's slavery laws suggests that Wisconsin's claimed power in *Abelman v. Booth*, 62 U.S. 506, 507 (1859) was not an unfounded departure. The Wisconsin courts had assumed a power to issue habeas relief to a prisoner held by federal authorities for abetting a fugitive slave in violation of the 1850 Fugitive Slave Act.

45. 46 U.S. at 631–32 (Grier, J.).

46. *Miln*, 36 U.S. at 158 (Story, J., dissenting).

47. The License Cases, 46 U.S. at 607 (Catron, J., concurring).

48. 40 U.S. 449 (1841).

49. There were two vacancies on the Court, as Barbour had died, and Catron missed the argument due to illness. 40 U.S. at 517. Only one justice argued that the Mississippi constitutional provision was invalidated by the Commerce Clause because slaves were articles of commerce. 40 U.S. at 517 (Baldwin, J.). Schwartz, "An Error and an Evil," 993–94, explains the justices' varying views in detail.

50. 40 U.S. at 508.

51. The License Cases, 46 U.S. at 629–30 (Woodbury, J.), quoting Prigg v. Pennsylvania, 41 U.S. (16 Pet.) 625 (1842).

52. Lightner, *Slavery and the Commerce Power*, 82–84.

53. The Passenger Cases, 48 U.S. at 427 (Wayne, J.).

54. 48 U.S. at 466–68, 474 (Taney, C.J., dissenting).

55. 48 U.S. at 508 (Daniel, J.) (majority's construction of trade treaty constitutes an "invasion of [states'] domestic security" by permitting "British subjects to land within the territory of any of the States cargoes of negroes from Jamaica, Hayti, or Africa"); id. at 525–26 (Woodbury, J.) (asserting right of states to exclude "slaves, or, what is still more common in America, in Free States as well as Slave States, [to] exclude colored emigrants, though free").

56. 48 U.S. at 457 (Grier, J., concurring).

57. 48 U.S. at 428–29 (Wayne, J., concurring).

58. 53 U.S. 299 (1852).

59. 53 U.S. at 320.

60. 44 U.S. 151 (1845).

61. 44 U.S. at 178 (McLean, J., dissenting); id. at 159 (argument of Attorney General Nelson).

62. 44 U.S. at 170.

63. 55 U.S. 568 (1853).
64. 55 U.S. at 571, 575, 573–74. *Gibbons* was mentioned once, in a string citation.
65. 55 U.S. at 574.
66. 55 U.S. at 574. See also Sinnot v. Davenport, 63 U.S. 227, 241–42 (1859) (relying on *Gibbons* to strike down an Alabama law imposing monetary fines on interstate steamboat operators who failed to preregister their vessels in the port of Mobile prior to entry).
67. Finkelman, *Supreme Injustice,* 140–41. Finkelman states that Margaret and her children disappeared from the historical record after they were sold.
68. U.S. Const. art. IV, § 2, cl. 3.
69. Somerset v. Stewart, 98 E.R. 499 (1772).
70. Finkelman, *Supreme Injustice,* 132, 146–50.
71. Morris, *Free Men All.*
72. Fehrenbacher, *Slaveholding Republic,* 246.
73. 41 U.S. 539 (1842).
74. 41 U.S. at 612–17, 622.
75. 41 U.S. at 627–30, 635, 656–58 (dissents of Taney, Thompson, and Daniel).
76. Story, *Commentaries* (1833 ed.), 3:677; Cover, *Justice Accused,* 239–41.
77. 41 U.S. at 618–19.
78. 41 U.S. at 621–25. Story cited the Marshall Court decisions in *Houston v. Moore, Martin v. Hunter's Lessee,* and *Sturges v. Crowninshield.*
79. 41 U.S. at 585 (argument of counsel) (quoting Story, *Commentaries,* § 1238).
80. Finkelman, *Supreme Injustice,* 142–44.
81. 41 U.S. at 611–12.
82. 41 U.S. at 639.
83. Finkelman, *Supreme Injustice,* 145–50.
84. 60 U.S. 393 (1857).
85. 60 U.S. at 407.
86. U.S. Const. art. IV, § 2, cl. 1.
87. The Taney Court, once again, issued multiple opinions. Taney's opinion for the Court was joined by Justices Wayne, Nelson, Grier, and Campbell. Writing separately, Daniel merely rehashed Taney's arguments and Catron reached the same result through different reasoning. The two Whig justices, McLean and Curtis, dissented.
88. The Marshall Court had decided that the federal government could govern territories as if it were a state government with general powers in *American Insurance Co. v. Canter,* 26 U.S. 511 (1828). Taney devoted five pages to an unpersuasive effort to distinguish *Canter. Dred Scott,* 60 U.S. at 442–46.
89. 60 U.S. at 448–49.
90. *McCulloch,* 17 U.S. at 418, 422.
91. Dred Scott v. Sandford, 60 U.S. at 440.
92. Dred Scott v. Sandford, 60 U.S. at 543 (McLean, J., dissenting). McLean, perhaps relying on memory, placed quotation marks around his own approximation of Marshall's actual language. Compare id. at 542 (McLean, J., dissenting) ("the degree of its necessity is a question of legislative discretion, not of judicial cognizance"), with *McCulloch,* 17 U.S. at 423 ("to inquire into the degree of its necessity, would be . . . to tread on legislative ground").
93. 62 U.S. 506 (1859).
94. 62 U.S. at 524–25.
95. 62 U.S. at 517, 520–21.
96. 55 U.S. 13 (1852).
97. *Prigg,* 41 U.S. at 625.
98. Graber, *Dred Scott,* 3–8; Allen, *Dred Scott Case,* 5–6.

Chapter 6

1. LCJS, 2:466, 171.
2. LCJS, 2:468, 402.
3. Thayer, *Marshall*, 58–59; LCJS 1:227.
4. E.g., Farber, *Lincoln's Constitution*, 99; Levinson, "They Whisper," 1093; Amar, "Sovereignty and Federalism," 1454–55.
5. In a December 1839 speech advocating a new national bank, Lincoln noted that "the Supreme Court—that tribunal which the Constitution has itself established to decide Constitutional questions—has solemnly decided that such a bank is constitutional." His argument that the Bank is "necessary and proper" to executing congressional powers only loosely tracks *McCulloch's* discussion, and goes beyond it to assert that the primary constitutional justification for a national bank is that it is necessary and proper to the taxing and spending powers, and to creating a uniform national currency. CWL, 1:160, 171–72. See also id. 1:307 ("a national Bank . . . is highly necessary and proper to the establishment and maintenance of a sound currency"). Lincoln placed greater emphasis on the Bank's affirmation by the first Congress, Washington, and later Madison. CWL, 1:312 (Campaign Circular from Whig Committee, Mar. 4, 1843); 1:333 (Speeches in Virginia, Illinois, Feb. 22, 1844). Lincoln was familiar with at least some of the documentary record, quoting at length from Jefferson's cabinet memo to Washington opposing the First Bank. CWL, 1:502 (House speech of July 27, 1848). He once cited *McCulloch* in a brief in a case involving a state tax on one of his clients, a federally chartered railroad. Burlingame, *Abraham Lincoln*, 2:336.
6. "Will you not graciously allow us to do with the Dred Scott decision precisely as you did with the Bank decision?" Speech at Springfield, Jul. 17, 1858, CWL, 2:519. See also First Debate, at Ottawa, Aug. 21, 1858; Fifth Debate, at Galesburg, Oct. 7, 1858; Sixth Debate, at Quincy, Oct. 13, 1858; CWL, 3:28, 232, 278.
7. See, e.g., Burlingame, *Abraham Lincoln*, 2:570. Burlingame points out that the Gettysburg Address, for instance, shows influence from Daniel Webster's "Second Reply to Hayne," ("people's government, made for the people, made by the people, and answerable to the people"); Theodore Parker's sermon, "Democracy is Direct Self-government, over all the people, for all the people, by all the people"; and Galusha Grow's July 4, 1861 speech ("Fourscore years ago").
8. First Inaugural, CWL, 4:268.
9. First Inaugural, CWL, 4:265.
10. First Inaugural, CWL, 4:264.
11. CWL, 4:267–68.
12. McPherson, *Battle Cry*, 232, 308–12. Lincoln received 39.65% of the total popular vote, and 59.4% of the electoral vote. https://uselectionatlas.org/RESULTS/
13. CWL, 4:426.
14. Foreman, *World on Fire*, 98–99.
15. Lincoln, July 4, 1861 message to Congress, CWL, 4:439.
16. Gettysburg Address, CWL, 7:17–22.
17. MacPherson, *Battle Cry*, 450; Currie, "Civil War Congress," 1142–51; Curry, *Blueprint for Modern America*, 11, 75–148.
18. Burlingame, *Lincoln*, 2:220.
19. Curry, *Blueprint for Modern America*, 181–86; McPherson, *Battle Cry*, 444–47; Ritter, *Goldbugs and Greenbacks*, 29–30.
20. U.S. Const. art. I., § 8, cl. 5.
21. This requires reading two clauses together: the power "to borrow money on the credit of the United States," which implies issuing notes or bonds, and the power "to provide for the punishment of counterfeiting the securities . . . of the United States"—again, Treasury notes or bonds. U.S. Const. art. I., § 8, cls. 2, 6.
22. Ritter, *Goldbugs and Greenbacks*, 73–74.

23. U.S. Const. art. I, § 10, cl.1 (emphasis added).

24. Bates to Spaulding, Jan. 6, 1862, in Spaulding, *Resource of War*, 15–16.

25. *Life and Accomplishments of Elbridge Gerry Spaulding*, Buffalo Architecture and Hist., last visited May 31, 2017, http://buffaloah.com/h/spauld.

26. Cong. Globe, 37th Cong., 3d Sess. 286 (Jan. 12, 1863) (Rep. Spaulding).

27. Cong. Globe, 37th Cong., 2d Sess. 688 (Feb. 6, 1862) (Rep. Stevens).

28. Cong. Globe, 37th Cong., 2d Sess. 679 (Feb. 6, 1862) (Rep. Kellogg).

29. Currie, "Civil War Congress," 1165; McPherson, *Battle Cry*, 440, 447.

30. 12 Stat. 318, §§ 2, 3; Currie, "Civil War Congress," 1141.

31. U.S. Const. art. III, § 3, cl. 2. The lifetime limitation on property forfeiture was intended to eliminate the monarchical practice of using treason prosecutions as a revenue-raising device.

32. Currie, "Civil War Congress," 1193–94; Curry, *Blueprint*, 95–98.

33. Cong. Globe, 27th Cong., 2d sess. 429 (Apr. 15, 1842). Adams argued that military commanders had the power "to emancipate all the slaves" in a war zone, whether in a case of invasion or war, "whether servile, civil, or foreign." Adams had deployed the argument in hope of dissuading southern Democrats from voting for war against Mexico.

34. Cong. Globe, 37th Cong., 2d sess. 346–48 (Jan. 15, 1862) (Rep. Bingham). Bingham expressly referred to Adams.

35. Cong. Globe, 37th Cong., 2d sess. 464 (Jan. 23, 1862) (Rep. Van Horn).

36. Cong. Globe, 37th Cong., 2d Sess. 803 (Sen. Pearce) (implied powers are those necessary and proper to express ones); 1761 (1862) (Sen. Davis) (same); 1630 (1862) (Rep. Nixon) (emancipation power is incidental to war power).

37. For citations to *Brown v. United States*, 12 U.S. (8 Cranch) 110 (1814), in support of congressional confiscation power, see Cong. Globe, 37th Cong., 2d Sess. 1559–60 (Apr. 7, 1862) (Sen. Trumbull); 1862 (Rep. Sheffield); 1874 (Sen. Wilmot). See also Cong. Globe, 37th Cong., 2d Sess. 551 (Rep. Pendleton) (citing *Craig v. Missouri*); 1860 (Sen. Browning) (citing *Fletcher v. Peck*).

38. Burlingame, *Lincoln*, 2:333–35.

39. CWL, 5:433–36. He also cited section 10, which prohibited the return of fugitive slaves to owners who had not forsworn rebellion.

40. Whiting, *War Powers*, 37.

41. Whiting's argument on Congressional power tracked Bingham's January 15 speech. His reference to *McCulloch* came in a lengthy near-verbatim extract from Spaulding's January 28 speech introducing the Legal Tender Act, copying even an erroneous page citation to Kent's *Commentaries*. Compare Whiting, *War Powers*, 34–37, with Cong. Globe, 37th Cong., 2d Sess. 526 (Jan. 28, 1862) (Rep. Spaulding).

42. Compare Neely, *Triumph*, 80–85 (Whiting created a "personal myth" that has "fooled us into taking Whiting too seriously") with Burlingame, *Lincoln*, 362. Burlingame speculates that Whiting "may have" influenced Lincoln, but asserts that "Charles Sumner, Henry Ward Beecher, and other antislavery militants had endorsed Adams's dictum" that the war power authorized emancipation. The earliest mention of Whiting's book found in a database of period newspapers was a bookseller's advertisement in the Boston Daily *Advertiser*, Nov. 5, 1862, p. 2, col. 8. https://infoweb-newsbank-com.

43. CWL, 6:28–30.

44. Ex parte Merryman, 17 F. Cas. 144 (1861); Burlingame, 2:151 (Lincoln ignored the ruling); Simon, *Lincoln and Taney*, 221 (Taney on secession); White, *Law in American History*, 1:432–33.

45. 67 U.S. 635 (1863).

46. Swisher, *Taney*, 570, 572–75. Art. I, § 8, cl. 2 authorizes Congress "to borrow money on the credit of the United States."

47. U.S. Const. art. I, § 8, cl. 12.

48. Roger B. Taney, "Thoughts on the Conscription Law of the United States" (unpublished legal opinion, 1863), in Anderson, *Military Draft*, 207, 213.

49. *McCulloch*, 17 U.S. at 415.

Chapter 7

1. Foner, *Reconstruction*.

2. Foner, *Reconstruction*.

3. U.S. Const. amend. XIII, § 2; amend. XIV, § 5; amend. XV, § 2.

4. Katzenbach v. Morgan, 384 U.S. 641 651 (1966); see, e.g., Amar, *America's Constitution*, 361–62; Tribe, *American Constitutional Law*, 805; Engel, "*McCulloch* Theory," 118–19.

5. Vorenberg, *Final Freedom*, 189–91; Fairman, *Reconstruction and Reunion*, 1:1156–59; Pope, "Thirteenth Amendment," 433–34.

6. 62 U.S. 506, 517 (1859). Thomas Hart Benton, a leading critic of *McCulloch* in the Senate who strategized on how best to overrule it, advocated "appropriate legislation" to remove federal subtreasury deposits from state banks that suspended specie payments. 14 Reg. Deb. 1,195 (1837). See also S. Doc. 512, at 718 (1833) (letter of Gov. Lumpkin) (proposing that Georgia legislature enact "appropriate legislation" to eject the Cherokee nation from the state); Cong. Globe, 26th Cong., 1st Sess. 484 (1840) (Sen. Lumpkin) (states can protect debtors "by their insolvent laws, and other appropriate legislation"); Cong. Globe, 33d Cong., 2d Sess. 1036 (1855) (Sen. Cooper) (bill on import duties should be examined carefully "to secure just and appropriate legislation"); Cong. Globe, 36th Cong., 1st Sess. 6 (1859) (Sen. Mason) (suggesting "appropriate legislation" to prevent recurrence of raids on federal armories like that of John Brown).

7. Constitutional scholars have tended to work backward from these post-ratification debates in 1866 to simply assume that the framers of the Thirteenth Amendment in 1864–65 had *McCulloch* in mind. See, e.g., Caminker, "Appropriate Means-Ends Constraints," 1159 and n. 164.

8. 14 Stat. 27, § 1. The current version of the law is codified as 42 U.S.C. § 1981.

9. MPP, 8:3605–6.

10. United States v. Rhodes, 27 F. Cas. 785, 794 (1866 Civil Rights Act "gives only certain civil rights. Whether it was competent for congress to confer political rights also, involves a different inquiry."); Brandwein, *Judicial Settlement*, 71.

11. Sumner, *Works*, 14:355, 384, 426; Fairman, *Reconstruction and Reunion*, 1:1164–93; Brandwein, *Judicial Settlement*, 63–65.

12. Cong. Globe 39th Cong., 1st sess. 1118 (Mar. 1, 1866).

13. 27 F. Cas. 785 (1866).

14. 27 F. Cas. at 794, 791–92.

15. Cong. Globe, 39th Cong., 1st Sess. 1094 (Feb. 28, 1866).

16. 17 Stat. 13. Its main provision is generally known as "section 1983" for its codification in the U.S. Code. See 42 U.S.C. § 1983. It is also known as the Third Enforcement Act or the Ku Klux Klan Act. Foner, *Reconstruction*, 454–55.

17. In support: Cong. Globe, 42d Cong., 1st Sess. 333 (1871) (Rep. Hoar) (1871 Civil Rights Act); Cong. Globe, 42d Cong., 1st Sess. 476 (1871) (Rep. Dawes) (1871 Civil Rights Act); Cong. Globe, 42d Cong., 1st Sess. 202 (1871) (Rep. Snyder) (1871 Civil Rights Act); 3 Cong. Rec. 2,979–80 (1875) (Rep. Hale) (1875 Civil Rights Act); 2 Cong. Rec. 1,414 (1874) (Rep. Lawrence) (same). In opposition: 42d Cong., 1st Sess. 87 (1871) (Rep. Storm) (1871 Civil Rights Act); Cong. Globe, 42d Cong., 1st Sess. 648–49 (1871) (Sen. Davis) (1871 Civil Rights Act); Cong. Globe, 42d Cong., 1st Sess. 695 (1871) (Sen. Thurman) (1871 Civil Rights Act); 2 Cong. Rec. 5,4084–85 (1874) (Sen. Thurman) (1875 Civil Rights Act); Cong. Globe, 39th Cong., 1st Sess. 933–34 (1866) (Sen. Davis) (in support of Johnson's veto of Freedman's Bureau bill); Cong. Globe, 40th Cong., 2d Sess. 586 (1868) (Rep. Eldridge) (against reconstruction bill).

18. See, e.g., Cong. Globe, 39th Cong., 1st Sess. 474 (Jan. 29, 1866) (Sen. Trumbull).

19. Sumner, *Works*, 14:355, 385, 429.

20. App. to the Cong. Globe, 39th Cong., 1st Sess. 122 (1866) (Sen. Sumner) (HR 51 reapportionment amendment); Cong. Globe, 40th Cong., 2d Sess. 596 (Feb. 3, 1868) (Rep. Boutwell) (implied powers to legislate readmission of rebel states); Cong. Globe, 40th Cong., 2d Sess. 2664 (1868) (Sen. Conkling) (same); Cong. Globe, 40th Cong., 2d Sess. 929 (1868) (Sen. Stewart) (implied war powers); Cong. Globe, 39th Cong., 1st Sess. 908 (1866) (Rep. Lawrence) (reconstruction bill); 40th Cong., 2d Sess. 545 (1868) (Rep. Beck) (Congress's power to legislate for readmitted states); Cong. Globe, 38th Cong., 2d Sess. 77–78 (1864) (Sen. Davis) (citing *McCulloch* in opposition to bill to emancipate families of Black soldiers); Cong. Globe, 38th Cong., 1st Sess. 2020 (1864) (Sen. Davis) (citing *McCulloch* against power to issue legal tender paper money); Cong. Globe, 39th Cong., 1st Sess. 276 (1866) (Rep. Baker) (bill to incorporate a federal insurance corporation for homesteaders). *McCulloch* was cited by several members in support of stringent loyalty oaths for returning members of Congress from former rebel states. Cong. Globe, 40th Cong., 2d Sess. 660 (1868) (Sen. Stewart). Cong. Globe, 40th Cong., 2d Sess. 894–94 (1868) (Rep. Dawes). Cong. Globe, 40th Cong., 2d Sess. 910 (1868) (Rep. Cook).

21. See, e.g., Cong. Globe, 39th Cong., 1st Sess. 474 (Jan. 29, 1866) (Sen. Trumbull) (supporting 1866 Civil Rights Act). On the proportion of lawyers, see Aynes, "39th Congress," 1024–25.

22. Coquillette and Kimball, *Battlefield of Merit*, 132, 230–31.

23. Caminker, "Appropriate Means-Ends Constraints," 1158–66; Engel, "*McCulloch* Theory."

24. Although the breadth of the Necessary and Proper Clause is expressed on its face, many courts and commentators over the years have read it as though it were limited to "the foregoing powers." On this point, and the Clause's proper interpretation, see John Mikhail's illuminating study. Mikhail, "Necessary and Proper Clauses."

25. See Cong. Globe, 39th Cong., 1st sess. 1294 (Rep. Wilson) (1866); Brandwein, Judicial Settlement, 35–37. *Prigg v. Pennsylvania*, 41 U.S. 539 (1842), is discussed in Chapter 5.

26. Barnett, "Career of Chase," 656–76; Friedman, "Salmon P. Chase," JUSSC, 2:551–55.

27. 74 U.S. 71 (1869).

28. 74 U.S. at 76.

29. 74 U.S. 700 (1869).

30. 74 U.S. at 720, 725 (emphasis added).

31. The alternative amendment procedure requires a national constitutional convention called by Congress on the application of two-thirds of the states. U.S. Const. art. V.

32. 83 U.S. 36 (1873).

33. Although not detailed in the Court's opinion, the scattering of butcher shops willy-nilly throughout New Orleans, with the animal wastes they generated, had indeed presented a major health problem. There was also an underlying race element, as the challengers were white butchers who resented the biracial makeup of the monopoly consortium, and had themselves tried to monopolize the trade to exclude black competitors. Brandwein, *Judicial Settlement*, 56; Ross, *Samuel Freeman Miller*, 189–200.

34. The Slaughter-House Cases, 83 U.S. at 76.

35. 83 U.S. at 77–78.

36. Brandwein, *Judicial Settlement*, 70–74. For earlier and more general descriptions of the rights typology, see Hyman and Wiecek, *Equal Justice*, 395–97; Tushnet, "Politics of Equality," 884–90.

37. Section 2 allowed states to deny the right to vote in federal elections, but imposed a penalty by providing that excluded voting-age males (presumably those excluded on the basis of race) would not be counted toward congressional or electoral college representation.

38. Brandwein, *Judicial Settlement*, 60–67, 75–86; Foner, *Reconstruction*, 255–56, 289.

39. Strauder v. West Virginia, 100 U.S. 303 (1880); Ex parte Virginia 100 U.S. 339 (1880).

40. Ex parte Siebold, 100 U.S. 371 (1880); see also United States v. Reese, 92 U.S. 214, 218 (1876) (suggesting Congress can legislate to prevent state race discrimination in voting).

41. Siebold, 100 U.S. 371; Ex parte Yarbrough, 110 U.S. 651 (1884). The idea that post–Civil War federal authority extended to "every inch" of American "soil" is discussed in Chapter 8.

42. See, e.g., United States v. Reese, 92 U.S. 214 (1876); United States v. Harris, 106 U.S. 629 (1883).

43. Lane, *The Day Freedom Died*, 90–109, 265–66.

44. 92 U.S. 542, 556 (1876).

45. Welke, "When All the Women Were White," 266–77; Scott, "Public Rights, Social Equality," 790–98; Brandwein, *Judicial Settlement*, 72–73.

46. Brandwein, 66–69.

47. 18 Stat. 335, §§ 1, 2.

48. 109 U.S. 3 (1883).

49. 109 U.S. at 13–14, 24.

50. 94 U.S. 113 (1877).

51. The Civil Rights Cases, 109 U.S. at 43 (Harlan, J., dissenting).

52. 109 U.S. at 19.

53. 163 U.S. 537 (1896).

54. United States v. Morrison, 529 U.S. 598, 602 (2000); see also Heart of Atlanta Motel v. United States, 379 U.S. 241 (1964). These are discussed in Chapters 12 and 13.

55. The Civil Rights Cases, 109 U.S. at 51 (Harlan, J., dissenting).

56. Nelson, *Fourteenth Amendment*, 133–36. Nelson speaks of segregation rather than using the specific category of "social rights."

57. The doctrine of "severability" or "separability" recognizing this practice was by 1883 "an elementary principle." Allen v. Louisiana, 103 U.S. 80, 83–84 (1880).

58. The Civil Rights Cases, reporters' summary, 109 U.S. at 3–5.

59. Brief for Plaintiff's in Error at 5, 7, 14–15; Brief for Defendant in Error at 2–5, Robinson v. Memphis & Charleston R. Co., reprinted in Kurland, Landmark Briefs, 8:358, 360, 367–68, 391–94; see also Welke, "When All the Women Were White," 279–80, 306.

60. The Civil Rights Cases, 109 U.S. at 26.

61. 109 U.S. at 10, 19.

62. 109 U.S. at 60 (Harlan, J., dissenting). In the *Trade-mark Cases*, 100 U.S. 82 (1879), the Court considered multiple powers of Congress before striking the law down, even though the law identified no particular constitutional basis. See also Woods v. Cloyd W. Miller Co., 333 U.S. 138, 140–41, 144 (1948) ("The question of the constitutionality of action taken by Congress does not depend on recitals of the power which it undertakes to exercise"). In *EEOC v. Wyoming*, 460 U.S. 226 (1983), the Court noted that Congress had power to enact the federal age-discrimination statute under the Commerce Clause even though it had purported to rely on section 5 of the Fourteenth Amendment. See 460 U.S. at 244 n. 18.

63. The Civil Rights Cases, 109 U.S. at 25–26.

64. 109 U.S. at 60 (Harlan, J., dissenting). Michael Klarman suggests that many people drew a distinction between segregation and complete exclusion from facilities. Under this view, the statutory language "full and equal and enjoyment" may have been interpreted to allow "separate but equal" accommodations in theaters, etc. Although state-mandated Jim Crow laws were still a few years away, private business owners of various sorts were already pursuing this policy, and courts were already developing doctrine to the effect that segregation was a reasonable policy for the comfort of patrons. Klarman, *Jim Crow*, 19–22. But there is no indication in the congressional debates that Sumner's public accommodations law contemplated "separate but equal" facilities as opposed to desegregated ones. Mrs. Robinson was kicked out of the ladies' car, not kicked off the train, and neither she nor the defendant suggested that the 1875 Civil Rights Act was inapplicable to "mere" segregation as opposed to complete exclusion.

65. 95 U.S. 485 (1878).

66. 95 U.S. at 489–50; Scott, "Public Rights, Social Equality," 792–93; Palmore, "Interstate Jim Crow," 1777–78; Foner, *Reconstruction*, 370–71.

67. *DeCuir*, 95 U.S. at 489–90.
68. Klarman, *Jim Crow*, 20–21.
69. 73 U.S. 35 (1868).
70. *DeCuir*, 95 U.S. at 490.
71. Brief of the Plaintiff in Error at 53, Hall v. DeCuir, 95 U.S. 485.
72. 133 U.S. 587 (1890).
73. The Court claimed that the Mississippi Supreme Court had authoritatively interpreted the law that way. 133 U.S. at 591. That was true, but that fact failed to make sense of the passenger/carrier distinction or to distinguish *DeCuir*. See Louisville, N. O. and T. R. Co. v. State, 6 So. 203, 204 (1889).
74. *Louisville,* 133 U.S. at 593–95.
75. 230 U.S. 126, 132–33 (1913).
76. Klarman, *Jim Crow,* 24–25; Brandwein, *Judicial Settlement,* 69–70; Palmore, "Interstate Jim Crow." Brandwein shows that even Republican members of Congress who voted for the 1875 Civil Rights Act were at best lukewarm about its merits, and supported it to honor Sumner's memory. But unless one argues that these lukewarm Republicans *wanted* the law struck down—which seems truly strange and is not what Brandwein argues—then my criticism of the *Civil Rights Cases* holds.
77. Scott, "Public Rights, Social Equality," 780.
78. Jackson, *Judicial Supremacy,* 315; Magliocca, *Andrew Jackson,* 2–3.
79. Gillman, Graber, and Whittington, *American Constitutionalism,* 720. The Act of February 8, 1894, 28 Stat. 36, repealed numerous voting rights provisions. An 1877 civil rights repeal bill passed by a Democratic Congress had been vetoed by Republican President Hayes. Carr, *Federal Protection,* 45–46.

Chapter 8

1. *McCulloch v. Maryland,* 17 U.S. (4 Wheat.) 316, 404 (1819).
2. The Legal Tender Cases, 79 U.S. 457, 555 (1871) (Bradley, J., concurring).
3. Howe, *American Whigs,* 28–29, 133–35, 219–37; Howe, *What Hath God Wrought,* 570–612.
4. 75 U.S. 603 (1870).
5. Prior to 1870, the Court had struck down acts of Congress in five cases, but none based on a supposed Commerce Clause limitation. *Marbury v. Madison* invalidated a law purportedly expanding the grounds for Supreme Court original jurisdiction, but did not suggest that Congress had exceeded one of its enumerated powers. *Dred Scott* invalidated the Missouri Compromise, an issue that did not involve the Commerce Clause. *Cummings v. Missouri,* 71 U.S. 316 (1867) and *Ex parte Garland,* 71 U.S. 333 (1867), struck down a post-rebellion loyalty oath law as violating the Bill of Attainder and Ex Post Facto clauses and the president's pardon power. In *United States v. DeWitt* (1869), striking down a federal regulation of flammable lighting oils, the Court did not acknowledge the commerce power issue, and focused on the taxing power.
6. 79 U.S. 457 (1871).
7. The value of a banknote comprised at least three elements: the creditworthiness of the issuing institution, with a discount reflecting the risk that the bank would fail to redeem the note in specie; the transaction cost of physically redeeming a note for specie; and the supply of paper currency relative to the demand for it, compared to the supply and demand for specie.
8. Unger, *Greenback Era,* 17–22. The 1875 Resumption Act promised to redeem legal tender notes in gold as of 1879. Ritter, *Goldbugs and Greenbacks,* 286.
9. Butler v. Horwitz, 74 U.S. 258 (1869). See also Bank v. Supervisors, 74 U.S. 26 (1869) (greenbacks held exempt from state taxation); Lane County v. Oregon, 74 U.S. 71 (1869) (greenbacks were not legal tender for payment of state taxes); Bronson v. Rodes, 74 U.S. 229 (1869) (Legal Tender Act did not apply to pre-enactment debts).

10. *Hepburn*, 75 U.S. at 611. Compare Marbury v. Madison, 5 U.S. (1 Cranch) 137, 177 (1803). ("It is emphatically the province and duty of the judicial department to say what the law is").

11. *Hepburn*, 75 U.S. at 613–14.

12. 75 U.S. at 614–15, quoting *McCulloch*, 17 U.S. at 421, 423.

13. 75 U.S. at 615, 617, 620–21.

14. 75 U.S. at 618, 622–25.

15. See U.S. Const., art. I, § 10, cl. 1 (impairment of contracts prohibition), amend. V (due process clause). Three years later, in the *Slaughterhouse Cases*, 83 U.S. 36 (1873), four dissenting justices (Chase, Swayne, Field, and Bradley) expressly supported the idea that the due-process clause could bar at least some economic regulations, but the majority rejected this view.

16. *Hepburn*, 75 U.S. at 622, 625.

17. 75 U.S. 533 (1869).

18. *Veazie Bank*, 75 U.S. at 548–49.

19. 72 U.S. 462, 471 (1867) (Congress lacked power to regulate intrastate commerce "except such as is *strictly incidental* to the exercise of powers clearly granted").

20. 24 F. Cas. 337 (1867).

21. 24 F. Cas. 337. See United States v. Rhodes, 27 F. Cas. 785 (1866).

22. 75 U.S. at 615.

23. Benedict, "Chase and Constitutional Politics," 487.

24. *Hepburn*'s effort to constitutionalize a "hard-money" (i.e., gold-backed currency) policy might also have resonated with traditional Jacksonians, though the politics of hard versus soft money was itself in a confused state of flux as Jacksonians were "emerg[ing] from the [Civil] war years with enthusiastic faith" in paper money. Hammond, *Sovereignty and an Empty Purse*, 356.

25. See Chapter 13.

26. *Hepburn*, 75 U.S. at 628–29 (Miller, J., dissenting).

27. Miller and the two other dissenters, Davis and Swayne, had been infuriated by what they perceived as Chase's manipulative and overbearing conduct behind the scenes in the *Hepburn* case. When *Hepburn* was argued, there was already one Court vacancy and the retirement of Grier, whose mental faculties had been impaired by a series of strokes, was imminent. But Chase ignored Miller's entreaties to postpone deciding the constitutionality of the Legal Tender Act until the Court was at full strength, probably realizing that new Court appointments would tip the balance in favor of the Act. Instead, Chase pushed the decision forward, and browbeat the mentally infirm Grier into changing his vote to win a 5-3 majority to strike down the law. Grier retired the week before the controversial five-to-three decision was announced. Miller, "Statement of Facts," 46, 61, 69–71; Fairman, Reconstruction and Reunion, 1:716–19. Miller's anger at Chase boiled over two months later when Chase, in Miller's words, "resorted to all the stratagems of the lowest political trickery" to prevent re-argument of the Legal Tender issue before a full nine-justice Court. Miller to William Pitt Ballinger, Apr. 12, 1870, Miller Correspondence; Ross, *Samuel Freeman Miller*, 184.

28. *Hepburn*, 75 U.S. at 627–31 (Miller, J., dissenting).

29. 75 U.S. at 627–28, 635, 638–39.

30. 75 U.S. at 637–38.

31. 79 U.S. 457 (1871).

32. 79 U.S. at 531.

33. 79 U.S. at 539–40, 542.

34. 79 U.S. at 532–33, 534–35.

35. 79 U.S. at 544, 547.

36. Thayer, "Legal Tender," 84.

37. The Legal Tender Cases, 79 U.S. at 544–46.

38. 79 U.S. at 550–52.

39. 79 U.S. at 555–56, 560, 567–68.

40. 79 U.S. at 570–71 (Chase, C. J., dissenting).

41. William Nelson argues that Marshall's approach was to defer to congressional choices on contested policy matters, limiting constitutional principles to "widely shared values." Nelson, "Eighteenth-Century Background," 901–902.
42. The Legal Tender Cases, 79 U.S. at 582 (Chase, C.J., dissenting).
43. 79 U.S. at 542–43.
44. 77 U.S. 557, 566 (1871).
45. Searight v. Stokes, 44 U.S. 151 (1845).
46. Hare, *American Constitutional Law*, v–vi.
47. 73 U.S. 35 (1868).
48. Black, *Structure and Relationship*, 13–17.
49. *Crandall*, 73 U.S. at 43–44, 45.
50. 91 U.S. 367 (1876).
51. 91 U.S. at 371–74. A single, inglorious citation to *McCulloch*, without discussion, appears at the end of a string of cases introduced by "We also refer to. . . ." Id. at 373.
52. 93 U.S. 130, 136 (1876).
53. 93 U.S. at 136.
54. 96 U.S. 1 (1878).
55. 96 U.S. at 11.
56. 100 U.S. 371 (1880).
57. 100 U.S. at 394–95. See also Tennessee v. Davis, 100 U.S. 257, 263 (1879) ("The United States is a government with authority extending over the whole territory of the Union, acting upon the States and upon the people of the States").
58. Currie, "Civil War Congress," 1145–46; Curry, *Blueprint for Modern America*, 116–36.
59. 127 U.S. 1 (1888).
60. 127 U.S. at 39.
61. Warren, *Supreme Court*, 3:359.
62. 76 U.S. 41 (1869).
63. 76 U.S. at 44. Brief for United States at 6, United States v. Dewitt, 76 U.S. 41 (1869) (citing *McCulloch*).
64. 100 U.S. 82 (1879).
65. 100 U.S. at 93, 95.
66. 128 U.S. 1 (1888).
67. 128 U.S. at 17–18.

Chapter 9

1. Hepburn v. Griswold, 75 U.S. 603, 629 (1870) (Miller, J., dissenting).
2. 110 U.S. 651, 658 (1884).
3. Miller, *Constitution of the United States*, 389–91.
4. By Gray: Julliard v. Greenman, 110 U.S. 421 (1884) (legal tender paper money); Van Brocklin v. Tennessee, 117 U.S. 151 (1886) (repossession of public lands from homesteaders); Logan v. United States, 144 U.S. 263, 283 (1892) (protection of federal prisoner from lynching); Fong Yue Ting v. United States 130 U.S. 581, 603–4 (1892) (deportation and exclusion of immigrants); Luxton v. North River Bridge, 153 U.S. 525, 529 (1894) (condemnation of private property for federal internal improvements). By Harlan: Interstate Commerce Commission v. Brimson, 154 U.S. 447, 472 (1894) (statutory authorization for ICC to issue subpoenas). Harlan relied on *McCulloch* in his dissents in the *Civil Rights Cases*, as seen in Chapter 7, in *United States v. E.C. Knight Co.*, 156 U.S. 1, 33 (1895), discussed below, and in later majority opinions in *Champion v. Ames*, 188 U.S. 321 (1903), and *Northern Securities Co. v. United States*, 193 U.S. 197 (1904), discussed in Chapter 10.
5. Holmes to Sir Frederick Pollock, *Holmes-Pollock Letters*, 2:7–8. Holmes is also reputed to have called Harlan "the last of the tobacco-spittin' judges," but this may be apocryphal. I have found

no confirming primary source, nor anyone recounting the epithet who cites a primary source. See, e.g., Yarbrough, *Judicial Enigma*, viii; Biddle, *Holmes*, 107–8.

6. Louis Filler, "Horace Gray," in JUSSC, 2:669. For example, a contemporary newspaper account of the *Pollock* case, striking down the federal income tax law, suggested Gray visibly smirked and exchanged scornful whispers with Justice Field in open court while Harlan read his dissent. Yarbrough, *Judicial Enigma*, 175.

7. Yarbrough, *Judicial Enigma*, 6, quoting Harlan, autobiographical letter.

8. Thomas A. Marshall was the son of John Marshall's cousin and close friend, Humphrey. The Chief Justice once wrote a recommendation letter on behalf of "my nephew Thomas" to Henry Clay. Smith, *Marshall*, 499.

9. Richard Olney, "Memoir of Horace Gray," quoted in Spector, "Justice Horace Gray," 184.

10. Spector, 181–200; Filler, "Horace Gray," JUSSC, 2:667–70; Coquillette and Kimball, *Battlefield of Merit*, 170–173 (Harvard curriculum); Peppers, "Lost Law Clerks," 19–23.

11. 110 U.S. 421 (1884)

12. Act of May 31, 1878, 20 Stat. 87.

13. *Julliard*, 110 U.S. at 441, 438–39.

14. Frankfurter, "John Marshall," 219.

15. See *Julliard*, 110 U.S. at 445–46.

16. 29 U.S. (4 Pet.) 410 (1830).

17. 17 U.S. (4 Wheat.) 122 (1819).

18. *Julliard*, 110 U.S. at 441–44.

19. Coquillette and Kimball, *Battlefield of Merit*, 49–58, 63–64; White, *Law in American History*, 1:286–87; 2:312–15; Friedman, *History of American Law*, 318–22.

20. Coquillette and Kimball, 344–51, 385–87, 400–407; White, *Law in American History*, 2:328–30.

21. Coquillette and Kimball, 167–68, 351–60; LaPiana, *Logic and Experience*, 22–28, 96–109.

22. LaPiana, 79–99, 144–48; White, *Law in American History*, 2:330–331; Friedman, *History of American Law*, 606–20.

23. Friedman, 618–23; White, *Tort Law in America*, 20–37.

24. Coquillette and Kimball, *Battlefield of Merit*, 157, 166–68.

25. Pomeroy, *Constitutional Law*, 166–69; see also Hare, *American Constitutional Law*, 1:105.

26. Kent, *Commentaries*, 1:242 n. a (3rd ed. 1836).

27. Kent, *Commentaries*, 1:251 (2d ed. 1832).

28. See Kent, *Commentaries*, 1:266–68 (2d ed. 1832); 1:266–70 (6th ed. 1848); 1:268–71 (14th ed. 1896). Kent's *Commentaries* went through fourteen editions in the nineteenth century, with a fifteenth published after a hundred-year hiatus, starting in 1997. According to Holmes, the sixth edition of 1848 was the last one written by Kent himself (and published the year after his death). "Editor's Preface," in Kent, *Commentaries* (12th ed. 1873).

29. Kent, 1:254 n. 1 (12th ed. 1873).

30. On Cooley's works and influence, see Carrington, "Thomas McIntyre Cooley," 386.

31. Cooley, *Constitutional Limitations*, 63.

32. Cooley, *Principles of Constitutional Law*, 28, 91–93. Cooley omitted *McCulloch* entirely from an introductory chapter with such *McCulloch*-related topics as "By whom [the Constitution] adopted," "The Union Indissoluble," "the Constitution a Grant of Powers," "It is Supreme," and "the Territories." Id., at 20, 26, 28, 29, 31, 36 For the rejection of compact theory, Cooley cites *McCulloch* in the middle of a long string of Marshall Court cases. He suggests they were of less moment than Webster's speeches, Jackson's anti-nullification proclamation, elective branch activity, public opinion, and the Reconstruction Amendments. Id. at 28.

33. See, e.g., Von Holst, *Constitutional Law*, 54, 117, 121 (recognizing *McCulloch* only as an intergovernmental taxation case); Tiedeman, *Police Power* 315, 603–10, 636–37 (treating *Legal Tender Cases* as the leading decision on implied powers).

34. Wilson, *Congressional Government*, 22–23.

35. *Roosevelt and Frankfurter: Correspondence*, 25.

36. Thayer also published a famous work on evidence law, *A Preliminary Treatise on Evidence at the Common Law*, Boston: Little, Brown, 1898.

37. Thayer, "Origin and Scope." See Introduction to One Hundred Years of Judicial Review: The Thayer Centennial Symposium, 88 Nw. U. L. Rev. i (1993) (quoting Henry P. Monaghan, "Marbury and the Administrative State," 83 Colum. L. Rev. 1, 7 [1983]). The symposium was celebrating the centennial of Thayer's article.

38. According to the *Nation* review, Thayer's "skillful linking together of the developed steps of each topic, and the copious annotation from all sources give this book the character of an original work." The Nation, Apr. 11, 1895. Brandeis wrote to Thayer that the book "brings me a wealth of learning and of ideas. . . . I regret only that . . . your own opinions are not more frequently expressed." Brandeis to Thayer, Aug. 27, 1894. Thayer Papers, Box 17, Folder 1.

39. Thayer, *Cases*, 1:266–70, 272–85. The three excerpts are federalism passages from Marshall's opinions in *Sturges v. Crowninshield* and *Gibbons v. Ogden*, and Kent's opinion in *Livingston v. Van Ingen*, 9 Johns. 507 (1812).

40. Schwartz, "Misreading," 9 n. 21.

41. Cases on Constitutional Law: For the Use of the Class in Constitutional Law at the Harvard Law School, 1892–93. *The Making of Modern Law.* Gale. 2017. Gale, Cengage Learning. http://galenet.galegroup.com. The eighteen-page pamphlet does not identify an instructor or author, but it was clearly Thayer's work, as it almost exactly matches the outline in Thayer's teaching notebook for his 1891–92 Constitutional Law course. Thayer Papers, Box 2, Folder 7. Thayer's casebook very closely tracks the syllabus, though with a few significant changes, such as the changed placement of *McCulloch*.

42. Thayer, "Legal Tender," 73–97.

43. Thayer, "Origin and Scope," 138.

44. Peppers, "Lost Law Clerks," 30. That Thayer and his son Ezra Ripley Thayer had a close but difficult relationship, is reflected in the tenor of their correspondence. See, e.g., E.R. Thayer to J.B. Thayer, Aug. 28, 1891, in which Ezra abjectly apologizes and castigates himself for missing a train that prevented him from attending one of his father's lectures. Thayer Papers, Box 18, Folder 19.

45. See, e.g., Thayer to Gray, Feb. 16, 1879 (praising one of Gray's opinions); Thayer to Gray, Mar. 6, 1880 (requesting a copy of Gray's article on *Dred Scott*); Horace Gray Papers, Library of Congress. Gray to Thayer, Nov. 17, 1900 ("your forthcoming article on Marshall in the Atlantic"), Thayer Papers, Box 14, Folder 1.

46. Thayer, *John Marshall*, 83, 85.

47. Thayer Papers, Boxes 13–14 (Marshall biography materials); Hook, "Thayer," 8.

48. Waite's public service consisted of a few brief stints in state government and several months as one of three U.S. representatives before an 1872 international arbitration tribunal. Louis Filler, "Morrison R. Waite," in JUSSC, 2:611–15.

49. Frankfurter, *Commerce Clause*, 79; Filler, JUSSC, 2:611; Stephenson, "Waite Court," 481–83.

50. Fiss, *Troubled Beginnings*, 22–23.

51. Joseph P. Bradley to Stephen Field, Apr. 30, 1888, Bradley Papers, Box 3, Folder 13. Bradley's file copy of the letter, which he noted was sent on June 2, 1888, contained the following crossed-out sentence: "All [members of the Court] would have been satisfied with the appointment of our senior Justice, our brother Miller, but it could hardly be expected that The President would appoint any person outside of his own political party."

52. E.g., Downes v. Bidwell, 182 U.S. 244, 259 and passim (1901); id. at 353 (Fuller, C.J., dissenting).

53. Magliocca, *Tragedy of Bryan*, 39–47; Sanders, *Roots of Reform*, 128–35; Ross, *Muted Fury*, 37, 131.

54. Magliocca, *Tragedy of Bryan*, 52; Paul, *Conservative Crisis* at 196.

55. Tiedeman, *Police Power*, vi–viii.

56. Quoted in Paul, *Conservative Crisis*, 61–64, 70–71, 78–81. Paul's excellent survey contains literally dozens of such examples from this time period.

57. Sanders, *Roots of Reform*, 33–34, 101; Ross, *Muted Fury*, at 12, 25–31; Magliocca, *Tragedy of Bryan*, 33.

58. "The United States shall guarantee to every state in this union a republican form of government, and shall protect each of them against invasion; and on application of the legislature, or of the executive (when the legislature cannot be convened) against domestic violence." U.S. Const., art. IV, § 4.

59. Paul, *Conservative Crisis*, 133–38; Magliocca, *Tragedy of Bryan*, 56–58.

60. 156 U.S. 1 (1895).

61. 158 U.S. 564 (1895).

62. Pollock v. Farmers' Loan and Trust Co., 157 U.S. 429, 650–651, *modified*, 158 U.S. 601 (1895).

63. Magliocca, *Tragedy of Bryan*, 70–92.

64. *Debs*, 158 U.S. at 582, 578.

65. *E.C. Knight*, 156 U.S. at 12.

66. See, e.g., Covington & Cincinnati Bridge Co. v. Kentucky, 154 U.S. 204. 209–10 (1894); McCall v. California, 136 U.S. 104, 113 (1890); Nathan v. Louisiana, 49 U.S. 73, 82 (1850).

67. *E.C. Knight*, 156 U.S. at 13, 14.

68. 156 U.S. at 39 (Harlan, J., dissenting).

69. An Act to reduce taxation, to provide revenue for the Government, and for other purposes. 28 Stat. 509, Aug. 27, 1894.

70. U.S. Const., art. I, §9 cl. 4.

71. 157 U.S. at 586.

72. 157 U.S. at 532 (argument of Choate).

73. 157 U.S. at 553 (argument of Choate).

74. 157 U.S. at 554; Magliocca, *Tragedy of Bryan*, 78–82; Douglas, "Rhetorical Uses of Marbury," 394 (2003); Whittington and Rinderle, "Marbury and the Canon," 825.

75. *Pollock*, 157 U.S. at 586.

76. Pollock v. Farmers' Loan & T. Co., on rehearing ("*Pollock II*"), 158 U.S. 601, 637 (1895).

77. Fiss, *Troubled Beginnings*, 77 n.7; Paul, *Conservative Crisis*, 198–206.

78. *Pollock II*, 158 U.S. at 617.

79. Democratic Party platform 1896, http://www.presidency.ucsb.edu/platforms.php; Friedman, *Will of the People*, 173–87; Paul, *Conservative Crisis*, 221–37; Ross, *Muted Fury*, 28–48.

80. MPP, 14:6456.

81. LCJS, 1:vii, 345.

82. Report of the Twenty-Second Annual Meeting of the American Bar Ass'n (Aug. 28–30, 1899).

83. LCJS, 1:385.

84. LCJS, 2:201, 89, 29.

85. Magliocca, *Tragedy of Bryan*, 94–97.

86. Blight, *Race and Reunion*, 37–38, 91, 251–300.

87. LCJS, 1:47–48.

88. LCJS, 2:135.

89. LCJS, 1:xvi.

90. Holmes, *Collected Legal Papers*, 270.

Chapter 10

1. McCulloch v. Maryland, 17 U.S. (4 Wheat.) 316, 419 (1819).

2. 198 U.S. 45 (1905).

3. The number of citations to *McCulloch* on issues of implied powers, nationalism, and constitutional interpretation—that is, not counting intergovernmental taxation cases—rose steadily between 1895 and 1925, both in raw numbers and as a percentage of published Court opinions. See Appendix 1, Figures 1.1 and 1.2.

4. Magliocca, *Tragedy of Bryan*, 138–48; Blum, *Progressive Presidents*; Link, *Wilson and the Progressive Era*; Purcell, *Progressive Constitution*, 11–38.

5. Haines, *Judicial Supremacy*, 497, quoting John Woodward, "The Courts and the People" (1907); see Purcell, *Progressive Constitution*, 15–16, 22–23.

6. Ransom, *Majority Rule*, xiii–xiv; Roosevelt, "Introduction" in id., at 13–14.

7. Hand, "Due Process," 508; Pound, "Liberty of Contract," 479–81; Frankfurter, "Hours of Labor," 370–371. See Wiecek, *Classical Legal Thought*, 187–201; Ross, *Muted Fury*, 135–36; Gerhardt, "Rhetoric of Judicial Critique," 596; Snyder, "Frankfurter and Popular Constitutionalism," 356–58.

8. Croly, *Promise of American Life*, 22–23; Bowers, *Jefferson and Hamilton*, v; see Peterson, *Jefferson Image*, 333–45; Wiecek, *Classical Legal Thought*, 187–91.

9. Democratic Party Platform, Jul. 4, 1900. http://www.presidency.ucsb.edu/ws/index.php?pid=29587

10. Erman, *Almost Citizens*, 8–46.

11. 182 U.S. 244, 267–68 (1901). The issue in *Downes* was whether the constitutional requirement of uniform taxes applied to the territory of Puerto Rico; the Court held that it did not.

12. Thayer, "Origin and Scope," 151.

13. Snyder, "Frankfurter and Popular Constitutionalism," 352; Snyder, *House of Truth*, 73, 126.

14. Felix Frankfurter, "John Marshall," 225.

15. Snyder, *House of Truth*, 566–67.

16. Thayer, "Our New Possessions," 464–65.

17. Thayer, 468–70.

18. According to student notes from the class, "12 H.L.R. 469–470 discusses previous remarks," referring to Thayer's lecture on *McCulloch*. See Typescript of Lecture Notes of Professor James B. Thayer's Lectures in Constitutional Law, 19; Harvard Law School Library, Historical and Special Collections, Hollis number 004180327. A handwritten note on its cover page by Eugene Wambaugh, Thayer's former student and successor as Constitutional Law professor, describes the class notes as an illicit student study outline for Thayer's course that was "confiscated" pursuant to the policy of Dean James Barr Ames.

19. Blum, *Progressive Presidents*, 30–50; Link, *Wilson and the Progressive Era*, 18–21; Ruiz, "Roosevelt and Wilson," 159–77.

20. Roosevelt, "Beveridge's Marshall."

21. Roosevelt to Lodge, Jul. 10, 1902. Theodore Roosevelt Papers, Library of Congress Manuscript Division.

22. Roosevelt, "Beveridge's Marshall."

23. Bowers, *Beveridge*, 1–30, 34–35 (Beveridge moved by *McCulloch*), 79–97, 118–22.

24. Cong. Rec., Jan. 9, 1900, p. 711.

25. Bowers, *Beveridge*, 223–37, 384–403, 545–62.

26. The one book-length biography of Marshall that had previously been published, Allan B. Magruder's *John Marshall* (1895), was regarded as amateur work. Edward Corwin disdained it as the poorest entry in Henry Cabot Lodge's *American Statesmen* series. Corwin, *Marshall*, 233–34.

27. Beveridge, *Marshall*, 1:v.

28. Bowers, *Beveridge*, 559–61; Corwin, *Marshall*, 233; http://www.pulitzer.org/winners/albert-j-beveridge.

29. Beveridge, *Marshall*, 4:282, 3:vi, 4:168, 295–96, 301.

30. Beveridge, 4:295.

31. Beveridge, 4:308.

32. Balkin, "Marshall's Greatness," 1337–38.

33. Frankfurter, *Justice Holmes*, 88.

34. Sanders, *Rediscovering the Progressive Era*, 1294.

35. Pure Food and Drug Act of 1906, 34 Stat. 768.

36. 45 Cong. Rec. 7,7686 (1910) (Rep. Burgess). See also 40 Cong. Rec. 6,5685 (Apr. 23, 1906) (Sen. La Follette) (power to regulate intrastate rail rates); 42 Cong. Rec. 7,6392 (1908) (reprinting H.R. Rep. No. 60-1514) (power to acquire lands for national forests); 45 Cong. Rec. 4,3902 (1910) (Rep. Martin) (in support of antitrust enforcement); Report of the Employers' Liability and Workmen's Compensation Commission. Vol. 2: Hearings and Briefs with Table of Cases and General Index, Sen. Doc. No. 62-338, at 80–82, 98, 166 (1912); Control of Corporations, Persons, and Firms Engaged in Interstate Commerce, Report of the Committee on Interstate Commerce, 62d Cong., 1498 (report of Edgar Farrar) (power to build roads); Sen. Rep. No. 65-125, at 8–9 (1917) (power to impose military draft); Extension of Provisions of the Food and Drugs Act: Hearing on S. 3011 Before the Senate Committee on Agriculture and Forestry, 66th Cong. 78 (1919) (statement of Wm. M. Williams).
37. 193 U.S. 197 (1904).
38. 193 U.S. at 336.
39. 193 U.S. at 368–70 (White, J., dissenting).
40. 193 U.S. at 400–401, 402–3.
41. 193 U.S. at 347, 349.
42. See, e.g., Coronado Coal Company v. United Mine Workers 268 U.S. 295 (1925); Purcell, *Progressive Constitution*, 70–71, 85–86.
43. Addyston Pipe and Steel Co. v. United States, 175 U.S. 211 (1899) (multiple firms); Standard Oil Co. of New Jersey v. United States, 221 U.S. 1 (1911) (single firm).
44. Stafford v. Wallace, 258 U.S.495, 518–19 (1922); Swift Co. v. United States, 196 U.S. 375, 396–97 (1905).
45. United States v. Lopez, 514 U.S. 549, 558 (1995).
46. 234 U.S. 342 (1914).
47. See, e.g., Tribe, *Constitutional Law*, 811; Epstein, "Commerce Power," 1416–21. To pro–New Deal justice Robert Jackson, the *Shreveport Rate Cases* "began a different mode of thinking" by allowing judicial Commerce Clause interpretations "to be determined by the economic effects." Jackson, "Memorandum for Mr. Costelloe re Wickard Case," Jun. 19, 1942, at 2, Jackson Papers, Box 125. This "has made the mechanical application of legal formulas no longer feasible." Wickard v. Filburn, 317 U.S. 111, 123–24 (1942) (per Jackson, J.).
48. Johnson v. Southern Pac. Co., 196 U.S. 1 (1904).
49. 207 U.S. 463 (1908).
50. 207 U.S. at 504.
51. 207 U.S. at 504 (Peckham, J., joined by Fuller, C.J., and Brewer, J., concurring).
52. 207 U.S. at 532.
53. Act of April 22, 35 Stat. 65.
54. 223 U.S. 1 (1912).
55. 208 U.S. 161 (1908).
56. 208 U.S. at 177, 178.
57. Texas & N. O. R. Co. v. Bhd. of R. & S.S. Clerks, 281 U.S. 548 (1930).
58. McDermott v. Wisconsin, 228 U.S. 115, 128 (1913).
59. 188 U.S. 321 (1903).
60. 188 U.S. at 354, 355, 357.
61. 188 U.S. at 365 (Fuller, C.J., dissenting).
62. 188 U.S. at 357–58 (internal quotations omitted).
63. 188 U.S. at 365 (Fuller, C.J., dissenting).
64. Hipolite Egg Co. v. United States, 220 U.S. 45 (1911) (impure food and drugs); Hoke v. United States, 227 U.S. 308 (1913) (sex trafficking); Weber v. Freed, 239 U.S. 325 (1915) (pictorial representations of prize fights); Brooks v. United States, 267 U.S. 432 (1925) (stolen vehicles).
65. 41 Cong. Rec. 2, 1871 (Jan. 29, 1907) (Sen. Beveridge); Braeman, "Beveridge and the Child Labor Bill."

66. 247 U.S. 251 (1918).
67. 247 U.S. at 271.
68. 247 U.S. at 272–73, 274, 275.
69. 247 U.S. at 273, 275.
70. See, e.g., *Hammer v. Dagenhart*, 247 U.S. at 278-81 (Holmes, J., dissenting); Rabin, "Federal Regulation," 1229–36; Pushaw and Nelson, "Narrow Interpretation," 707; Raoul Berger, "Judicial Manipulation," 711–12.
71. See Friedman, *Will of the People*, 181–82, 472 n. 138 (analyzing the literature).

Chapter 11

1. Lincoln, July 4, 1861 message to Congress, CWL, 4:426.
2. Shesol, *Supreme Power*, 19.
3. *McCulloch v. Maryland*, 17 U.S. (4 Wheat.) 316, 408 (1819).
4. 285 U.S. 262 (1932).
5. 285 U.S. at 278.
6. 285 U.S. at 311.
7. Alter, *Defining Moment*, 250–74; Schlesinger, *New Deal*, 4–21.
8. 291 U.S. 502 (1934).
9. 290 U.S. 398, 426 (1934).
10. Morehead v. New York ex rel. Tipaldo, 298 U.S. 587 (1936).
11. *Nebbia*, 291 U.S. at 532.
12. *Blaisdell*, 290 U.S. at 442–43.
13. Stone to Hughes, Dec. 13, 1933, Stone Papers, Box 75; Blaisdell, No. 370, Cardozo's unpublished concurring opinion; Hughes to Stone, Jan. 4, 1934; Stone to Hughes, Jan. 4, 1934; G. A. Jenkins, undated memo to file, Home Bldg. & Loan Ass'n v. Blaisdell, #370; Stone papers, Box 62.
14. H. J. Res. 192, 73d Cong., 1st Sess., Jun 5. 1933. In the 1970s, the United States discontinued redemption of U.S. dollars for gold in transactions with foreign governments and ceased valuing dollars in terms of gold, finally taking U.S. currency off the gold standard.
15. Shesol, *Supreme Power*, 99–100; Magliocca, "Gold Clause Cases," 1243.
16. 294 U.S. 240, 303 (1935).
17. 294 U.S. at 302.
18. 294 U.S. 330 (1935).
19. 294 U.S. at 357–58.
20. In two cases, the Court found that Congress had delegated excessive legislative powers to the president. Panama Refining Co. v. Ryan, 293 U.S. 388 (1935); A.L.A. Schechter Poultry Corporation v. United States, 295 U.S. 495 (1935). The Court also ruled unconstitutional Roosevelt's firing of a Federal Trade Commissioner, a conservative holdover from the Hoover administration whose economic views were out of step with the Administration's. Humphrey's Executor v. United States, 295 U.S. 602 (1935).
21. Louisville Joint Stock Land Bank v. Radford, 295 U.S. 555 (1935). The Court struck down a similar state law shortly before this. W. B. Worthen Co. v. Kavanaugh, 295 U.S. 56 (1935).
22. 295 U.S. 330, 369–72, 374 (1935).
23. 295 U.S. 495 (1935).
24. 295 at 544–47.
25. 295 U.S. at 554 (Cardozo, J., concurring).
26. 297 U.S. 288, 326 (1936).
27. 297 U.S. 1 (1936).
28. 297 U.S. at 66, 73.
29. 297 U.S. at 70–75.
30. 297 U.S. at 63, 68–69.

31. Stone to Frankfurter, Jun. 3, 1936, Stone Papers, Box 13; Frankfurter to Stone, Oct. 26, 1939, Stone Papers, Box 74; Mason, *Stone*, 254.

32. *Butler*, 297 U.S. at 78–79, 83 (Stone, J., dissenting).

33. 297 U.S. at 84, 85 (Stone, J., dissenting).

34. See Mason, *Stone*, 79 (Stone's son Marshall); 86 (teaching at Columbia). His scholarship focused on trusts, equity jurisprudence, and legal education. HeinOnline search, Nov. 23, 2018. https://home.heinonline.org/content/law-journal-library/. Stone was not an uncritical admirer of John Marshall. On intergovernmental tax immunity, Stone wrote, "everything was either black or white" to Marshall. Stone to Irving Brant, May 1, 1937, Stone Papers, Box 7. And in correspondence regarding the *Blaisdell* case, Stone observed that Marshall's decisions on debtor relief and the contracts clause were outmoded. Stone to Hughes, Dec. 12, 1933, Stone Papers, Box 75 ("We are thus confronted with a problem permeating the entire economic structure, of which Chief Justice Marshall probably never had any conception"). Stone claimed John Marshall Harlan as his namesake in a letter to Irving Brant, Apr. 27, 1937, Stone Papers, Box 7. It seems implausible, however, that Stone's New Hampshire Yankee parents in 1872, the year of Stone's birth, would even have heard of John Marshall Harlan, then a state politician in Kentucky whose Supreme Court appointment was five years away.

35. Brief for the United States at vii, 241–42, United States v. Butler.

36. Brief for the United States at 262–63, 273, United States v. Butler.

37. Telegram, Frankfurter to Stone, Jan. 7, 1936, Stone Papers, Box 13.

38. In an *aide memoire* on *Butler*, Stone wrote that he was forced to write his dissent over a few days when the Court's law library was closed for New Year's, and "[t]he whole history of the case was characterized by inadequate discussion and great haste in the production and circulation of the opinions." Memorandum re No. 401, Feb. 4, 1936; Stone Papers, Box 62.

39. Thomas Reed Powell, "Some Aspects of Constitutionalism and Federalism," 14 N.C.L. Rev. 1, 16 (1935). Of this article, Stone wrote to Powell, "I shall be reading your North Carolina Bar Association address with interest whenever it puts in an appearance." Stone to Powell, Jan. 22, 1936, Stone Papers, Box 24.

40. Stone to Beard, Apr. 16, 1936; Beard to Stone, Apr. 19, 1936; Stone to Beard, Apr. 23, 1936; Stone Papers, Box 6. Stone had begun the correspondence with a confusingly worded question in a letter dated March 24, which Beard apparently mislaid or did not see.

41. *Historical Statistics of the United States, 1789–1945: A Supplement to the Statistical Abstract of the United States.* 1954. Washington, DC: United States Dept of Commerce.

42. 298 U.S. 238 (1936).

43. 298 U.S. 587 (1936).

44. Hughes wrote separately to state that he would have upheld the price regulations. 298 U.S. at 319–20 (Hughes, C.J.).

45. *Carter Coal*, 298 U.S. at 291–93.

46. 298 U.S. 326–28 (Cardozo, J., dissenting).

47. 298 U.S. at 298.

48. See, e.g., *Carter Coal*, 298 U.S. at 291; Petitioner's Brief at 80, *Carter Coal*; United States v. Butler, 297 U.S. at 69; Amicus Brief of Farmers' Independence Council of America at 8, United States v. Butler; Brief for Petitioners at 87–88, 138–39, *Schechter Poultry*, 295 U.S. 495; Respondent's Brief at 17, R.R. Ret. Bd. v. Alton R. Co., 295 U.S. 330 (1935).

49. *McCulloch*, 17 U.S. at 423.

50. See *Schechter Poultry*, 295 U.S. at 507–8. The district court opinion's discussion of *McCulloch* is found in the Transcript of Record, 145.

51. I base this claim on a review of more than fifty law review articles published between 1931 and 1940. From a database search of a few hundred articles citing *McCulloch*, I selected those with titles relevant to judicial review of New Deal legislation. I found only one article suggesting an implied commerce theory, and that relegated to a single sentence in a footnote. Robert L. Stern, "That Commerce Which Concerns More States Than One," 47 Harv. L. Rev. 1335,

1347 n. 40 (1934). Another article cited *McCulloch* to argue that Congress's power to enact the 1934 Securities Exchanges Act could be implied from the borrowing clause. P. Tennent Norton, Jr., "Constitutionality of Federal Regulation of Stock Exchanges," 24 Geo. L.J. 20, 25–26 (1935). For examples of articles citing *McCulloch* as generic support for New Deal laws, see, e.g., Maurice M. Feuerlicht, "Interstate Commerce Clause and NRA," 9 Ind. L.J. 434, 445–46 (1934); N. Henry Josephs, "The Federal Constitution in Time of Emergency," 11 N.Y.U. L. Q. Rev. 499, 509 (1934); Horace Russell, "Constitutionality of the Federal Home Loan System," 24 Geo. L.J. 910 (1936). See also Harrison J. Barrett, "Is There a National Police Power?" 14 B.U. L. Rev. 243, 264 (1934).

52. Albert Russell Ellingwood, "The New Deal and the Constitution," 28 Ill. L. Rev. 729, 731–32 (1934).

53. Hamilton and Adair, *Power to Govern*; Corwin, "Power to Prohibit Commerce," 503.

54. Snyder, "Frankfurter and Popular Constitutionalism," 352–54, 366–67.

55. Frankfurter, *Commerce Clause*, 112–14.

56. Frankfurter, "Justice Brandeis," 38–39.

57. 277 U.S. 438 (1928).

58. 277 U.S. at 465, 472 (Brandeis, J., dissenting).

59. Mason, "Justice Brandeis," 839.

60. Corwin, "Moratorium over Minnesota," 314–15 (1934).

61. Quoted in Crews, *Corwin and the American Constitution*, 23.

62. Corwin, *Commerce Power*, ix.

63. Corwin, 18–19, 4.

64. Mason, "Yesterday and Today," 36.

65. Haines, "Judicial Review," 817–24, 843–44. See also Stern, "That Commerce," 1344–45.

66. Swisher, *Taney*, 505.

67. Boudin, "Marshall and Taney." See Boudin, *Government by Judiciary*.

68. Boudin, "Marshall and Taney," 880, 893, 896, 899–900.

69. See also Lerner, "John Marshall" (1939).

70. Frankfurter, *Commerce Clause*, 66, 68, 69.

71. Frankfurter, 70, 73.

72. Corwin, *Commerce Power*, 135, 140 (emphasis in original).

73. Brief for Government Officers at 135–36, 183, Carter v. Carter Coal, 298 U.S. 238 (1936).

74. Arnold to Corwin, Oct. 5, 1936, quoted in Crews, *Corwin*, 25.

75. Shesol, *Supreme Power*, 206–7, 348.

76. A clear example from recent memory was the Court's decision in *Eisner v. Macomber*, 252 U.S. 189 (1920), which narrowed the scope of the Sixteenth Amendment by holding that stock dividends were not taxable income.

77. *Carter Coal*, 298 U.S. at 298.

Chapter 12

1. Carter v. Carter Coal, 298 U.S. 238, 291 (1936).

2. *Addresses of Franklin D. Roosevelt*, 6:118, 121.

3. S. 1392, 75th Cong. (1937)

4. Shesol, *Supreme Power*, 505.

5. Jackson, *Judicial Supremacy*, 315. Gerard Magliocca has insightfully developed this theme in several works. See Magliocca, *William Jennings Bryan*; Magliocca, *Andrew Jackson*.

6. 301 U.S. 379 (1937).

7. 301 U.S. 1 (1937).

8. Jackson, *Judicial Supremacy*, v. See Kalman, "New Deal(s)," 2168–85 (analyzing historiographical debate).

9. United States v. Lopez, 514 U.S. 549, 601–2 (1995) (Thomas, J., concurring).

10. E.g., Ackerman, *We the People*, 312–16, 342–43; Kramer, *The People Themselves*, 219–20; Graber, *American Constitutionalism*, 151–53, 169–73.

11. 301 U.S. 1 (1937).

12. 301 U.S. at 25–27. The Court did not mean to signal that the NLRA would apply only to the largest business enterprises. In a companion case, the Court also upheld the application of the NLRA to a clothing manufacturer that did $1.75 million worth of business in 1935 (equivalent to around $32 million in 2018 dollars), around 90% of it to out-of-state buyers. Friedman-Harry Marks Clothing Co. v. NLRB, 301 U.S. 58, 72 (1937). Hughes's opinion simply relied on "the reasons stated" in *Jones & Laughlin Steel*. The Court also found it important that the clothing workers were represented by a significant interstate union. *Friedman-Harry Marks Clothing Co.*, 301 U.S. at 73–74.

13. 301 U.S. at 36–37.

14. 77 U.S. 557 (1871).

15. *Jones & Laughlin Steel*, 301 U.S. at 37.

16. 301 U.S. at 37.

17. Coan, *Rationing the Constitution*, 55-75.

18. This point has been meticulously demonstrated by Barry Cushman, in *Rethinking the New Deal Court*. My account aligns with Cushman's, largely following his trail through the same archival files. We diverge in that Cushman, whose project was different from mine, does not explore the decisive role of Stone in the New Deal transition, and I believe he understates the revolutionary quality of *Darby*, placing primary emphasis on *Wickard*. See Cushman, *New Deal Court*, 208–9.

19. Brant to Stone, Apr. 15, 1937, Stone Papers, Box 7.

20. 310 U.S. 381 (1940).

21. 310 U.S. at 394.

22. Similarly, in *United States v. Rock Royal Co-operative*, 307 U.S. 533, 568 and n. 37 (1939), the Court upheld regulation of intrastate milk prices "intermingled" with interstate milk sales, on the authority of the *Shreveport Rate Cases* and other *Lochner*-era precedents.

23. 304 U.S. 144 (1938). Footnote 4 of that opinion, the joint product of Stone and his brilliant law clerk and later Columbia law professor Louis Lusky, was written to address the problem that less deferential review might still be appropriate for laws that infringe fundamental rights or reflect "prejudice against discrete and insular minorities," which "seriously to curtail the operation of those political processes ordinarily to be relied upon to protect minorities. . . ." Here, the citation reads, "Compare McCulloch v. Maryland, 4 Wheat. 316, 428; South Carolina v. Barnwell Bros., 303 U.S. 177, 184, n. 2, and cases cited." *Carolene Products*, 304 U.S. at 152 n. 4. Stone apparently cited *McCulloch* because he read its taxation holding as asserting the structural principle that majorities cannot shift their costs onto unrepresented citizens of other states; the cited *Barnwell Bros.* reference made the same point. See Lusky, "Footnote Redux," 1103–1104 and App.; Coenen, "Footnote Four," 805.

24. 312 U.S. 100 (1941).

25. Darby Lumber's brief cited *Hammer* eight times and *Carter Coal* nineteen times. See Brief of Appellee at v–vi, United States v. Darby Lumber Co., 312 U.S. 100 (1941).

26. Brief for the United States at 71–72, United States v. Darby Lumber Co., 312 U.S. 100 (1941),

27. Brief for the United States at 69, 96, *Darby Lumber Co.*

28. Justice Frank Murphy noted that "McReynolds is sound asleep mouth open and Stone is dozing away." Conference notes, "## 82 and 330, O[ct] T[erm] 1940," Murphy Papers, Roll 123. The justices also discussed a companion case, *Opp Cotton Mills v. Administrator*, 312 U.S. 126 (1941), which raised both the commerce power issue and a challenge to the authority of the administrator of the Wage and Hour Division.

29. Conference notes, "## 82 and 330, O[ct] T[erm] 1940," Murphy Papers, Roll 123; Conference notes, Dec. 12, 1940, "No. 82, U. S. v. F. W. Darby Lumber Co," Douglas Papers, Box 52, Folder 1.

30. Conference notes, Murphy Papers, Roll 123; Conference notes, Douglas Papers, Box 52, Folder 1.

31. Conference notes, Murphy Papers, Roll 123; Conference notes, Douglas Papers, Box 52, Folder 1.

32. Simon, *FDR and Hughes*, 383–86.

33. Hughes to Stone, Jan. 27, 1941, Stone Papers, Box 66.

34. Conference notes, "## 82 and 330, O[ct] T[erm] 1940," Murphy Papers, Roll 123; Conference notes, Dec. 12, 1940, "No. 82, U. S. v. F. W. Darby Lumber Co," Douglas Papers, Box 52, Folder 1.

35. I do not mean to assert that the New Deal was a revolution in the social and political sense, something that present-day historians seriously doubt. See Kalman, "New Deal(s)," 2198–201. I do assert that it was a revolution in the narrower and more rarified world of constitutional law.

36. Hughes, join memo, Stone Papers, Box 62. In this era, the justices typically indicated their agreement to draft opinions with handwritten notes on the back of a printed draft opinion circulated by the writing justice.

37. McReynolds retired in on January 31, 1941, the Friday before *Darby* was announced. Ward, *Deciding to Leave*, 142. As Stone's case file contains no join memo from McReynolds, presumably he did not officially participate in the decision.

38. *Darby*, 312 U.S. at 113.

39. *Darby*, 312 U.S. at 113–14, 124.

40. *Darby*, 312 U.S. at 118–21.

41. 312 U.S. at 119–20.

42. Join memos, United States v. Darby Lumber Co., Stone Papers, Box 66.

43. 315 U.S. 110 (1942).

44. Brief of the United States at 23–24 (emphasis added), *Wrightwood Dairy*, 315 U.S. 110.

45. *Wrightwood Dairy*, 315 U.S. at 121.

46. 315 U.S. at 118–19.

47. 315 U.S. at 119.

48. At conference, Stone said, "The use of the word 'direct' from Schechter case gives trouble. I think it meant what majority of Ct. said in Schechter case." Conf notes Nos. 744 and 783, United States v. Wrightwood Dairy Co., Murphy Papers, Roll 123. See *Wrightwood Dairy*, 315 U.S. at 124.

49. *Wrightwood Dairy*, 315 U.S. at 125.

50. Frankfurter join memo, Wrightwood Dairy; Stone Papers, Box 68. The opinion's first four pages (through 315 U.S. at 120) covered Stone's entire discussion of *McCulloch, Gibbons*, and the Commerce Clause.

51. 317 U.S. 111 (1942).

52. Brief for the Appellee on Re-argument at 10, 12, Wickard v. Filburn.

53. Appellant's Brief at 42–43, 45, 50, Wickard v. Filburn.

54. Cushman, *New Deal Court*, 212–22.

55. The source is William O. Douglas's conference notes. Stone presented the case by summarizing the government's argument as saying "it is regulating commerce, since purpose is to regulate crop which moves in commerce—have to take control of whole crop—if he can feed this to stock, then it affects commerce." Douglas continued, "C.J. finds it difficult to say as a matter of logic & economics that that is not means of regulating commerce—perhaps indispensable—raises question where regulation of commerce ends—can regulate intrastate where it has fair relation to commerce—said that in milk [*Wrightwood Dairy*] case—this case closely parallel [to] *Darby* case." Although it is customary for the Chief Justice to vote last, Stone disclosed up front that he "does not care for the result" in the lower court. Conference notes, May 7, 1942, No. 1080, Wickard v. Filburn; Douglas Papers, Box 78, Folder 9.

56. Douglas Docket Book, 1941 Term, p. 478, Douglas Papers, Box 63; Murphy Docket Book, 1941 Term, Murphy Papers, Box 104. Roberts initially passed, though he expressed

"doubt" about the lower court's decision. Reed recused himself. Murphy Conference Notes, Roll 125.

57. Wickard v. Filburn, No. 1080, May 22, 1942 (unpublished opinion), 11, 9–10; Jackson Papers, Box 125.

58. Wickard v. Filburn, No. 1080, May 22, 1942 (unpublished opinion), 11–12, 13; Jackson Papers, Box 125.

59. Join memos (Byrnes, Frankfurter); Stone, "Memorandum in re No. 1080—Wickard v. Filburn," May 25, 1942; Jackson to Stone, May 25, 1942; Douglas to Jackson, May 25, 1942; Stone, "Memorandum in re No. 1080—Wickard v. Filburn," May 27, 1942; Jackson Papers, Box 125.

60. "[First] Memorandum for Mr. Costelloe re Wickard case," Jun. 19, 1942, at 1–6; Jackson Papers, Box 125.

61. "[Second] Memorandum for Mr. Costelloe re Wickard case," Jul. 10, 1942, at 8, 14–15, 18, 20; Jackson Papers, Box 125.

62. Appellant's Brief (on re-argument) at 43–44, 45–48, Wickard v. Filburn, 317 U.S. 111 (1942).

63. Undated note, Stern to Jackson; Jackson to Stern, Nov. 18, 1942; Jackson Papers, Box 125. The article was Robert L. Stern, "That Commerce Which Concerns More States Than One," 47 Harv. L. Rev. 1335 (1934).

64. 317 U.S. at 127–28.

65. 317 U.S. at 120 (citing Gibbons v. Ogden, 22 U.S. 1, 194–95, 197 [1824]).

66. Wickard, 317 U.S. at 124–25.

67. 317 U.S. at 123–25.

68. Gibbons, 22 U.S. at 10–11 (argument of Webster).

69. Join memo (Stone); Jackson Papers, Box 125.

70. Douglas conference notes, No. 59—"Wickard, Secy of Agriculture v. Filburn," Oct. 17, 1942; Douglas Papers, Box 78, Folder 9; Murphy conference notes, "No. 59 OT 1942" ("It is appropriate regulation of something that does affect commerce"); Murphy Papers, Roll 127.

71. Murphy Conference Notes, "No. 59 OT 1942," Murphy Papers, Roll 127.

72. Jackson had severely criticized the Court's direct/indirect distinction and its obsession with identifying economic activities as "local" in his 1941 book The Struggle for Judicial Supremacy. See Cushman, New Deal Court, 215.

73. Wrightwood Dairy, 315 U.S. at 118–19.

74. Darby, 312 U.S. at 115–17.

75. Wickard, 317 U.S. at 119–20.

76. 317 U.S. at 129.

77. Kalman, Legal Realism at Yale, 222; White, Tort Law, 143–45; Eskridge and Frickey, "Legal Process," 2033–51.

78. Joint Resolution Designating the Month of September 1955 as John Marshall Bicentennial Month, and Creating a Commission to Supervise and Direct the Observance of Such Month, 68 Stat. 702 (1954); Final Report of the U.S. Commission for the Celebration of the Two Hundredth Anniversary of the Birth of John Marshall (Dec. 31, 1955) at 16; Proclamation 3102, Jul. 13, 1955.

79. Final Report, 17–22, 30, 45–49. The commission oversaw widespread outreach to the state and local governments, schools and civic associations, and a media blitz distributing "50,000 pieces of publicity material" to print and broadcast media, including full-scale features in major publications such as The New York Times and Time magazine. The U.S. Postal Service issued a commemorative stamp.

80. Eisenhower, "The Spirit of John Marshall: Crusader for Ordered Liberty and Justice," 41 ABA L.J. 1005, 1006 (Nov. 1955).

81. 41 ABA L.J. 1005, 1009 (Nov. 1955).

82. Final Report, at 1.

83. Frankfurter, "John Marshall," 218–19.

84. 336 U.S. 77, 90 (1949) (Frankfurter, J., concurring).

85. Nat'l Mut. Ins. Co. v. Tidewater Transfer Co., 337 U.S. 583, 647 (1949) (Frankfurter, J., dissenting).

86. Youngstown Sheet & Tube Co. v. Sawyer, 343 U.S. 579, 596 (1952) (Frankfurter, J., concurring).

87. Reid v. Covert, 354 U.S. 1, 43 (1957) (Frankfurter, J., concurring).

88. Frankfurter, "John Marshall," 222.

89. Schmidt, "Section 5's Forgotten Years," 53–64.

90. H.R. 2232, § 2(a), 79th Cong. 1st sess. (1946); Konvitz, *Constitution and Civil Rights*, 91.

91. Exec. Ord. 9608, Dec. 5, 1946, in *To Secure These Rights*.

92. *To Secure These Rights*, 106–7.

93. *To Secure These Rights*, 108–9.

94. "Major Legislation by 79th Congress," CQ Researcher, http://library.cqpress.com/cqresearcher/document.php?id=cqresrre1946080300.

95. Schmidt, "Section 5's Forgotten Years," 57–72.

96. E.g., Eskridge and Ferejohn, "Super-Statutes," 1240–1242.

97. 379 U.S. 241 (1964).

98. 379 U.S. 294 (1964).

99. Appellee's Brief at i–ii, Katzenbach v. McClung, 379 U.S. 294 (1964).

100. *Heart of Atlanta Motel*, 379 U.S. at 258.

101. See *Heart of Atlanta Motel*, 379 U.S. at 253 (quoting Senate hearing report to the effect that "these conditions had become so acute as to require the listing of available lodging for Negroes in a special guidebook"); *McClung*, 379 U.S. at 303–4.

102. *Heart of Atlanta Motel*, 379 U.S. at 253–55, 258.

103. *McClung*, 379 U.S. at 303–4.

104. *Heart of Atlanta Motel*, 379 U.S. at 276–77 (Black, J., concurring); id. at 280–281 (Douglas, J., concurring); id. at 293 (Goldberg, J., concurring).

105. See United States v. Morrison, 529 U.S. 598 (striking down key provision of Violence Against Women Act of 1994).

106. The Civil Rights Cases, 109 U.S. 3, 51–52 (1883) (Harlan, J., dissenting); United States v. Reese, 92 U.S. 214, 253 (1876) (Hunt, J., dissenting).

107. *Heart of Atlanta Motel*, 379 U.S. at 280–281 (Douglas, J., concurring) ("Fourteenth amendment rights"); id. at 276–77 (Black, J., concurring) ("In view of the Thirteenth, Fourteenth, and Fifteenth Amendments, it is not possible to deny that the aim of protecting Negroes from discrimination is also a legitimate end.").

108. 383 U.S. 301 (1966).

109. 383 U.S. at 324 (emphasis added), 326–27.

110. 384 U.S. 641 (1966).

111. Katzenbach v. Morgan, 384 U.S. at 651.

112. 384 U.S. at 648–49.

113. United States v. Guest, 383 U.S. 745, 784 (1966) (Brennan, J., concurring in part, dissenting in part). A key issue in *Guest* was whether 18 U.S.C. § 241 applied to a conspiracy by private persons to threaten or intimidate black Americans to keep them from equal enjoyment of state-owned facilities. In a strangely fractured decision, a five-justice majority held that the indictment sufficiently alleged state-actor involvement. Yet six justices, in two separate three-justice opinions, agreed that "the specific language of § 5 empowers the Congress to enact laws punishing all conspiracies—with or without state action—that interfere with Fourteenth Amendment rights." Id. at 762 (Clark, J., joined by Black and Fortas, JJ., concurring); accord id. at 784 (Brennan, J., joined by Warren, C.J., and Douglas, J., concurring in part, dissenting in part).

Chapter 13

1. See Appendix 1, Figure 1.1.
2. *McCulloch v. Maryland*, 17 U.S. (4 Wheat.) 316, 420–421 (1819). See also *Gibbons v. Ogden*, 22 U.S. (9 Wheat.) 1, 222 (1824) (narrow construction would "explain away the constitution of our country, and leave it, a magnificent structure, indeed, to look at, but totally unfit for use").
3. In the thirty-three-year period from January 1937 to December 1969, 22 new justices were appointed to the Court, a turnover rate of 0.667 per year, compared with 17 new justices appointed in the forty-nine years from 1970 to 2018, or 0.347 per year. Epstein, et al., *Supreme Court Compendium*, 294–95.
4. Roberts is, in my view, as conservative as Rehnquist, whom he replaced. Alito and Kavanagh may be slightly more conservative than O'Connor and Kennedy, respectively, but all four were solid Republican appointees. Sonya Sotomayor replaced the liberal David Souter, and Elena Kagan the liberal John Paul Stevens.
5. 462 U.S. 919, 941 (1974)
6. 505 U.S. 144, 158–59 (1992).
7. Ariz. State Legis. v. Ariz. Indep. Redistricting Comm'n, 135 S. Ct. 2652, 2677 (2015); id. at 2680 (Roberts, C.J., dissenting); Horne v. Dep't of Agric., 135 S. Ct. 2419, 2428 (2015); United States v. Windsor, 570 U.S. 744, 765 (2013).
8. 514 U.S. 779 (1995).
9. 560 U.S. 126 (2010).
10. 560 U.S. at 133, 149.
11. See United States v. O'Brien, 391 U.S. 367, 377–78 (1968) (recognizing this chain of inference).
12. See Coan, *Rationing the Constitution*, 55-75.
13. 521 U.S. 507 (1997).
14. 494 U.S. 872 (1990).
15. Boerne, 521 U.S. at 520, 530. RFRA remains good law as applied to the federal government, however. See Burwell v. Hobby Lobby Stores, Inc., 134 S. Ct. 2751 (2014).
16. 529 U.S. 598 (2000).
17. 529 U.S. at 619, 627.
18. 570 U.S. 529 (2015).
19. 570 U.S. at 593 (Ginsburg, J., dissenting)
20. 570 U.S. at 544.
21. 570 U.S. at 567 (Ginsburg, J., dissenting).
22. 514 U.S. 549 (1995).
23. 514 U.S. at 564–65.
24. *Morrison*, 529 U.S. at 615–18.
25. *Lopez*, 514 U.S. at 615 (Souter, J., dissenting); id. at 627–28 (Breyer, J., dissenting); *Morrison*, 529 U.S. at 642–43 (Souter, J., dissenting).
26. *Lopez*, 514 U.S. at 555; *Morrison*, 529 U.S. at 608.
27. *Jones & Laughlin Steel*, 301 U.S. at 37, quoting *Schechter*, 295 U.S. at 554 (Cardozo, J., concurring).
28. Schwartz, "An Error and an Evil," 939, 1011.
29. 545 U.S. 1 (2005).
30. 21 U.S.C. §§ 801, 844.
31. 21 U.S.C. § 844(a). See *Lopez*, 514 U.S. at 580 (Kennedy, J., concurring).
32. *Raich*, 545 U.S. at 26.
33. 545 U.S. at 36–37, 39, 40 (Scalia, J., concurring in the judgment).
34. 567 U.S. 519 (2012).
35. See *Lopez*, 514 U.S. at 555; *Wickard*, 317 U.S. at 120; *Wrightwood Dairy*, 315 U.S. at 119; *Darby*, 312 U.S. at 120–121.

36. *NFIB*, 567 U.S. at 691 (Scalia, Kennedy, Thomas, and Alito, JJ., dissenting).

37. Randy Barnett, *Understanding Justice Scalia's Concurring Opinion in* Raich, Volokh Conspiracy (Mar. 9, 2012, 4:13 PM), http://volokh.com/2012/03/09/understanding-justice-scalias-concurring-opinion-in-raich/.

38. 567 U.S. at 560.

39. 567 U.S. at 559.

40. Schwartz, "A Question Perpetually Arising," 624–44.

41. The Affordable Care Act Cases, Oral Argument, Mar. 27, 2012, https://www.oyez.org/cases/2011/11-393.

Conclusion

1. 298 U.S. 238, 297 (1936).

2. This interpretation is consistent with, though different in detail and emphasis from, the revisionists who see *Lochner* era jurisprudence as "neo-Jacksonian." To them, the *Lochner* era was characterized by a Jacksonian hostility to "class legislation." To me, the key point is the ongoing hostility to implied commerce powers motivated by slavery in the antebellum period, and laissez faire and state control of race after Reconstruction.

3. Compare Barnett, "Original Meaning of the Commerce Clause," with Balkin, "Commerce." I say "properly understood" because contesting my point about the breadth of implied commerce powers requires a narrow reading of the Commerce Clause combined with a strained reading of *McCulloch* to produce a narrow and eccentric definition of "Necessary and Proper." See Barnett, 146–47.

4. Holmes, *Collected Legal Papers*, 270; LCJS 1:208.

SELECTED BIBLIOGRAPHY

List of Abbreviations

AHP   Hamilton, Alexander. *The Papers of Alexander Hamilton.* Vols. 7–8.
New York: Columbia University Press, 1961–87.

CIC   Currie, David P. *The Constitution in Congress.* Vol 1: *The Federalist Period, 1789–1801.*
Vol. 2: *The Jeffersonians, 1801–1829.* Vol. 3: *Democrats and Whigs, 1829–1861.* Vol.
4: *Descent into the Maelstrom, 1829–1861.* Chicago; London: University of Chicago
Press, 1997–2005.

CWL   Lincoln, Abraham. *The Collected Works of Abraham Lincoln.* 8 vols. New Brunswick,
NJ: Rutgers University Press, 1953–1955.

HCP   Clay, Henry. *The Papers of Henry Clay.* 11 vols. Lexington: University Press of
Kentucky, 1961–92.

JMP   Marshall, John. *The Papers of John Marshall.* 12 vols. Chapel Hill, NC: University of
North Carolina Press, 1974–.

JUSSC   Friedman, Leon, and Fred L. Israel, eds. *The Justices of the United States Supreme
Court: Their Lives and Major Opinions.* 3 vols. New York: Chelsea House, 1997.

LCJS   Dillon, John F. *John Marshall: Life, Character and Judicial Services: As Portrayed in the
Centenary and Memorial Addresses and Proceedings throughout the United States on
Marshall Day, 1901*[. . .]. 3 vols. Chicago: Callaghan, 1903.

MPP   Compilation of the Messages and Papers of the Presidents. Compiled by James
D. Richardson. New York: Bureau of National Literature, 22 vols. (1789–1929).
HeinOnline. https://home.heinonline.org/

Manuscript Collections and Databases

America's Historical Newspapers. https://infoweb-newsbank-com.
Bradley, Joseph P. U.S. Supreme Court Justice Papers. New Jersey Historical Society, Newark, New
    Jersey.
Douglas, William O. Papers. Library of Congress, Washington, DC.
Harlan, John Marshall. Papers. Library of Congress, Washington, DC.
Jackson, Robert H. Papers. Library of Congress, Washington, DC.

Jefferson, Thomas. *The Papers of Thomas Jefferson.* Edited by James P. McClure and J. Jefferson Looney. Digital Edition. University of Virginia Press. https://www.upress.virginia.edu/rotunda.

Miller, Samuel F. Correspondence, 1854–1887. Library of Congress, Washington, DC.

Murphy, Frank. Papers, 1908–1949. Bentley Historical Library, University of Michigan, Ann Arbor, Michigan.

Stone, Harlan Fiske. Papers, 1889–1953. Library of Congress, Washington, DC.

Thayer, James Bradley. Papers. Harvard Law School Library, Historical and Special Collections.

U.S. Supreme Court Records and Briefs, 1832–1978. *The Making of Modern Law.* https://www.gale.com/primary-sources/making-of-modern-law.

Books and Edited Book Chapters

Ackerman, Bruce A. *We the People.* Cambridge, MA: Belknap Press of Harvard University Press, 1991.

Allen, Austin. *Origins of the Dred Scott Case : Jacksonian Jurisprudence and the Supreme Court, 1837–1857.* Athens, GA: University of Georgia Press, 2006.

Alter, Jonathan. *The Defining Moment: FDR's Hundred Days and the Triumph of Hope.* New York: Simon and Schuster, 2006.

Amar, Akhil Reed. *America's Constitution: A Biography.* New York: Random House, 2005.

Anderson, Martin, ed. *The Military Draft: Selected Readings on Conscription.* Stanford, CA: Hoover Institution, 1982.

Balkin, Jack M., and Sanford Levinson, eds. *Legal Canons.* New York: New York University Press, 2000.

Baxter, Maurice G. *The Steamboat Monopoly: Gibbons v. Ogden, 1824.* New York: Knopf, 1972.

Belknap, Michal R. *Securing the Enactment of Civil Rights Legislation: Civil Rights Act of 1964.* New York: Garland, 1991.

Beth, Loren P. *John Marshall Harlan: The Last Whig Justice.* Lexington, KY: University Press of Kentucky, 1992.

Beveridge, Albert J. *The Life of John Marshall.* 4 vols. Boston: Houghton Mifflin, 1916-19.

Black, Charles L., Jr. *Structure and Re7lationship in Constitutional Law.* Baton Rouge: Louisiana State University Press, 1969.

Blight, David W. *Race and Reunion: The Civil War in American Memory.* Cambridge, MA; London: Harvard University Press, 2001.

Blum, John M. *The Progressive Presidents: Roosevelt, Wilson, Roosevelt, Johnson.* New York: W.W. Norton, 1980.

Boudin, Louis B. *Government by Judiciary.* New York: W. Godwin, 1932.

Bowers, Claude G. *Beveridge and the Progressive Era.* New York: Literary Guild, 1932.

Bowers, Claude G. *Jefferson and Hamilton; the Struggle for Democracy in America.* Boston; New York: Houghton Mifflin, 1925.

Brandwein, Pamela. *Rethinking the Judicial Settlement of Reconstruction.* New York: Cambridge University Press, 2011.

Burlingame, Michael. *Abraham Lincoln a Life.* 2 Vols. Baltimore: Johns Hopkins University Press, 2008.

Butterfield, L.H., Wendell D. Garrett, and Marjorie Sprague, eds. *Adams Family Correspondence.* 13 vols. Cambridge, MA: Belknap Press of Harvard University Press, 1963.

Calhoun, John C., ed. Richard K. Crallé. *The Works of John C. Calhoun.* New York: D. Appleton, 1863–64.

Carr, Robert Kenneth. *Federal Protection of Civil Rights: Quest for a Sword.* Ithaca, NY: Cornell University Press, 1947.

Chemerinsky, Erwin. *Constitutional Law: Principles and Policies.* 3rd ed. New York: Aspen, 2006.

Chernow, Ron. *Alexander Hamilton.* New York: Penguin Books, 2005.

Clayton, Cornell W., and Howard Gillman, eds. *Supreme Court Decision-Making: New Institutionalist Approaches*. Chicago: University of Chicago Press, 1999.

Coan, Andrew. *Rationing the Constitution: How Judicial Capacity Shapes Supreme Court Decision-Making*. Cambridge: Harvard University Press, 2019.

Cooley, Thomas McIntyre. *The General Principles of Constitutional Law in the United States of America*. Boston: Little, Brown, 1880.

Cooley, Thomas McIntyre. *Treatise on Constitutional Limitations Which Rest upon the Legislative Power of the States of the American Union*. Boston: Little, Brown, 1868.

Corwin, Edward S. *The Commerce Power versus States Rights: "Back to the Constitution."* Princeton, NJ: Princeton University Press; London: H. Milford, Oxford University Press, 1936.

Corwin, Edward S. *John Marshall and the Constitution: A Chronicle of the Supreme Court*. New Haven, CT: Yale University Press, 1920.

Coquillette, Daniel R., and Bruce A. Kimball. *On the Battlefield of Merit: Harvard Law School, the First Century*. Cambridge, MA: Harvard University Press. 2015.

Cover, Robert M. *Justice Accused: Antislavery and the Judicial Process*. New Haven, CT: Yale University Press, 1975.

Crews, Kenneth D. *Edward S. Corwin and the American Constitution: A Bibliographical Analysis*. Westport, CT: Greenwood, 1985.

Croly, Herbert D. *The Promise of American Life*. Cambridge, MA: Belknap Press of Harvard University Press, 1965.

Curry, Leonard P. *Blueprint for Modern America: Non-Military Legislation of the First Civil War Congress*. Nashville, TN: Vanderbilt University Press, 1968.

Cushman, Barry. *Rethinking the New Deal Court: The Structure of a Constitutional Revolution*. New York: Oxford University Press, 1998.

Elkins, Stanley M., and Eric McKitrick. *The Age of Federalism*. New York: Oxford University Press, 1993.

Ellis, Richard E. *Aggressive Nationalism: McCulloch v. Maryland and the Foundation of Federal Authority in the Young Republic*. New York: Oxford University Press, 2007.

Epstein, Lee, Jeffrey A. Segal, Harold J. Spaeth, and Thomas G. Walker. *The Supreme Court Compendium: Data, Decisions, and Developments*. 5th ed. Los Angeles: SAGE/CQ Press, 2012.

Erman, Sam. *Almost Citizens: Puerto Rico, the U.S. Constitution, and Empire*. New York: Cambridge University Press, 2019.

Farber, Daniel A., and Suzanna Sherry. *A History of the American Constitution*. 2nd ed. St. Paul: Thomson/West, 2005.

Farber, Daniel A. *Lincoln's Constitution*. Chicago: University of Chicago Press, 2003.

Fairman, Charles. *Reconstruction and Reunion, 1864–88*. 2 vols. New York: Macmillan, 1987.

Fehrenbacher, Don E. *Slaveholding Republic: An Account of the United States Government's Relations to Slavery*. New York; Oxford: Oxford University Press, 2001.

Finkelman, Paul. *Supreme Injustice: Slavery in the Nation's Highest Court*. Cambridge, MA: Harvard University Press, 2018.

Fiss, Owen M. *Troubled Beginnings of the Modern State, 1888–1910*. The Oliver Wendell Holmes Devise: History of the Supreme Court of the United States, vol. 8. New York: Macmillan, 1993.

Foner, Eric. *Reconstruction: America's Unfinished Revolution, 1863–1877*. New York: Perennial Classics, 2002.

Foreman, Amanda. *A World on Fire: Britain's Crucial Role in the American Civil War*. New York: Random House, 2010.

Frankfurter, Felix. *The Commerce Clause under Marshall, Taney and Waite*. Chapel Hill: University of North Carolina Press, 1937.

Frankfurter, Felix. *Mr. Justice Holmes and the Supreme Court*. Cambridge, MA: Harvard University Press, 1938.

Friedman, Barry. *The Will of the People: How Public Opinion Has Influenced the Supreme Court and Shaped the Meaning of the Constitution*. New York: Farrar, Straus and Giroux, 2009.

Friedman, Lawrence M. *A History of American Law*. 2nd ed. New York: Simon and Schuster, 1985.

Gillman, Howard, Mark A. Graber, and Keith E. Whittington. *American Constitutionalism*. 2d ed. New York: Oxford University Press, 2017.

Gillman, Howard. *The Constitution Besieged: The Rise and Demise of Lochner Era Police Powers Jurisprudence*. Durham, NC: Duke University Press, 1993.

Graber, Mark A. *Dred Scott and the Problem of Constitutional Evil*. Cambridge, MA; New York: Cambridge University Press, 2006.

Graber, Mark A. *A New Introduction to American Constitutionalism*. Oxford; New York: Oxford University Press, 2013.

Gunther, Gerald. *John Marshall's Defense of McCulloch v. Maryland*. Stanford, CA: Stanford University Press, 1969.

Gutzman, Kevin Raeder. *Virginia's American Revolution: From Dominion to Republic, 1776–1840*. Lanham, MD: Lexington Books, 2007.

Haines, Charles Grove. *The American Doctrine of Judicial Supremacy*. New York: Macmillan, 1914; 2d ed. Berkeley: University of California Press, 1932.

Hamilton Walton H., and Adair, Douglass. *The Power to Govern; the Constitution—Then and Now*. New York: W. W. Norton, 1937; reprint New York: Da Capo Press, 1972.

Hammond, Bray. *Banks and Politics in America, from the Revolution to the Civil War*. Princeton, NJ: Princeton University Press, 1957.

Hammond, Bray. *Sovereignty and an Empty Purse: Banks and Politics in the Civil War*. Princeton, NJ: Princeton University Press, 1970.

Hare, J.I. Clark, *American Constitutional Law*. 2 vols. Boston: Little, Brown, 1889.

Haskins, John Lee, and Herbert Alan Johnson. *Foundations of Power: John Marshall, 1801–15*. New York: Macmillan; London: Collier Macmillan, 1981.

Hobson, Charles F. *The Great Chief Justice: John Marshall and the Rule of Law*. Lawrence: University Press of Kansas, 1996.

Holmes, Oliver Wendell [Jr.], *Collected Legal Papers*. New York: Harcourt, Brace and Howe, 1920; reprint New York: Peter Smith, 1952.

Howe, Daniel Walker. *The Political Culture of the American Whigs*. Chicago: University of Chicago Press, 1979.

Howe, Daniel Walker. *What Hath God Wrought: The Transformation of America, 1815–1848*. New York: Oxford University Press, 2009.

Hoffer, Peter Charles, Williamjames Hull Hoffer, and N.E.H. Hull. *The Federal Courts: An Essential History*. New York: Oxford University Press, 2016.

Hurst, James Willard. *A Legal History of Money in the United States, 1774–1970*. Lincoln: University of Nebraska Press, 1973.

Hyman, Harold, and William M. Wiecek. *Equal Justice under Law: Constitutional Development, 1835–1875*. New York: Harper and Row, 1982.

Jackson, Robert H. *The Struggle for Judicial Supremacy: A Study of a Crisis in American Power Politics*. New York: A.A. Knopf, 1941.

Kalman, Laura. *Legal Realism at Yale, 1927–1960*. Chapel Hill: University of North Carolina Press, 1986.

Karst, Kenneth L. *Belonging to America: Equal Citizenship and the Constitution*. New Haven, CT: Yale University Press, 1989.

Kent, James. *Commentaries on American Law*. 2d ed., 1832; 3rd ed., 1836; 6th ed., 1848; 12th ed., 1873; 14th ed., 1896.

Killenbeck, Mark Robert. *M'Culloch v. Maryland: Securing a Nation*. Lawrence: University Press of Kansas, 2006.

Klarman, Michael J. *From Jim Crow to Civil Rights: The Supreme Court and the Struggle for Racial Equality*. Oxford; New York: Oxford University Press, 2004.

Konvitz, Milton R. *The Constitution and Civil Rights*. New York: Columbia University Press, 1954.

Kramer, Larry. *The People Themselves: Popular Constitutionalism and Judicial Review*. Oxford; New York: Oxford University Press, 2004.

Lane, Charles. *The Day Freedom Died: The Colfax Massacre, the Supreme Court, and the Betrayal of Reconstruction*. New York: Henry Holt, 2008.

LaPiana, William P. *Logic and Experience: The Origin of Modern American Legal Education*. New York: Oxford University Press, 1994.

Lightner, David L. *Slavery and the Commerce Power: How the Struggle against the Interstate Slave Trade Led to the Civil War*. New Haven, CT: Yale University Press, 2006.

Link, Arthur S. *Woodrow Wilson and the Progressive Era, 1910–1917*. New American Nation Series. New York: Harper, 1954.

Llewellyn, Karl N. *The Common Law Tradition: Deciding Appeals*. Boston: Little, Brown, 1960.

Lomazoff, Eric. *Reconstructing the National Bank Controversy: Politics and Law in the Early American Republic*. Chicago: University of Chicago Press, 2018.

Magliocca, Gerard N. *Andrew Jackson and the Constitution: The Rise and Fall of Generational Regimes*. Lawrence: University Press of Kansas, 2007.

Magliocca, Gerard N. *The Tragedy of William Jennings Bryan: Constitutional Law and the Politics of Backlash*. New Haven: Yale University Press, 2011.

Magruder, Allan Bowie. *John Marshall*. Boston; New York: Houghton Mifflin, 1885.

Marcus, Maeve, and James J. Perry, eds. *The Documentary History of the Supreme Court of the United States, 1789–1800*. New York: Columbia University Press, 1985–2007.

Marshall, John. *The Life of George Washington*. Vol. 5. Philadelphia: C.P. Wayne, 1807.

Mason, Alpheus T. *Harlan Fiske Stone: Pillar of the Law*. New York: Viking, 1956.

McCloskey, Robert G., and Sanford Levinson. *The American Supreme Court*. Chicago: University of Chicago Press, 2005.

McCloskey, Robert G. *The Modern Supreme Court*. Cambridge, MA: Harvard University Press, 1972.

McPherson, James M. *Battle Cry of Freedom: The Civil War Era*. New York: Ballantine Books, 1989.

Miller, Samuel F. "A statement of facts relating to the order of the Supreme Court of the United States for a re-argument of the Legal-Tender Question, in April, 1870." In *Miscellaneous Writings of the Late Hon. Joseph P. Bradley, Associate Justice of Supreme Court of the United States*, edited by Charles Bradley. Newark, NJ: L.J. Hardham, 1901.

Miller, Samuel Freeman. *Lectures on the Constitution of the United States*. New York: Banks, 1893.

Morgan, Donald G. *Justice William Johnson, the First Dissenter; the Career and Constitutional Philosophy of a Jeffersonian Judge*. Columbia: University of South Carolina Press, 1954.

Morris, Thomas D., *Free Men All: The Personal Liberty Laws of the North, 1780–1861*. Baltimore: Johns Hopkins University Press, 1974.

Neely, Mark E. *Lincoln and the Triumph of the Nation: Constitutional Conflict in the American Civil War*. Chapel Hill: University of North Carolina Press, 2011.

Nelson, William E. *The Fourteenth Amendment: From Political Principle to Judicial Doctrine*. Cambridge, MA: Harvard University Press, 1988.

Newmyer, R. Kent. *John Marshall and the Heroic Age of the Supreme Court*. Baton Rouge: Louisiana State University Press, 2001.

Novak, William J. *The People's Welfare: Law and Regulation in Nineteenth-Century America*. Chapel Hill: University of North Carolina Press, 1996.

Paul, Arnold M. *Conservative Crisis and the Rule of Law: Attitudes of Bar and Bench, 1887–1895*. New York: Harper and Row, 1969.

Peppers, Todd C. "Birth of an Institution: Horace Gray and the Lost Law Clerks." In *In Chambers: Stories of Supreme Court Law Clerks and Their Justices*, edited by Todd C. Peppers and Artemus Ward, 17–41. Charlottesville; London: University of Virginia Press, 2013.

Peterson, Merrill D. *The Great Triumvirate: Webster, Clay, and Calhoun*. New York: Oxford University Press, 1987.

Peterson, Merrill D. *The Jefferson Image in the American Mind*. Charlottesville: University Press of Virginia, 1998.

Pomeroy, John Norton. *An Introduction to the Constitutional Law of the United States.* Indianapolis, IN: Bowen-Merrill, 1888.

Purcell, Edward A. *Brandeis and the Progressive Constitution: Erie, the Judicial Power, and the Politics of the Federal Courts in Twentieth-Century America.* New Haven, CT: Yale University Press, 2000.

Ransom, William L. *Majority Rule and the Judiciary.* New York: C. Scribner's Sons, 1912; reprint New York: Da Capo, 1971.

Remini, Robert V. *Andrew Jackson and the Bank War; A Study in the Growth of Presidential Power.* New York: Norton, 1967.

Ritter, Gretchen. *Goldbugs and Greenbacks: The Antimonopoly Tradition and the Politics of Finance in America.* New York: Cambridge University Press, 1997.

Roosevelt, Franklin D. *Roosevelt and Frankfurter: Their Correspondence, 1928–1945.* Boston: Little, Brown, 1967.

Roosevelt, Franklin D. *The Public Papers and Addresses of Franklin D. Roosevelt.* New York: Random House, 13 vols. 1938–1945.

Ross, Michael A. *Justice of Shattered Dreams: Samuel Freeman Miller and the Supreme Court during the Civil War Era.* Baton Rouge: Louisiana State University Press, 2003.

Ross, William G. *A Muted Fury: Populists, Progressives, and Labor Unions Confront the Courts, 1890–1937.* Princeton, NJ: Princeton University Press, 1994.

Sanders, M. Elizabeth. *Roots of Reform: Farmers, Workers, and the American State, 1877–1917.* Chicago: University of Chicago Press, 1999.

Schlesinger, Arthur M., Jr. *The Coming of the New Deal, 1933–1935.* Boston: Houghton Mifflin, 2003.

Shesol, Jeff. *Supreme Power: Franklin Roosevelt vs. the Supreme Court.* New York: W.W. Norton, 2010.

Simon, James F. *FDR and Chief Justice Hughes.* New York: Simon and Schuster, 2012.

Simon, James F. *Lincoln and Chief Justice Taney: Slavery, Secession, and the President's War Powers.* New York: Simon and Schuster, 2006.

Smith, Jean Edward. *John Marshall: Definer of a Nation.* New York: H. Holt, 1996.

Snyder, Brad. *The House of Truth: A Washington Political Salon and the Foundations of American Liberalism.* New York, NY: Oxford University Press, 2017.

Spaulding, E.G. *A Resource of War—The Credit of the Government Made Immediately Available: History of the Legal Tender Paper Money Issued during the Great Rebellion . . . Buffalo: Express Printing Company, 1869;* reprint Westport, CT: Greenwood Press, 1971.

Stone, Geoffrey R., Louis M. Seidman, Cass R. Sunstein, Mark V. Tushnet, and Pamela S. Karlan. *Constitutional Law.* 6th ed. New York: Aspen Publishers, 2009.

Story, Joseph. *Commentaries on the Constitution of the United States: With a Preliminary Review of the Constitutional History of the Colonies and States, before the Adoption of the Constitution.* 2 vols. Boston: Hilliard, Gray, and Co., 1833; 4th ed., Boston: Little, Brown, and Co, 1873.

Sunstein, Cass R. *Radicals in Robes: Why Extreme Right-Wing Courts Are Wrong for America.* New York: Basic Books, 2005.

Swisher, Carl Brent. *Roger B. Taney.* New York: Macmillan, 1935.

Taylor, John. *Construction Construed and Constitutions Vindicated.* Richmond: Shepherd and Pollard, 1820; reprint New York: Da Capo, 1970.

Thayer, James Bradley. *Cases on Constitutional Law: with Notes.* 2 vols. Cambridge: C.W. Sever, 1894–95.

Thayer, James Bradley. *John Marshall.* Boston: Houghton, Mifflin, 1901.

Tiedeman, Christopher G. *A Treatise on the Limitations of Police Power in the United States: Considered from Both a Civil and Criminal Standpoint.* St. Louis: F.H. Thomas Law Book, 1886.

Tribe, Laurence H. *American Constitutional Law.* 3rd ed. New York: Foundation Press, 2000.

Unger, Irwin. *The Greenback Era: A Social and Political History of American Finance, 1865–1879.* Princeton, NJ: Princeton University Press, 1964.

United States. Constitutional Convention. *Jonathan Elliot's Debates in the Several State Conventions on the Adoption of the Federal Constitution as Recommended by the General Convention at Philadelphia in 1787.* Cumberland, VA: J. River Press, 1989.

United States. President's Committee on Civil Rights. *To Secure These Rights: The Report of the President's Committee on Civil Rights*. Washington, DC: United States Government Printing Office, 1947.

Urofsky, Melvin I. (ed.). *Documents of American Constitutional and Legal History*. Philadelphia: Temple University Press, 1989.

Van Cleve, George. *A Slaveholders' Union: Slavery, Politics, and the Constitution in the Early American Republic*. Chicago: University of Chicago Press, 2010.

Von Holst, H. *The Constitutional Law of the United States of America*. Chicago: Callaghan, 1887.

Vorenberg, Michael. *Final Freedom: The Civil War, the Abolition of Slavery, and the Thirteenth Amendment*. Cambridge; New York: Cambridge University Press, 2001.

Ward, Artemus. *Deciding to Leave: The Politics of Retirement from the United States Supreme Court*. Albany: State University of New York Press, 2003.

Webster, Daniel. *The Papers of Daniel Webster*. Vol. 2, *Speeches and Formal Writings*. Hanover, NH: Published for Dartmouth College by the University Press of New England, 1974–89.

Whalen, Charles W. *The Longest Debate: A Legislative History of the 1964 Civil Rights Act*. Washington, DC: Seven Locks, 1985.

White, G. Edward. *Law in American History*. Oxford; New York: Oxford University Press, 2012.

White, G. Edward. *The Marshall Court and Cultural Change, 1815–35*. The Oliver Wendell Holmes Devise: History of the Supreme Court of the United States, Vols. 3–4. New York: Macmillan; London: Collier Macmillan, 1988.

White, G. Edward. *Tort Law in America: An Intellectual History*. Oxford; New York: Oxford University Press, 1980.

Whiting, William. *The war powers of the President, and the legislative powers of Congress in relation to rebellion, treason and slavery*. Boston: J. L. Shorey, 1862.

Whittington, Keith E. *Political Foundations of Judicial Supremacy: The Presidency, the Supreme Court, and Constitutional Leadership in U.S. History*. Princeton, NJ: Princeton University Press, 2007.

Wiecek, William M. *The Lost World of Classical Legal Thought: Law and Ideology in America, 1886–1937*. New York: Oxford University Press, 1998.

Wilson, Woodrow. *Congressional Government: A Study in American Politics*. Boston: Houghton Mifflin, 1885.

Yarbrough, Tinsley E. *Judicial Enigma: The First Justice Harlan*. New York: Oxford University Press, 1995.

Articles

Amar, Akhil Reed. "Of Sovereignty and Federalism." *Yale Law Journal* 96, no. 7 (1987): 1425–520.

Ammon, Harry. "The Richmond Junto, 1800–1824." *Virginia Magazine of History and Biography* 61, no. 4 (1953): 395–418.

Aynes, Richard L. "The 39th Congress (1865–1867) and the 14th Amendment: Some Preliminary Perspectives." *Akron Law Review* 42, no. 4 (2009): 1025.

Balkin, Jack M., and Sanford Levinson. "The Canons of Constitutional Law." *Harvard Law Review* 111, no. 4 (1998): 963–1022.

Balkin, Jack M. "Commerce." *Michigan Law Review* 109, no. 1 (2010): 1–51.

Balkin, Jack M. "The Use That the Future Makes of the Past: John Marshall's Greatness and Its Lessons for Today's Supreme Court Justices." *William and Mary Law Review* 43, no. 4 (2002): 1321–38.

Barnett, Randy E. "From Antislavery Lawyer to Chief Justice: The Remarkable but Forgotten Career of Salmon P. Chase." *Case Western Law Review* 63, no. 3 (2013): 653–702.

Barnett, Randy E. "The Original Meaning of the Commerce Clause." *University of Chicago Law Review* 68, no. 1 (2001): 101–47.

Barrett, Harrison J. "Is There a National Police Power; If So, What Is Its Relation to the Recent Federal Statutes Affecting Industry and Trade Generally, Particularly the National Industrial Recovery Act?" *Boston University Law Review* 14, no. 2 (1934): [i]–292.

Beach, Rex. "Spencer Roane and the Richmond Junto." *William and Mary Quarterly* 22, no. 1 (1942): 1–17.

Benedict, Michael Les. "Salmon P. Chase and Constitutional Politics." *Law and Social Inquiry* 22, no. 2 (1997): 487.

Berger, Raoul. "Judicial Manipulation of the Commerce Clause." *Texas Law Review* 74, no. 4 (1996): 695–718.

Boudin, Louis B. "John Marshall and Roger B. Taney." *Georgetown Law Journal* 24, no. 4 (1936): 864–909.

Braeman, John. "Albert J. Beveridge and the First National Child Labor Bill." *Indiana Magazine of History* 60, no. 1 (1964): 1–36.

Caminker, Evan. "Appropriate Means-Ends Constraints on Section 5 Powers." *Stanford Law Review* 53, no. 5 (2001): 1127–99.

Carrington, Paul D. "The Constitutional Law Scholarship of Thomas McIntyre Cooley." *American Journal of Legal History* 41, no. 3 (1997): 368–99.

Coenen, Dan T. "The Future of Footnote Four." *Georgia Law Review* 41, no. 3 (2007): 797–841.

Collins, Michael G. "M'Culloch and the Turned Comma." *Green Bag* 12, no. 3 (Spring 2009): 265–75.

Corwin, Edward S. "Congress's Power to Prohibit Commerce a Crucial Constitutional Issue." *Cornell Law Quarterly* 18, no. 4 (1933): 477–506.

Corwin, Edward S. "Moratorium over Minnesota." *University of Pennsylvania Law Review and American Law Register* 82, no. 4 (1934): 311–16.

Currie, David P. "The Civil War Congress." *University of Chicago Law Review* 73, no. 4 (2006): 1131–226.

Currie, David P. "The Constitution in the Supreme Court: State and Congressional Powers, 1801–1835." *University of Chicago Law Review* 49, no. 4 (1982): 887–975.

Currie, David P. "The Constitution in the Supreme Court: The New Deal, 1931–1940." *University of Chicago Law Review* 54, no. 2 (1987): 504–55.

Currie, David P. "The Constitution in the Supreme Court: The Powers of the Federal Courts, 1801–1835." *University of Chicago Law Review* 49, no. 3 (1982): 646–724.

Douglas, Davison M. "The Rhetorical Uses of Marbury v. Madison: The Emergence of a 'Great Case.'" *Wake Forest Law Review* 38, no. 2 (2003).

Ellingwood, Albert Russell. "New Deal and the Constitution." *Illinois Law Review* 28, no. 6 (1934): 729–51.

Engel, Steven A. "The McCulloch Theory of the Fourteenth Amendment: City of Boerne v. Flores and the Original Understanding of Section 5." *Yale Law Journal* 109, no. 1 (1999): 115.

Epstein, Richard A. "The Proper Scope of the Commerce Power." *Virginia Law Review* 73, no. 8 (1987): 1387-1455.

Eskridge, William N., Jr., and John Ferejohn. "Super-Statutes Special Symposium Issue: Congress and the Constitution." *Duke Law Journal* 50 (2000–2001): 1215–76.

Eskridge, William N., and Philip P. Frickey, "The Making of 'The Legal Process.'" *Harvard Law Review* 107, no. 8 (1994): 2031–55.

Fallon, Richard H. "How to Choose a Constitutional Theory." *California Law Review* 87, no. 3 (1999): 535–79.

Frankfurter, Felix, and James M. Landis. "Business of the Supreme Court of the United States—A Study in the Federal Judicial System I." *Harvard Law Review* 38, no. 8 (1925): 1005–59.

Frankfurter, Felix. "Hours of Labor and Realism in Constitutional Law." *Harvard Law Review* 29, no. 1 (1916): 353–71.

Frankfurter, Felix. "John Marshall and the Judicial Function." *Harvard Law Review* 69, no. 2 (1955): 217–38.

Frankfurter, Felix. "Mr. Justice Brandeis and the Constitution." *Harvard Law Review* 45, no. 1 (1931): 33–111.

Feuerlicht, Maurice M. Jr. "Interstate Commerce Clause and NRA." *Indiana Law Journal* 9, no. 7 (1934–33): 434–55.

Gerhardt, Michael J. "The Rhetoric of Judicial Critique: From Judicial Restraint to the Virtual Bill of Rights." *William and Mary Bill of Rights Journal* 10, no. 3 (2002): 585, 596.

Gillman, Howard. "More on the Origins of the Fuller Court's Jurisprudence: Reexamining the Scope of Federal Power over Commerce and Manufacturing in Nineteenth-Century Constitutional Law." *Political Research Quarterly* 49, no. 2 (1996): 415–37.

Graber, Mark A. "The Collapse of the New Deal Conceptual Universe." *Maryland Law Review* 77 (2017): 108–46.

Graber, Mark A. "Federalist or Friends of Adams: The Marshall Court and Party Politics." *Studies in American Political Development* 12, no. 2 (1998): 229-66.

Graber, Mark A. "Naked Land Transfers and American Constitutional Development." *Vanderbilt Law Review* 53, no.1 (2000): 73-121.

Graber, Mark A. "The Passive-Aggressive Virtues: Cohens v. Virginia, and the Problematic Establishment of Judicial Power." *Constitutional Commentary* 12, no. 1 (1995): 67–92.

Graber, Mark. "Overruling *McCulloch?*" *Arkansas Law Review* 71, no. 4 (2019): 79–127.

Graber, Mark. Review of "*Origins of the Dred Scott Case: Jacksonian Jurisprudence and the Supreme Court, 1837–1857*" by Austin Allen. *Law and History Review* 25, no. 3 (2007): 671–73.

Haines, Charles Grove. "Judicial Review of Acts of Congress and the Need for Constitutional Reform." *Yale Law Journal* 45, no. 5 (1936): 816–56.

Hall, Aaron R. "Reframing the Fathers' Constitution: The Centralized State and Centrality of Slavery in the Confederate Constitutional Order." *Journal of Southern History* 83, no. 2 (2017): 255–96.

Hand, Learned. "Due Process of Law and the Eight-Hour Day." *Harvard Law Review* 21, no. 1 (1908): 495, 508.

Hobson, Charles. "Defining the Office: John Marshall as Chief Justice." *University of Pennsylvania Law Review* 154, no. 6 (2006): 1421–61.

Hook, Jay. "A Brief Life of James Bradley Thayer." *Northwestern University Law Review* 88, no. 1 (1993): 1–8.

Huebner, Timothy S. "The Consolidation of State Judicial Power: Spencer Roane, Virginia Legal Culture, and the Southern Judicial Tradition." *Virginia Magazine of History and Biography* 102, no. 1 (1994): 47–72.

Jackson, Vicki C. "Federalism and the Court: Congress as the Audience?" *Annals of the American Academy of Political and Social Science* 574 (2001): 145.

Johnson, Calvin. "The Dubious Enumerated Powers Doctrine." *Constitutional Commentary* 22, no. 1 (Spring 2005): 25–96.

Josephs, N. Henry. "The Federal Constitution in Time of Emergency." *New York University Law Quarterly Review* 11, no. 4 (1934): 499–537.

Kalman, Laura. "Law, Politics, and the New Deal(s)." *Yale Law Journal* 108, no. 8 (1999): 2165–13.

Killenbeck, Mark. "All Banks in Like Manner Taxed? Maryland and the Second Bank of the United States." *Journal of Supreme Court History* 44, no. 2 (forthcoming 2019).

Klarman, Michael J. "How Great Were the 'Great' Marshall Court Decisions?" *Virginia Law Review* 87 (2001): 75.

LaCroix, Alison L. "The Interbellum Constitution: Federalism in the Long Founding Moment." *Stanford Law Review* 67, no. 2 (2015): 397-445.

Lerner, Max. "John Marshall and the Campaign of History." *Columbia Law Review* 39, no. 3 (1939): 396–431.

Levinson, Sanford. "They Whisper: Reflections on Flags, Monuments, and State Holidays, and the Construction of Social Meaning in a Multicultural Society." *Chicago-Kent Law Review* 70, no. 3 (1995): 1079–15.

Lusky, Louis. "Footnote Redux: A Carolene Products Reminiscence." *Columbia Law Review* 82, no. 6 (1982): 1093–1109.

Magliocca, Gerard N. "The Gold Clause Cases and Constitutional Necessity." *Florida Law Review* 64, no. 5 (2012).

Magliocca, Gerard N. "A New Approach to Congressional Power: Revisiting the Legal Tender Cases." *Georgetown Law Journal* 95, no. 1 (2006): 119–70.

Magliocca, Gerard N. "Veto! The Jacksonian Revolution in Constitutional Law." *Nebraska Law Review* 78, no. 2 (1999): 205–62.

Mason, Alpheus T. "Mr. Justice Brandeis and the Constitution." *University of Pennsylvania Law Review and American Law Register* 80, no. 6 (1932): 799–841.

Mason, Alpheus T. "Supreme Court of Yesterday and Today: A Government of Men and Not of Laws." *New Jersey State Bar Association Quarterly* 1 (1934): 25–40.

Mikhail, John. "The Necessary and Proper Clauses." *Georgetown Law Journal* 102, no. 4 (2014): 1045–132.

Miller, F. Thornton. "John Marshall versus Spencer Roane: A Reevaluation of Martin v. Hunter's Lessee." *Virginia Magazine of History and Biography* 96, no. 3 (1988): 297–314.

Monaghan, Henry P. "'Marbury' and the Administrative State." *Columbia Law Review* 83, no. 1 (1983): 1–34.

Nelson, William E. "The Eighteenth-Century Background of John Marshall's Constitutional Jurisprudence." *Michigan Law Review* 76, no. 6 (May 1978): 893.

Newmyer, R. Kent. "John Marshall, McCulloch v. Maryland, and the Southern States' Rights Tradition." *John Marshall Law Review* 33, no. 4 (1999): 875.

Norton, P. Tennent Jr. "Constitutionality of Federal Regulation of Stock Exchanges." *Georgetown Law Journal* 24 (1935–36): 20–68.

Palmore, Joseph R. "The Not-So-Strange Career of Interstate Jim Crow: Race, Transportation, and the Dormant Commerce Clause, 1878–1946." Note. *Virginia Law Review* 83 (1997): 1773–818.

Pound, Roscoe. "Liberty of Contract." *Yale Law Journal* 18, no. 7 (1909): 454, 479–81.

Pope, James Gray. "Section 1 of the Thirteenth Amendment and the Badges and Incidents of Slavery." *UCLA Law Review* 65, no. 2 (2018): 433–34.

Primus, Richard. "'The Essential Characteristic': Enumerated Powers and the Bank of the United States." *Michigan Law Review* 117, no. 3 (2018): 415–97.

Primus, Richard. "The Gibbons Fallacy." *University of Pennsylvania Journal of Constitutional Law* 19, no. 3 (2016): 567–620.

Pushaw, Robert J., Jr., and Grant S. Nelson. "A Critique of the Narrow Interpretation of the Commerce Clause." *Northwestern University Law Review* 96, no. 2 (2002): 695–720.

Rabin, Robert L. "Federal Regulation in Historical Perspective." *Stanford Law Review* 38, no. 5 (1986): 1189–326.

Roosevelt, Theodore. "Beveridge's Life of Marshall." *The Outlook*, Jul. 7, 1917. http://www.theodore-roosevelt.com/treditorials.html.

Ruiz, George W. "The Ideological Convergence of Theodore Roosevelt and Woodrow Wilson." *Presidential Studies Quarterly* 19, no. 1 (1989): 159–77.

Russell, Horace. "Constitutionality of the Federal Home Loan System." *Georgetown Law Journal* 24, no. 4 (1936): 910–34.

Sanders, Elizabeth. "Rediscovering the Progressive Era Symposium: Reflections on Progressive Constitutionalism: Theory, Practice and Critique." *Ohio State Law Journal* 72 (2011): 1281–94.

Schmidt, Christopher W. "Section 5's Forgotten Years: Congressional Power to Enforce the Fourteenth Amendment before Katzenbach v. Morgan." *Northwestern University Law Review* 118, no. 1 (2018): 47–108.

Schwartz, David S. "An Error and An Evil: the Strange History of Implied Commerce Powers." *American University Law Rview* 68, no. 3 (2019): 927–1014.

Schwartz, David S. "Misreading McCulloch v. Maryland." *University of Pennsylvania Journal of Constitutional Law* 18, no. 1 (2015): 1–94.

Schwartz, David S. "A Question Perpetually Arising: Implied Powers, Capable Federalism, and the Limits of Enumerationism." *Arizona Law Review* 59, no. 3 (2017): 573–646.

Scott, Rebecca J. "Public Rights, Social Equality, and the Conceptual Roots of the Plessy Challenge." *Michigan Law Review* 106, no. 5 (2008): 777–804.

Snyder, Brad. "Frankfurter and Popular Constitutionalism." *U.C. Davis Law Review* 47, no. 1 (2013): 343–418.

Spector, Robert M. "Legal Historian on the United States Supreme Court: Justice Horace Gray, Jr., and the Historical Method." *American Journal of Legal History* 12, no. 3 (1968): 181–210.

Stern, Robert L., "The Commerce Clause and the National Economy, 1933-1946." *Harvard Law Review* 59, no. 5 (1946): 645–69.

Stern, Robert L. "That Commerce Which Concerns More States Than One." *Harvard Law Review* 47, no. 8 (1934): 1335–66.

Thayer, James B. "Legal Tender." *Harvard Law Review* 1, no. 2 (1887): 73–97.

Thayer, James B. "The Origin and Scope of the American Doctrine of Constitutional Law." *Harvard Law Review* 7, no. 3 (1893): 129–56.

Thayer, James Bradley. "Our New Possessions." *Harvard Law Review* 12, no. 7 (1899): 464–85.

Tushnet, Mark V. "The Politics of Equality in Constitutional Law: The Equal Protection Clause, Dr. Du Bois, and Charles Hamilton Houston." *Journal of American History* 74, no. 3 (1987): 884–903.

Welke, Barbara. "When All the Women Were White, and All the Blacks Were Men: Gender, Class, Race, and the Road to 'Plessy,' 1855–1914." *Law and History Review* 13, no. 2 (October 1, 1995): 261–316.

Weinberg, Louise. "Fear and Federalism." *Ohio Northern University Law Review* 23 no. 4 (1997): 1295.

White, G. Edward. "Looking at Holmes Looking at Marshall." *Massachusetts Legal History: A Journal of the Supreme Judicial Court Historical Society* 7 (2001): 63–80.

Whittington, Keith E. "Judicial Review of Congress before the Civil War." *Georgetown Law Journal* 97, no. 5 (2009): 1257.

Whittington, Keith E., and Amanda Rinderle. "Making a Mountain out of a Molehill—Marbury and the Construction of the Constitutional Canon." *Hastings Constitutional Law Quarterly* 39 (2010–2011): 823–60.

Williams, Norman R. "The Dormant Commerce Clause: Why *Gibbons v. Ogden* Should Be Restored to the Canon." *Saint Louis University Law Journal* 49, no. 3 (2005): 817–34.

Williams, Norman R. "*Gibbons.*" *New York University Law Review* 79, no. 4 (2004): 1398–499.

Woodward, John. "The Courts and the People." *Columbia Law Review* 7, no. 8 (1907): 559–72.

Other Sources

The Affordable Care Act Cases, Oral Argument, March 27, 2012. https://www.oyez.org/cases/2011/11-393.

Johnson, Samuel, *A Dictionary of the English Language: A Digital Edition of the 1755 Classic by Samuel Johnson.* https://johnsonsdictionaryonline.com/.

Levinson, Sanford. "A Close Reading of McCulloch v. Maryland," Course Description, Harvard Law School online catalogue, Fall 2014. Last visited Nov. 28, 2018. http://www.law.harvard.edu / academics/curriculum/catalog/index.html?o=67026

Mikhail, John. "Fixing the Constitution's Implied Powers." Balkinization (blog), Oct. 25, 2018. https://balkin.blogspot.com/2018/10/fixing-constitutions-implied-powers.html.

Mikhail, John. "McCulloch's Strategic Ambiguity." Unpublished manuscript, Nov. 16, 2018..

Vermeule, Adrian. "Living It Up." *The New Republic*, Aug. 1, 2010. https://newrepublic.com/article/76600/living-it.

INDEX

For the benefit of digital users, indexed terms that span two pages (e.g., 52–53) may, on occasion, appear on only one of those pages.